Easy Grammar Plus

Wanda C. Phillips

Easy Grammar Systems
P. O. Box 25970
Scottsdale, Arizona 85255

www.easygrammar.com

Printed in the United States

Dedication

To the professors at George Fox University—where faith and learning are integrated

A student workbook entitled **Easy Grammar Plus Student Workbook** is available. This workbook does not include an answer key or strategies for effective teaching. In addition, tests are not included.

Easy Grammar Plus Student Test Booklet is now available; this contains a pre-assessment test, all unit tests and cumulative tests, and a post-assessment test.

Correlation pages for **Easy Grammar Plus** and **Easy Grammar Plus Student Workbook** have been placed throughout this textbook. Also, a correlation of teacher edition pages and workbook pages has been placed at the back of this text.

TABLE OF CONTENTS

TO THE TEACHER: Assessment Information

EXTREMELY IMPORTANT

An assessment is provided on the next eight pages.
(Answers are on pages 681-686).

1. Please allow students to take this assessment before beginning any lessons. Although the assessment is eight pages in length, it should not take students long to complete. For the pre-assessment, you may want to tell students to leave an answer blank if they don't know it. (This usually places students in a more relaxed mode.)

2. Score the assessment and review it for information regarding the level of each student's understanding.

(I recommend that you do not share the pre-assessment results with students. If the score is low, a student may feel deflated before he begins this approach to grammar concepts and usage. Students' scores on last year's standardized tests may be reviewed to determine areas of strengths and weaknesses, also.)

3. After scoring the pre-assessment, please store it somewhere to be retrieved **after** the student takes it as a post-assessment. After you have scored the post-assessment, share both results with students so that they can see their increase in understanding. This is positive in that students can visualize the product of their work and can **internalize success**. (Consider ***individual conferences*** to discuss the pre-assessment and post-assessment results.)

SCORING: I have provided one method of scoring in the answer key that follows this test. You will note that I place more points in usage than I do on such items as identification of nouns. You may disagree. Please feel free to determine which areas you consider most important and to create your own scoring rubric. However, be sure that you use the same method of scoring for **both** the pre-assessment and the post-assessment. This assessment has been designed mainly as a tool to help students visualize their academic growth.

Note: Deletion of prepositional phrases has only been suggested (not graded) on the assessment. I recommend that you use this process all year so that it becomes an automatic tool.

Name________________________________ **Assessment**

Date________________________________ **Pre-Post**

A. Clauses:

Directions: Place **DC** if the words form a dependent clause; place **IC** if the words form an independent clause. Write **No** if the words do not form any type of clause.

1. ______ After you buy your ticket.

2. ______ After dinner at a fast-food restaurant.

3. ______ After we finish, let's make popsicles.

4. ______ The team flew to Los Angeles after the game.

B. Sentences, Fragments, and Run-Ons:

Directions: Write **S** if the words form a sentence. Write **F** if the words form a fragment. Write **R-O** if the words form a run-on.

1. ______ Lana doesn't like kiwis, she prefers pineapples.

2. ______ Stop.

3. ______ When their parents went to a neighborhood party.

4. ______ Within two hours of hearing about the flood, rescuers responded.

5. ______ Kira drove to the airport, parked, went to ticketing, but she had left her purse in her truck and had to return to it and so she missed her flight.

C. Sentence Types:

Directions: Place correct punctuation at the end of each sentence and write the sentence type on the line.

1. ________________________ Is Tamarindo in Costa Rica

2. ________________________ Yikes! We're lost

3. ________________________ Please remain quiet

4. ________________________ They live on Shell Avenue

D. Business Letters:

Directions: Label the boldfaced part of this business letter ***and*** punctuate the salutation (greeting) correctly.

September 21, 20—

Easy Grammar Systems
Post Office Box 100 ______________________________
Scottsdale, AZ 85255

Dear Mr. Phipps

E. Capitalization:

Directions: Write a capital letter above any word that should be capitalized.

1. have governor t. loon and those from the house of representatives met today?
2. in the summer, they like to eat fish tacos at a mexican restaurant on shell beach.
3. the oldest african-american church was started in the east in 1813 by peter spencer.
4. he studied french history, reading, and biology 101 at cambria college in july.
5. the demacane corporation moved just south of pinnacle peak last tuesday.
6. during thanksgiving weekend, both dad and i read <u>strangers from my native land</u>.
7. take ventura freeway north to see hearst castle and to attend the templeton grape festival.
8. his brother, a banker, speaks japanese and flies to asia on thailand airlines.
9. a delaware company that worked with nasa is located on moonwalker road.
10. did james cook claim the hawaiian islands for the british empire?
11. some pioneers left new england to settle near the salt river in the arizona territory.
12. does the university of virginia foundation run the boar's head inn?

F. Punctuation:

Directions: Insert needed punctuation.

1. His address is 10 South Street Austin TX 78705
2. Joys aunt a teacher bought a newly remodeled home
3. On May 24 2006 they were married in a small country chapel

4. Emma asked Tate do you need an old branding iron
5. Yes I want to see the movie entitled Struck Twice by Lightning
6. During the last week of September we went to Alaska said Kim
7. Yeah Emily exclaimed My race is next
8. Although Allen is a nurse hes interested in doctors rights
9. Fight Against Bacteria is an article in the magazine entitled Health World
10. The town built the following a childrens hospital a large park and a zoo
11. The team will leave at noon and the band will follow within two hours
12. By the way are you going with us to Missoula Montana next fall
13. The fair is next week however I cant attend

G. Subjects and Verbs:

Directions: Underline the subject once and the verb or verb phrase twice.

Note: Crossing out prepositional phrases will help you.

1. I have purchased a new watercolor by a Western artist.
2. Did anyone find a cat with long gray fur?
3. Before the basketball game, several players were given extra practice.
4. I am definitely sad about your lost hamster.
5. Your brother shouldn't have gone to the library by himself.

H. Contractions:

Directions: Write the contraction.

1. does not - ___________
2. they are - ___________
3. I have - ___________
4. how is - ___________
5. have not - ___________
6. you will - ___________

I. Subject-Verb Agreement:

Directions: Underline the subject once. Underline the verb that agrees twice.

1. Carmello and Bo (was, were) in Ohio recently.
2. Someone in the last few rows (have, has) a cell phone turned on.

3. The girls with the cute, little beagle puppy (like, likes) to walk him.

4. Neither the ladies nor the man with them (want, wants) dessert.

5. One of the watermelons (is, are) ready to cut.

J. Irregular Verbs:

Directions: Circle the correct verb.

1. Have you (spoke, spoken) to your friends about it?
2. He should not have (did, done) that.
3. Carlo has not ever (ridden, rode) a horse.
4. I may have (ate, eaten) too much.
5. Their alarm clock has (rang, rung) three times.
6. They have (drove, driven) to the coast.
7. Have you (drunk, drank) green tea?
8. A sign must have (fell, fallen) during the storm.
9. The couple has (chosen, chose) a house with an old barn.
10. (Lie, Lay) on the floor by the fire.
11. We should have (took, taken) our dogs to the lake with us.
12. The city of Vancouver was (began, begun) in 1792 by the British.
13. They may have (went, gone) to a baseball game.
14. I should have (brung, brang, brought) my camera.
15. Have Mr. and Mrs. Cole (flew, flown) to Dover?
16. The sleepy child had (laid, lain) on the floor.
17. The church's stained-glass window was (broken, broke).
18. That shovel must have (frozen, froze) in the snow.
19. Many doctors must have (came, come) to the conference late.
20. (Sit, Set) beside me!
21. I (saw, seen) him at the mall.
22. Many horses have (ran, run) in that famous race.
23. A reporter had (wrote, written) about the lost diamond mine.

K. Tenses:

Directions: Underline the subject once and the verb or verb phrase twice. Write the tense in the blank.

1. ____________________ I am leaving soon.
2. ____________________ I left early.
3. ____________________ They had left for New York City at noon.
4. ____________________ Chase will leave on vacation next week.
5. ____________________ Abigail always leaves food on her plate.

L. Common and Proper Nouns:

Directions: Place a ✓ if the noun is abstract.

1. ___ jar 2. ___ respect 3. ___ promise 4. ___ air

M. Singular and Plural Nouns:

Directions: Write the correct spelling of each plural noun.

1. loss - ____________________
2. wrench - ____________________
3. leaf - ____________________
4. robbery- ____________________
5. deer - ____________________
6. display - ____________________
7. excitement - ____________________
8. potato - ____________________
9. badge- ____________________
10. chief - ____________________

N. Possessive Nouns:

Directions: Write the possessive in each blank.

1. a cart used by more than one workman - ____________________
2. a market set up by more than one farmer- ____________________
3. a home belonging to Tom and Lori- ____________________
4. computers owned by a company - ____________________
5. a playroom used by more than one child - ____________________

O. Identifying Nouns:

Directions: Circle any nouns.

1. Many strong winds blow through this village and its meadows and into a deep cave.

P. Usage and Knowledge:

1. Circle the correct answer: Josh did the sanding (himself, hisself).
2. Write an interjection: ______________________________
3. Write a gerund: ________________________________
4. Write the antecedent of the possessive pronoun:

   Someone shouted his name over a loudspeaker. ____________________
5. Circle a reflexive pronoun: We did it ourselves, and nobody helped!

Q. Identifying Adjectives:

Directions: Circle any adjective.

1. One glossy photograph had French swans on a very lovely lake.

R. Degrees of Adjectives:

Directions: Circle the correct answer.

1. The road by my cousin's house is the (curvier, curviest) one in the county.
2. She is the (more talkative, most talkative) twin.
3. This shell feels (rougher, roughest) than that one.
4. Of the entire family, Tara seems (more timid, most timid, timider, timidest).

S. Adverbs:

Directions: Circle the correct answer.

1. You did (good, well).
2. I don't feel (good, well).
3. Ron hardly ever has (no, any) extra change.
4. You are speaking too (loud, loudly).
5. She doesn't know (anybody, nobody) in her new school.
6. Their truck runs (good, well).

T. Identifying Adverbs:

Directions: Circle any adverbs.

1. Tammy and her sister always play so nicely together.

U. Degrees of Adverbs:

Directions: Circle the correct answer.

1. Of the two girls, Ellen jumps (farther, farthest).
2. Mia wins (more often, most often, oftener, oftenest) than her friend.
3. The injured player walked (more lightly, most lightly) on his right foot.
4. The dog barked (more ferociously, most ferociously) at the third car.
5. Bo played (worse, worser, worst, worsest) during the second game.

W. Pronouns:

Directions: Circle the correct answer.

1. Pam and (she, her) donated blood.
2. (Who, Whom) did you call?
3. The flowers were for Sara and (I, me).
4. (Them, Those) cookies are too hard.
5. One of the girls left (her, their) books by the bench.
6. The coach and (we, us) practiced dribbling.
7. (Me and my friend, My friend and I, My friend and me) will help.
8. Annie and (they, them) walked to the ice cream shop.
9. The first one to present an award was (he, him).
10. Lance will call (we, us) boys after dinner.
11. Our cousins are (they, them) with the sheep dog.
12. The leader handed (she, her) a large manila envelope.
13. (Who, Whom) has a colored pencil?
14. Both of the street sweepers ate (his, their) snacks.
15. The winners are Nat and (me, I).
16. The debate was between Karen and (he, him).
17. Please give (they, them) my message.

W. Nouns and Pronouns Used as Subjects, Direct Objects, Indirect Objects, Objects of the Preposition, and Predicate Nominatives:

Directions: Look at the boldfaced word and decide how it is used in the sentence. Write **S.** for subject, **D.O.** for direct object, **I.O.** for indirect object, **O.P.** for object of the preposition, and **P.N.** for predicate nominative.

1. _____ Quit bothering **me**!

2. _____ Their **grandparents** live in Florida.

3. _____ Jenny always earns **money** for her school clothes.

4. _____ Tad became a **bricklayer**.

5. _____ Stay away from the **alley**.

6. _____ Give the **waiter** a tip.

EASY GRAMMAR PLUS

This book is based on **SUCCESS**, student success. When students actually **LEARN**, they feel good about themselves. You can tell "Johnny" how terrific he is, and that's fine. However, unless "Johnny" builds on his own personal successes, "he" will soon feel inadequate despite your praises.

Forgive my repetition, but emphasis must be placed on **SUCCESS.** Over the years, I have seen most of my students succeed in English. Their understanding of grammar and usage increased greatly. Many students came to me and said, "I really like English now. It makes sense. I just didn't understand it before this class." It was then that the idea of this book developed.

The sole purpose of Easy Grammar Plus is to provide students with grammar *tools*. With these *tools*, students will learn to speak and write properly.

Easy Grammar Plus includes unit reviews, cumulative reviews, unit tests, and cumulative tests.

Who cannot teach Easy Grammar Plus **successfully?**

A. If you absolutely HATE English, stop. I didn't say *dislike*. Even if you dislike(d) English, this approach will work for you. In fact, you will have success, too!

B. Anyone can teach Easy Grammar Plus.

What if I get lost?

A. You won't if you follow the guidelines listed on the next page.

B. This is a very simplistic and thorough approach to grammar and usage.

Guidelines to Successful Use of Easy Grammar Plus

TWO MUSTS:

A. Insist on MASTERY learning.

In mastery learning, the student fully understands the concept and is able to use it when the need arises. It's like tying your shoe; once learned, no one has to reteach you every time you do it.

B. Students must memorize and learn fifty prepositions. This is the first step and is basic to Easy Grammar Plus. Those fifty prepositions are involved with nearly every aspect of grammar. Mastery learning begins with PREPOSITIONS.

OTHER GUIDELINES:

A. You certainly may duplicate the pages of this book. Workbooks containing these pages are available for student use. Students need *hands-on* experience in English, too!

B. Encourage your students. Be positive about English; the influence you have is amazing.

C. Discuss your students' successes with them. They will be thrilled to acknowledge their hard work and the good feeling that hard work has produced.

ADDITIONAL NOTE:

You may wish to teach this material out of sequence. The author recommends teaching the prepositional unit first. After completion of that unit, you may wish to teach capitalization and punctuation*. If this is your choice, you will, of course, want to teach the verb unit next. The remainder of the book should be taught in order. This is necessary because many concepts are interrelated.

*A book from the Daily Grams: Guided Review Aiding Mastery Skills series is highly recommended as a ten minute **daily review** of capitalization, punctuation, grammar, and sentence combining. (See last page.)

PAGE 3 = WORKBOOK PAGE 1

THE STUDENT MUST LEARN THE 50 PREPOSITIONS.* The prepositions must be memorized and listed. A dictionary definition of a preposition has been provided here. As you can see, it's very complicated. However, some teachers like to present a written definition.

By definition, a preposition is "a relation or function word...that connects a lexical word, usually a noun, or pronoun, or a syntactic construction to another element of the sentence, as to a verb, to a noun, or to an adjective..."

-Webster's New World Dictionary

You may want to divide the list where appropriate and learn them in groups. Be sure to test students daily by asking them to list prepositions. Use whatever techniques with which you are comfortable (prizes, candy, etc.) to insure learning. This list is basic to the success of the rest of the Easy Grammar Plus program and must be learned.

*The preposition list on page four actually contains fifty-three prepositions. Instruct students to list 50; the extra three might be counted as additional points. (There are, of course, more than 53 prepositions in the English language. The list contains those commonly used.)

Note: Both grammar and writing are important; a synthesis of the two is ideal. Easy Writing by Wanda C. Phillips teaches students how to write more complex sentences.

PREPOSITIONS:

about
above
across
after
against
along
amid
among
around
at
atop
before
behind
below
beneath
beside
between
beyond
but (meaning except)
by
concerning
down
during
except
for
from
in
inside
into
like
near
of
off
on
onto
out
outside
over
past
regarding
since
through
throughout
to
toward
under
underneath
until
up
upon
with
within
without

PAGE 7 = WORKBOOK PAGE 2

PREPOSITION BINGO INSTRUCTIONS

To the Teacher:

A. Place each preposition on a one inch square piece of construction paper. (Laminate for durability.) Place squares in a container.

B. Give each student a blank "bingo" card.

Playing the game:

A. Have students fill in each blank with their choice of prepositions. (See sample page.)

B. Use scrap paper pieces for "corn."

C. You will select a preposition from your envelope or box.
   1. Say the preposition.
   2. Use the preposition in a prepositional phrase.

D. The student who gets "Bingo" first is the winner. If you are playing "Blackout," the student who covers his/her entire board first is the winner.

beside	past	into	from	about
up	through	after	against	to
without	during	FREE	of	below
regarding	off	under	near	with
except	before	toward	down	concerning

		FREE		

Name________________________________

WORKBOOK PAGE 3

Date________________________________

PREPOSITIONS

Directions: Unscramble the following prepositions.

1. twih- WITH
2. stap- PAST
3. ta- AT
4. nagol- ALONG
5. fof- OFF
6. no- ON
7. duren- UNDER
8. nagasit- AGAINST
9. denboy- BEYOND
10. toni- INTO
11. mrof- FROM
12. ot- TO
13. nithwi- WITHIN
14. tebewen- BETWEEN
15. foereb- BEFORE
16. socasr- ACROSS
17. pu- UP
18. boeva- ABOVE
19. diam- AMID
20. wolbe- BELOW
21. ethuneadnr- UNDERNEATH
22. tluin- UNTIL
23. wnod- DOWN
24. rane- NEAR
25. fro- FOR
26. ni- IN
27. dibneh- BEHIND
28. nupo- UPON
29. tthouiw- WITHOUT
30. tafre- AFTER
31. darnou- AROUND
32. goman- AMONG
33. beedis- BESIDE
34. ringdu- DURING
35. vroe- OVER
36. theeabn- BENEATH
37. gotuhrh- THROUGH
38. ubato- ABOUT
39. poat- ATOP
40. tub- BUT

Name________________________________ **PREPOSITIONS**

Date________________________________

Directions: Unscramble the following prepositions.

1. twih-____________________
2. stap-____________________
3. ta-____________________
4. nagol-____________________
5. fof-____________________
6. no-____________________
7. duren-____________________
8. nagasit-____________________
9. denboy-____________________
10. toni-____________________
11. mrof-____________________
12. ot-____________________
13. nithwi-____________________
14. tebewen-____________________
15. foereb-____________________
16. socasr-____________________
17. pu-____________________
18. boeva-____________________
19. diam-____________________
20. wolbe-____________________
21. ethuneadnr-____________________
22. tluin-____________________
23. wnod-____________________
24. rane-____________________
25. fro-____________________
26. ni-____________________
27. dibneh-____________________
28. nupo-____________________
29. tthouiw-____________________
30. tafre-____________________
31. darnou-____________________
32. goman-____________________
33. beedis-____________________
34. ringdu-____________________
35. vroe-____________________
36. theeabn-____________________
37. gotuhrh-____________________
38. ubato-____________________
39. poat-____________________
40. tub-____________________

Name________________________________ **PREPOSITIONS**

WORKBOOK PAGE 4

Date________________________________

Directions: Unscramble the following prepositions.

1. yb-______BY______________
2. uto-______OUT______________
3. dinesi-__INSIDE______________
4. egninrcnoc-_CONCERNING____
5. petcex-__EXCEPT____________
6. kiel-______LIKE______________
7. fo-______OF______________
8. deotuis-_OUTSIDE____________
9. cines- ___SINCE______________
10. drwtao-__TOWARD____________
11. gindrager-_REGARDING______
12. oouuhhttgr-THROUGHOUT_____

Name________________________________ **PREPOSITIONS**

Date________________________________

Directions: Unscramble the following prepositions.

1. yb-____________________
2. uto-____________________
3. dinesi-____________________
4. egninrcnoc-____________________
5. petcex-____________________
6. kiel-____________________
7. fo-____________________
8. deotuis-____________________
9. cines-____________________
10. drwtao-____________________
11. gindrager-____________________
12. oouuhhttgr-____________________

WORKBOOK PAGE 5

<u>A PREPOSITIONAL PHRASE BEGINS WITH A PREPOSITION AND ENDS WITH A NOUN OR PRONOUN.</u> That noun or pronoun is called the object of the preposition.

after dinner	(<u>after</u> is the preposition)
	(<u>dinner</u> is the object of the preposition)
	(<u>after dinner</u> is the prepositional phrase)
without you	(<u>without</u> is the preposition)
	(<u>you</u> is the object of the preposition)
	(<u>without you</u> is the prepositional phrase)

PREPOSITIONAL PHRASES WILL NOT BE THE SUBJECT OR VERB OF THE SENTENCE. *

WORKBOOK PAGE 6

HOW TO TEACH SUBJECTS:

After crossing out all prepositional phrases, find **who** or **what** the sentence is about.

A. The man with his son walked toward me.

The man ~~with his son~~ walked ~~toward me~~.

B. Some of the ducklings waddled past us.

Some ~~of the ducklings~~ waddled ~~past us~~.

C. A book of stamps lay on the table.

A book ~~of stamps~~ lay ~~on the table~~.

HOW TO TEACH VERBS:

After finding the subject of the sentence, decide **what happened** or **what "Is"** in the sentence. Remember: *The verb will never be in a prepositional phrase.*

A. The man ~~with his son~~ walked ~~toward us~~.

B. Some ~~of the ducklings~~ waddled ~~toward us~~.

C. A book ~~of stamps~~ lay ~~on the table~~.

*This will hold true 99% of the time.

Name_______________________________ **PREPOSITIONS**

WORKBOOK PAGE 7

Date________________________________

Directions: Cross out any prepositional phrases. Underline the subject once and the verb twice.

1. The shoppers went ~~into the store.~~
2. A blender fell ~~on the floor.~~
3. We walked ~~between the aisles~~ ~~of the supermarket~~.
4. ~~During the storm~~ we held ~~onto the side~~ ~~of the boat~~.
5. ~~Outside our home~~ a pine tree grows.
6. He stepped ~~behind the door~~.
7. The vacationers went ~~to the beach~~.
8. ~~Throughout the day~~ the rain came ~~in the window~~.
9. The price ~~of soda~~ is ~~over a dollar~~.
10. ~~Past the large sign~~ is a windmill.
11. The report ~~concerning smoking~~ is ~~in my desk~~.
12. All students ~~except Juan~~ rode ~~to school~~ ~~on a bus~~.
13. The child went ~~up the ladder~~ and ~~down the slide~~.
14. The lettuce is ~~inside the refrigerator~~ ~~by the milk carton~~.
15. ~~After the television program~~ ~~about snakes~~, we rode ~~on our bikes~~ ~~to the zoo~~.

Name________________________________ **PREPOSITIONS**

Date________________________________

Directions: Cross out any prepositional phrases. Underline the subject once and the verb twice.

1. The shoppers went into the store.
2. A blender fell on the floor.
3. We walked between the aisles of the supermarket.
4. During the storm we held onto the side of the boat.
5. Outside our home a pine tree grows.
6. He stepped behind the door.
7. The vacationers went to the beach.
8. Throughout the day the rain came in the window.
9. The price of soda is over a dollar.
10. Past the large sign is a windmill.
11. The report concerning smoking is in my desk.
12. All students except Juan rode to school on a bus.
13. The child went up the ladder and down the slide.
14. The lettuce is inside the refrigerator by the milk carton.
15. After the television program about snakes, we rode on our bikes to the zoo.

PAGE 17 = WORKBOOK PAGE 11

A PREPOSITIONAL PHRASE BEGINS WITH A PREPOSITION AND ENDS WITH A NOUN OR PRONOUN. That noun or pronoun is called the object of the preposition.

to the store (Store is the object of the preposition.)

with me (Me is the object of the preposition.)

Sometimes the preposition will have compound objects. This means that there will be two or more nouns or pronouns following the preposition.

to the store and post* office (Store and office are objects of the preposition.)

*Note that you include only the noun (office); the describing word is not part of the object of the preposition.

with John and me (John and me are objects of the preposition.)

Name________________________________ **PREPOSITIONS**

WORKBOOK PAGE 8

Date_________________________________

Directions: Cross out any prepositional phrases. Underline the subject once and the verb twice.

1. ~~After school~~ we walked ~~to the library~~.

2. Mary sits ~~behind you~~ ~~in science class~~.

3. The plane flew ~~above the clouds~~.

4. Jane lives ~~across the street~~ ~~from me~~.

5. ~~Down the road~~ galloped the horse.

6. We went ~~to the beach~~.

7. Some boys crawled ~~under the car~~.

8. The pump is ~~behind the barn~~.

9. They stopped ~~along the road~~ ~~for five minutes~~.

10. ~~During skiing season~~ our family went ~~to a lodge~~ ~~for a weekend~~.

11. The cars travel ~~below the river~~ and ~~through the tunnel~~.

12. The telephone rang ~~in the middle~~ ~~of the night~~.

13. ~~Below the sink~~ is the garbage can.

14. Everyone ~~except Mary~~ left ~~by noon~~.

15. ~~Within ten minutes~~ ~~of the call~~, my dad arrived ~~in our driveway~~.

Name________________________________ **PREPOSITIONS**

Date________________________________

Directions: Cross out any prepositional phrases. Underline the subject once and the verb twice.

1. After school we walked to the library.
2. Mary sits behind you in science class.
3. The plane flew above the clouds.
4. Jane lives across the street from me.
5. Down the road galloped the horse.
6. We went to the beach.
7. Some boys crawled under the car.
8. The pump is behind the barn.
9. They stopped along the road for five minutes.
10. During skiing season our family went to a lodge for a weekend.
11. The cars travel below the river and through the tunnel.
12. The telephone rang in the middle of the night.
13. Below the sink is the garbage can.
14. Everyone except Mary left by noon.
15. Within ten minutes of the call, my dad arrived in our driveway.

Name_______________________________ **PREPOSITIONS**
WORKBOOK PAGE 9
Date_______________________________

Directions: Cross out any prepositional phrases. Underline the subject once and the verb/verb phrase twice.

Remember: Sometimes the preposition will have a compound object.

1. We take our vacation ~~in July and August~~.

2. The gift was ~~from John and his sister~~.

3. The ball rolled ~~between the chair and the sofa~~.

4. ~~In the spring or summer~~, I visit our friends ~~for a week~~.

5. The librarian gave the books ~~to Tom and me~~.

6. The meal ~~of steak and potatoes~~ was eaten ~~at our favorite diner~~.

7. The taxi driver left ~~without his change or a tip~~ ~~from the passsenger~~.

8. That good reader likes stories ~~about horses and reptiles~~.

9. ~~Down streets and alleys~~ trotted the owner ~~in search~~ ~~of his lost pet~~.

10. ~~During a trip to the zoo~~, the child stared ~~at the lions and the tigers~~.

11. ~~Above the door and windows~~ was a shelf ~~for plants~~.

12. All friends ~~but Susan and Bill~~ came ~~to the party~~.

13. The band leader returned ~~within five or ten minutes~~.

14. ~~Before lunch and dinner~~ the parent reads ~~to the children~~.

15. ~~Beyond the Earth and its moon~~ are other planets.

Name________________________________ **PREPOSITIONS**

Date________________________________

Directions: Cross out any prepositional phrases. Underline the subject once and the verb/verb phrase twice.

Remember: Sometimes the preposition will have a compound object.

1. We take our vacation in July and August.
2. The gift was from John and his sister.
3. The ball rolled between the chair and the sofa.
4. In the spring or summer, I visit our friends for a week.
5. The librarian gave the books to Tom and me.
6. The meal of steak and potatoes was eaten at our favorite diner.
7. The taxi driver left without his change or a tip from the passsenger.
8. That good reader likes stories about horses and reptiles.
9. Down streets and alleys trotted the owner in search of his lost pet.
10. During a trip to the zoo, the child stared at the lions and the tigers.
11. Above the door and windows was a shelf for plants.
12. All friends but Susan and Bill came to the party.
13. The band leader returned within five or ten minutes.
14. Before lunch and dinner the parent reads to the children.
15. Beyond the Earth and its moon are other planets.

PAGE 23 = WORKBOOK PAGE 11

There sometimes is a compound subject in a sentence. Compound subject means there are two or more subjects in the sentence.

A. During the snow storm, the boys and girls rushed home.

~~During the snow storm~~, the boys and girls rushed home.

B. Neither my dad nor my mother went to Mexico City.

Neither my dad nor my mother went ~~to Mexico City~~.

C. Ms. Jones, Mr. Raimo, and Mrs. Burnhart will be in the office from nine until five.

Ms. Jones, Mr. Raimo, and Mrs. Burnhart will be ~~in the office from nine until five~~.

Name________________________________

WORKBOOK PAGE 12

Date________________________________

PREPOSITIONS

Compound Subjects

Directions: Cross out any prepositional phrases. Underline the subject once and the verb/verb phrase twice.

1. ~~Outside the building~~, the cats and dogs played.

2. The burglar and his helper walked ~~toward me~~.

3. The broken cup and saucer were ~~under the table~~.

4. Milk or juice came ~~with the meal~~.

5. ~~Up the tree~~ scurried a squirrel and a chipmunk.

6. ~~Across the Golden Gate Bridge~~ sped the cars and trucks.

7. Neither my hand nor my foot hurt ~~after the injury~~.

8. My cousin and her roommate moved ~~across the hall~~ ~~to a larger apartment~~.

9. ~~Within a week~~ the detective and the other police officer solved the crime.

10. Gloria and Robert married ~~underneath the elm~~ ~~in our backyard~~.

11. ~~After the fire~~ ~~in our home~~, friends and neighbors came ~~with boxes~~.

12. Knives and forks were ~~in the drawer~~ ~~under the counter.~~

13. ~~On the entryway table~~ are a candle and a plant.

14. The teacher and the principal talked ~~about geography~~.

15. ~~For breakfast~~, cereal, pancakes, and toast were served.

Name________________________________

Date________________________________

PREPOSITIONS
Compound Subjects

Directions: Cross out any prepositional phrases. Underline the subject once and the verb/verb phrase twice.

1. Outside the building, the cats and dogs played.
2. The burglar and his helper walked toward me.
3. The broken cup and saucer were under the table.
4. Milk or juice came with the meal.
5. Up the tree scurried a squirrel and a chipmunk.
6. Across the Golden Gate Bridge sped the cars and trucks.
7. Neither my hand nor my foot hurt after the injury.
8. My cousin and her roommate moved across the hall to a larger apartment.
9. Within a week the detective and the other police officer solved the crime.
10. Gloria and Robert married underneath the elm in our backyard.
11. After the fire in our home, friends and neighbors came with boxes.
12. Knives and forks were in the drawer under the counter.
13. On the entryway table are a candle and a plant.
14. The teacher and the principal talked about geography.
15. For breakfast, cereal, pancakes, and toast were served.

Do not stress correct verb phrases at this point. Remember that verbs have not yet been covered as a separate unit. However, explain a verb phrase and give students these helping verbs.

DO NOT EXPECT STUDENTS TO MEMORIZE BOTH THE LIST OF PREPOSITIONS AND THE HELPING VERBS AT THE SAME TIME. STUDENTS WILL BE EXPECTED TO MEMORIZE THE HELPING VERBS UNDER THE VERB SECTION.

WORKBOOK PAGE 10

List of helping verbs:

do
does
did

has
have
had

is
am
are
was
were
be
being
been

may
must
might

should
could
would

shall
will
can

WORKBOOK PAGE 13

NOT is never a verb. Do not underline NOT as part of the verb phrase.

A. The child ~~with the red hair~~ did not sit ~~beside me~~.

B. He should not have given his comb ~~to me~~.

C. This house is not ~~for sale~~.

Note: I recommend that you have students **box** not or n't. This prevents a student from underlining not (n't) as part of the verb phrase.

Name________________________________ **PREPOSITIONS**
WORKBOOK PAGE 14 Helping Verbs
Date________________________________

Directions: Cross out any prepositional phrases. Underline the subject once and the verb/verb phrase twice.

Reminder: Not is an adverb. Do not underline NOT as part of the verb.

1. The swimmers were not competing ~~for ribbons~~.

2. ~~In the afternoon~~ the tots did not take a nap.

3. We will not go ~~to the mountains~~ ~~during the rainy season~~.

4. You should not go ~~before noon~~.

5. The bird would not fly ~~near me~~.

6. The corn was not ~~in the barn~~.

7. The children may not play ~~outside the house~~ ~~during the storm~~.

8. You must not drive ~~through the tunnel~~ ~~without bright headlights~~.

Reminder: In the word CANNOT, underline only the CAN.

9. I cannot understand your answer.

10. ~~Without food~~, your body cannot function.

Reminder: If NOT appears N'T, do not underline the N'T.

11. Some cars haven't been sold ~~at the auction~~.

12. The doctor didn't write a prescription ~~for her patient~~.

13. Shouldn't the officers leave ~~after the program~~?

14. ~~From my point of view~~, you don't deserve a prize ~~for that~~.

15. I won't go ~~without you~~.

Name________________________________

Date________________________________

PREPOSITIONS
Helping Verbs

Directions: Cross out any prepositional phrases. Underline the subject once and the verb/verb phrase twice.

Reminder: Not is an adverb. Do not underline NOT as part of the verb.

1. The swimmers were not competing for ribbons.
2. In the afternoon the tots did not take a nap.
3. We will not go to the mountains during the rainy season.
4. You should not go before noon.
5. The bird would not fly near me.
6. The corn was not in the barn.
7. The children may not play outside the house during the storm.
8. You must not drive through the tunnel without bright headlights.

Reminder: In the word CANNOT, underline only the CAN.

9. I cannot understand your answer.
10. Without food, your body cannot function.

Reminder: If NOT appears N'T, do not underline the N'T.

11. Some cars haven't been sold at the auction.
12. The doctor didn't write a prescription for her patient.
13. Shouldn't the officers leave after the program?
14. From my point of view, you don't deserve a prize for that.
15. I won't go without you.

PAGE 31 = WORKBOOK PAGE 15

Sometimes *to* will come before a verb. TO + VERB is an infinitive; TO + VERB IS NOT A PREPOSITIONAL PHRASE.

To dance, to sing, to yell, to be, to leave, to go are examples of infinitives. Do NOT cross them out as prepositional phrases. Place an infinitive in parenthesis.

Example: I like (to sing) ~~in the morning~~.

A. in the morning - a prepositional phrase

B. to sing - infinitive (to + verb)

Note: Instruct students to place an infinitive in parenthesis. This will refrain students from crossing out infinitives.

Name________________________________
WORKBOOK PAGE 16
Date________________________________

PREPOSITIONS
Infinitives

Directions: Cross out any prepositional phrases. Underline the subject once and the verb/verb phrase twice. Place each infinitive in parenthesis.

Reminder: TO + VERB = INFINITIVE. Do not cross out an infinitive.

Example: I like (to go) ~~to the movies~~.

1. ~~At night~~ he wants (to leave) ~~by bus~~.
2. The child decided (to run) ~~to the baseball game~~.
3. ~~After dinner~~ the guests desire (to enjoy) some coffee.
4. The artist likes (to paint) ~~during the morning~~.
5. The teams wanted (to practice) ~~after school~~.
6. She forgot (to look) ~~for her lost watch~~.
7. The rider hopes (to be) ~~in the rodeo~~.
8. ~~For an hour~~ the customers waited ~~for dinner~~.
9. His uncle pretended (to twist) his arm.
10. They like (to play) ~~against that team~~.
11. The diplomat waited (to hear) the end ~~of the speech~~.
12. The cheerleader ran (to catch) the bus ~~for the game~~.
13. ~~Before the game~~ the spectators rose (to sing) the national anthem.
14. ~~During the parade~~ the marcher stopped (to rest) ~~for a moment~~.
15. A few ~~of the guests~~ ~~at the wedding~~ wanted (to dance) ~~with the bride~~.

Name________________________________

Date________________________________

PREPOSITIONS
Infinitives

Directions: Cross out any prepositional phrases. Underline the subject once and the verb/verb phrase twice. Place each infinitive in parenthesis.

Reminder: TO + VERB = INFINITIVE. Do not cross out an infinitive.

Example: I like (to go) ~~to the movies~~.

1. At night he wants to leave by bus.
2. The child decided to run to the baseball game.
3. After dinner the guests desire to enjoy some coffee.
4. The artist likes to paint during the morning.
5. The teams wanted to practice after school.
6. She forgot to look for her lost watch.
7. The rider hopes to be in the rodeo.
8. For an hour the customers waited for dinner.
9. His uncle pretended to twist his arm.
10. They like to play against that team.
11. The diplomat waited to hear the end of the speech.
12. The cheerleader ran to catch the bus for the game.
13. Before the game the spectators rose to sing the national anthem.
14. During the parade the marcher stopped to rest for a moment.
15. A few of the guests at the wedding wanted to dance with the bride.

PAGE 35 = WORKBOOK PAGE 17

In an imperative sentence, the subject is (You).

I. An imperative sentence gives a command.

II. (You) is termed ***YOU UNDERSTOOD***. It is written at the beginning of the sentence, underlined, and placed in parenthesis.

EXAMPLES:

A. Go down the street.

(You) Go ~~down the street~~.

B. Please look at me.

(You) Please look ~~at me~~.

C. Put the scissors in the drawer.

(You) Put the scissors* ~~in the drawer~~.

*Some students will want to underline scissors as the subject.

1. Lead them to see that it is an imperative sentence and review that (You) will be the subject.

2. Ask the questions, "Are the scissors putting?" No. Help the students to see that **YOU** are putting.

Name______________________________ **PREPOSITIONS**

WORKBOOK PAGE 18 Imperative

Date______________________________

Directions: Cross out any prepositional phrases. Underline the subject once and the verb/verb phrase twice.

Reminder: In an imperative sentence (command), the subject is often (You).

(You)
1. Put the packages ~~from my grandparents~~ ~~on the kitchen table~~.

(You)
2. ~~During the thunderstorm~~, light the candles.

(You)
3. Tell the class ~~about your summer~~.

(You)
4. Sit ~~between Tracy and my brother~~ ~~during the game~~.

(You)
5. Jump ~~on the wagon~~.

(You)
6. Look ~~under the sink~~ ~~for the paper bag~~.

(You)
7. ~~After class~~ give the teacher your paper.

(You)
8. Walk ~~toward me~~.

(You)
9. ~~From the town square~~, drive three miles ~~to the inn~~.

(You)
10. Stop ~~in the middle~~ ~~of the road~~.

(You)
11. Pay ~~for the tour~~ ~~inside the museum~~.

(You)
12. Hurry ~~down the hall~~ ~~for your next meeting~~.

(You)
13. ~~Near the end~~ ~~of the year~~, take a trip ~~to Paris~~.

(You)
14. Go ~~into the apartment~~ ~~for an umbrella~~.

(You)
15. ~~In January~~ send the children ~~to the nurse~~ ~~for a hearing test~~.

Name________________________________

Date________________________________

PREPOSITIONS
Imperative Sentences

Directions: Cross out any prepositional phrases. Underline the subject once and the verb/verb phrase twice.

Reminder: In an imperative sentence (command), the subject is often (<u>You</u>).

1. Put the packages from my grandparents on the kitchen table.

2. During the thunderstorm, light the candles.

3. Tell the class about your summer.

4. Sit between Tracy and my brother during the game.

5. Jump on the wagon.

6. Look under the sink for the paper bag.

7. After class give the teacher your paper.

8. Walk toward me.

9. From the town square, drive three miles to the inn.

10. Stop in the middle of the road.

11. Pay for the tour inside the museum.

12. Hurry down the hall for your next meeting.

13. Near the end of the year, take a trip to Paris.

14. Go into the apartment for an umbrella.

15. In January send the children to the nurse for a hearing test.

Name________________________________ **PREPOSITIONS**

WORKBOOK PAGE 19

Date________________________________

Directions: Cross out any prepositional phrases. Underline the subject once and the verb/verb phrase twice.

1. John walked ~~along the trail~~ ~~during the summer~~.

2. ~~In one cage~~ we saw a huge bird ~~from the jungles~~ ~~of Brazil~~.

3. A rose bush ~~with sharp thorns~~ grew ~~inside our fence~~.

4. She divided the candy ~~among the children~~ ~~at the party~~.

5. The boys will go ~~across the street~~, ~~through the alley~~, and ~~into the park~~.

6. ~~Beyond that hill~~ is a house ~~without a roof~~.

7. ~~Near that city~~ and ~~past a mountain~~ is a pot ~~of gold~~ ~~for you~~.

8. ~~Along the muddy road~~ and ~~against the rain~~, the lady walked ~~underneath an umbrella~~.

9. ~~Above the third shelf~~, you will find books ~~about Abe Lincoln~~ and ~~concerning other aspects~~ ~~of American history~~.

10. ~~In the middle~~ ~~of the party~~, the lady dashed ~~out the door~~ ~~without her coat~~.

11. ~~Beneath the tree~~ slumbered an old man ~~with his dog~~.

12. The lad darted ~~beyond his mother's reach~~ ~~during the game~~.

    (You)
13. Walk ~~past the gate~~ and ~~through the door~~ to find a beautiful room ~~without furniture~~.

14. The dessert was stored ~~in the refrigerator~~ ~~until the end~~ ~~of the meal~~.

15. ~~Behind me~~ sat a clown ~~with his balloons and lollipops~~.

Name________________________________ **PREPOSITIONS**

Date________________________________

Directions: Cross out any prepositional phrases. Underline the subject once and the verb/verb phrase twice.

1. John walked along the trail during the summer.
2. In one cage we saw a huge bird from the jungles of Brazil.
3. A rose bush with sharp thorns grew inside our fence.
4. She divided the candy among the children at the party.
5. The boys will go across the street, through the alley, and into the park.
6. Beyond that hill is a house without a roof.
7. Near that city and past a mountain is a pot of gold for you.
8. Along the muddy road and against the rain, the lady walked underneath an umbrella.
9. Above the third shelf, you will find books about Abe Lincoln and concerning other aspects of American history.
10. In the middle of the party, the lady dashed out the door without her coat.
11. Beneath the tree slumbered an old man with his dog.
12. The lad darted beyond his mother's reach during the game.
13. Walk past the gate and through the door to find a beautiful room without furniture.
14. The dessert was stored in the refrigerator until the end of the meal.
15. Behind me sat a clown with his balloons and lollipops.

PREPOSITION VERSUS ADVERB

Do not confuse the students. Emphasize that a preposition must be part of a prepositional phrase. In other words, it must have a noun or pronoun closely following the preposition. If there is no noun or pronoun, then the preposition is not crossed out. Do NOT bother to explain that the word (preposition) is then an adverb.

Examples:

A. The dog squeezed in through the doggie door.

The dog squeezed in* ~~through the doggie door.~~

**In* cannot be a preposition because there is no noun or pronoun following it. A preposition must have an object.

B. After lunch the guests walked out into the garden.

~~After lunch~~ the guests walked out* ~~into the garden.~~

**Out* is not a preposition. It does not have a noun or pronoun (object of the preposition).

Name_______________________________ **PREPOSITIONS**
WORKBOOK PAGE 20 Preposition or Adverb?
Date_______________________________

Directions: Cross out any prepositional phrases. Underline the subject once and the verb/verb phrase twice.

1. The bird flew in and out ~~among the branches~~ ~~of the oak tree~~.

2. She looked up ~~in the sky~~.

3. Do you live near ~~to me~~?

4. The tourists went down ~~into the caverns~~.

5. The model strolled in and looked ~~around the room~~.

6. The child dashed over ~~to the edge~~ ~~of the canyon~~.

7. ~~During the hayride~~, the leader jumped off ~~of the wagon~~.

8. Someone ~~like Jane~~ may come over ~~for a visit~~.

9. ~~In the breeze~~, the flower swayed up and down.

10. Dad will come along ~~on the picnic~~ tomorrow.

11. Our family went outside to take a picture.

12. (You) Go in ~~through the side entrance~~.

13. He crawled ~~below the deck~~ and remained inside.

14. The secretary and the accountant walked around and found the missing notebook ~~in the trash can~~.

15. The oven has been turned off ~~for an hour and thirty minutes~~.

Name_______________________________

Date_______________________________

PREPOSITIONS
Preposition or Adverb?

Directions: Cross out any prepositional phrases. Underline the subject once and the verb/verb phrase twice.

1. The bird flew in and out among the branches of the oak tree.

2. She looked up in the sky.

3. Do you live near to me?

4. The tourists went down into the caverns.

5. The model strolled in and looked around the room.

6. The child dashed over to the edge of the canyon.

7. During the hayride, the leader jumped off of the wagon.

8. Someone like Jane may come over for a visit.

9. In the breeze, the flower swayed up and down.

10. Dad will come along on the picnic tomorrow.

11. Our family went outside to take a picture.

12. Go in through the side entrance.

13. He crawled below the deck and remained inside.

14. The secretary and the accountant walked around and found the missing notebook in the trash can.

15. The oven has been turned off for an hour and thirty minutes.

PAGE 45 = WORKBOOK PAGE 21

Helpful Hints

I. Words that end in ly are usually adverbs. They are not prepositions.

Examples: A. We went into the pool carefully.

ADV.
We went ~~into the pool~~ carefully.

B. Slowly the banker walked into the vault.

ADV.
Slowly the banker walked ~~into the vault~~.

II. If you are not sure if a word is part of the verb, try putting TO in front of the word. If you cannot divide it into present (today), and past (yesterday) tenses, the word probably is not a verb.

Examples: A. The pie was good.

Can you say "To Good"? Today I good; yesterday I gooded. Good does not make sense here, and thus, good is not part of the verb.

The pie was good.

B. Marty was happy.

Can you say "To Happy"? Today I happy; yesterday I happied. Happy does not make sense here, and thus, happy is not part of the verb.

Marty was happy.

Name________________________________ **PREPOSITIONS**

WORKBOOK PAGE 22

Date________________________________

Directions: Cross out any prepositional phrases. Underline the subject once and the verb/verb phrase twice.

1. ~~In the bushes~~ ~~along the road~~ stood an elephant ~~with purple spots~~ ~~in front of his eyes~~.

2. You may go ~~at noon~~ ~~except Saturdays~~.

3. ~~Until Christmas~~, the shoppers will travel ~~through stores~~, ~~across streets~~, ~~between cars~~ ~~in parking lots~~, and ~~past decorated windows~~ ~~in search~~ ~~of the perfect gift~~.

4. ~~At the beginning~~ ~~of the year~~, students must learn rules ~~concerning the playground~~ and ~~regarding the lunch line~~.

5. ~~On the fifth~~ ~~of November~~, everyone ~~but my brother and sister~~ should arrive ~~in Phoenix~~ ~~by plane~~.

6. ~~During the football game~~, many spectators sat ~~behind the goal posts~~ and went frequently ~~to the snack bar~~.

7. ~~Near the museum~~ stands a statue ~~of Paul Bunyon and his ox~~.

(You)

8. Go ~~down the street~~ ~~for a cup~~ ~~of milk~~.

9. You may not go ~~between the buildings~~ or ~~outside the school campus~~ ~~from eight o'clock~~ ~~until four o'clock~~.

10. The can ~~of soup~~ is ~~below the sink~~, ~~above the stove~~, or ~~beside the refrigerator~~.

11. ~~Over the bridge~~, ~~under the freeway~~, and ~~through the field~~ ran the team.

12. ~~After the game~~, the girls ~~in the blue sweaters~~ walked ~~to the auditorium~~.

13. ~~After class~~ you must go ~~out the door~~ and ~~into the street~~ ~~for a parade~~.

14. The book ~~concerning politics~~ is ~~against discrimination~~.

15. ~~By noon~~ we had walked ~~over a mile~~ ~~beyond our goal~~.

Name______________________________ **PREPOSITIONS**

Date______________________________

Directions: Cross out any prepositional phrases. Underline the subject once and the verb/verb phrase twice.

1. In the bushes along the road stood an elephant with purple spots in front of his eyes.
2. You may go at noon except Saturdays.
3. Until Christmas, the shoppers will travel through stores, across streets, between cars in parking lots, and past decorated windows in search of the perfect gift.
4. At the beginning of the year, students must learn rules concerning the playground and regarding the lunch line.
5. On the fifth of November, everyone but my brother and sister should arrive in Phoenix by plane.
6. During the football, game many spectators sat behind the goal posts and went frequently to the snack bar.
7. Near the museum stands a statue of Paul Bunyon and his ox.
8. Go down the street for a cup of milk.
9. You may not go between the buildings or outside the school campus from eight o'clock until four o'clock.
10. The can of soup is below the sink, above the stove, or beside the refrigerator.
11. Over the bridge, under the freeway, and through the field ran the team.
12. After the game, the girls in the blue sweaters walked to the auditorium.
13. After class you must go out the door and into the street for a parade.
14. The book concerning politics is against discrimination.
15. By noon we had walked over a mile beyond our goal.

Name______________________________ **PREPOSITIONS**
WORKBOOK PAGE 23
Date______________________________

Directions: Cross out any prepositional phrases. Underline the subject once and the verb/verb phrase twice.

1. ~~Over that hill~~ and ~~past the bridge~~ jogged a lady ~~with her new dog~~.

2. ~~Throughout the night~~ the security guard walked ~~from store~~ ~~to store~~.

3. The meeting ~~concerning the new town hall~~ met ~~at the library~~.

4. ~~During the celebration~~ everyone ~~except Mother~~ flew ~~to San Diego~~.

5. ~~On the moonlit night~~, the deer appeared ~~in a field~~ ~~by the quiet stream~~.

6. The student walked ~~out the door~~ ~~among his friends~~ ~~during graduation practice~~.

7. The treasure was buried ~~underneath a tree~~ ~~near the railroad car~~.

8. The movie star walked ~~among the fans~~ and ~~across the street~~ ~~to the theater~~.

9. ~~Out the door~~ and ~~into the car~~ scurried the woman ~~with her brown briefcase~~.

10. ~~During the carnival~~, the small child squirmed out ~~of the reach~~ ~~of his parents~~.

11. The person ~~beside me~~ plays a flute ~~in our band~~.

12. The dancers waltzed ~~off the floor~~ and went outside ~~for some cool air~~.

(You)
13. Go ~~to the snack bar~~ ~~before the movie~~.

14. The swimmer dived ~~off the board~~ and swam ~~toward me~~.

15. ~~From 5 o'clock~~ ~~until 8 o'clock~~, I wandered ~~around the building~~ to find my mother.

Name________________________________ **PREPOSITIONS**

Date________________________________

Directions: Cross out any prepositional phrases. Underline the subject once and the verb/verb phrase twice.

1. Over that hill and past the bridge jogged a lady with her new dog.

2. Throughout the night the security guard walked from store to store.

3. The meeting concerning the new town hall met at the library.

4. During the celebration everyone except Mother flew to San Diego.

5. On the moonlit night, the deer appeared in a field by the quiet stream.

6. The student walked out the door among his friends during graduation practice.

7. The treasure was buried underneath a tree near the railroad car.

8. The movie star walked among the fans and across the street to the theater.

9. Out the door and into the car scurried the woman with her brown briefcase.

10. During the carnival, the small child squirmed out of the reach of his parents.

11. The person beside me plays a flute in our band.

12. The dancers waltzed off the floor and went outside for some cool air.

13. Go to the snack bar before the movie.

14. The swimmer dived off the board and swam toward me.

15. From 5 o'clock until 8 o'clock, I wandered around the building to find my mother.

Name________________________________ **PREPOSITIONS**

WORKBOOK PAGE 24

Date________________________________

Directions: Cross out any prepositional phrases. Underline the subject once and the verb/verb phrase twice.

1. Some spectators ~~in the back row~~ ~~of the rodeo~~ jeered ~~at the clowns~~ ~~after the last event~~.

2. ~~Around the house~~ and ~~across the street~~ ran a little squirrel ~~with an acorn~~ ~~in his mouth~~.

3. ~~During the storm~~, the wind blew ~~inside the house~~ ~~from the north~~.

4. Our maid cleaned the top ~~of the counter~~ and looked ~~amid the groceries~~ ~~throughout the refrigerator~~.

5. We will be ~~at the mall~~ ~~by the fountain~~ ~~within an hour~~.

6. Three ~~of the students~~ were ~~against shorter vacations~~ ~~for teachers~~.

7. The letters ~~for Lani and Jacy~~ ~~concerning college~~ and ~~regarding admission costs~~ were ~~outside the house~~ ~~in the mailbox~~.

8. All cars ~~except the blue one~~ were sold ~~before noon~~ ~~by that salesman~~.

9. ~~Between you and me~~, the crickets were singing ~~in the oleander~~ ~~after the rain~~.

10. Our plane flew ~~through a storm~~ ~~over the Rio Grande River~~.

11. The yacht sailed ~~across the Potomac River~~ and ~~under the Mason Bridge~~.

(You)

12. Do not go ~~past the line~~ ~~until the end~~ ~~of the game~~.

13. All ~~of my cousins~~ ~~except John~~ went ~~to the zoo~~ ~~without their jackets~~.

14. ~~Down the slopes~~ ~~toward the Swiss village~~ came the mountain climbers.

15. The matter ~~concerning the parking ticket~~ was decided ~~by the judge~~ ~~at the court~~ ~~on Monday~~.

Name________________________________ **PREPOSITIONS**

Date________________________________

Directions: Cross out any prepositional phrases. Underline the subject once and the verb/verb phrase twice.

1. Some spectators in the back row of the rodeo jeered at the clowns after the last event.

2. Around the house and across the street ran a little squirrel with an acorn in his mouth.

3. During the storm, the wind blew inside the house from the north.

4. Our maid cleaned the top of the counter and looked amid the groceries throughout the refrigerator.

5. We will be at the mall by the fountain within an hour.

6. Three of the students were against shorter vacations for teachers.

7. The letters for Lani and Jacy concerning college and regarding admission costs were outside the house in the mailbox.

8. All cars except the blue one were sold before noon by that salesman.

9. Between you and me, the crickets were singing in the oleander after the rain.

10. Our plane flew through a storm over the Rio Grande River.

11. The yacht sailed across the Potomac River and under the Mason Bridge.

12. Do not go past the line until the end of the game.

13. All of my cousins except John went to the zoo without their jackets.

14. Down the slopes toward the Swiss village came the mountain climbers.

15. The matter concerning the parking ticket was decided by the judge at the court on Monday.

Name________________________________ **PREPOSITIONS**

WORKBOOK PAGE 25

Date________________________________

Directions: Cross out any prepositional phrases. Underline the subject once and the verb/verb phrase twice.

1. ~~In the early morning~~, the birds chirped ~~in the back~~ ~~of the house~~ ~~near the pond~~.

2. ~~After this year~~, the students must go ~~to the lakes~~ ~~for a short vacation~~.

3. We walked ~~through the forest~~, ~~past the old mill~~, and ~~between two highways~~.

(You)

4. Place the boxes ~~over the sink~~ or ~~under the cupboard~~.

5. ~~Without your help~~, I would lose ~~at chess and checkers~~.

6. The man threw his fishing pole ~~to his friend~~ ~~across the stream~~.

7. Many ~~of the cows~~ were lying ~~in the field~~ ~~after the storm~~.

8. ~~Behind the woods~~ and ~~over that hill~~, you will find a prize ~~in a pile~~ ~~of rubble~~.

(You)

9. Look ~~across the street~~ and ~~down the road~~ ~~before crossing~~.

10. ~~From the looks~~ ~~of the weather~~, the children should not go ~~outside the house~~.

11. ~~Before the meeting~~, the group talked ~~about women's liberation~~.

12. Up ~~above the rooftops~~ is a beautiful full moon ~~with a haze~~ ~~around it~~.

(You)

13. Don't tell anyone ~~about the decision~~ ~~concerning the talent show and the puppet production.~~

14. ~~Atop the fence~~ ~~at the edge~~ ~~of the town~~ sat a hobo ~~throughout the hot day~~ ~~in July~~.

15. ~~Before recess~~, groups ~~of students~~ were not allowed to go out ~~into the hallway~~ ~~without the teacher~~.

Name______________________________

PREPOSITIONS

Date______________________________

Directions: Cross out any prepositional phrases. Underline the subject once and the verb/verb phrase twice.

1. In the early morning, the birds chirped in the back of the house near the pond.
2. After this year, the students must go to the lakes for a short vacation.
3. We walked through the forest, past the old mill, and between two highways.
4. Place the boxes over the sink or under the cupboard.
5. Without your help, I would lose at chess and checkers.
6. The man threw his fishing pole to his friend across the stream.
7. Many of the cows were lying in the field after the storm.
8. Behind the woods and over that hill, you will find a prize in a pile of rubble.
9. Look across the street and down the road before crossing.
10. From the looks of the weather, the children should not go outside the house.
11. Before the meeting, the group talked about women's liberation.
12. Up above the rooftops is a beautiful full moon with a haze around it.
13. Don't tell anyone about the decision concerning the talent show and the puppet production.
14. Atop the fence at the edge of the town sat a hobo throughout the hot day in July.
15. Before recess, groups of students were not allowed to go out into the hallway without the teacher.

Name________________________________ **PREPOSITIONS**

WORKBOOK PAGE 26

Date________________________________

Directions: Cross out any prepositional phrases. Underline the subject once and the verb/verb phrase twice.

1. ~~After the session~~ ~~with the band leader~~, the team didn't want to go ~~without you~~.

2. ~~Within the hour~~, the mail person delivered a box ~~for Mrs. Hill~~.

3. Archaeologists ~~with dedication~~ dig ~~for days~~ ~~in search~~ ~~of artifacts~~.

4. ~~Beyond the wall~~ there is a lovely puppy ~~from your dad~~.

5. ~~Around the turn~~ ~~in the road~~ and ~~about two miles~~ ~~down the road~~, there is located an old inn.

6. ~~During the American Revolution~~, Paine wrote a book ~~concerning liberty and justice~~.

7. Johnathon lives near ~~to you~~, ~~past that old bridge~~, and ~~under an oak tree~~.

8. (You) Find the marbles ~~under the sink~~, ~~beneath the first shelf~~, ~~below the bathroom vanity~~, or ~~underneath a rock~~ ~~in the front yard~~.

9. ~~Over the bridge~~, ~~past the toll booth~~, and ~~through the tunnel~~, the cars ~~of New York~~ travel.

10. His statement ~~regarding our defense~~ was good.

11. ~~In the middle~~ ~~of the mutiny~~, Columbus's men saw birds and knew ~~about land~~.

12. He went up ~~in the elevator~~ and out ~~onto the observation deck~~.

13. (You) Give the message ~~about her illness~~ ~~to your mother~~ today ~~after school~~.

14. A few ~~of the games~~ were played ~~during the evening hours~~ ~~before dark~~.

15. Did any ~~of the mothers~~ fill ~~in the forms~~ ~~about the children's health records~~?

Name________________________________ **PREPOSITIONS**

Date________________________________

Directions: Cross out any prepositional phrases. Underline the subject once and the verb/verb phrase twice.

1. After the session with the band leader, the team didn't want to go without you.
2. Within the hour, the mail person delivered a box for Mrs. Hill.
3. Archaeologists with dedication dig for days in search of artifacts.
4. Beyond the wall there is a lovely puppy from your dad.
5. Around the turn in the road and about two miles down the road, there is located an old inn.
6. During the American Revolution, Paine wrote a book concerning liberty and justice.
7. Johnathon lives near to you, past that old bridge, and under an oak tree.
8. Find the marbles under the sink, beneath the first shelf, below the bathroom vanity, or underneath a rock in the front yard.
9. Over the bridge, past the toll booth, and through the tunnel, the cars of New York travel.
10. His statement regarding our defense was good.
11. In the middle of the mutiny, Columbus's men saw birds and knew about land.
12. He went up in the elevator and out onto the observation deck.
13. Give the message about her illness to your mother today after school.
14. A few of the games were played during the evening hours before dark.
15. Did any of the mothers fill in the forms about the children's health records?

Name________________________________ **PREPOSITIONS**

WORKBOOK PAGE 27

Date_________________________________

Directions: Cross out any prepositional phrases. Underline the subject once and the verb/verb phrase twice.

1. ~~After the game~~, the team ate ~~at a restaurant~~ ~~on the freeway~~.

2. ~~During the class~~, a student pitched a book ~~out the window~~.

3. The girl stumbled ~~over a rock~~ and was taken ~~to emergency~~.

4. The ladies and men ~~of the photography club~~ met ~~at the library~~ ~~at seven o'clock~~ ~~in the evening~~.

5. ~~In October~~, the teacher gave a test ~~about fractions~~.

6. ~~Through the forest~~ and ~~past the old mill~~ lives a carpenter ~~with his horse and dog~~.

7. ~~In July~~, school is not ~~in session~~.

8. (You)
Come ~~into the house~~ and take ~~off your shoes~~ ~~in the kitchen~~.

9. ~~During the spring break~~, the members ~~of our club~~ visited Maine.

10. (You)
Quietly and carefully remove the boxes ~~from the premises~~.

11. The meal ~~of meat loaf, au gratin potatoes, and beans~~ was good.

12. The lid ~~of the tea kettle~~ was closed.

13. ~~After the sale~~, every woman went ~~into the store~~, ~~down the escalator~~, and ~~to the bargains~~ ~~in the basement~~.

14. The picture ~~of Martha Washington~~ hung ~~in the closet~~ ~~by the fireplace~~.

15. The walls ~~of the mansion~~ were ~~of gold and marble~~.

Name________________________________ **PREPOSITIONS**

Date________________________________

Directions: Cross out any prepositional phrases. Underline the subject once and the verb/verb phrase twice.

1. After the game, the team ate at a restaurant on the freeway.
2. During the class, a student pitched a book out the window.
3. The girl stumbled over a rock and was taken to emergency.
4. The ladies and men of the photography club met at the library at seven o'clock in the evening.
5. In October, the teacher gave a test about fractions.
6. Through the forest and past the old mill lives a carpenter with his horse and dog.
7. In July, school is not in session.
8. Come into the house and take off your shoes in the kitchen.
9. During the spring break, the members of our club visited Maine.
10. Quietly and carefully remove the boxes from the premises.
11. The meal of meat loaf, au gratin potatoes, and beans was good.
12. The lid of the tea kettle was closed.
13. After the sale, every woman went into the store, down the escalator, and to the bargains in the basement.
14. The picture of Martha Washington hung in the closet by the fireplace.
15. The walls of the mansion were of gold and marble.

Name________________________________ **PREPOSITION REVIEW**

WORKBOOK PAGE 28

Date________________________________

A. **Infinitives:**

Directions: Cross out any prepositional phrases. Underline the subject once and the verb/verb phrase twice. Place any infinitive in parenthesis ( ).

1. Marnie's mother and father want (to go) ~~to New York~~ ~~during the summer~~.

2. A group ~~of parents~~ went ~~into the auditorium~~ (to hear) several speakers.

3. They like (to eat) lunch ~~at that cafe~~ ~~on Brock Street~~.

4. The reporter decided (to interview) the mayor ~~of our town~~.

5. His sister pretended (to be) angry ~~with him~~.

6. Their car did **not** need (to remain) ~~in the repair shop~~ ~~for a long time~~.

7. Many tourists stopped (to read) brochures ~~about Pearl Harbor~~.

B. **Verb Phrases:**

Directions: Cross out any prepositional phrases. Underline the subject once and the verb/verb phrase twice.

1. The garbage truck has stopped ~~near the corner~~ ~~of Washington Street~~.

2. May I sit ~~between Todd and you~~ ~~for ten minutes~~?

3. Everyone ~~but John~~ must have taken his bathing suit ~~with him~~.

4. We will be rowing ~~on the lake~~ ~~after sunset~~ today.

5. Does the policeman attend the church ~~beside the new park~~?

6. Your name should **not** have been written ~~in cursive~~.

7. Mark's friend can**not** come ~~until the end~~ ~~of the winter~~.

Name________________________________

Date________________________________

PREPOSITION REVIEW

A. **Infinitives:**

Directions: Cross out any prepositional phrases. Underline the subject once and the verb/verb phrase twice. Place any infinitive in parenthesis ( ).

1. Marnie's mother and father want to go to New York during the summer.
2. A group of parents went into the auditorium to hear several speakers.
3. They like to eat lunch at that cafe on Brock Street.
4. The reporter decided to interview the mayor of our town.
5. His sister pretended to be angry with him.
6. Their car did not need to remain in the repair shop for a long time.
7. Many tourists stopped to read brochures about Pearl Harbor.

B. **Verb Phrases:**

Directions: Cross out any prepositional phrases. Underline the subject once and the verb/verb phrase twice.

1. The garbage truck has stopped near the corner of Washington Street.
2. May I sit between Todd and you for ten minutes?
3. Everyone but John must have taken his bathing suit with him.
4. We will be rowing on the lake after sunset today.
5. Does the policeman attend the church beside the new park?
6. Your name should not have been written in cursive.
7. Mark's friend cannot come until the end of the winter.

Name________________________________ **PREPOSITION REVIEW**

WORKBOOK PAGE 29

Date________________________________

C. **Imperative Sentences:**

Directions: Cross out any prepositional phrases. Underline the subject once and the verb/verb phrase twice.

1. (You) Give this tip ~~to the waiter~~ ~~in the checkered shirt~~.

2. (You) Remove your shoes ~~at the door~~, please.

3. (You) ~~Near the end~~ ~~of the day~~, please take a bath.

4. (You) Follow the interstate highway ~~through the tunnels~~.

5. (You) Drive ~~to the side~~ ~~of the road~~ immediately.

6. (You) ~~After the meeting~~, hand a pamphlet ~~to everyone~~ ~~but Mr. Barton~~.

7. (You) Sit ~~across the table~~ ~~from me~~ ~~during the luncheon~~ ~~with those guests~~.

D. **Compound Objects:**

Directions: Cross out any prepositional phrase(s). Underline the subject once and the verb/verb phrase twice.

1. Mrs. Little stepped ~~into the rain~~ ~~without a hat or an umbrella~~.

2. A young lady ~~with red hair~~ sat ~~between Mary and me~~.

3. A package ~~from Grandma and Grandpa~~ was delivered ~~before lunch~~.

4. ~~In July, August, or September~~, their family will visit Montana.

5. Flowers grow ~~along the walk and driveway~~ ~~of the new home~~.

6. One ~~of the houses~~ ~~by the sea~~ won't be completed ~~until fall or winter~~.

7. (You) Go ~~past the library and police station~~ (to reach) the courthouse.

Name________________________________

Date________________________________

PREPOSITION REVIEW

C. **Imperative Sentences:**

Directions: Cross out any prepositional phrases. Underline the subject once and the verb/verb phrase twice.

1. Give this tip to the waiter in the checkered shirt.
2. Remove your shoes at the door, please.
3. Near the end of the day, please take a bath.
4. Follow the interstate highway through the tunnels.
5. Drive to the side of the road immediately.
6. After the meeting, hand a pamphlet to everyone but Mr. Barton.
7. Sit across the table from me during the luncheon with those guests.

D. **Compound Objects:**

Directions: Cross out any prepositional phrases. Underline the subject once and the verb/verb phrase twice.

1. Mrs. Little stepped into the rain without a hat or an umbrella.
2. A young lady with red hair sat between Mary and me.
3. A package from Grandma and Grandpa was delivered before lunch.
4. In July, August, or September, their family will visit Montana.
5. Flowers grow along the walk and driveway of the new home.
6. One of the houses by the sea won't be completed until fall or winter.
7. Go past the library and police station to reach the courthouse.

Name_______________________________
WORKBOOK PAGE 30
Date_______________________________

PREPOSITION REVIEW

E. **Compound Subjects:**

Directions: Cross out any prepositional phrases. Underline the subject once and the verb/verb phrase twice.

1. Doug and his new bride vacationed ~~in Florida~~.

2. ~~During the fair~~, a country singer and his band performed ~~for a huge crowd~~.

3. A bowl ~~of various fruits~~ and a plate ~~of cheeses~~ are ~~beside the crackers~~.

4. ~~Underneath the steps of a small cottage~~ lay a tawny cat and a black dog.

5. Ted's brother and friend chased ~~around the park on roller blades~~.

6. Some businesswomen and politicians are meeting (to discuss) the economy.

7. The attorneys and the judge went ~~into the chambers for a private discussion~~.

F. **Compound Verbs:**

Directions: Cross out any prepositional phrases. Underline the subject once and the verb/verb phrase twice.

1. The instructor stood ~~among the students~~ and chatted ~~with them~~.

2. Did the technician fix the television or tell Kurt (to buy) another?

3. Some children walked ~~along the road~~ and picked flowers.

4. ~~After supper~~, we cleared the table and rinsed our dishes.

5. (You) Go ~~inside the shed~~ and get sponges and a pail ~~for water~~, please.

6. My glass duck ~~from Aunt Betty~~ has fallen ~~on the stairs~~ and has broken ~~into many pieces~~.

7. Everyone ~~but Jonah~~ stood and cheered ~~for the contestants~~.

Name______________________________

Date______________________________

PREPOSITION REVIEW

E. **Compound Subjects:**

Directions: Cross out any prepositional phrases. Underline the subject once and the verb/verb phrase twice.

1. Doug and his new bride vacationed in Florida.

2. During the fair, a country singer and his band performed for a huge crowd.

3. A bowl of various fruits and a plate of cheeses are beside the crackers.

4. Underneath the steps of a small cottage lay a tawny cat and a black dog.

5. Ted's brother and friend chased around the park on roller blades.

6. Some businesswomen and politicians are meeting to discuss the economy.

7. The attorneys and the judge went into the chambers for a private discussion.

F. **Compound Verbs:**

Directions: Cross out any prepositional phrases. Underline the subject once and the verb/verb phrase twice.

1. The instructor stood among the students and chatted with them.

2. Did the technician fix the television or tell Kurt to buy another?

3. Some children walked along the road and picked flowers.

4. After supper, we cleared the table and rinsed our dishes.

5. Go inside the shed and get sponges and a pail for water, please.

6. My glass duck from Aunt Betty has fallen on the stairs and has broken into many pieces.

7. Everyone but Jonah stood and cheered for the contestants.

Name________________________________

WORKBOOK PAGE 31

Date________________________________

PREPOSITION REVIEW

G. **Preposition or Adverb:**

Directions: Cross out any prepositional phrases. Underline the subject once and the verb/verb phrase twice. Label any adverb-Adv.

1. That small child often falls down (Adv.) ~~on his roller skates~~.
2. Lenny's brothers are playing outside (Adv.) ~~in the rain~~.
3. The dog went outside (Adv.) and ran around (Adv.) ~~in a circle~~.
4. (You) Please look up (Adv.) ~~toward the skylight~~ ~~in the ceiling~~.
5. The teenagers walked in (Adv.) and out (Adv.) ~~among the fair booths~~.
6. Are Annie and James lagging behind (Adv.) again?
7. One ~~of the players~~ ~~on the other team~~ came over (Adv.) (to talk) ~~to my brother~~.
8. We walked inside (Adv.) and looked ~~for a guide~~.
9. Rob will come along (Adv.) ~~with us~~.
10. Several girls rode by (Adv.) ~~on their bikes~~ and waved.
11. A frightened child would not (Adv.) come near (Adv.).
12. You may not (Adv.) go through (Adv.) ~~without a ticket.~~
13. (You) Please come by (Adv.) ~~in the morning~~.
14. The mother walked inside (Adv.) and checked the cake ~~in the oven~~.
15. She approached the table, looked underneath (Adv.), and found a giggling toddler.
16. The shopper looked both ways ~~at the intersection~~ and hurried across (Adv.).

Name________________________________

Date________________________________

PREPOSITION REVIEW

G. **Preposition or Adverb:**

Directions: Cross out any prepositional phrases. Underline the subject once and the verb/verb phrase twice. Label any adverb-Adv.

1. That small child often falls down on his roller skates.
2. Lenny's brothers are playing outside in the rain.
3. The dog went outside and ran around in a circle.
4. Please look up toward the skylight in the ceiling.
5. The teenagers walked in and out among the fair booths.
6. Are Annie and James lagging behind again?
7. One of the players on the other team came over to talk to my brother.
8. We walked inside and looked for a guide.
9. Rob will come along with us.
10. Several girls rode by on their bikes and waved.
11. A frightened child would not come near.
12. You may not go through without a ticket.
13. Please come by in the morning.
14. The mother walked inside and checked the cake in the oven.
15. She approached the table, looked underneath, and found a giggling toddler.
16. The shopper looked both ways at the intersection and hurried across.

Name______________________________ **PREPOSITIONS**

WORKBOOK PAGE 32

Date______________________________

Directions: Cross out any prepositional phrases. Underline the subject once and the verb/verb phrase twice.

1. ~~From June~~ ~~until the end~~ ~~of August~~, Carl lives ~~in Alabama~~.

2. Some boys and girls rode their bikes ~~along a path~~.

3. The man walked ~~behind a car~~ and ~~across the street~~.

4. The laughing girls jumped ~~into the stream~~ and chased each other ~~through the water~~.

5. (You) Finish your project ~~by the end~~ ~~of the week~~.

6. Everyone ~~except the senator~~ attended the meeting ~~concerning the proposed tax increase~~.

7. ~~During the wedding reception~~, the bride sat ~~near the groom and her attendants~~.

8. ~~Within a week~~, the detective had checked ~~with several witnesses~~.

9. Her dog likes (to lie) ~~upon a pillow~~ ~~throughout the afternoon~~.

10. One ~~of his cats~~ will **not** go outside ~~after a rainstorm~~.

11. ~~For several minutes~~, several toddlers danced around ~~in a circle~~.

12. ~~At five o'clock~~ ~~on June 1st~~, my aunt will be baptized ~~by her minister~~.

13. The discussion ~~between Lori and her mother~~ was ~~regarding their weekend plans~~.

14. One house ~~beside the museum~~ has been deserted ~~since last February~~.

15. That rancher walked out ~~beyond his corral~~ and stared ~~toward the woods~~.

Name________________________________ **PREPOSITIONS**

Date________________________________

Directions: Cross out any prepositional phrases. Underline the subject once and the verb/verb phrase twice.

1. From June until the end of August, Carl lives in Alabama.
2. Some boys and girls rode their bikes along a path.
3. The man walked behind a car and across the street.
4. The laughing girls jumped into the stream and chased each other through the water.
5. Finish your project by the end of the week.
6. Everyone except the senator attended the meeting concerning the proposed tax increase.
7. During the wedding reception, the bride sat near the groom and her attendants.
8. Within a week, the detective had checked with several witnesses.
9. Her dog likes to lie upon a pillow throughout the afternoon.
10. One of his cats will not go outside after a rainstorm.
11. For several minutes, several toddlers danced around in a circle.
12. At five o'clock on June 1st, my aunt will be baptized by her minister.
13. The discussion between Lori and her mother was regarding their weekend plans.
14. One house beside the museum has been deserted since last February.
15. That rancher walked out beyond his corral and stared toward the woods.

Name________________________________ **PREPOSITIONS**
WORKBOOK PAGE 33
Date________________________________

Directions: Cross out any prepositional phrases. Underline the subject once and the verb/verb phrase twice.

1. ~~Without hesitation~~, the rabbit hopped ~~underneath some brush~~.

2. Dad looked ~~above the stove~~ ~~for a fire extinguisher~~.

3. The readers searched ~~among the shelves~~ ~~for books~~ ~~about frogs and toads~~.

4. (You) Clean the glass ~~under the coffee table~~ ~~with this sponge~~.

5. ~~Before the parade~~, everyone walked ~~toward the town square~~.

6. The company has displayed all ~~of its products~~ ~~but the new cleanser~~.

7. Your jacket has fallen down ~~behind the green flowered sofa~~.

8. (You) Place these washcloths and towels ~~in the cupboard~~ ~~beneath the sink~~.

9. Their grandparents ~~from Colorado~~ stay inside ~~during the winter~~.

10. Yesterday, the skater fell down and rolled ~~off the low curb~~ .

11. Miss Jones and her friend walk ~~past the park~~ ~~on their way~~ ~~to the gym~~.

12. The athlete jumped ~~over a hurdle~~ and darted ~~for the finish line~~.

13. Insects ~~like grasshoppers, centipedes, and dragonflies~~ do**n't** scare them.

14. ~~At the beginning~~ ~~of the class~~, Mrs. Harmon talked ~~about the Middle East~~.

15. The chimney sweep laid his tools ~~against the fireplace~~ and peered ~~up the chimney~~.

Name_______________________________ **PREPOSITIONS**

Date_______________________________

Directions: Cross out any prepositional phrases. Underline the subject once and the verb/verb phrase twice.

1. Without hesitation, the rabbit hopped underneath some brush.

2. Dad looked above the stove for a fire extinguisher.

3. The readers searched among the shelves for books about frogs and toads.

4. Clean the glass under the coffee table with this sponge.

5. Before the parade, everyone walked toward the town square.

6. The company has displayed all of its products but the new cleanser.

7. Your jacket has fallen down behind the green flowered sofa.

8. Place these washcloths and towels in the cupboard beneath the sink.

9. Their grandparents from Colorado stay inside during the winter.

10. Yesterday, the skater fell down and rolled off the low curb .

11. Miss Jones and her friend walk past the park on their way to the gym.

12. The athlete jumped over a hurdle and darted for the finish line.

13. Insects like grasshoppers, centipedes, and dragonflies don't scare them.

14. At the beginning of the class, Mrs. Harmon talked about the Middle East.

15. The chimney sweep laid his tools against the fireplace and peered up the chimney.

Name________________________________

Date________________________________

PREPOSITION TEST

Directions: Cross out any prepositional phrases. Underline the subject once and the verb/verb phrase twice.

1. One ~~of the men~~ leaned ~~against the door~~ ~~during the discussion~~.
2. Several dogs ~~at the veterinarian's office~~ were lying ~~by their owners' feet~~.
3. Kerry stood ~~in the rain~~ and waited along ~~with the other bus riders~~.
4. ~~After the accident~~, a policeman walked ~~toward the damaged car~~.
5. Claude and his aunt live ~~near the park~~ ~~on Houston Avenue~~.
6. ~~Before the school carnival~~, many students carried chairs ~~into a tent~~.
7. His nearest neighbor lives ~~across the field~~ and ~~past some water tanks~~.
8. (You) Please place this poster ~~regarding water safety~~ ~~above the door~~.
9. You may **not** go outside ~~without your coat, hat, and boots~~.
10. ~~Throughout the spring~~, nine robins played ~~underneath our willow tree~~.
11. A model stood ~~among the ladies~~ and instructed them ~~about proper nutrition~~.
12. Some horses were running around ~~in the field~~ ~~between the barn and the house~~.
13. Everyone ~~but the tall man~~ ~~in the blue wool suit~~ remained ~~for the banquet~~.
14. ~~After the meeting~~, Mom and her friend will help ~~with refreshments~~ ~~until nine o'clock~~.
15. Large dogs ~~like shepherds and retrievers~~ are**n't** allowed ~~within the gated area~~.

Name________________________________

Date________________________________

PREPOSITION TEST

Directions: Cross out any prepositional phrases. Underline the subject once and the verb/verb phrase twice.

1. One of the men leaned against the door during the discussion.

2. Several dogs at the veterinarian's office were lying by their owners' feet.

3. Kerry stood in the rain and waited along with the other bus riders.

4. After the accident, a policeman walked toward the damaged car.

5. Claude and his aunt live near the park on Houston Avenue.

6. Before the school carnival, many students carried chairs into a tent.

7. His nearest neighbor lives across the field and past some water tanks.

8. Please place this poster regarding water safety above the door.

9. You may not go outside without your coat, hat, and boots.

10. Throughout the spring, nine robins played underneath our willow tree.

11. A model stood among the ladies and instructed them about proper nutrition.

12. Some horses were running around in the field between the barn and the house.

13. Everyone but the tall man in the blue wool suit remained for the banquet.

14. After the meeting, Mom and her friend will help with refreshments until nine o'clock.

15. Large dogs like shepherds and retrievers aren't allowed within the gated area.

PAGE 73 = WORKBOOK PAGE 34

SUGGESTIONS FOR MASTERY LEARNING

Keep in mind that the goal of your teaching is to insure mastery learning. Therefore, review is necessary to the program. You want your students to have concepts learned in long-term memory. Unit reviews and cumulative reviews are located at the end of each unit to aid in realizing this goal. Of course, testing, both unit and cumulative, will help you determine if mastery is being achieved. If you discover that a student lacks understanding, it is suggested that you reteach the non-mastered concept.

You will note that the student has not been asked to determine if the prepositional phrase serves as an adjective or an adverb in the sentence. Because students have not been introduced to adjectives or adverbs at this point, it only confuses students to introduce this concept now.

DIRECT OBJECTS

Students must understand that direct objects receive the action of the verb. Although occasionally a prepositional phrase may serve as a direct object, it occurs so seldom that, once again, students are instructed to cross out prepositional phrases and not label those as direct objects.

Direct Objects:

1. The easiest way to insure understanding of direct objects is for you to actually *do* an action. I have had success with suddenly throwing an eraser across the room.

   D.O.
   The teacher threw an eraser.

   What was the object that the teacher threw? Eraser, then, is the direct object; the eraser received the action.

   Use other overt actions to aid learning:

   A. I kicked the desk. (What received the action?)
   B. I pulled Jane's hair. (What received the action?)
   C. I tossed the pencil. (What received the action?)

   You may want to ask students to *do* examples. Peers can determine the direct object.

2. Review the concept of direct objects by giving similar examples at the beginning of each English class. Never assume that all have mastered a concept automatically.

3. The success factor is high with direct objects. In Easy Grammar direct objects are taught immediately after prepositions for two reasons:

   A. Crossing out prepositional phrases helps to determine if a direct object is in the sentence. You have fewer words left in the sentence so students tend not to become frustrated.
   B. Since the concept of direct objects can be understood easily, more success is internalized by the student.

Name______________________________ **DIRECT OBJECTS**

WORKBOOK PAGE 35

Date______________________________

Directions: Cross out any prepositional phrases. Underline the subject once and the verb/verb phrase twice. Label direct object(s)- D.O.

D.O.
1. The child grabbed the toy ~~from his brother.~~

D.O.
2. Susan chose the pink dress ~~for the dance~~.

D.O.
3. ~~After dinner~~ Father washed the dishes.

D.O.
4. We ate bananas ~~for breakfast~~.

D.O.
5. The girl hit the ball ~~to left field~~.

D.O.
6. The cook fried an egg ~~in that frying pan~~.

D.O.
7. ~~During the ceremony~~, the speaker presented an award ~~to the student~~.

D.O.
8. The other school played a game ~~against our school~~.

D.O.
9. The plumber took her tools ~~with her~~.

D.O.
10. The gardener chased the rabbits ~~off his property~~.

D.O.
11. The baby threw the rattle ~~onto the floor~~.

D.O.
12. The officer parked the car ~~near the police station~~.

D.O.
13. ~~At that restaurant~~ the waiters carry large trays.

D.O.
14. The hikers carried their packs ~~across town~~.

(You) D.O.
15. Set the groceries ~~by the microwave oven~~.

Name________________________________ **DIRECT OBJECTS**

Date________________________________

Directions: Cross out any prepositional phrases. Underline the subject once and the verb/verb phrase twice. Label direct object(s)-D.O.

1. The child grabbed the toy from his brother.
2. Susan chose the pink dress for the dance.
3. After dinner Father washed the dishes.
4. We ate bananas for breakfast.
5. The girl hit the ball to left field.
6. The cook fried an egg in that frying pan.
7. During the ceremony, the speaker presented an award to the student.
8. The other school played a game against our school.
9. The plumber took her tools with her.
10. The gardener chased the rabbits off his property.
11. The baby threw the rattle onto the floor.
12. The officer parked the car near the police station.
13. At that restaurant the waiters carry large trays.
14. The hikers carried their packs across town.
15. Set the groceries by the microwave oven.

PAGE 77 = WORKBOOK PAGE 36

Direct Objects

A sentence may contain compound direct objects. This means that there are two or more direct objects within a sentence.

Examples:

A. The toddler chased the dog and cat around the house.

D.O. D.O.
The toddler chased the dog and cat ~~around the house~~.

B. The artist drew birds, flowers, and butterflies in the painting.

D.O. D.O. D.O.
The artist drew birds, flowers, and butterflies ~~in the painting~~.

Name________________________________ **DIRECT OBJECTS**

WORKBOOK PAGE 37

Date________________________________

Directions: Cross out any prepositional phrases. Underline the subject once and the verb/verb phrase twice. Label the direct object(s)-D.O.

D.O. D.O.
1. We ate bacon and eggs ~~for breakfast~~.

D.O. D.O.
2. The traveler dropped his luggage and his keys ~~beside me~~.

D.O. D.O.
3. ~~Within an hour~~, the detective had caught the burglar and his accomplice.

D.O. D.O.
4. ~~During the sale~~, my mother purchased a new blouse and some earrings.

D.O. D.O.
5. Nikki and Dakota baked cookies and coconut pie ~~for the bake sale~~.

D.O. D.O.
6. The farmer planted tomatoes and peppers ~~in his garden~~.

(You) D.O. D.O.
7. Take fried chicken and potato salad ~~on the picnic~~.

D.O. D.O.
8. ~~Before his trip~~, the pilot ironed his pants and shirt.

D.O. D.O.
9. You will find the mop or broom ~~in the laundry room~~.

D.O. D.O.
10. Are you buying French fries and a soda ~~at our favorite restaurant~~?

D.O. D.O.
11. Some ~~of the students~~ took their books and notebooks ~~with them~~.

D.O. D.O.
12. The shopper selected fish and broccoli ~~for dinner~~.

D.O. D.O.
13. A couple received a toaster and a blender ~~for a wedding gift~~.

D.O. D.O.
14. I placed toys and other junk ~~under my bed~~.

D.O. D.O.
15. ~~Over the door~~ we hung ribbons and balloons ~~for the birthday party~~.

Name______________________________ **DIRECT OBJECTS**

Date______________________________

Directions: Cross out any prepositional phrases. Underline the subject once and the verb/verb phrase twice. Label the direct object(s)-D.O.

1. We ate bacon and eggs for breakfast.
2. The traveler dropped his luggage and his keys beside me.
3. Within an hour, the detective had caught the burglar and his accomplice.
4. During the sale, my mother purchased a new blouse and some earrings.
5. Nikki and Dakota baked cookies and coconut pie for the bake sale.
6. The farmer planted tomatoes and peppers in his garden.
7. Take fried chicken and potato salad on the picnic.
8. Before his trip, the pilot ironed his pants and shirt.
9. You will find the mop or broom in the laundry room.
10. Are you buying French fries and a soda at our favorite restaurant?
11. Some of the students took their books and notebooks with them.
12. The shopper selected fish and broccoli for dinner.
13. A couple received a toaster and a blender for a wedding gift.
14. I placed toys and other junk under my bed.
15. Over the door we hung ribbons and balloons for the birthday party.

PAGE 81 = WORKBOOK PAGE 38

VERBS

The verb of a sentence expresses an action or simply states a fact.

Examples: Jenny cut down the old oak tree. (action)

Waiters set the table for the buffet. (action)

Our senator is happy about the new law. (fact)

My brother was in a bad mood. (fact)

Verbs that simply state a fact are often called **state of being verbs.**

<u>VERBS</u>

There are two main types of verbs: **action and linking**. Action verbs do exactly what the term implies. Action verbs show action. You will note that in order to have a direct object, the sentence must contain an action verb.

Linking verbs are difficult. First, they do not show action. They do exactly what their name implies. They link two parts in the sentence. They link the subject with either a noun or pronoun (called a predicate nominative) or with an adjective (called a predicate adjective).*

*Linking verbs will be discussed on page 125. Students must learn a basic list.

PAGE 82 = WORKBOOK PAGE 39
PAGE 83 = WORKBOOK PAGE 40

CONTRACTIONS

To contract means to draw together. Thus, in forming contractions, we draw together two words to make one word. We do this by dropping some letter or letters and inserting an apostrophe (') where the letter(s) is(are) missing.

Suggestions:

A. Make sure that your apostrophe looks like an apostrophe and not a chicken scratch mark.

B. Place the apostrophe exactly where the letter(s) are missing.

C. The contraction should be written in broken form so that mistakes are avoided.

This *don' t* Not This *don't*

Contractions =	verb	+	word
don't	do	+	not
doesn't	does	+	not
didn't	did	+	not
hasn't	has	+	not
haven't	have	+	not
hadn't	had	+	not
isn't	is	+	not
aren't	are	+	not
wasn't	was	+	not
weren't	were	+	not
mustn't	must	+	not
mightn't	might	+	not
shouldn't	should	+	not
couldn't	could	+	not
wouldn't	would	+	not
won't	will	+	not
can't	can	+	not

Contractions =	word	+	verb
I'm	I	+	am
I've	I	+	have
I'd	I	+	would
I'll	I	+	will
you'll	you	+	will
they'll	they	+	will
we'll	we	+	will
he's	he	+	is
he'd	he	+	would
she's	she	+	is
they've	they	+	have
they're	they	+	are
it's	it	+	is
who's	who	+	is
what's	what	+	is
where's	where	+	is
here's	here	+	is
there's	there	+	is

Name________________________________ **VERBS**

WORKBOOK PAGE 41 Contractions

Date________________________________

Directions: Write the contraction in the space provided.

Example: What's — What is your name?

1. Here's — Here is your order.
2. won't — The emergency kit will not fit into the glove compartment of his car.
3. couldn't — The guests could not finish their dessert.
4. I've — I have so much to accomplish.
5. wasn't — The macrame was not completed until last weekend.
6. he'd — I think that he would be happier in a warmer climate.
7. We'll — We will take the chair lift to the mountain slope.
8. hasn't — The shipment of cameras has not arrived.
9. They're — They are finished with their latest report.
10. isn't — Our antique china closet is not refinished.
11. You'll — You will want a green rug for the living room.
12. can't — This blanket cannot be washed.
13. What's — What is the name of your new friend?
14. don't — Some of your test answers do not make sense.
15. wouldn't — Our saw would not cut into that piece of hard wood.

Name______________________________

Date______________________________

VERBS
Contractions

Directions: Write the contraction in the space provided.

Example: What's What is your name?

1. ______________________ Here is your order.

2. ______________________ The emergency kit will not fit into the glove compartment of his car.

3. ______________________ The guests could not finish their dessert.

4. ______________________ I have so much to accomplish.

5. ______________________ The macrame was not completed until last weekend.

6. ______________________ I think that he would be happier in a warmer climate.

7. ______________________ We will take the chair lift to the mountain slope.

8. ______________________ The shipment of cameras has not arrived.

9. ______________________ They are finished with their latest report.

10. ______________________ Our antique china closet is not refinished.

11. ______________________ You will want a green rug for the living room.

12. ______________________ This blanket cannot be washed.

13. ______________________ What is the name of your new friend?

14. ______________________ Some of your test answers do not make sense.

15. ______________________ Our saw would not cut into that piece of hard wood.

Name________________________________ **VERBS**

WORKBOOK PAGE 42 Contractions

Date________________________________

Directions: Write the contraction in the space provided.

Example: ___How's___ How is your father?

1. ___Don't___ Do not go fishing without me.

2. ___I'll___ I told him that I will be there at four o'clock.

3. ___Where's___ Where is the Alamo?

4. ___aren't___ Some of the sheep are not being herded by the dog.

5. ___She's___ She is a very capable woodcarver.

6. ___didn't___ The blue house did not get painted this summer.

7. ___They've___ They have just returned from a trip to China.

8. ___it's___ Do you think it is acceptable to send flowers to a young man?

9. ___There's___ There is no milk for my cereal.

10. ___hadn't___ Fortunately many of the artifacts had not broken.

11. ___wasn't___ I was not informed of the problem.

12. ___I'll___ Our leader explained that I will give the speech at the next assembly.

13. ___shouldn't___ If you should not choose to go, Mary will take your place.

14. ___Here's___ Here is your missing assignment.

15. ___who's___ Have you met the person who is director of our recreation club?

Name________________________________

Date________________________________

VERBS
Contractions

Directions: Write the contraction in the space provided.

Example: ____How's________ How is your father?

1. ______________________ Do not go fishing without me.

2. ______________________ I told him that I will be there at four o'clock.

3. ______________________ Where is the Alamo?

4. ______________________ Some of the sheep are not being herded by the dog.

5. ______________________ She is a very capable woodcarver.

6. ______________________ The blue house did not get painted this summer.

7. ______________________ They have just returned from a trip to China.

8. ______________________ Do you think it is acceptable to send flowers to a young man?

9. ______________________ There is no milk for my cereal.

10. ______________________ Fortunately many of the artifacts had not broken.

11. ______________________ I was not informed of the problem.

12. ______________________ Our leader explained that I will give the speech at the next assembly.

13. ______________________ If you should not choose to go, Mary will take your place.

14. ______________________ Here is your missing assignment.

15. ______________________ Have you met the person who is director of our recreation club?

VERBS

The student must memorize these twenty-three helpers and list them.

Be sure that the student has complete mastery of these auxiliary (helping) verbs. Remember, **mastery is our goal**. Once again, asking students to list them for a quiz or test grade is suggested. Use methods with which you are comfortable to insure student mastery of this list.

List of Auxiliary (Helping) Verbs

DO	**HAS**	**IS**	**MAY**
DOES	**HAVE**	**AM**	**MUST**
DID	**HAD**	**ARE**	**MIGHT**
		WAS	**SHOULD**
		WERE	**COULD**
		BE	**WOULD**
		BEING	**SHALL**
		BEEN	**WILL**
			CAN

WORKBOOK PAGE 43

VERB PHRASES

Sometimes two or more words make up a verb. This is called a verb phrase.

The last word in a verb phrase is called the **main verb**; other words are called **auxiliary (helping) verbs.***

Verb Phrase	=	helping verb(s)	+	main verb
should go	=	**should**	+	**go**
has been given	=	**has been**	+	**given**
will be leaving	=	**will be**	+	**leaving**

In a declarative (statement) sentence, the verb phrase is usually together.

Example: That window must have been broken by a rock.

must have been + broken

In an interrogative (question) sentence, the verb phrase is often split.

Example: Have my jeans been washed yet?

Have been + washed

WORKBOOK PAGE 44

***Students are expected to memorize and learn the auxiliary (helping) verbs.**

Name______________________________ **VERBS**

WORKBOOK PAGE 45 Verb Phrases

Date______________________________

Directions: Cross out any prepositional phrases. Underline the subject once and the verb/verb phrase twice. Place the auxiliary (helping) verb(s) and the main verb of each sentence on the line indicated.

Example: The car will not start! ___will___ ___start___

		HELPING VERB(S)	MAIN VERB
1.	Will you answer the phone?	will	answer
2.	Dr. Jones must have shown your sister the x-rays.	must have	shown
3.	May Connie and I leave now?	May	leave
4.	There must have been an accident ~~on this corner~~.	must have	been
5.	Did Katy return her imperfect briefcase?	Did	return
6.	Was any chair sold ~~for fifty dollars~~?	Was	sold
7.	Peter should not have stayed ~~at the park~~.	should have	stayed
8.	My student has had strep throat three times this year.	has	had
9.	Doesn't your dad cook breakfast every Saturday morning?	Does	cook
10.	They could fix the light ~~after working hours~~.	could	fix
11.	I'm searching ~~for the word in the dictionary~~.	am	searching
12.	Has anyone seen the Egyptian pyramids?	Has	seen
13.	The jury might decide the verdict today.	might	decide
14.	I shall inform you ~~of my decision.~~	shall	inform
15.	That would never have occurred ~~to me~~.	would have	occurred

Name_______________________________

Date_______________________________

VERBS
Verb Phrases

Directions: Cross out any prepositional phrases. Underline the subject once and the verb/verb phrase twice. Place the auxiliary (helping) verb(s) and the main verb of each sentence on the line indicated.

Example: The car will not start! ___will___ ___start___

		HELPING VERB(S)	MAIN VERB
1.	Will you answer the phone?	________	________
2.	Dr. Jones must have shown your sister the x-rays.	________	________
3.	May Connie and I leave now?	________	________
4.	There must have been an accident on this corner.	________	________
5.	Did Katy return her imperfect briefcase?	________	________
6.	Was any chair sold for fifty dollars?	________	________
7.	Peter should not have stayed at the park.	________	________
8.	My student has had strep throat three times this year.	________	________
9.	Doesn't your dad cook breakfast every Saturday morning?	________	________
10.	They could fix the light after working hours.	________	________
11.	I'm searching for the word in the dictionary.	________	________
12.	Has anyone seen the Egyptian pyramids?	________	________
13.	The jury might decide the verdict today.	________	________
14.	I shall inform you of my decision.	________	________
15.	That would never have occurred to me.	________	________

Name________________________________

WORKBOOK PAGE 46

Date________________________________

VERBS

Verb Phrases

Directions: Cross out any prepositional phrases. Underline the subject once and the verb/verb phrase twice. Place the auxiliary (helping) verb(s) and the main verb of each sentence on the line provided.

Example: We have gone often. ___have___ ___gone___

	Sentence	HELPING VERBS	MAIN VERB
1.	These apples must have been grown ~~in Pennsylvania~~.	must have been	grown
2.	Sissy will not be attending her class reunion.	will be	attending
3.	Were the investors planning a convention ~~in Lake Tahoe~~?	Were	planning
4.	I might have lost my new tennis racket.	might have	lost
5.	Which ~~of the fabrics~~ do you like?	do	like
6.	Whose car has been parked ~~at the bottom of the hill~~?	has been	parked
7.	Those plants should be watered daily.	should be	watered
8.	Have you been ~~in the Sears Tower in Chicago~~?	Have	been
9.	The jeweler would not remove the diamond necklace ~~from the window display~~.	would	remove
10.	Who will be coming ~~to the graduation dance~~?	will be	coming
11.	The photographer has taken a family portrait.	has	taken
12.	Am I expected ~~at the Brown's home for dinner~~?	Am	expected
13.	You are wearing my favorite color.	are	wearing
14.	~~By dusk~~, we will have been ~~in this car for five hours~~.	will have	been
15.	Shall I ask my parents ~~for their approval~~?	Shall	ask

Name________________________________

Date________________________________

VERBS
Verb Phrases

Directions: Cross out any prepositional phrases. Underline the subject once and the verb/verb phrase twice. Place the auxiliary (helping) verb(s) and the main verb of each sentence on the line provided.

Example: We have gone often. ___have___ ___gone___

		HELPING VERBS	MAIN VERB
1.	These apples must have been grown in Pennsylvania.	____________	____________
2.	Sissy will not be attending her class reunion.	____________	____________
3.	Were the investors planning a convention in Lake Tahoe?	____________	____________
4.	I might have lost my new tennis racket.	____________	____________
5.	Which of the fabrics do you like?	____________	____________
6.	Whose car has been parked at the bottom of the hill?	____________	____________
7.	Those plants should be watered daily.	____________	____________
8.	Have you been in the Sears Tower in Chicago?	____________	____________
9.	The jeweler would not remove the diamond necklace from the window display.	____________	____________
10.	Who will be coming to the graduation dance?	____________	____________
11.	The photographer has taken a family portrait.	____________	____________
12.	Am I expected at the Brown's home for dinner?	____________	____________
13.	You are wearing my favorite color.	____________	____________
14.	By dusk, we will have been in this car for five hours.	____________	____________
15.	Shall I ask my parents for their approval?	____________	____________

VERBS

In regular verbs, the past and the past participle are the same. The past tense is formed by adding ed to the verb (bark-barked).

Examples:

Infinitive	Present	Past	Past Participle
to walk	walk(s)	walked	(had) walked
to jump	jump(s)	jumped	(had) jumped
to grab	grab(s)	grabbed	(had) grabbed
to boast	boast(s)	boasted	(had) boasted

IRREGULAR VERBS

Irregular verbs do not add ed to the past tense (fall-fell). Usually the past tense and the past participle form are not the same (spoke-spoken).

Examples:

Infinitive	Present	Past	Past Participle
to run	run(s)	ran	(had) run
to know	know(s)	knew	(had) known
to bring	bring(s)	brought	(had) brought*

*You will note that the past and the past participle forms of to bring are the same. However, to bring qualifies as an irregular verb because ed is not added to form the past tense.

PAGE 97 = WORKBOOK PAGE 49
PAGE 98 = WORKBOOK PAGE 50

The following two pages contain a list of irregular verbs and their forms. Students should be expected to master this list.

IRREGULAR VERBS

Infinitive	Present	Past	Present Participle	Past Participle*
To be	is, am, are	was, were	being	been
To beat	beat(s)	beat	beating	beaten
To begin	begin(s)	began	beginning	begun
To blow	blow(s)	blew	blowing	blown
To break	break(s)	broke	breaking	broken
To bring	bring(s)	brought	bringing	brought
To burst	burst(s)	burst	bursting	burst
To buy	buy(s)	bought	buying	bought
To choose	choose(s)	chose	choosing	chosen
To come	come(s)	came	coming	come
To do	do, does	did	doing	done
To drink	drink(s)	drank	drinking	drunk
To drive	drive(s)	drove	driving	driven
To eat	eat(s)	ate	eating	eaten
To fall	fall(s)	fell	falling	fallen
To fly	fly, flies	flew	flying	flown
To freeze	freeze(s)	froze	freezing	frozen
To give	give(s)	gave	giving	given
To go	go, goes	went	going	gone
To grow	grow(s)	grew	growing	grown
To have	have, has	had	having	had
To hang	hang(s)	hanged, hung	hanging	hanged, hung
To know	know(s)	knew	knowing	known
To lay	lay(s)	laid	laying	laid
To leave	leave(s)	left	leaving	left

*Uses a helping verb such as has, have, or had.

IRREGULAR VERBS

Infinitive	Present	Past	Present Participle	Past Participle*
To lie	lie(s)	lay	lying	lain
To ride	ride(s)	rode	riding	ridden
To ring	ring(s)	rang	ringing	rung
To rise	rise(s)	rose	rising	risen
To run	run(s)	ran	running	run
To see	see(s)	saw	seeing	seen
To set	set(s)	set	setting	set
To shake	shake(s)	shook	shaking	shaken
To shrink	shrink(s)	shrank	shrinking	shrunk
To sing	sing(s)	sang	singing	sung
To sink	sink(s)	sank	sinking	sunk
To sit	sit(s)	sat	sitting	sat
To speak	speak(s)	spoke	speaking	spoken
To spring	spring(s)	sprang	springing	sprung
To steal	steal(s)	stole	stealing	stolen
To swim	swim(s)	swam	swimming	swum
To swear	swear(s)	swore	swearing	sworn
To take	take(s)	took	taking	taken
To teach	teach(es)	taught	teaching	taught
To throw	throw(s)	threw	throwing	thrown
To wear	wear(s)	wore	wearing	worn
To write	write(s)	wrote	writing	written

*The past participle form is the form of the verb used with <u>have</u>, <u>has</u>, or <u>had</u>.

PAGE 100 = WORKBOOK PAGE 51
PAGE 101 = WORKBOOK PAGE 52

The following page is designed for the teacher to dictate various infinitives. The student then fills in all blanks. It is suggested that the student be instructed to write HAS, HAVE, and HAD above the past participle column and to select one of those verb helpers to be included throughout the past participle column. This insures understanding of the "helper + past participle" concept.

Example: has, have, had

INFINITIVE	PRESENT	PAST	PAST PARTICIPLE
to see	see(s)	saw	(had) seen
to go	go (es)	went	(had) gone

Name________________________________ **VERB FORMS**

Date________________________________

Directions: Place the correct verb form(s) in the space provided.

INFINITIVE	PRESENT	PAST	PAST PARTICIPLE

Name________________________________ **VERB FORMS**

Date________________________________

Directions: Place the correct verb form(s) in the space provided.

INFINITIVE	PRESENT	PAST	PAST PARTICIPLE

Name______________________________ **IRREGULAR VERBS**

WORKBOOK PAGE 53

Date______________________________

Directions: Cross out any prepositional phrases. Underline the subject once and the verb/verb phrase twice.

Example: I should have (chose, chosen) a newer car.

1. The flag had (flew, flown) ~~at half mast~~.

2. We have (choose, chosen) a new sofa.

3. The pupil had not (brang, brought) the homework.

4. Has the lamp been (broke, broken)?

5. The graduate was (gave, given) a gift.

6. Has the choir ever (sung, sang) that tune?

7. We could have (run, ran) another mile.

8. Our family had (drove, driven) ~~to Arcadia National Park~~.

9. The seamstress should have (boughten, bought) more fabric.

10. ~~By the end of the contest~~, the contestants will have (ate, eaten) ~~at least two pies~~.

11. I could have (drank, drunk) a gallon ~~of water~~.

12. Their bus must have already (came, come).

13. Has your blouse (shrank, shrunk) ~~in the laundry~~?

14. Jordy could have (wore, worn) your costume ~~to the party~~.

15. Has the sun (rose, risen) earlier than usual?

Name________________________________ **IRREGULAR VERBS**

Date_________________________________

Directions: Cross out any prepositional phrases. Underline the subject once and the verb/verb phrase twice.

Example: I should have (chose, chosen) a newer car.

1. The flag had (flew, flown) at half mast.
2. We have (choose, chosen) a new sofa.
3. The pupil had not (brang, brought) the homework.
4. Has the lamp been (broke, broken)?
5. The graduate was (gave, given) a gift.
6. Has the choir ever (sung, sang) that tune?
7. We could have (run, ran) another mile.
8. Our family had (drove, driven) to Arcadia National Park.
9. The seamstress should have (boughten, bought) more fabric.
10. By the end of the contest, the contestants will have (ate, eaten) at least two pies.
11. I could have (drank, drunk) a gallon of water.
12. Their bus must have already (came, come).
13. Has your blouse (shrank, shrunk) in the laundry?
14. Jordy could have (wore, worn) your costume to the party.
15. Has the sun (rose, risen) earlier than usual?

Name_______________________________ **IRREGULAR VERBS**

WORKBOOK PAGE 54

Date_______________________________

Directions: Cross out any prepositional phrases. Underline the subject once and the verb/verb phrase twice.

Example: The speaker has (come, came) early.

1. Our balloons have (burst, bursted).

2. Has the president (shook, shaken) your hand?

3. The laundry had been (hang, hung) ~~on the clothesline~~.

4. That ship must have (sank, sunk) ~~during the battle~~.

5. They have (stole, stolen) that idea ~~from another company~~.

6. The boxer (sprang, sprung) ~~to his feet during the count~~.

7. I may have (did, done) the problem incorrectly.

8. Ice cubes were (froze, frozen) ~~in pretty trays~~.

9. My opponent has (beat, beaten) me ~~at the game of chess~~.

10. She (began, begun) (to feel) ill.

11. Wind may have (blew, blown) the table over.

12. Has the puppy (laid, lain) there long?

13. He must have (saw, seen) me ~~at the dance~~.

14. A rock was (threw, thrown) ~~through the large window~~.

15. Several children (swam, swum) ~~in the lake~~.

Name________________________________ **IRREGULAR VERBS**

Date________________________________

Directions: Cross out any prepositional phrases. Underline the subject once and the verb/verb phrase twice.

Example: The speaker has (come, came) early.

1. Our balloons have (burst, bursted).
2. Has the president (shook, shaken) your hand?
3. The laundry had been (hang, hung) on the clothesline.
4. That ship must have (sank, sunk) during the battle.
5. They have (stole, stolen) that idea from another company.
6. The boxer (sprang, sprung) to his feet during the count.
7. I may have (did, done) the problem incorrectly.
8. Ice cubes were (froze, frozen) in pretty trays.
9. My opponent has (beat, beaten) me at the game of chess.
10. She (began, begun) to feel ill.
11. Wind may have (blew, blown) the table over.
12. Has the puppy (laid, lain) there long?
13. He must have (saw, seen) me at the dance.
14. A rock was (threw, thrown) through the large window.
15. Several children (swam, swum) in the lake.

Name________________________________ **IRREGULAR VERBS**

WORKBOOK PAGE 55

Date________________________________

Directions: Cross out any prepositional phrases. Underline the subject once and the verb/verb phrase twice.

Example: He has (gave, given) me his old hat.

1. In July our neighbors had (went, gone) to Europe.

2. Have you (rode, ridden) the gray mare?

3. A mountain climber must have (ran, run) into difficulty.

4. Has Grandma (knew, known) your parents for a long time?

5. George should **not** have (wrote, written) the note.

6. The naughty child (sank, sunk) down into the seat.

7. A witness was (swore, sworn) in by the judge.

8. Records were (broke, broken) during the Olympics.

9. You should have (chose, chosen) something more practical.

10. Had he (ate, eaten) before surgery?

11. The soloist (sung, sang) very loudly.

12. The real estate agent must have (brung, brought) thirty people through our home.

13. Some of my classmates (done, did) their homework at school.

14. Our brother would **not** have (drunk, drank) milk with each meal.

15. Jason should have (went, gone) earlier.

Name________________________________ **IRREGULAR VERBS**

Date________________________________

Directions: Cross out any prepositional phrases. Underline the subject once and the verb/verb phrase twice.

Example: He has (gave, given) me his old hat.

1. In July our neighbors had (went, gone) to Europe.
2. Have you (rode, ridden) the gray mare?
3. A mountain climber must have (ran, run) into difficulty.
4. Has Grandma (knew, known) your parents for a long time?
5. George should not have (wrote, written) the note.
6. The naughty child (sank, sunk) down into the seat.
7. A witness was (swore, sworn) in by the judge.
8. Records were (broke, broken) during the Olympics.
9. You should have (chose, chosen) something more practical.
10. Had he (ate, eaten) before surgery?
11. The soloist (sung, sang) very loudly.
12. The real estate agent must have (brung, brought) thirty people through our home.
13. Some of my classmates (done, did) their homework at school.
14. Our brother would not have (drunk, drank) milk with each meal.
15. Jason should have (went, gone) earlier.

Name________________________________ **IRREGULAR VERBS**

WORKBOOK PAGE 56

Date________________________________

Directions: Cross out any prepositional phrases. Underline the subject once and the verb/verb phrase twice.

Example: The balloon should not have (bursted, burst) so easily.

1. The bestseller should have been (given, gave) ~~to my mother~~.

2. Hot dogs were (chose, chosen) ~~for the lunch menu~~.

3. The mail must have (came, come) early.

4. He might have (gone, went) ~~to the symphony~~ ~~after dinner~~.

5. Has the road map (fallen, fell) ~~on the floor~~ ~~of the car~~?

6. ~~During the early hours~~, the repairman (done, did) his tasks.

7. The papers ~~on the sofa~~ have (lain, lay) there all day.

8. ~~By December~~ the business lady will have (flew, flown) 50,000 miles.

9. Has a copy ~~of this test~~ been (ran, run)?

10. You should have (saw, seen) the look ~~on his face~~.

11. A florist had (spoke, spoken) ~~about flower arrangements~~ ~~at our gardening meeting~~.

12. I (seen, saw) Joe ~~at the basketball game~~.

13. The clothes were (shaken, shook) ~~after removal~~ ~~from the dryer~~.

14. Was the accident victim (took, taken) ~~to a local hospital~~?

15. The sweepstakes winner has (written, wrote) a clever jingle.

Name_______________________________ **IRREGULAR VERBS**

Date_______________________________

Directions: Cross out any prepositional phrases. Underline the subject once and the verb/verb phrase twice.

Example: The balloon should not have (bursted, burst) so easily.

1. The bestseller should have been (given, gave) to my mother.
2. Hot dogs were (chose, chosen) for the lunch menu.
3. The mail must have (came, come) early.
4. He might have (gone, went) to the symphony after dinner.
5. Has the road map (fallen, fell) on the floor of the car?
6. During the early hours, the repairman (done, did) his tasks.
7. The papers on the sofa have (lain, lay) there all day.
8. By December the business lady will have (flew, flown) 50,000 miles.
9. Has a copy of this test been (ran, run)?
10. You should have (saw, seen) the look on his face.
11. A florist had (spoke, spoken) about flower arrangements at our gardening meeting.
12. I (seen, saw) Joe at the basketball game.
13. The clothes were (shaken, shook) after removal from the dryer.
14. Was the accident victim (took, taken) to a local hospital?
15. The sweepstakes winner has (written, wrote) a clever jingle.

In order to teach the confusing verbs **sit/set**, **rise/raise**, and **lie/lay** with greater ease and understanding, a review of direct objects is necessary. The following pages contain worksheets for this purpose.*

*Hopefully, prepositions are, at this point, in long-term memory. However, a few students may need to refer back to their original preposition list.

Name________________________________ **DIRECT OBJECTS**

WORKBOOK PAGE 57

Date________________________________

Directions: Cross out any prepositional phrases. Underline the subject once and the verb/verb phrase twice. Label direct object(s)-D.O.

D.O.
1. I put the casserole ~~into the oven~~.

D.O.
2. The campers made a fire ~~at night~~.

D.O.
3. We cleaned the pool ~~after the dust storm~~.

D.O.
4. ~~Before dawn~~, the farmer milked the cows.

D.O.
5. ~~During the emergency~~, the lifeguard pulled the child ~~from the water~~.

D.O. D.O.
6. Mary chased Susan and her friend ~~around the room~~.

D.O.
7. Santa left the gifts ~~under the tree~~.

D.O.
8. A traveler caught a taxi ~~to the bus terminal~~.

D.O.
9. ~~Within two minutes~~ the monkey had eaten three bananas.

D.O.
10. A handyman placed paneling ~~on the wall~~ ~~in our den~~.

D.O.
11. Several ~~of the squirrels~~ had hidden nuts ~~in the tree~~.

D.O.
12. ~~At noon~~ we should have eaten more pizza.

D.O.
13. Has John or Grace taken the test today?

D.O.
14. Roofers placed new shingles ~~on the house~~.

(You) D.O. D.O.
15. Take this envelope and that package ~~to the post office~~.

Name________________________________

DIRECT OBJECTS

Date________________________________

Directions: Cross out any prepositional phrases. Underline the subject once and the verb/verb phrase twice. Label direct object(s)-D.O.

1. I put the casserole into the oven.
2. The campers made a fire at night.
3. We cleaned the pool after the dust storm.
4. Before dawn, the farmer milked the cows.
5. During the emergency, the lifeguard pulled the child from the water.
6. Mary chased Susan and her friend around the room.
7. Santa left the gifts under the tree.
8. A traveler caught a taxi to the bus terminal.
9. Within two minutes the monkey had eaten three bananas.
10. A handyman placed paneling on the wall in our den.
11. Several of the squirrels had hidden nuts in the tree.
12. At noon we should have eaten more pizza.
13. Has John or Grace taken the test today?
14. Roofers placed new shingles on the house.
15. Take this envelope and that package to the post office.

Name______________________________ **DIRECT OBJECTS**

WORKBOOK PAGE 58

Date______________________________

Directions: Cross out any prepositional phrases. Underline the subject once and the verb/verb phrase twice. Label the direct object(s)-D.O.

1. The coach carried the injured player (D.O.) ~~off the field~~.
2. ~~At the soda fountain~~ each ~~of us~~ ate a sundae (D.O.).
3. Have you seen my watch (D.O.) anywhere?
4. Birds ate the seeds (D.O.) ~~in our garden~~.
5. They bought a new tape (D.O.) ~~for their collection~~.
6. Dr. Abernathy gave sugarless lollipops (D.O.) ~~to his young patients~~.
7. Have you dialed the phone (D.O.)?
8. I cannot bring my whistle (D.O.) or horn (D.O.) ~~to your house~~.
9. The ladies' club served coffee (D.O.) and tea (D.O.) ~~at the end of the meeting~~.
10. We will not cut the grass (D.O.) ~~until evening~~.
11. (You) Give your book (D.O.) ~~to the new student~~.
12. The housekeeper washed the floors (D.O.) and dusted the furniture (D.O.).
13. Did you send me a card (D.O.) ~~on my birthday~~?
14. Someone hid my keys (D.O.) ~~under the table~~ and scribbled the walls (D.O.) ~~with purple and green crayons~~.
15. Is the milkman delivering milk (D.O.) ~~in your neighborhood~~?

Name________________________________ **DIRECT OBJECTS**

Date________________________________

Directions: Cross out any prepositional phrases. Underline the subject once and the verb/verb phrase twice. Label the direct object(s)-D.O.

1. The coach carried the injured player off the field.
2. At the soda fountain each of us ate a sundae.
3. Have you seen my watch anywhere?
4. Birds ate the seeds in our garden.
5. They bought a new tape for their collection.
6. Dr. Abernathy gave sugarless lollipops to his young patients.
7. Have you dialed the phone?
8. I cannot bring my whistle or horn to your house.
9. The ladies' club served coffee and tea at the end of the meeting.
10. We will not cut the grass until evening.
11. Give your book to the new student.
12. The housekeeper washed the floors and dusted the furniture.
13. Did you send me a card on my birthday?
14. Someone hid my keys under the table and scribbled the walls with purple and green crayons.
15. Is the milkman delivering milk in your neighborhood?

PAGE 117 = WORKBOOK PAGE 59
PAGE 118 = WORKBOOK PAGE 60
PAGE 119 = WORKBOOK PAGE 61

SIT/SET
LIE/LAY
RISE/RAISE

Note: The next few pages contain an explanation of sit/set, lie/lay, and rise/raise. *To set, to lay,* and *to raise* usually are followed by direct objects and are taught in this manner. It is extremely helpful for a student to spot a direct object and know that the correct form will be to set/to lay/to raise (from choices given).

Unfortunately, as in many other English areas, there are exceptions, and I have included some. However, even with the numerous exceptions, I think that having students seek out direct objects is extremely beneficial. If we can encourage students to think about the meaning of sit/set, lie/lay, and rise/ raise, few mistakes will be made.

SIT/SET

To sit: means to rest
To set: means to place or to put

FORMS:

Infinitive	Present	Past	Present Participle	Past Participle
To sit	sit(s)	sat	sitting	(had) sat
To set	set(s)	set	setting	(had) set

If students understand direct objects, they should have no trouble with sit/set.

Two basic items for sit/set:

A. Both *sit* and *set* are irregular verbs and must be learned.

B. *Set* requires a direct object.*

Examples:

He is (sitting, setting) on the porch.

He is (sitting, setting) on the porch. (There is no direct object in the sentence. Thus, *sitting* is used. In addition, *resting* can be inserted for *sitting*.)

The librarian (sit, set) the books down.

The librarian (sit, set) the books down. (Because *books* is the direct object, the answer has to be *set*. In addition, *put* can be inserted for *set*.)

Unfortunately, there are times when *to set* will NOT have a direct object. Give full attention to the meaning of *place* or *put*. If *placed* can be inserted for *set*, use a form of *to set*.

Example: Fried chicken had been (sat, set) in the basket.
(placed)

*In most cases

RISE/RAISE

To rise: means to go up (without help)
To raise: means to go up (with help)

FORMS:

Infinitive	Present	Past	Present Participle	(has, have, had) Past Participle
To rise	rise(s)	rose	rising	(had) risen
To raise	raise(s)	raised	raising	(had) raised

If students understand direct objects, they will have no trouble with rise/raise.*

Two basic items for rise/raise:

A. To rise is an irregular verb; its forms need to be mastered.
To raise is a regular verb.

B. *Raise* requires a direct object.**

Examples:

The sourdough bread is (rising, raising). There is no direct object so the answer has to be *rising*.

The sourdough bread is (rising, raising).

D.O.
The charity organization (rose, raised) money for the needy.
The object the organization raised was *money*. Thus money is the direct object. The choice must be *raised*.

The charity organization (rose, raised) money for the needy.

* Go back to direct objects for a review.
**In most cases.

Example: The flag had been (risen, raised) at sunrise.

Keep in mind that *to raise* implies with help. The flag needed help; it could not have gone up on its own. Therefore, *to raise* is correct even though there is no direct object in the sentence.

LIE/LAY

To lie: means to rest or recline
To lay: means to place or to put

FORMS:

Infinitive	Present	Past	Present Participle	(has, have, had) Past Participle
To lie	lie(s)	lay	lying	(had) lain
To lay	lay(s)	laid	laying	(had) laid

Lie/lay is one of the most difficult concepts in English. The past tense of *to lie* and the present tense of *to lay* are the same.

Two basic items for lie/lay:

A. Lie/Lay are irregular verbs and must be mastered.

B. *Lay* will have a direct object.*

Examples:

A pig is (lying, laying) in the mud.

A pig is (lying, laying) ~~in the mud~~. — There is no direct object in the sentence so the answer has to be *lying*.

D.O.

We (lay, laid) the envelope on your desk yesterday.

We (lay, laid) ** the envelope on your desk yesterday. — The object we laid on the desk was an envelope. Thus envelope is a direct object.

*Go back to direct objects for a review.

**Be sure you understand that *laid* will have a direct object. However, at times, *to lay* will NOT have a direct object.

Example: A magazine had been (lain, laid) there by Martha.
To lay means to place. You can insert *placed* for *laid* in the sentence without changing its meaning. Thus in some cases, direct objects will be missing.

Name________________________________ **SIT/SET**
WORKBOOK PAGE 62 **LIE/LAY**
Date________________________________ **RISE/RAISE**

Directions: Cross out any prepositional phrases. Underline the subject once and the verb/verb phrase twice. Label any direct object(s)-D.O.

Reminder: To Set/To Lay/To Raise will have direct object(s).*

1. She often (lies, lays) ~~in the hammock~~ (to read).

D.O.
2. The farmer's daughter (rose, raised) a pig ~~for her project~~.

D.O.
3. Candace (lay, laid) tile ~~in the bathroom~~.

4. Our mail was (lying, laying) ~~on the kitchen counter~~.

5. Have you (sat, set) there long?

6. Every afternoon, the retired man (lies, lays) ~~by the pool~~.

D.O.
7. The crowd (rose, raised) its voice ~~in protest~~.

D.O.
8. Walter (sits, sets) his lunch ~~by the door~~ each evening.

9. We had been (rising, raising) early.

D.O.
10. Father (lay, laid) the infant ~~in the crib~~.

11. Your paper is (lying, laying) ~~by the front door~~.

12. She (sat, set) quietly ~~on the red velvet chair~~.

D.O.
13. The volunteer fire company (rose, raised) money ~~for a new engine~~.

14. Aunt Robyn (sits, sets) ~~for a daily meditation~~.

D.O.
15. The clerk (lay, laid) my package ~~on the counter~~.

*Most of the time.

Name________________________________

Date________________________________

SIT/SET
LIE/LAY
RISE/RAISE

Directions: Cross out any prepositional phrases. Underline the subject once and the verb/verb phrase twice. Label any direct object(s)-D.O.

Reminder: To Set/To Lay/To Raise will have direct object(s).*

1. She often (lies, lays) in the hammock to read.
2. The farmer's daughter (rose, raised) a pig for her project.
3. Candace (lay, laid) tile in the bathroom.
4. Our mail was (lying, laying) on the kitchen counter.
5. Have you (sat, set) there long?
6. Every afternoon, the retired man (lies, lays) by the pool.
7. The crowd (rose, raised) its voice in protest.
8. Walter (sits, sets) his lunch by the door each evening.
9. We had been (rising, raising) early.
10. Father (lay, laid) the infant in the crib.
11. Your paper is (lying, laying) by the front door.
12. She (sat, set) quietly on the red velvet chair.
13. The volunteer fire company (rose, raised) money for a new engine.
14. Aunt Robyn (sits, sets) for a daily meditation.
15. The clerk (lay, laid) my package on the counter.

*Most of the time.

Name________________________________ **SIT/SET**
WORKBOOK PAGE 63 **LIE/LAY**
Date________________________________ **RISE/RAISE**

Directions: Cross out any prepositional phrases. Underline the subject once and the verb/verb phrase twice. Label any direct object(s)-D.O.

Reminder: To Set/To Lay/To Raise will have direct object(s).

D.O.
Example: They were (rising, raising) their hands (to show) agreement.

D.O.
1. The race car driver (sat, set) the keys ~~on the hood of the car~~.

2. A gray horse was (lying, laying) ~~in an open meadow~~.

3. We (sit, set) down (to eat) lunch.

4. Smoke (rose, raised) ~~up the chimney~~.

D.O.
5. The baker (sat, set) the pie ~~in the pantry~~.

6. Applesauce bread was (rising, raising).

D.O.
7. Martin (sits, sets) his toothbrush ~~in the medicine cabinet~~.

8. The sun had (risen, raised) ~~at six o'clock~~.

D.O.
9. Did Hannah (sit, set) the record ~~for the long jump?~~

10. Our spaniel has (lain, laid) ~~in that spot~~ all afternoon.

11. My dance partner (sits, sets) next ~~to me in science class~~.

D.O.
12. We (lay, laid) the records ~~on the stereo cabinet~~.

13. A famous clothes designer was (sitting, setting) ~~among many guests~~.

14. Prices ~~of shoes and socks~~ have (risen, raised) ~~in the last year~~.

D.O.
15. Mother and Dad (lay, laid) towels ~~by the pool~~.

Name_________________________________ **SIT/SET**
LIE/LAY
Date _________________________________ **RISE/RAISE**

Directions: Cross out any prepositional phrases. Underline the subject once and the verb/verb phrase twice. Label any direct object(s)-D.O.

Reminder: To Set/To Lay/To Raise will have direct object(s).

D.O.
Example: They were (rising, raising) their hands (to show) agreement.

1. The race car driver (sat, set) the keys on the hood of the car.
2. A gray horse was (lying, laying) in an open meadow.
3. We (sit, set) down to eat lunch.
4. Smoke (rose, raised) up the chimney.
5. The baker (sat, set) the pie in the pantry.
6. Applesauce bread was (rising, raising).
7. Martin (sits, sets) his toothbrush in the medicine cabinet.
8. The sun had (risen, raised) at six o'clock.
9. Did Hannah (sit, set) the record for the long jump?
10. Our spaniel has (lain, laid) in that spot all afternoon.
11. My dance partner (sits, sets) next to me in science class.
12. We (lay, laid) the records on the stereo cabinet.
13. A famous clothes designer was (sitting, setting) among many guests.
14. Prices of shoes and socks have (risen, raised) in the last year.
15. Mother and Dad (lay, laid) towels by the pool.

IRREGULAR VERB *TO BE*

Students need to **memorize** and **master** the conjugation of *to be.*

is, am, are, was, were, be, being, been

Once again, use appropriate methods to insure mastery learning. Listing them is an effective way. (Students will be thrilled that these memorization lists are getting shorter!)

Present Tense:

Singular: **is** (The boy **is** nice.)

am (I **am** here.) ***Am*** is used only with the **I** pronoun.

Plural: **are** (The classes **are** interesting.)

Past Tense:

Singular: **was** (The person **was** alone.)

Plural: **were** (Some loons **were** on the lake.)

PAGE 124 = WORKBOOK PAGE 64
PAGE 125 = WORKBOOK PAGE 65

LINKING VERBS

Linking verbs DO NOT SHOW ACTION. They link the subject with a noun or pronoun, or they link the subject with an adjective (describing word).

Examples: His mother is an accountant.

The winners of the game were they in blue shirts.

Mary became sick after the high jump.

There are three easy aspects of linking verbs:

A. Linking verbs never show action.

B. Linking verbs always link the subject with something.

C. Linking verbs appear as a separate list.

The following list of linking verbs must be **memorized** and **mastered**:

*to feel	to become	to remain
to taste	to seem	to appear
to look	to sound	to stay
to smell	to grow	to be (is, am, are, was, were, be, being, been)

To check if a verb (other than *to be*) is serving as a linking verb in a sentence, replace the verb with a form of *to be*. If the sentence makes sense and the meaning is not changed, the verb serves as a linking verb.

Examples: Joe seemed angry today.

Joe was angry today.

*High-utility linking verbs are included in this list.

LINKING VERBS

In order to teach linking verbs, you must introduce two new terms: predicate nominative and predicate adjective.

A **predicate nominative** is a noun (naming word) or a pronoun (I, he, she, we, they, who, you, or it) that is the same as the subject of the sentence. **Predicate nominative = P.N.**

Examples: My dad is the track coach at school. (P.N.)

Ms. Brody became our teacher. (P.N.)

Predicate nominatives are easy to check. Simply invert the sentence starting with the word after the verb in a declarative sentence, tag on the verb, and add the complete subject. (Rather than going through all of the preceeding explanation, simply instruct students to "invert" the sentence and give many examples. Students quickly understand this process.)

Example: My dad is the track coach at school. (P.N.)

Check: The track coach at school is my dad.

If a form of *to be* does not appear as the linking verb in the sentence, you will need to replace the existing linking verb with an appropriate form of *to be*.

Example: Ms. Brody became our teacher.

Ms. Brody was our teacher.

Check: Our teacher was Ms. Brody.

A sentence may contain a compound predicate nominative.

Example: My best subjects are history and math. (P.N. P.N.)

Check: History and math are my best subjects.

PAGE 126 = WORKBOOK PAGE 66
PAGE 127 = WORKBOOK PAGE 67

LINKING VERBS

Predicate Nominatives:

In an interrogative sentence, the predicate nominative may be more difficult to find. Follow this method: turn the question into a statement, mark the sentence (subject, verb, and predicate nominative), and "invert" the statement to check it.

Example: Is Hannah the girl in the striped blouse?

P.N.

Hannah is the girl in the striped blouse.

Check: The girl in the striped blouse is Hannah.

Example: Are you the new secretary for student council?

P.N.

You are the new secretary for student council.

Check: The new secretary is* you.

*Sometimes the present form of *to be* (is, am, are) must be inserted when checking for predicate nominatives.

Example: Was Ralph the last person to see him?

P.N.

Ralph was the last person to see him.

Check: The last person to see him was Ralph.

Example: Did your nephew become a doctor?

P.N.

Your nephew did become a doctor.

Check: The doctor was your nephew. Was the doctor your nephew?

Name________________________________

WORKBOOK PAGE 68

Date________________________________

LINKING VERBS

Predicate Nominatives

Directions: Cross out any prepositional phrases. Underline the subject once and the verb/verb phrase twice. Label the predicate nominative(s) in each sentence. Then, write the inverted form of the sentence on the line provided.

P.N.

Example: My brother is the boy ~~in the first row~~.

Check: The boy is my brother.

P.N.

1. Monica was the winner ~~of the contest~~.

The winner was Monica.

P.N.

2. My favorite food is pie.

Pie is my favorite food.

P.N.

3. Our doctor was Dr. Strom.

Dr. Strom was our doctor.

P.N.

4. Their dessert was a banana split.

A banana split was their dessert.

P.N.

5. My cousin is Freddy.

Freddy is my cousin.

P.N.

6. Jane became my favorite aunt.

My favorite aunt (is) Jane.

P.N. P.N.

7. The swimmers were Beth and her friend.

Beth and her friend were the swimmers.

P.N.

8. My dog remained my pal ~~throughout life~~.

My pal (was) my dog.

P.N.

9. Ms. Armstrong is the speaker today.

The speaker today is Ms. Armstrong.

P.N.

10. Bill has been our neighbor ~~for years~~.

Our neighbor has been Bill.

Name_______________________________

Date_______________________________

LINKING VERBS
Predicate Nominatives

Directions: Cross out any prepositional phrases. Underline the subject once and the verb/verb phrase twice. Label the predicate nominative(s) in each sentence. Then, write the inverted form of the sentence on the line provided.

P.N.
Example: My brother is the boy ~~in the first row.~~
Check: The boy is my brother.

1. Monica was the winner of the contest.

____

2. My favorite food is pie.

____

3. Our doctor was Dr. Strom.

____

4. Their dessert was a banana split.

____

5. My cousin is Freddy.

____

6. Jane became my favorite aunt.

____

7. The swimmers were Beth and her friend.

____

8. My dog remained my pal throughout life.

____

9. Ms. Armstrong is the speaker today.

____

10. Bill has been our neighbor for years.

____

PAGE 131 = WORKBOOK PAGE 69

LINKING VERBS

Predicate Adjectives:

A predicate adjective is a **describing word** that occurs **after the verb** and goes back to describe the **subject** of the sentence.

In order for a word to be a predicate adjective, you must have the following:

A. The sentence must contain a linking verb.
B. The adjective must go back and describe the subject of the sentence.

Examples:

P.A.
My wagon is red. (red wagon)

P.A.
The man felt* sick. (sick man)

P.A.
Sharp cheese tastes good. (good cheese)

P.A.
Birds ~~in our backyard~~ sounded happy. (happy birds)

Note: In the sentence, "John wore a blue shirt.", blue is NOT a predicate adjective. The verb *wore* is NOT a linking verb, and blue describes the shirt, NOT the subject, John.

Compound Predicate Adjectives:

There may be more than one predicate adjective in a sentence.

Examples:

P.A. P.A. P.A.
Our flag is red, white, and blue. (red flag) (white flag) (blue flag)

P.A. P.A.
The tired child became sleepy and restless. (sleepy child) (restless child)

---

*Remember that an aid to checking if the verb is linking is to see if you can insert a form of *to be* for the verb. If you can, the verb generally will be a linking verb. (The man felt (was) sick.)

Name______________________________ **LINKING VERBS**

WORKBOOK PAGE 70 Predicate Adjectives

Date______________________________

Directions: Cross out any prepositional phrases. Underline the subject once and the verb/verb phrase twice. Label the predicate adjective(s) in each sentence. On the line after the sentence, write the predicate adjective(s) with the subject.

Example: My dog is brown. (P.A.: brown) ______ brown dog ______

1. Our tractor is yellow. (P.A.: yellow) ______ yellow tractor ______
2. Sandpaper usually feels rough ~~to the touch~~. (P.A.: rough) ______ rough sandpaper ______
3. ~~After the verdict~~, her face grew pale. (P.A.: pale) ______ pale face ______
4. His plan sounded superb. (P.A.: superb) ______ superb plan ______
5. That person certainly looks suspicious ~~to me~~. (P.A.: suspicious) ______ suspicious person ______
6. The dress ~~in the closet~~ was once purple. (P.A.: purple) ______ purple dress ______
7. Your lasagna tastes spicy. (P.A.: spicy) ______ spicy lasagna ______
8. Hair should be soft and shiny. (P.A.: soft; P.A.: shiny) ______ soft and shiny hair ______
9. The motorist seemed unaware ~~of the accident~~. (P.A.: unaware) ______ unaware motorist ______
10. Grandpa grows tired easily. (P.A.: tired) ______ tired Grandpa ______
11. Their friends remained tense ~~throughout the entire movie~~. (P.A.: tense) ______ tense friends ______
12. The cookies smelled burned. (P.A.: burned) ______ burned cookies ______
13. The customer had become angry quickly. (P.A.: angry) ______ angry customer ______
14. Those plums were delicious. (P.A.: delicious) ______ delicious plums ______
15. The baby stayed happy ~~during the entire shopping trip~~. (P.A.: happy) ______ happy baby ______

Name________________________________

Date________________________________

LINKING VERBS
Predicate Adjectives

Directions: Cross out any prepositional phrases. Underline the subject once and the verb/verb phrase twice. Label the predicate adjective(s) in each sentence. On the line after the sentence, write the predicate adjective(s) with the subject.

Example: My dog is brown. (P.A.: brown) ______brown dog______

1. Our tractor is yellow. ________________________________
2. Sandpaper usually feels rough to the touch. ________________________
3. After the verdict, her face grew pale. ________________________
4. His plan sounded superb. ________________________________
5. That person certainly looks suspicious to me. ________________________
6. The dress in the closet was once purple. ________________________
7. Your lasagna tastes spicy. ________________________________
8. Hair should be soft and shiny. ________________________________
9. The motorist seemed unaware of the accident. ________________________
10. Grandpa grows tired easily. ________________________________
11. Their friends remained tense throughout the entire movie. ______________

    ____
12. The cookies smelled burned. ________________________________
13. The customer had become angry quickly. ________________________
14. Those plums were delicious. ________________________________
15. The baby stayed happy during the entire shopping trip.________________

PAGE 135 = WORKBOOK PAGE 71

ACTION OR LINKING VERBS

Students need to "think" about the verb. Often they will readily see that the verb shows action (yells, talked, etc.). Because the students are required to memorize linking verbs, they will immediately recognize that *know* cannot be a linking verb. *Know* is not one of their linking verbs. *Know,* therefore, has to be an action verb.

Some verbs can serve both as action and linking verbs.

Example: Joan tasted the soup. (action)

This drink tastes bitter. (linking)

Suggestion: Instruct students to insert a form of *to be* (is, am, are, was, were) for the verb. If the sentence meaning is not changed, the verb is usually linking.

Examples: Joan tasted the soup.

Joan was the soup. (*Tasted* is not a linking verb here. The sentence meaning is changed by inserting *was*.)

This drink tastes bitter.

This drink is bitter. (*Tastes* is a linking verb. In inserting *is*, the sentence meaning is not changed.)

What became of him?

What was of him? (*Became* is not a linking verb here. Inserting *was* changes the sentence meaning.)

Name________________________________ **VERBS**

WORKBOOK PAGE 72 Action or Linking?

Date________________________________

Directions: Cross out any prepositional phrases. Underline the subject once and the verb/verb phrase twice. Place an A on the line if the verb shows action. Place L on the line if the verb is linking. Above linking verbs, write a form of *to be* (is, am, are, was, were) as a check.

Example: __L__ Despite the medicine, the patient remained (was) ill.

1. __A__ The diner choked ~~on a piece of steak~~.
2. __L__ Suzanne grew (was) excited ~~about her new career~~.
3. __A__ An insect bit me.
4. __L__ His eyes looked (were) glazed.
5. __A__ We smelled the flowers.
6. __A__ The mother looked ~~at the messy house~~ ~~with displeasure~~.
7. __L__ Your taco smells (is) good.
8. __L__ The electrician seemed (was) sad ~~about your decision~~.
9. __A__ The seventh grader grew four inches ~~during the summer~~.
10. __A__ We tasted several strange foods ~~at the international restaurant~~.
11. __A__ The custodian felt his way ~~down a darkened hall~~.
12. __L__ The puppy stayed (was) little ~~for nearly a year~~.
13. __A__ Melissa threw the ball ~~to the pitcher~~.
14. __L__ Our family felt (was) happy ~~about our new canary~~.
15. __A__ Missionaries ~~from Africa~~ stayed ~~with me~~ ~~for a week~~.

Name________________________________

Date________________________________

VERBS

Action or Linking?

Directions: Cross out any prepositional phrases. Underline the subject once and the verb/verb phrase twice. Place an A on the line if the verb shows action. Place L on the line if the verb is linking. Above linking verbs, write a form of *to be* (*is, am, are, was, were*) as a check.

Example: __L__ Despite the medicine, the patient remained ill. (was)

1. _____ The diner choked on a piece of steak.
2. _____ Suzanne grew excited about her new career.
3. _____ An insect bit me.
4. _____ His eyes looked glazed.
5. _____ We smelled the flowers.
6. _____ The mother looked at the messy house with displeasure.
7. _____ Your taco smells good.
8. _____ The electrician seemed sad about your decision.
9. _____ The seventh grader grew four inches during the summer.
10. _____ We tasted several strange foods at the international restaurant.
11. _____ The custodian felt his way down a darkened hall.
12. _____ The puppy stayed little for nearly a year.
13. _____ Melissa threw the ball to the pitcher.
14. _____ Our family felt happy about our new canary.
15. _____ Missionaries from Africa stayed with me for a week.

PAGE 139 = WORKBOOK PAGE 73

SUBJECT-VERB AGREEMENT

If the subject is singular (only one), the verb will be singular. In a regular verb (one that adds ed to form past time, e.g. walk/ walked), you add s to the verb when the subject is singular.

Examples: Our maid cleans the room.

My father works hard.

The teller counts the money.

In most irregular verbs, the same rule applies. Simply add s to the verb.

Examples: The runner breaks a record.

A thief steals a car.

He speaks well.

In a few irregular verbs, es is added to the verb.

Examples: The baby goes to sleep early.

Mother teaches an exercise class.

Name______________________________ **VERBS**

WORKBOOK PAGE 74 Subject-Verb Agreement

Date______________________________

Directions: Cross out any prepositional phrases. Underline the subject once and the verb twice.

1. The dentist (clean, cleans) my teeth ~~during my yearly visit~~.
2. My grandmother (plant, plants) tulips ~~in her garden~~.
3. ~~After lunch~~ our family (plan, plans) to go ~~to the store~~.
4. ~~In biology class~~, Susan (sit, sits) ~~beside me~~.
5. Every afternoon the swimmer (dive, dives) ~~into the pool~~.
6. She (change, changes) a flat tire easily.
7. A friend ~~of my mother's~~ (collect, collects) dolls.
8. The worker (drive, drives) ~~onto the freeway~~ ~~on the way~~ ~~to his job~~.
9. That restaurant (serve, serves) lunch ~~from noon~~ ~~until five o'clock~~.
10. The bird (hop, hops) ~~by the water fountain~~ ~~during the morning~~.
11. ~~Near the furniture factory~~ (live, lives) a hobo ~~with his dog~~.
12. Our brother (pretend, pretends) to be a monster.
13. Their niece (serve, serves) dessert ~~after every dinner~~.
14. ~~Before a nap~~, that child (scream, screams) ~~at the top of his lungs~~.
15. A stack ~~of old newspapers~~ (stand, stands) ~~on the porch~~.

Name______________________________________

Date______________________________________

VERBS

Subject-Verb Agreement

Directions: Cross out any prepositional phrases. Underline the subject once and the verb twice.

1. The dentist (clean, cleans) my teeth during my yearly visit.
2. My grandmother (plant, plants) tulips in her garden.
3. After lunch our family (plan, plans) to go to the store.
4. In biology class, Susan (sit, sits) beside me.
5. Every afternoon the swimmer (dive, dives) into the pool.
6. She (change, changes) a flat tire easily.
7. A friend of my mother's (collect, collects) dolls.
8. The worker (drive, drives) onto the freeway on the way to his job.
9. That restaurant (serve, serves) lunch from noon until five o'clock.
10. The bird (hop, hops) by the water fountain during the morning.
11. Near the furniture factory (live, lives) a hobo with his dog.
12. Our brother (pretend, pretends) to be a monster.
13. Their niece (serve, serves) dessert after every dinner.
14. Before a nap, that child (scream, screams) at the top of his lungs.
15. A stack of old newspapers (stand, stands) on the porch.

PAGE 143 = WORKBOOK PAGE 75

SUBJECT-VERB AGREEMENT

If the subject is plural (more than one), do not add s to the verb.

Examples: Tigers (roam, roams) in the countryside.

Our trees (blossom, blossoms) in the spring.

In most irregular verbs, you do not add s to the verb if the subject is plural.

Examples: The players (sit, sits) in the circle.

Her mother and she (swim, swims) every day.

If a compound subject (two or more) is joined by *or*, follow these rules:

A. If the subject closer to the verb is singular, add s to the verb.
Example: His daughters or **son** **needs** a ride home.

B. If the subject closer to the verb is plural, don't add s to the verb.
Example: His son or **daughters** **need** a ride home.

Name________________________________ **VERBS**

WORKBOOK PAGE 76 Subject-Verb Agreement

Date________________________________

Directions: Cross out any prepositional phrases. Underline the subject once and the correct verb twice.

1. Three lawyers (comes, come) here ~~for lunch~~.
2. Margaret and her cousin (fly, flies) ~~to Detroit~~ each summer.
3. Mary and Bill (arrives, arrive) ~~at school~~ ~~before anyone~~.
4. The women (eat, eats) here often.
5. Tom's uncle (owns, own) a travel agency ~~in our city~~.
6. Both the fifth grade team and the sixth grade team (win, wins) often.
7. The new computers (works, work) well.
8. They (hear, hears) weird sounds ~~from the deserted shack.~~
9. The tennis rackets (remain, remains) ~~in the closet~~ ~~during the winter months~~.
10. The hikers (walks, walk) ten miles a day.
11. The members ~~of our group~~ (wants, want) a field trip ~~to the museum~~.
12. Spectators (line, lines) the streets ~~for the Rose Bowl Parade~~.
13. Horses and cows (lives, live) ~~in the same barn~~.
14. Firemen (practice, practices) CPR ~~throughout their career~~.
15. Father and Mother (leaves, leave) their offices early ~~on Fridays~~.

Name________________________________

Date________________________________

VERBS

Subject-Verb Agreement

Directions: Cross out any prepositional phrases. Underline the subject once and the correct verb twice.

1. Three lawyers (comes, come) here for lunch.
2. Margaret and her cousin (fly, flies) to Detroit each summer.
3. Mary and Bill (arrives, arrive) at school before anyone.
4. The women (eat, eats) here often.
5. Tom's uncle (owns, own) a travel agency in our city.
6. Both the fifth grade team and the sixth grade team (win, wins) often.
7. The new computers (works, work) well.
8. They (hear, hears) weird sounds from the deserted shack.
9. The tennis rackets (remain, remains) in the closet during the winter months.
10. The hikers (walks, walk) ten miles a day.
11. The members of our group (wants, want) a field trip to the museum.
12. Spectators (line, lines) the streets for the Rose Bowl Parade.
13. Horses and cows (lives, live) in the same barn.
14. Firemen (practice, practices) CPR throughout their career.
15. Father and Mother (leaves, leave) their offices early on Fridays.

Name________________________________ **VERBS**
WORKBOOK PAGE 77
Date________________________________

Directions: Cross out any prepositional phrases. Underline the subject once and the verb/verb phrase twice.

Example: We packed and left ~~for the cabin~~.

1. Bob was leaving ~~in a hurry~~.

2. The clown jumped and nearly fell.

3. Have you seen my books and notebook?

4. The pitcher wants a starting position ~~in the game~~.

5. I had baked a pie and had eaten almost all ~~of it~~ ~~by four o'clock~~.

6. Ms. Brant's class might be going, too.

7. The spider had spun an intricate web.

8. She declared her innocence and then fainted.

9. Should you have been given a larger size?

10. Several square dancers will be performing ~~at the rodeo~~.

11. Jill is Greg's cousin.

12. Has the librarian been reading that new book?

13. You should have come ~~with us~~ ~~to the parade~~.

14. Grandma may be home now.

15. I must finish or accept a last prize.

Name________________________________

Date________________________________

VERBS

Directions: Cross out any prepositional phrases. Underline the subject once and the verb/verb phrase twice.

Example: We packed and left ~~for the cabin~~.

1. Bob was leaving in a hurry.
2. The clown jumped and nearly fell.
3. Have you seen my books and notebook?
4. The pitcher wants a starting position in the game.
5. I had baked a pie and had eaten almost all of it by four o'clock.
6. Ms. Brant's class might be going, too.
7. The spider had spun an intricate web.
8. She declared her innocence and then fainted.
9. Should you have been given a larger size?
10. Several square dancers will be performing at the rodeo.
11. Jill is Greg's cousin.
12. Has the librarian been reading that new book?
13. You should have come with us to the parade.
14. Grandma may be home now.
15. I must finish or accept a last prize.

Name________________________________ **VERBS**
WORKBOOK PAGE 78
Date________________________________

Directions: Cross out any prepositional phrases. Underline the subject once and the verb/verb phrase twice.

Example: The gorilla has grown rapidly.

1. We cut out pictures and pasted them ~~on large sheets of paper~~.
2. Could you build a volcano ~~for the science project~~?
3. May the children wait until later ~~in the week~~?
4. Some teenagers are walking ~~to the park~~ (to play) tennis.
5. He would not answer the question immediately.
6. Some ~~of the plants~~ have withered and died ~~during the night~~.
7. Our judges will be selecting the grand prize winner ~~in an hour~~.
8. Several had never seen the Golden Gate Bridge.
9. Alice's friend had ridden her bike ~~to the store~~.
10. The French toast will taste delicious ~~with maple syrup~~.
11. A beautiful model traveled ~~to Sweden~~ and appeared ~~in a fashion show~~.
12. The news reporter asked a few questions and then stated her opinion.
13. Dad's office was broken into and robbed ~~during the night~~.
14. We wash our hair and brush our teeth ~~at bedtime~~.
15. Your grandpa should have been traveling ~~with a companion~~.

Name________________________________ **VERBS**

Date________________________________

Directions: Cross out any prepositional phrases. Underline the subject once and the verb/verb phrase twice.

Example: The <u>gorilla</u> <u>has grown</u> rapidly.

1. We cut out pictures and pasted them on large sheets of paper.
2. Could you build a volcano for the science project?
3. May the children wait until later in the week?
4. Some teenagers are walking to the park to play tennis.
5. He would not answer the question immediately.
6. Some of the plants have withered and died during the night.
7. Our judges will be selecting the grand prize winner in an hour.
8. Several had never seen the Golden Gate Bridge.
9. Alice's friend had ridden her bike to the store.
10. The French toast will taste delicious with maple syrup.
11. A beautiful model traveled to Sweden and appeared in a fashion show.
12. The news reporter asked a few questions and then stated her opinion.
13. Dad's office was broken into and robbed during the night.
14. We wash our hair and brush our teeth at bedtime.
15. Your grandpa should have been traveling with a companion.

Name________________________________ **VERBS**

WORKBOOK PAGE 79

Date________________________________

Directions: Cross out any prepositional phrases. Underline the subject once and the verb/verb phrase twice.

Example: Cars and trucks were stopped ~~on the freeway~~.

1. The boys scrambled ~~up the ladder~~ and scurried ~~over the roof~~.

2. Most ~~of the candidates~~ were not ~~in attendance~~.

3. The winter temperature may fall ~~below zero~~ ~~in Chicago~~.

4. The kids watched cartoons and then ate their lunch.

(You)

5. Go ~~to the store~~ and get some bananas and detergent.

6. The tiger leaped ~~upon the truck~~ and growled ~~in the window~~.

7. The cheerleader should have attended the workshop.

8. The bunch ~~of carrots~~ was lying ~~on the counter~~.

9. Our family might have gone earlier that day.

10. May he or she be permitted to delay the tournament ~~for a day~~?

11. The designer chose a fabric and then changed his mind.

12. The students had gone ~~to the auditorium~~ and had sat quietly.

13. The cyclist has traveled ~~throughout Europe~~.

14. Most ~~of us~~ must have done well ~~on the examination~~.

15. Cyrus cannot go ~~to the movie~~ or ~~to the dance~~ ~~at school~~.

Name________________________________ **VERBS**

Date________________________________

Directions: Cross out any prepositional phrases. Underline the subject once and the verb/verb phrase twice.

Example: Cars and trucks were stopped ~~on the freeway~~.

1. The boys scrambled up the ladder and scurried over the roof.
2. Most of the candidates were not in attendance.
3. The winter temperature may fall below zero in Chicago.
4. The kids watched cartoons and then ate their lunch.
5. Go to the store and get some bananas and detergent.
6. The tiger leaped upon the truck and growled in the window.
7. The cheerleader should have attended the workshop.
8. The bunch of carrots was lying on the counter.
9. Our family might have gone earlier that day.
10. May he or she be permitted to delay the tournament for a day?
11. The designer chose a fabric and then changed his mind.
12. The students had gone to the auditorium and had sat quietly.
13. The cyclist has traveled throughout Europe.
14. Most of us must have done well on the examination.
15. Cyrus cannot go to the movie or to the dance at school.

Name________________________________ **VERBS**
WORKBOOK PAGE 80
Date________________________________

Directions: Cross out any prepositional phrases. Underline the subject once and the verb/verb phrase twice.

Example: The package should not have been delivered there.

1. Was Bill leaving ~~on the afternoon bus~~?

2. Either Joan or Susan won the election.

3. Sam crawled ~~in the window~~ and fell ~~on the floor~~.

4. That movie was good.

(You)
5. Please go away.

6. Shelly laughed then but cried later.

7. Did Tom, Betty, or Heather recognize the burglar?

8. One ~~of the ladies~~ left her purse and returned ~~for it~~.

9. He was vacationing ~~in Brazil~~ and found a peculiar rock.

10. Neither the bananas nor the grapes have been eaten.

11. He has been searching ~~for the lost treasure of Tahiti~~.

(You)
12. Stop and rest a few moments!

13. The police, the nurses, and the sanitation workers have renewed their contracts.

14. ~~In these days of fast foods~~, we don't always remember our grandparents' hard labor ~~in the kitchen~~.

15. ~~With guidance~~, the twins learned (to tie) their shoes and (to write) their names.

Name________________________________ **VERBS**

Date_________________________________

Directions: Cross out any prepositional phrases. Underline the subject once and the verb/verb phrase twice.

Example: The package should not have been delivered there.

1. Was Bill leaving on the afternoon bus?
2. Either Joan or Susan won the election.
3. Sam crawled in the window and fell on the floor.
4. That movie was good.
5. Please go away.
6. Shelly laughed then but cried later.
7. Did Tom, Betty, or Heather recognize the burglar?
8. One of the ladies left her purse and returned for it.
9. He was vacationing in Brazil and found a peculiar rock.
10. Neither the bananas nor the grapes have been eaten.
11. He has been searching for the lost treasure of Tahiti.
12. Stop and rest a few moments!
13. The police, the nurses, and the sanitation workers have renewed their contracts.
14. In these days of fast foods, we don't always remember our grandparents' hard labor in the kitchen.
15. With guidance, the twins learned to tie their shoes and to write their names.

Name_______________________________ **VERBS**

WORKBOOK PAGE 81

Date_______________________________

Directions: Cross out any prepositional phrases. Underline the subject once and the verb/verb phrase twice.

Example: Did you cut the apple ~~into two pieces~~?

1. Neither Mary nor John has brought the homework.
2. When did the class leave ~~for the field trip~~?
3. Glenn's dad was ill last week.
4. Were Pat and her nephew skiing last weekend?
5. That group ~~of students~~ should have eaten earlier ~~in the day~~.
6. ~~With clenched teeth~~, the determined wrestler grabbed his opponent and pinned him.
7. Either you must clean the garage or park your car ~~in the street~~.
8. (You) Go ~~to the office~~, get some papers, and pass them out immediately.
9. Will some ~~of the secretaries~~ be going ~~to lunch~~ ~~with us~~?
10. Each ~~of the lawyers~~ must take his work home ~~with him~~.
11. Many men fought and died ~~at the Alamo~~.
12. ~~Within minutes~~, the team ~~of basketball players~~ finished and left.
13. Were the clowns or the trapeze artists funnier?
14. This is nice ~~of you~~ (to go).
15. Both my foot and my leg had been injured ~~in the accident~~.
16. You must go now or plan ~~on spending the night~~.
17. Will any ~~of the books~~ be returned today?
18. Several ministers and deacons met and discussed church activities.
19. A hand-carved cradle had been made ~~by her father's uncle~~.
20. Your pool should not have been cleaned ~~before the storm~~.

Name____________________________________ **VERBS**

Date____________________________________

Directions: Cross out any prepositional phrases. Underline the subject once and the verb/verb phrase twice.

Example: Did you cut the apple ~~into two pieces~~?

1. Neither Mary nor John has brought the homework.
2. When did the class leave for the field trip?
3. Glenn's dad was ill last week.
4. Were Pat and her nephew skiing last weekend?
5. That group of students should have eaten earlier in the day.
6. With clenched teeth, the determined wrestler grabbed his opponent and pinned him.
7. Either you must clean the garage or park your car in the street.
8. Go to the office, get some papers, and pass them out immediately.
9. Will some of the secretaries be going to lunch with us?
10. Each of the lawyers must take his work home with him.
11. Many men fought and died at the Alamo.
12. Within minutes, the team of basketball players finished and left.
13. Were the clowns or the trapeze artists funnier?
14. This is nice of you to go.
15. Both my foot and my leg had been injured in the accident.
16. You must go now or plan on spending the night.
17. Will any of the books be returned today?
18. Several ministers and deacons met and discussed church activities.
19. A hand-carved cradle had been made by her father's uncle.
20. Your pool should not have been cleaned before the storm.

PAGE 157 = WORKBOOK PAGE 82

VERB TENSES

Tenses mean time. Present tense, of course, signifies present time. Although present can mean "at this moment," it is easier to use the term, *today,* as a point of reference for present tense.

PRESENT TENSE NEVER HAS A HELPING (AUXILIARY) VERB.
(Repeat this fact until mastery of the idea is insured.)

1. If the student knows that the present tense never has a helper, he/she will not believe that the following sentence is present tense although it sounds like the present tense.

   The dog is barking.

   A. This sentence cannot be the present tense because there is a helping verb in the sentence. The entire verb phrase becomes *is barking*.

   B. The verb phrase, *is barking*, is actually a separate tense called the progressive tense.

2. To form the present tense, remove the *to* from the infinitive.

To speak = speak	(Today they speak.)
To talk = talk	(Today the boys talk.)
To push = push	(Today the vendors push the carts.)

Note that this holds true if the subject is plural (more than one).

To form the present tense with a singular subject, add s (and in some cases es) to the verb infinitive minus *to*.

To speak = speaks	(The guest speaks today.)
To talk = talks	(Today the boy talks.)
To push = pushes	(Today a vendor pushes his cart.)

VERB TENSES

WORKBOOK PAGE 83

PAST TENSE: Past tense indicates time that has occurred. Although past can mean less than a second ago, it is easier to use the term, *yesterday*, as a point of reference for past tense.

PAST TENSE NEVER HAS A HELPING (AUXILIARY) VERB.
(Repeat this fact until mastery of the concept is insured.)

1. If the student knows that the past tense never has a helping verb, she/he will not believe that the following sentence is past tense.

   Father has gone.

   A. This sentence cannot be the past tense because there is a helping verb in the sentence. The entire verb phrase is *has gone*.

   B. The verb phrase, *has gone*, is actually a separate tense called the perfect tense.

2. To form the past tense, teach two rules:

   A. **To form the past tense of regular verbs, add ed to the verb.**

   walk/walked love/loved

   B. **To form the past tense of irregular verbs, change the verb to its appropriate form.***

   speak/spoke bring/brought

*Refer to page 95.

FUTURE TENSE

WORKBOOK PAGE 84

Future tense indicates time yet to occur. It may be a second or a century from the moment.

There are two auxiliary (helping) verbs used with the future tense:

SHALL

WILL

Examples: I shall go to bed later.

Will Stan go with us tonight?

Note: Although it has become acceptable to use *will* with any subject, *shall* is generally reserved for the pronouns, *I* and *we*.

Stress with students that *shall* or *will* must be used with the verb to form the future tense.

THE FUTURE TENSE ALWAYS HAS THE HELPING VERBS WILL OR SHALL.*

Examples: The wind will probably blow hard tonight.

The dental assistant will find your chart.

Shall I ask for help?

*Although this concept seems easy, many students find it difficult. Ascertain that mastery learning is occurring.

Name________________________________ **VERBS**
WORKBOOK PAGE 85 Tenses
Date________________________________

Directions: Cross out any prepositional phrases. Underline the subject once and the verb/verb phrase twice. Write present, past, or future in the space provided to indicate the sentence tense.

Example: ___future___ The cobbler will repair my shoes.

1. ___present___ Some people persuade easily.
2. ___future___ We will persuade you (to stay).
3. ___past___ My counselor persuaded me (to attend) college.

1. ___future___ It will seem lonely ~~without you~~.
2. ___present___ That author seems lost ~~in thought~~.
3. ___past___ The answer seemed unsuitable ~~for the question~~.

1. ___present___ Arizona lies east ~~of California~~.
2. ___future___ I will lie ~~in the sun~~ ~~for ten minutes~~.
3. ___past___ The king lay ~~on the royal bed~~.

1. ___present___ ~~After playing~~, the children pick up all ~~of their toys~~.
2. ___past___ Josh picked ~~on other children~~ constantly.
3. ___future___ Frances will pick you up ~~after your appointment~~.

1. ___present___ Randy goes ~~to ballet classes~~ ~~on Tuesday~~.
2. ___future___ Will you go ~~with us~~?
3. ___past___ Our parents went ~~to Hawaii~~ this morning.

Name________________________________

Date________________________________

VERBS
Tenses

Directions: Cross out any prepositional phrases. Underline the subject once and the verb/verb phrase twice. Write present, past, or future in the space provided to indicate the sentence tense.

Example: ____future____ The cobbler will repair my shoes.

1. ________________ Some people persuade easily.
2. ________________ We will persuade you to stay.
3. ________________ My counselor persuaded me to attend college.

1. ________________ It will seem lonely without you.
2. ________________ That author seems lost in thought.
3. ________________ The answer seemed unsuitable for the question.

1. ________________ Arizona lies east of California.
2. ________________ I will lie in the sun for ten minutes.
3. ________________ The king lay on the royal bed.

1. ________________ After playing, the children pick up all of their toys.
2. ________________ Josh picked on other children constantly.
3. ________________ Frances will pick you up after your appointment.

1. ________________ Randy goes to ballet classes on Tuesday.
2. ________________ Will you go with us?
3. ________________ Our parents went to Hawaii this morning.

Name________________________________ **VERBS**

WORKBOOK PAGE 86 Tenses

Date________________________________

Directions: Cross out any prepositional phrases. Underline the subject once and the verb/verb phrase twice. Write present, past, or future in the space provided to indicate the sentence tense.

Example: ____present____ Some workers want higher wages.

1. ____present____ Small children often bring pets ~~to school~~.
2. ____future____ One person will bring juice ~~to the party~~.
3. ____past____ Susan brought her friends ~~to church~~.

1. ____past____ Workmen delivered the furniture ~~on Friday~~.
2. ____present____ Mother delivers speeches ~~about safe driving~~.
3. ____future____ We will deliver your pizza ~~in twenty minutes~~.

1. ____present____ I drink too much soda.
2. ____past____ A few cows drank water ~~from the pond~~.
3. ____future____ The nutritionist will drink milk ~~for lunch~~.

1. ____present____ My father enjoys letters ~~to the editor~~.
2. ____future____ Will you enjoy the trip alone?
3. ____past____ The rock stars enjoyed the concert.

1. ____future____ Someone will write ~~to you~~ ~~concerning the matter~~.
2. ____past____ The boss wrote a letter ~~of explanation~~ ~~to his employees~~.
3. ____present____ Tom and Sheila write well.

Name________________________________ **VERBS**

Tenses

Date________________________________

Directions: Cross out any prepositional phrases. Underline the subject once and the verb/verb phrase twice. Write present, past, or future in the space provided to indicate the sentence tense.

Example: ____present____ Some workers want higher wages.

1. ________________ Small children often bring pets to school.

2. ________________ One person will bring juice to the party.

3. ________________ Susan brought her friends to church.

1. ________________ Workmen delivered the furniture on Friday.

2. ________________ Mother delivers speeches about safe driving.

3. ________________ We will deliver your pizza in twenty minutes.

1. ________________ I drink too much soda.

2. ________________ A few cows drank water from the pond.

3. ________________ The nutritionist will drink milk for lunch.

1. ________________ My father enjoys letters to the editor.

2. ________________ Will you enjoy the trip alone?

3. ________________ The rock stars enjoyed the concert.

1. ________________ Someone will write to you concerning the matter.

2. ________________ The boss wrote a letter of explanation to his employees.

3. ________________ Tom and Sheila write well.

Name________________________________ **VERBS**

WORKBOOK PAGE 87 Tenses

Date________________________________

Directions: In the space provided, place the required verb/verb phrase.

Example: ____will paint____ I (future of paint) later.

1. ____will taste____ Dinner (future of taste) good tonight.
2. ____climbed____ Kannan (past of climb) a mountain.
3. ____runs____ The horse (present of run) fast.
4. ____will begin____ The speaker (future of begin) soon.
5. ____broke____ Some cars (past of break) down.
6. ____will dance____ Those girls (future of dance) for us.
7. ____laughed____ Everybody (past of laugh).
8. ____knits____ Lana (present of knit) daily.
9. ____flew____ We (past of fly) on a jet.
10. ____will be____ School (future of be) over in June.
11. ____build____ Some (present of build) sand castles.
12. ____gave____ A company (past of give) out balloons.
13. ____chose____ I (past of choose) my partner.
14. ____works____ The sculptor (present of work) each day.
15. ____crawled____ The divers (past of crawl) to safety.

Name________________________________

Date________________________________

VERBS
Tenses

Directions: In the space provided, place the required verb/verb phrase.

Example: ___will paint___ I (future of paint) later.

1. ____________________ Dinner (future of taste) good tonight.
2. ____________________ Kannan (past of climb) a mountain.
3. ____________________ The horse (present of run) fast.
4. ____________________ The speaker (future of begin) soon.
5. ____________________ Some cars (past of break) down.
6. ____________________ Those girls (future of dance) for us.
7. ____________________ Everybody (past of laugh).
8. ____________________ Lana (present of knit) daily.
9. ____________________ We (past of fly) on a jet.
10. ____________________ School (future of be) over in June.
11. ____________________ Some (present of build) sand castles.
12. ____________________ A company (past of give) out balloons.
13. ____________________ I (past of choose) my partner.
14. ____________________ The sculptor (present of work) each day.
15. ____________________ The divers (past of crawl) to safety.

Name______________________________

WORKBOOK PAGE 88

Date______________________________

VERBS

Tenses

Directions: In the space provided, place the required verb/verb phrase.

Example: _____is_____ Today (present of be) my birthday.

1. _____will come_____ Santa (future of come) on Christmas Eve.
2. _____left_____ Martha (past of leave) her home at two o'clock.
3. _____likes_____ Barton (present of like) his new toy.
4. _____went_____ Sharon (past of go) to her practice.
5. _____bring_____ They (present of bring) their mother here.
6. _____will help_____ Andrew (future of help) with the cleaning.
7. _____arrived_____ The box (past of arrive) in April.
8. _____will buy_____ I (future of buy) a new car.
9. _____rang_____ Laughter (past of ring) out.
10. _____are_____ Alicia and he (present of be) my choices.
11. _____swam_____ The duck (past of swim) in the pond.
12. _____will try_____ Mountain climbers (future of try) again.
13. _____talks_____ Kathy (present of talk) constantly.
14. _____will close_____ The public pool (future of close) today.
15. _____drove_____ The constant noise (past of drive) me crazy.

Name______________________________

Date______________________________

VERBS

Tenses

Directions: In the space provided, place the required verb/verb phrase.

Example: _____is_____ Today (present of be) my birthday.

1. ____________________ Santa (future of come) on Christmas Eve.
2. ____________________ Martha (past of leave) her home at two o'clock.
3. ____________________ Barton (present of like) his new toy.
4. ____________________ Sharon (past of go) to her practice.
5. ____________________ They (present of bring) their mother here.
6. ____________________ Andrew (future of help) with the cleaning.
7. ____________________ The box (past of arrive) in April.
8. ____________________ I (future of buy) a new car.
9. ____________________ Laughter (past of ring) out.
10. ____________________ Alicia and he (present of be) my choices.
11. ____________________ The duck (past of swim) in the pond.
12. ____________________ Mountain climbers (future of try) again.
13. ____________________ Kathy (present of talk) constantly.
14. ____________________ The public pool (future of close) today.
15. ____________________ The constant noise (past of drive) me crazy.

PAGE 169 = WORKBOOK PAGE 89

PERFECT TENSE

The perfect tense uses the past participle form.

Perfect Tense = *to have* + past participle *

To have:

Present:	have has
Past:	had
Future:	will have or shall have

Steps in forming the perfect tense:

1. Decide the past participle form of the given verb.

   Examples: to give = given   to place = placed

2. Decide the correct form of *to have*. If future perfect is required, use the future of *to have* (will have). Past perfect requires the past of *to have* (had). In forming the present perfect, either have or has will be used in order to make subject and verb agree.

3. Combine the *to have* form and the past participle form to make the perfect tense.

Perfect Tense (to know):

Present Perfect:	have known has known
Past Perfect:	had known
Future Perfect:	will have known or shall have known

*A review of past participles of irregular verbs is suggested.

Name________________________________ **VERBS**

WORKBOOK PAGE 90 Perfect Tense

Date________________________________

Directions: Cross out any prepositional phrases. Underline the subject once and the verb/verb phrase twice. Write present perfect, past perfect, or future perfect in the space provided to indicate tense.

Example: present perfect John has read fifty books.

1. past perfect — The truck had tipped over ~~on its side~~.

2. present perfect — She has tipped the waiter five dollars.

3. future perfect — ~~Within a few months~~, the informant will have provided the detectives ~~with information~~.

1. future perfect — ~~By June~~, we will have flown ~~across the Atlantic Ocean~~ four times.

2. present perfect — Have you ever flown ~~in a DC-10~~?

3. past perfect — Mother had flown ~~to San Francisco on a business trip~~.

1. present perfect — The track team has run the relay.

2. past perfect — Had the winner run ~~in a marathon~~ before?

3. future perfect — The Broadway show will have run ~~for a year in August~~.

1. future perfect — We will have nailed the entire fence ~~by the end of the day~~.

2. present perfect — Have you nailed the broken piece ~~of wood to the cabinet~~?

3. past perfect — Who had nailed ~~in the golden spike for the transcontinental railroad~~?

Name________________________________

Date________________________________

VERBS
Perfect Tense

Directions: Cross out any prepositional phrases. Underline the subject once and the verb/verb phrase twice. Write present perfect, past perfect, or future perfect in the space provided to indicate tense.

Example: present perfect ______ John has read fifty books.

1. ____________________ The truck had tipped over on its side.

2. ____________________ She has tipped the waiter five dollars.

3. ____________________ Within a few months, the informant will have provided the detectives with information.

1. ____________________ By June, we will have flown across the Atlantic Ocean four times.

2. ____________________ Have you ever flown in a DC-10?

3. ____________________ Mother had flown to San Francisco on a business trip.

1. ____________________ The track team has run the relay.

2. ____________________ Had the winner run in a marathon before?

3. ____________________ The Broadway show will have run for a year in August.

1. ____________________ We will have nailed the entire fence by the end of the day.

2. ____________________ Have you nailed the broken piece of wood to the cabinet?

3. ____________________ Who had nailed in the golden spike for the transcontinental railroad?

Name____________________________________ **VERBS**

WORKBOOK PAGE 91 Perfect Tense

Date____________________________________

Directions: Cross out any prepositional phrases. Underline the subject once and the verb/verb phrase twice. Write present perfect, past perfect, or future perfect in the space provided to indicate tense.

1. present perfect ______ They have chosen an alternate route ~~to St.Louis~~.
2. future perfect ______ Hopefully Janice and Paul will have chosen their course ~~of study~~ ~~by fall~~.
3. past perfect ______ Five judges had chosen the finalists.

1. present perfect ______ Margaret has joined a softball league.
2. past perfect ______ Had the twins joined 4-H last year?
3. future perfect ______ ~~After the wedding~~, the minister will have joined them ~~in holy matrimony~~.

1. future perfect ______ ~~By sunset~~, the motorist will have ridden five hundred miles.
2. past perfect ______ The excited children had ridden ~~in a hot air balloon~~.
3. present perfect ______ Have you ever ridden ~~in a Model T~~?

1. present perfect ______ Our package has arrived.
2. future perfect ______ All passengers will have arrived ~~by noon~~.
3. past perfect ______ The baby had arrived safely.

1. past perfect ______ My grandfather had seen Teddy Roosevelt.
2. present perfect ______ We have already seen the fireworks display.
3. future perfect ______ ~~By the end~~ ~~of the tour~~, our class will have seen most ~~of Washington, D. C~~.

Name____________________________________ **VERBS**

Perfect Tense

Date____________________________________

Directions: Cross out any prepositional phrases. Underline the subject once and the verb/verb phrase twice. Write present perfect, past perfect, or future perfect in the space provided to indicate tense.

1. ______________________ They have chosen an alternate route to St. Louis.
2. ______________________ Hopefully Janice and Paul will have chosen their course of study by fall.
3. ______________________ Five judges had chosen the finalists.

1. ______________________ Margaret has joined a softball league.
2. ______________________ Had the twins joined 4-H last year?
3. ______________________ After the wedding, the minister will have joined them in holy matrimony.

1. ______________________ By sunset, the motorist will have ridden five hundred miles.
2. ______________________ The excited children had ridden in a hot air balloon.
3. ______________________ Have you ever ridden in a Model T?

1. ______________________ Our package has arrived.
2. ______________________ All passengers will have arrived by noon.
3. ______________________ The baby had arrived safely.

1. ______________________ My grandfather had seen Teddy Roosevelt.
2. ______________________ We have already seen the fireworks display.
3. ______________________ By the end of the tour, our class will have seen most of Washington, D. C.

Name_______________________________ **VERBS**
WORKBOOK PAGE 92 Perfect Tense
Date_______________________________

Directions: In the space provided, place the required verb phrase.

Example: have seen I (present perfect of see) him.

1. has seen — The child (present perfect of see) me.
2. had seen — His father (past perfect of see) it twice.
3. will have seen — Someone (future perfect of see) the page.
4. have broken — Marvin and Greta (present perfect of break) a pitcher.
5. had broken — The players (past perfect of break) a record.
6. will have broken — They (future perfect of break) the tie.
7. had sung — The choir (past perfect of sing).
8. will have sung — My sister (future perfect of sing) by then.
9. have sung — Often I (present perfect of sing) for them.
10. will have run — The joggers (future perfect of run) a mile.
11. had run — A train (past perfect of run) out of steam.
12. has run — Number 4 (present perfect of run) in nearly every race.
13. had fallen — Some olives (past perfect of fall) from the tree.
14. has fallen — Cereal (present perfect of fall) on the floor.
15. will have fallen — Ten inches of snow (future perfect of fall) by evening.

Name________________________________ **VERBS**

Perfect Tense

Date________________________________

Directions: In the space provided, place the required verb phrase.

Example: ___have seen___ I (present perfect of see) him.

1. ____________________ The child (present perfect of see) me.

2. ____________________ His father (past perfect of see) it twice.

3. ____________________ Someone (future perfect of see) the page.

4. ____________________ Marvin and Greta (present perfect of break) a pitcher.

5. ____________________ The players (past perfect of break) a record.

6. ____________________ They (future perfect of break) the tie.

7. ____________________ The choir (past perfect of sing).

8. ____________________ My sister (future perfect of sing) by then.

9. ____________________ Often I (present perfect of sing) for them.

10. ____________________ The joggers (future perfect of run) a mile.

11. ____________________ A train (past perfect of run) out of steam.

12. ____________________ Number 4 (present perfect of run) in nearly every race.

13. ____________________ Some olives (past perfect of fall) from the tree.

14. ____________________ Cereal (present perfect of fall) on the floor.

15. ____________________ Ten inches of snow (future perfect of fall) by evening.

PAGE 177 = WORKBOOK PAGE 93

PROGRESSIVE TENSE*

The progressive tense uses the present participle form.

Progressive Tense = *to be* + present participle

To be:

Present:	am is are
Past:	was were
Future:	will be or shall be

Steps in forming the progressive tense:

1. Decide the present participle form of the given verb.

   Examples: to grow = growing   to yell = yelling

2. Decide the correct form of *to be*.

   A. Present progressive will use is, am, or are with the present participle.

   B. Past progressive will use was or were with the present participle.

   C. Future progressive will use shall be or will be with the present participle.

In forming the present progressive and past progressive, it is necessary to have subject and verb agreement.

Progressive Tense (to watch):

Present Progressive:	am watching is watching are watching
Past Progressive:	was watching were watching
Future Progressive:	will be watching or shall be watching

*Review present participle. Mastery learning may not be required.

Name____ **VERBS**
WORKBOOK PAGE 94 Progressive Tense
Date____

Directions: Cross out any prepositional phrases. Underline the subject once and the verb/verb phrase twice. Write present progressive (pres. pro.), past progressive (past pro.), or future progressive (fut. pro.) to indicate the tense of the sentence.

Example: past pro. A swan was swimming ~~across the lake~~.

1. pres. pro. A camel is lying ~~along the road~~.
2. past pro. Meat loaf was baking ~~in the oven~~.
3. fut. pro. We will be collecting cans this afternoon.
4. pres. pro. Monkeys are swinging ~~in the trees~~.
5. past pro. A frisky rabbit was nibbling the lettuce.
6. fut. pro. Will our class be going ~~on a field trip~~?
7. pres. pro. I am leaving ~~for Europe~~ tomorrow.
8. fut. pro. We will soon be learning how (to etch) glass.
9. past pro. The young girls were using different types ~~of makeup~~.
10. past pro. Birds were eating crumbs ~~in the yard~~.
11. fut. pro. Our club will be going there ~~on Friday~~.
12. pres. pro. My lower lip is burning.
13. pres. pro. I am learning ~~about yoga and karate~~.
14. past pro. The clown was dancing ~~for the small children~~.
15. pres. pro. Are you keeping a journal?

Name________________________________

Date________________________________

VERBS
Progressive Tense

Directions: Cross out any prepositional phrases. Underline the subject once and the verb/verb phrase twice. Write present progressive (pres. pro.), past progressive (past pro.), or future progressive (fut. pro.) to indicate the tense of the sentence.

Example: past pro. A swan was swimming ~~across the lake~~.

1. ____________________ A camel is lying along the road.
2. ____________________ Meat loaf was baking in the oven.
3. ____________________ We will be collecting cans this afternoon.
4. ____________________ Monkeys are swinging in the trees.
5. ____________________ A frisky rabbit was nibbling the lettuce.
6. ____________________ Will our class be going on a field trip?
7. ____________________ I am leaving for Europe tomorrow.
8. ____________________ We will soon be learning how to etch glass.
9. ____________________ The young girls were using different types of makeup.
10. ____________________ Birds were eating crumbs in the yard.
11. ____________________ Our club will be going there on Friday.
12. ____________________ My lower lip is burning.
13. ____________________ I am learning about yoga and karate.
14. ____________________ The clown was dancing for the small children.
15. ____________________ Are you keeping a journal?

Name________________________________ **VERBS**

WORKBOOK PAGE 95 Progressive Tense

Date________________________________

Directions: Cross out any prepositional phrases. Underline the subject once and the verb/verb phrase twice. Write present progressive (pres. pro.), past progressive (past pro.), or future progressive (fut. pro.) to indicate the tense of the sentence.

Example: pres. pro. They are listening very carefully.

1. past pro. Toys were lying all ~~over the floor~~.
2. pres. pro. The painter is adding the last few touches ~~to our wall~~.
3. pres. pro. Am I going, too?
4. past pro. The sky was growing dark.
5. fut. pro. Will I be choosing the best three essays?
6. pres. pro. Are you telling me the truth?
7. fut. pro. We will be hiking the canyon this month.
8. past pro. Were you skiing ~~at Aspen~~ last winter?
9. pres. pro. I am refinishing an antique chest.
10. past pro. The company was not sharing its profits.
11. past pro. Our family was camping last weekend.
12. fut. pro. The lakes will be freezing ~~during the winter months~~.
13. past pro. Five families were having a garage sale.
14. past pro. Smoke was rising ~~from several chimneys~~.
15. fut. pro. Will the cowboy artists be presenting any new works ~~at the fall showing~~?

Name________________________________

Date________________________________

VERBS

Progressive Tense

Directions: Cross out any prepositional phrases. Underline the subject once and the verb/verb phrase twice. Write present progressive (pres. pro.), past progressive (past pro.), or future progressive (fut. pro.) to indicate the tense of the sentence.

Example: pres. pro.__________ They are listening very carefully.

1. ______________________ Toys were lying all over the floor.
2. ______________________ The painter is adding the last few touches to our wall.
3. ______________________ Am I going, too?
4. ______________________ The sky was growing dark.
5. ______________________ Will I be choosing the best three essays?
6. ______________________ Are you telling me the truth?
7. ______________________ We will be hiking the canyon this month.
8. ______________________ Were you skiing at Aspen last winter?
9. ______________________ I am refinishing an antique chest.
10. ______________________ The company was not sharing its profits.
11. ______________________ Our family was camping last weekend.
12. ______________________ The lakes will be freezing during the winter months.
13. ______________________ Five families were having a garage sale.
14. ______________________ Smoke was rising from several chimneys.
15. ______________________ Will the cowboy artists be presenting any new works at the fall showing?

Name______________________________ **VERBS**
WORKBOOK PAGE 96 Tenses
Date______________________________

Directions: In the space provided, place the required verb/verb phrase.

Example:	spent	We (past of spend) too much money.
1.	will play	Abigail (future of play) in the tennis tournament.
2.	saw	The girls (past of see) the large flag.
3.	act	The children (present of act) in classroom plays.
4.	flew	Some flies (past of fly) around the honey.
5.	had served	Washington (past perfect of serve) two terms.
6.	has arrived	February (present perfect of arrive).
7.	will be running	In track, the members (future progressive of run.)
8.	had tried	Pontiac (past perfect of try) to unite the Indians.
9.	shall or will be celebrating	We (future progressive of celebrate) your anniversary.
10.	lies	The dog (present of lie) on a mat.
11.	will be receiving	Many students (future progressive of receive) good grades.
12.	will have left	A few (future perfect of leave) by the time you arrive.
13.	had bought	Joan (past perfect of buy) a card.
14.	bought	Joan (past of buy) a card.
15.	was buying	Joan (past progressive of buy) a card.

Name ______________________________

Date ______________________________

VERBS

Tenses

Directions: In the space provided, place the required verb/verb phrase.

Example: spent __________ We (past of spend) too much money.

1. ____________________ Abigail (future of play) in the tennis tournament.
2. ____________________ The girls (past of see) the large flag.
3. ____________________ The children (present of act) in classroom plays.
4. ____________________ Some flies (past of fly) around the honey.
5. ____________________ Washington (past perfect of serve) two terms.
6. ____________________ February (present perfect of arrive).
7. ____________________ In track, the members (future progressive of run.)
8. ____________________ Pontiac (past perfect of try) to unite the Indians.
9. ____________________ We (future progressive of celebrate) your anniversary.
10. ____________________ The dog (present of lie) on a mat.
11. ____________________ Many students (future progressive of receive) good grades.
12. ____________________ A few (future perfect of leave) by the time you arrive.
13. ____________________ Joan (past perfect of buy) a card.
14. ____________________ Joan (past of buy) a card.
15. ____________________ Joan (past progressive of buy) a card.

PAGE 185 = WORKBOOK PAGE 97

VERBS

Transitive or Intransitive?

A TRANSITIVE VERB WILL HAVE A DIRECT OBJECT.

Direct Object = Transitive

D.O.T. or DOT is a very easy way to remember that a transitive verb will have a direct object.

Remember: **A direct object receives the action of the verb.**

Examples: The child threw the **ball**. (Ball is the direct object; ball is what the child threw.)

Sally grabbed the **broom** from me. (Broom is the direct object; broom is what Sally grabbed.)

AN INTRANSITIVE VERB WILL NOT HAVE A DIRECT OBJECT.

The cat is up on the sink. (Intransitive Verb - no direct object)

We ran after the ice cream truck. (Intransitive Verb - no direct object. Even though ran is an action verb, there is no direct object in the sentence.)

The trees have been trimmed today. (Intransitive Verb - no direct object)

Name________________________________ **DIRECT OBJECTS**

WORKBOOK PAGE 98

Date________________________________

Directions: Cross out any prepositional phrases. Underline the subject once and the verb/verb phrase twice. Circle the direct object(s).

Direct objects are in boldfaced print.

Example: He paid **cash** ~~for the groceries~~.

1. The dentist gave sugarless **lollipops** ~~to his young patients~~.

2. You left your **keys** ~~in this drawer~~.

3. Brad grabbed his **coat** ~~from the front closet~~.

4. Jerry gave a **corsage** ~~to his mother~~ ~~for Mothers' Day~~.

5. We cooked **bacon** and **eggs** ~~for breakfast~~.

6. A nurse lifted the **baby** ~~into her arms~~.

7. Have you ever eaten **artichokes**?

8. An investor bought **land** ~~in Colorado~~.

9. The bachelor bought **towels** ~~for his new apartment~~.

10. Pat poured **juice** ~~into fancy, pink glasses~~.

11. I have given the waitress a large **tip**.

12. The custodian lowered the **flag** ~~after school~~.

13. They ride their **bikes** ~~on the sidewalk~~.

14. Peter climbs the **tree** often.

15. (You) Hang the **pictures** ~~on that wall~~.

Name________________________________ **DIRECT OBJECTS**

Date________________________________

Directions: Cross out any prepositional phrases. Underline the subject once and the verb/verb phrase twice. Circle the direct object(s).

Example: He paid **cash** ~~for the groceries~~.

1. The dentist gave sugarless lollipops to his young patients.
2. You left your keys in this drawer.
3. Brad grabbed his coat from the front closet.
4. Jerry gave a corsage to his mother for Mothers' Day.
5. We cooked bacon and eggs for breakfast.
6. A nurse lifted the baby into her arms.
7. Have you ever eaten artichokes?
8. An investor bought land in Colorado.
9. The bachelor bought towels for his new apartment.
10. Pat poured juice into fancy, pink glasses.
11. I have given the waitress a large tip.
12. The custodian lowered the flag after school.
13. They ride their bikes on the sidewalk.
14. Peter climbs the tree often.
15. Hang the pictures on that wall.

Name________________________________ **VERBS**

WORKBOOK PAGE 99 Transitive or Intransitive?

Date________________________________

Directions: Cross out any prepositional phrases. Underline the subject once and the verb/verb phrase twice.

Write the direct object of the sentence in the space provided. If there is no direct object, write none in the space provided. Then circle T if the verb is transitive and I if the verb is intransitive.

Answers are in boldfaced print.

Remember: Transitive verbs have direct objects. (D.O.T.) Intransitive verbs do not have direct objects.

Example: foot **T** I 1. I broke my foot.

doughnuts **T** I 1. The senior ate three doughnuts ~~for breakfast~~.

cars **T** I 2. Have you washed any cars lately?

none T **I** 3. The fireworks display was spectacular.

finger **T** I 4. I burned my finger ~~on the iron~~.

rides **T** I 5. Mother was given five rides ~~on that camel~~.

none T **I** 6. Eggs were cracked ~~into a large bowl~~.

none T **I** 7. Flour had been ground ~~for the griddle cakes~~.

whistle **T** I 8. ~~At the end of recess~~, a teacher blows a whistle.

none T **I** 9. The curtains have not been chosen.

none T **I** 10. My sandals are ~~of fine quality leather~~.

none T **I** 11. Priscilla flew ~~in a helicopter to the building site~~.

cheese **T** I 12. A cook's helper grated cheese ~~for a salad~~.

none T **I** 13. Your title is not centered ~~on the page~~.

(You)

none T **I** 14. Go!

train **T** I 15. That tour group will take a train ~~to Boise, Idaho~~.

Name______________________________

Date______________________________

VERBS
Transitive or
Intransitive?

Directions: Cross out any prepositional phrases. Underline the subject once and the verb/verb phrase twice.

Write the direct object of the sentence in the space provided. If there is no direct object, write none in the space provided. Then circle T if the verb is transitive and I if the verb is intransitive.

Remember: Transitive verbs have direct objects. (D.O.T.)
Intransitive verbs do not have direct objects.

Example: _foot_ (T) I 1. I broke my foot.

_______________ T I 1. The senior ate three doughnuts for breakfast.

_______________ T I 2. Have you washed any cars lately?

_______________ T I 3. The fireworks display was spectacular.

_______________ T I 4. I burned my finger on the iron.

_______________ T I 5. Mother was given five rides on that camel.

_______________ T I 6. Eggs were cracked into a large bowl.

_______________ T I 7. Flour had been ground for the griddle cakes.

_______________ T I 8. At the end of recess, a teacher blows a whistle.

_______________ T I 9. The curtains have not been chosen.

_______________ T I 10. My sandals are of fine quality leather.

_______________ T I 11. Priscilla flew in a helicopter to the building site.

_______________ T I 12. A cook's helper grated cheese for a salad.

_______________ T I 13. Your title is not centered on the page.

_______________ T I 14. Go!

_______________ T I 15. That tour group will take a train to Boise, Idaho.

Name______________________________ **VERBS**

WORKBOOK PAGE 100 Transitive or Intransitive?

Date______________________________

Directions: Cross out any prepositional phrases. Underline the subject once and the verb/verb phrase twice. Place a T in the space provided if the verb is transitive. Place an I in the space provided if the verb is intransitive.

Example: _T__ 1. The captain gave me a tour ~~of the ship~~.

Remember: A transitive verb has a direct object.

_I_____ 1. The Mississippi River flows ~~into the Gulf of Mexico~~.

_I_____ 2. (You) Go away!

_T_____ 3. I threw the crumpled paper ~~in the trash~~.

_I_____ 4. Those trees had been planted early ~~in the century~~.

_T_____ 5. Stella placed the vacuum cleaner ~~in the middle of the living room~~.

_T_____ 6. We planted geraniums ~~in the flower bed~~.

_I_____ 7. Those huskies are trained (to attack).

_T_____ 8. This house has three fire alarms.

_T_____ 9. Phil threw the ball ~~into the neighbor's yard~~.

_I_____ 10. Some crumbs had been thrown ~~to the birds~~.

_T_____ 11. Do you ever buy Indian jewelry?

_T_____ 12. An antique dealer bought four porcelain mugs ~~at the sale~~.

_I_____ 13. The telephone rang ~~for several minutes~~ and then stopped.

_T_____ 14. She carries her lunch ~~in a small yellow bag.~~

_I_____ 15. Our slides ~~of Japan~~ have been shown many times.

Name________________________________

Date________________________________

VERBS

Transitive or Intransitive?

Directions: Cross out any prepositional phrases. Underline the subject once and the verb/verb phrase twice. Place a T in the space provided if the verb is transitive. Place an I in the space provided if the verb is intransitive.

Example: _T__ 1. The captain gave me a tour ~~of the ship~~.

Remember: A transitive verb has a direct object.

__________ 1. The Mississippi River flows into the Gulf of Mexico.

__________ 2. Go away!

__________ 3. I threw the crumpled paper in the trash.

__________ 4. Those trees had been planted early in the century.

__________ 5. Stella placed the vacuum cleaner in the middle of the living room.

__________ 6. We planted geraniums in the flower bed.

__________ 7. Those huskies are trained to attack.

__________ 8. This house has three fire alarms.

__________ 9. Phil threw the ball into the neighbor's yard.

__________ 10. Some crumbs had been thrown to the birds.

__________ 11. Do you ever buy Indian jewelry?

__________ 12. An antique dealer bought four porcelain mugs at the sale.

__________ 13. The telephone rang for several minutes and then stopped.

__________ 14. She carries her lunch in a small yellow bag.

__________ 15. Our slides of Japan have been shown many times.

PAGE 193 = WORKBOOK PAGE 101

INDIRECT OBJECTS

An indirect object is the receiver of some direct objects.

D.O.
Example: Mother baked **me** a cake.

Rules for an Indirect Object:

1. **In order to have an indirect object in a sentence, there must be a direct object.**

   I.O. D.O.
   Example: Bill baked my mother some brownies.

2. **You can mentally insert *to* or *for* before an indirect object.**

   for
   Examples: A. Bill baked / my mother brownies.
   to
   B. The carrier handed / the lady a newspaper.

   Note: If to or for is actually written in the sentence, the noun or pronoun that follows is NOT an indirect object.

   Examples: A. He gave to Martha his umbrella.

   (Martha is not an indirect object.)

   B. Ms. Martin received for her neighbors their vacation mail.

   (Neighbors is not an indirect object.)

3. **A sentence containing a direct object does not have to contain an indirect object.**

   D.O.
   Examples: Did they send flowers? (No indirect object)

   I.O. D.O.
   Did they send the **winner** flowers? (Indirect Object)

4. **Compound indirect objects may occur in sentences.**

   I.O. I.O. D.O.
   Examples: A clown gave **Teresa** and **Donald** balloons.

   I.O. I.O. D.O.
   The chef prepared **Larry** and his **date** a meal.

Name________________________________

INDIRECT OBJECTS

WORKBOOK PAGE 102

Date________________________________

Directions: Cross out any prepositional phrases. Underline the subject once and the verb/verb phrase twice. Label the indirect object(s) I.O. and the direct object(s) D.O. in the following sentences.

Example: A seamstress made Frances Ann a flower girl dress. (I.O.: Frances Ann; D.O.: dress)

1. We sent the company proofs ~~of purchase~~ ~~for a free frisbee~~. (I.O.: company; D.O.: proofs)
2. Jackie ordered her husband a stereo ~~for their anniversary~~. (I.O.: husband; D.O.: stereo)
3. The collector gave us three new garbage cans. (I.O.: us; D.O.: cans)
4. The child draws his parents pretty pictures ~~at school~~. (I.O.: parents; D.O.: pictures)
5. The loan officer has often loaned them money. (I.O.: them; D.O.: money)
6. Will you send the shop owner my new address? (I.O.: owner; D.O.: address)
7. Has the rental agent found the young couple an apartment? (I.O.: couple; D.O.: apartment)
8. Each year the boss gives the employees a cash bonus. (I.O.: employees; D.O.: bonus)
9. I gave Terry your books ~~after the class~~. (I.O.: Terry; D.O.: books)
10. A gypsy had told Harriet an unusual story. (I.O.: Harriet; D.O.: story)
11. (You) Don't give anyone our tickets. (I.O.: anyone; D.O.: tickets)
12. She baked the family a pie. (I.O.: family; D.O.: pie)
13. Can you hand me your paper? (I.O.: me; D.O.: paper)
14. Someone ordered Mr. Jones and Mrs. Herb spark plugs ~~for their Model T~~. (I.O.: Mr. Jones; I.O.: Mrs. Herb; D.O.: plugs)
15. The termite inspector should have told us more information. (I.O.: us; D.O.: information)

Name___________________________________ **INDIRECT OBJECTS**

Date___________________________________

Directions: Cross out any prepositional phrases. Underline the subject once and the verb/verb phrase twice. Label the indirect object(s) I.O. and the direct object(s) D.O. in the following sentences.

Example: A seamstress made Frances Ann (I.O.) a flower girl dress (D.O.).

1. We sent the company proofs of purchase for a free frisbee.
2. Jackie ordered her husband a stereo for their anniversary.
3. The collector gave us three new garbage cans.
4. The child draws his parents pretty pictures at school.
5. The loan officer has often loaned them money.
6. Will you send the shop owner my new address?
7. Has the rental agent found the young couple an apartment?
8. Each year the boss gives the employees a cash bonus.
9. I gave Terry your books after the class.
10. A gypsy had told Harriet an unusual story.
11. Don't give anyone our tickets.
12. She baked the family a pie.
13. Can you hand me your paper?
14. Someone ordered Mr. Jones and Mrs. Herb spark plugs for their Model T.
15. The termite inspector should have told us more information.

Name________________________________ **INDIRECT OBJECTS**

WORKBOOK PAGE 103

Date________________________________

Directions: Decide where the indirect object is in each sentence. Place a / to or a / for where to or for should be inserted mentally.

Example: We sent / (to) Marshall shells from Florida.

1. That cashier gave / (to) Dr. King some change.
2. I prepared / (for) them a huge feast.
3. My friend sent / (to) you the proper forms.
4. Dad presented / (to) me a bike for my birthday.
5. The artist drew / (for) our company a sketch of the new building.
6. The librarian presented / (to) the child a reading award.
7. Laura asked / (to) the teacher a question.
8. A missionary gave / (to) the natives food.
9. Her company printed / (for) the customer twenty business cards.
10. The traffic officer presented / (to) the driver a speeding ticket.
11. Dad bakes / (for) us cookies every Tuesday afternoon.
12. I handed / (to) the teller five checks.
13. The corporation owner gives / (to) that charity organization a large donation each year.
14. Grandpa sent / (to) Rick and Barbara chocolate chip cookies at camp.
15. He fixed / (for) us a place to sleep for the night.

Name________________________________ **INDIRECT OBJECTS**

Date________________________________

Directions: Decide where the indirect object is in each sentence. Place a / to or a / for where to or for should be inserted mentally.

to
Example: We sent / Marshall shells from Florida.

1. That cashier gave Dr. King some change.

2. I prepared them a huge feast.

3. My friend sent you the proper forms.

4. Dad presented me a bike for my birthday.

5. The artist drew our company a sketch of the new building.

6. The librarian presented the child a reading award.

7. Laura asked the teacher a question.

8. A missionary gave the natives food.

9. Her company printed the customer twenty business cards.

10. The traffic officer presented the driver a speeding ticket.

11. Dad bakes us cookies every Tuesday afternoon.

12. I handed the teller five checks.

13. The corporation owner gives that charity organization a large donation each year.

14. Grandpa sent Rick and Barbara chocolate chip cookies at camp.

15. He fixed us a place to sleep for the night.

Name________________________________ **INDIRECT OBJECTS**

WORKBOOK PAGE 104

Date________________________________

Directions: Cross out any prepositional phrases. Underline the subject once and the verb/verb phrase twice. Label the indirect object I.O. and the direct object D.O.

I.O. D.O.
Example: We sent Marshall shells ~~from Florida~~.

I.O. D.O.
1. That cashier gave Dr. King some change.

I.O. D.O.
2. I prepared them a huge feast.

I.O. D.O.
3. My friend sent you the proper form.

I.O. D.O.
4. Dad presented me a bike ~~for my birthday~~.

I.O. D.O.
5. The artist drew our company a sketch ~~of the new building~~.

I.O. D.O.
6. The librarian presented the child a reading award.

I.O. D.O.
7. Laura asked the teacher a question.

I.O. D.O.
8. A missionary gave the natives food.

I.O. D.O.
9. Her company printed the customer twenty business cards.

I.O. D.O.
10. The traffic officer presented the driver a speeding ticket.

I.O. D.O.
11. Dad bakes us cookies every Tuesday afternoon.

I.O. D.O.
12. I handed the teller five checks.

I.O. D.O.
13. The corporation owner gives that charity organization a large donation each year.

I.O. I.O. D.O.
14. Grandpa sent Rick and Barbara chocolate chip cookies ~~at camp~~.

I.O. D.O.
15. He fixed us a place (to sleep) ~~for the night~~.

Name________________________________ **INDIRECT OBJECTS**

Date________________________________

Directions: Cross out any prepositional phrases. Underline the subject once and the verb/verb phrase twice. Label the indirect object I.O. and the direct object D.O.

I.O. D.O.

Example: We sent Marshall shells ~~from Florida~~.

1. That cashier gave Dr. King some change.
2. I prepared them a huge feast.
3. My friend sent you the proper form.
4. Dad presented me a bike for my birthday.
5. The artist drew our company a sketch of the new building.
6. The librarian presented the child a reading award.
7. Laura asked the teacher a question.
8. A missionary gave the natives food.
9. Her company printed the customer twenty business cards.
10. The traffic officer presented the driver a speeding ticket.
11. Dad bakes us cookies every Tuesday afternoon.
12. I handed the teller five checks.
13. The corporation owner gives that charity organization a large donation each year.
14. Grandpa sent Rick and Barbara chocolate chip cookies at camp.
15. He fixed us a place to sleep for the night.

Name________________________________ **VERB REVIEW**

WORKBOOK PAGE 105

Date________________________________

A. **Contractions:**

Directions: Write the contraction.

1. they will - they'll
2. it is - it's
3. had not - hadn't
4. we are - we're
5. does not - doesn't
6. I have - I've
7. should not - shouldn't
8. cannot - can't
9. they are - they're
10. what is - what's

B. **Auxiliary (Helping) Verbs:**

Directions: Write the 23 auxiliary verbs.

do, does, did has, have, had may, must, might should, would, could
shall, will, can is, am, are, was, were, be, being, been

C. **Verb Phrases:**

Directions: Cross out any prepositional phrases. Underline the subject once and the verb/verb phrase twice. Write the helping (auxiliary) verb(s) in the first column and the main verb in the second column.

	HELPING VERB(S)	MAIN VERB
1. He must have tripped ~~on a rock~~.	must have	tripped
2. A dentist should examine your teeth.	should	examine
3. May I purchase a ticket ~~for a ride~~?	May	purchase
4. ~~During the game~~, the player should have listened ~~to the coach~~.	should have	listened
5. The lady ~~with the small child~~ will **not** be remaining ~~at the meeting~~.	will be	remaining
6. Does anyone want (to go) along?	Does	want

Name_______________________________ **VERB REVIEW**

Date_______________________________

A. **Contractions:**
Directions: Write the contraction.

1. they will - ____________________
2. it is - ____________________
3. had not - ____________________
4. we are - ____________________
5. does not - ____________________
6. I have - ____________________
7. should not - ____________________
8. cannot - ____________________
9. they are - ____________________
10. what is - ____________________

B. **Auxiliary (Helping) Verbs:**
Directions: Write the 23 auxiliary verbs.

____

____

____

C. **Verb Phrases:**
Directions: Cross out any prepositional phrases. Underline the subject once and the verb/verb phrase twice. Write the helping (auxiliary) verb(s) in the first column and the main verb in the second column.

	HELPING VERB(S)	**MAIN VERB**
1. He must have tripped on a rock.	____________	____________
2. A dentist should examine your teeth.	____________	____________
3. May I purchase a ticket for a ride?	____________	____________
4. During the game, the player should have listened to the coach.	____________	____________
5. The lady with the small child will not be remaining at the meeting.	____________	____________
6. Does anyone want to go along?	____________	____________

Name________________________________ **VERB REVIEW**

WORKBOOK PAGE 106

Date________________________________

D. **Irregular Verbs Using Direct Objects:**

Directions: Cross out any prepositional phrases. Underline the subject once and the verb/verb phrase twice. Label any direct object-D.O.

D.O.

1. Dasha (sits, sets) her books ~~on the kitchen table~~.

2. Their dog was (lying, laying) ~~near the front door~~.

D.O.

3. That majorette (rose, raised) her baton (to begin) her routine.

4. (You) ~~During the assembly~~, please (sit, set) ~~beside the exit~~.

5. The girls have (laid, lain) ~~by the pool~~ ~~for one half hour~~.

D.O.

6. ~~With a look of relief~~, Manzo (sat, set) the packages ~~in the van~~.

7. Dough ~~for onion bread~~ (rises, raises) ~~in a very warm place~~.

E. **Linking Verbs:**

Directions: List the linking verbs (12 infinitives + 8).

to feel, to taste, to look, to smell, to appear, to become, to grow, to remain, to seem, to sound, to stay, to be, is, am, are, was, were, be, being, been

F. **Linking or Action Verbs?:**

Directions: Cross out any prepositional phrases. Underline the subject once and the verb/verb phrase twice. Write A in the space if the verb is action. Write L in the space if the verb is linking.

Remember: **Write *is, am, are, was,* or *were* above a verb that you think is linking. If the meaning of the sentence is not changed, the verb is usually linking.**

are

1. __L__ Orange blossoms smell very fragrant.

is

2. __L__ Casper's cousin seems very nice.

3. __A__ Yuri swept the floor ~~after dinner~~.

is

4. __L__ That curvy road looks dangerous.

5. __A__ The baker tasted a sample ~~of cheesecake~~.

Name________________________________ **VERB REVIEW**

Date________________________________

D. **Irregular Verbs Using Direct Objects:**
Directions: Cross out any prepositional phrases. Underline the subject once and the verb/verb phrase twice. Label any direct object-D.O.

1. Dasha (sits, sets) her books on the kitchen table.
2. Their dog was (lying, laying) near the front door.
3. That majorette (rose, raised) her baton to begin her routine.
4. During the assembly, please (sit, set) beside the exit.
5. The girls have (laid, lain) by the pool for one-half hour.
6. With a look of relief, Manzo (sat, set) the packages in the van.
7. Dough for onion bread (rises, raises) in a very warm place.

E. **Linking Verbs:**
Directions: List the linking verbs (12 infinitives + 8).

____

____

F. **Linking or Action Verbs?:**
Directions: Cross out any prepositional phrases. Underline the subject once and the verb/verb phrase twice. Write A in the space if the verb is action. Write L in the space if the verb is linking.

Remember: Write *is*, *am*, *are*, *was*, or *were* above a verb that you think is linking. If the meaning of the sentence is not changed, the verb is usually linking.

1. ______ Orange blossoms smell very fragrant.
2. ______ Casper's cousin seems very nice.
3. ______ Yuri swept the floor after dinner.
4. ______ That curvy road looks dangerous.
5. ______ The baker tasted a sample of cheesecake.

Name____________________________________ **VERB REVIEW**

WORKBOOK PAGE 107

Date____________________________________

G. **Linking Verbs/Predicate Adjectives:**

Directions: Cross out any prepositional phrases. Underline the subject once and the verb twice. Write Yes if the boldfaced word is a predicate adjective; write No if the boldfaced word isn't a predicate adjective.

Remember: Be sure to determine if the sentence contains a linking verb.

1. Yes This blanket feels (*is*) **scratchy**.

2. No Dawn and Jack baked a **delicious** pie.

3. Yes That cut ~~on your arm~~ looks (*is*) **painful**.

4. No They looked ~~in the **antique** chest~~ ~~for a picture album~~.

5. Yes His voice sounded (*was*) **faint** ~~from a distance~~.

H. **Linking Verbs/Predicate Nominatives:**

Directions: Place the predicate nominative in the space provided. Then, rewrite the sentence to prove it. If there is no predicate nominative, write none.

Remember: Be sure to determine if the sentence contains a linking verb.

1. Chicago His favorite city is Chicago.

   Proof: Chicago is his favorite city.

2. George Washington The leader of the Continental Army was George Washington.

   Proof: George Washington was the leader of the Continental Army.

3. None Mr. Thorton handed a paper to Danny.

   Proof: ____________________

4. secretary Sally Kenton became the club's secretary.

   Proof: The club's secretary became (was) Sally Kenton.

Name________________________________ **VERB REVIEW**

Date________________________________

G. **Linking Verbs/Predicate Adjectives:**
Directions: Cross out any prepositional phrases. Underline the subject once and the verb twice. Write Yes if the boldfaced word is a predicate adjective; write No if the boldfaced word isn't a predicate adjective.

Remember: Be sure to determine if the sentence contains a linking verb.

1. _______ This blanket feels **scratchy**.

2. _______ Dawn and Jack baked a **delicious** pie.

3. _______ That cut on your arm looks **painful**.

4. _______ They looked in the **antique** chest for a picture album.

5. _______ His voice sounded **faint** from a distance.

H. **Linking Verbs/Predicate Nominatives:**
Directions: Place the predicate nominative in the space provided. Then, rewrite the sentence to prove it. If there is no predicate nominative, write none.

Remember: Be sure to determine if the sentence contains a linking verb.

1. ________________ His favorite city is Chicago.

Proof: ____

2. ________________ The leader of the Continental Army was George Washington.

Proof: ____

3. ________________ Mr. Thorton handed a paper to Danny.

Proof: ____

4. ________________ Sally Kenton became the club's secretary.

Proof: ____

Name________________________________ **VERB REVIEW**

WORKBOOK PAGE 108

Date________________________________

I. **Subject/Verb Agreement:**

Directions: Cross out any prepositional phrases. Underline the subject once and the verb/verb phrase twice. Be sure that the subject and verb agree.

1. Margaret's jump rope (is, are) ~~on the floor~~.

2. Those acrobats (perform, performs) often.

3. The store manager and a clerk (counts, count) the money ~~at closing time~~.

4. Geese (fly, flies) south ~~for the winter~~.

5. One ~~of the mail carriers~~ (live, lives) ~~in Katie's neighborhood~~.

6. Everyone ~~without a partner~~ (need, needs) (to go) ~~to the end of the line~~.

J. **Tenses:**

Directions: Cross out any prepositional phrases. Underline the subject once and the verb/verb phrase twice. In the space provided, write the tense: *present*, *past*, or *future* .

1. ______present______ A letter ~~regarding the new library~~ is ~~on the desk~~.

2. ______future______ The meeting will be ~~after dinner~~.

3. ______future______ Shall I open this envelope ~~from the insurance company~~?

4. ______past______ His mother placed the ladder ~~against the house~~.

5. ______past______ Two eagles soared ~~above the trees~~.

6. ______present______ All ~~of Brian's relatives~~ live ~~in Toledo, Ohio~~.

Name______________________________

Date______________________________

VERB REVIEW

I. **Subject/Verb Agreement:**

Directions: Cross out any prepositional phrases. Underline the subject once and the verb/verb phrase twice. Be sure that the subject and verb agree.

1. Margaret's jump rope (is, are) on the floor.

2. Those acrobats (perform, performs) often.

3. The store manager and a clerk (counts, count) the money at closing time.

4. Geese (fly, flies) south for the winter.

5. One of the mail carriers (live, lives) in Katie's neighborhood.

6. Everyone without a partner (need, needs) to go to the end of the line.

J. **Tenses:**

Directions: Cross out any prepositional phrases. Underline the subject once and the verb/verb phrase twice. In the space provided, write the tense: *present*, *past*, or *future* .

1. ______________________________ A letter regarding the new library is on the desk.

2. ______________________________ The meeting will be after dinner.

3. ______________________________ Shall I open this envelope from the insurance company?

4. ______________________________ His mother placed the ladder against the house.

5. ______________________________ Two eagles soared above the trees.

6. ______________________________ All of Brian's relatives live in Toledo, Ohio.

Name______________________________ **VERB REVIEW**

WORKBOOK PAGE 109

Date______________________________

K. **Past Participles:**

Directions: Write the past participle form.

1. to bring - (had) brought
2. to leave - (had) left
3. to spring - (had) sprung
4. to eat - (had) eaten
5. to do - (had) done
6. to swim - (had) swum
7. to lie - (had) lain
8. to ride - (had) ridden
9. to wear - (had) worn
10. to shake - (had) shaken

L. **Verb Phrases/Irregular Verbs:**

Directions: Cross out any prepositional phrases. Underline the subject once and the verb/verb phrase twice.

1. Snow had (fallen, fell) ~~during the night~~.
2. Smoke has (rose, risen) ~~from the campfire~~.
3. ~~After church~~, their family had (went, gone) ~~to a friend's house~~.
4. Claudia and Michael were (chose, chosen) ~~for the play~~.
5. Has the bell (rang, rung) yet?
6. The banana peels had been (threw, thrown) ~~into the garbage~~.
7. A passenger must have (taken, took) the last seat ~~on the bus~~.
8. Marsh and his dad had (ran, run) a mile ~~before breakfast~~.
9. Awards were (gave, given) ~~to each contestant~~.
10. Wind had (blown, blew) ~~through the valley~~ ~~for several days~~.

Name________________________ **VERB REVIEW**

Date________________________

K. **Past Participles:**

Directions: Write the past participle form.

1. to bring - ____________________
2. to leave - ____________________
3. to spring - ____________________
4. to eat - ____________________
5. to do - ____________________
6. to swim - ____________________
7. to lie - ____________________
8. to ride - ____________________
9. to wear - ____________________
10. to shake - ____________________

L. **Verb Phrases/Irregular Verbs:**

Directions: Cross out any prepositional phrases. Underline the subject once and the verb/verb phrase twice.

1. Snow had (fallen, fell) during the night.
2. Smoke has (rose, risen) from the campfire.
3. After church, their family had (went, gone) to a friend's house.
4. Claudia and Michael were (chose, chosen) for the play.
5. Has the bell (rang, rung) yet?
6. The banana peels had been (threw, thrown) into the garbage.
7. A passenger must have (taken, took) the last seat on the bus.
8. Marsh and his dad had (ran, run) a mile before breakfast.
9. Awards were (gave, given) to each contestant.
10. Wind had (blown, blew) through the valley for several days.

Name________________________________ **VERB REVIEW**

WORKBOOK PAGE 110

Date________________________________

M. **Tenses:**

Directions: Cross out any prepositional phrases. Underline the subject once and the verb phrase twice. Write the tense in the space provided.

Be specific. Your answer will be one of the following: *present perfect, past perfect, future perfect, present progressive, past progressive,* or *future progressive.*

1. past perfect — The carpenter ~~in the red truck~~ had forgotten his tools.

2. present progressive — A dance student is purchasing new ballet shoes.

3. present perfect — Have you decided ~~about your summer plans~~?

4. past progressive — Several boys were yelling ~~to their friends~~.

5. future perfect — ~~By March~~, I shall have earned enough money ~~for a bicycle~~.

6. future progressive — Will you be eating ~~in the dining room~~?

N. **Verb Phrases:**

Directions: Cross out any prepositional phrases. Underline the subject once and the verb/verb phrase twice.

1. One ~~of June's cousins~~ has decided (to be) a dental hygienist.

2. Should**n't** Bianca have taken those yellow plastic bags ~~with her~~?

3. Is the bus driver returning ~~to the bus garage~~ ~~after her last stop~~?

4. ~~In May~~, electric car races will be held ~~at a nearby raceway~~.

5. (You) Cut this meat ~~into small pieces~~ and coat it ~~with flour~~ ~~for stew~~.

Name________________________________ **VERB REVIEW**

Date________________________________

M. **Tenses:**

Directions: Cross out any prepositional phrases. Underline the subject once and the verb phrase twice. Write the tense in the space provided.

Be specific. Your answer will be one of the following: *present perfect*, *past perfect*, *future perfect*, *present progressive*, *past progressive*, or *future progressive*.

1. ________________________________ The carpenter in the red truck had forgotten his tools.

2. ________________________________ A dance student is purchasing new ballet shoes.

3. ________________________________ Have you decided about your summer plans?

4. ________________________________ Several boys were yelling to their friends.

5. ________________________________ By March, I shall have earned enough money for a bicycle.

6. ________________________________ Will you be eating in the dining room?

N. **Verb Phrases:**

Directions: Cross out any prepositional phrases. Underline the subject once and the verb/verb phrase twice.

1. One of June's cousins has decided to be a dental hygienist.
2. Shouldn't Bianca have taken those yellow plastic bags with her?
3. Is the bus driver returning to the bus garage after her last stop?
4. In May, electric car races will be held at a nearby raceway.
5. Cut this meat into small pieces and coat it with flour for stew.

Name______________________________ **VERB TEST**

Date______________________________

A. Directions: Write each contraction.

1.	they will - they'll	12.	do not - don't
2.	I am - I'm	13.	I shall - I'll
3.	it is - it's	14.	cannot - can't
4.	was not - wasn't	15.	we are - we're
5.	you are - you're	16.	is not - isn't
6.	she would - she'd	17.	who is - who's
7.	could not - couldn't	18.	does not - doesn't
8.	will not - won't	19.	here is - here's
9.	they are - they're	20.	I have - I've
10.	you will - you'll	21.	are not - aren't
11.	she is - she's	22.	we are - we're

B. Directions: Circle the correct verb.
Answers are in boldfaced print.

1. Juan has (saw, **seen**) the Hope Diamond.
2. She (teached, **taught**) us how to dive properly.
3. The balls were (**thrown**, threw) into the center of the ring.
4. This mop has been (shook, **shaken**) several times.
5. Her mother must have (**come**, came) by to see her today.
6. Herbs were (**grown**, grew) in a box on the window sill.
7. The Harrison family may have (went, **gone**) water skiing.
8. They should have (rode, **ridden**) their bikes in the rain.
9. Jenny has (swam, **swum**) since her first birthday.
10. Have you ever (broke, **broken**) a bone?

Name________________________________ **VERB TEST**

Date________________________________

A. Directions: Write each contraction.

1. they will - ____________________
2. I am - ____________________
3. it is - ____________________
4. was not - ____________________
5. you are - ____________________
6. she would - ____________________
7. could not - ____________________
8. will not - ____________________
9. they are - ____________________
10. you will - ____________________
11. she is - ____________________
12. do not - ____________________
13. I shall - ____________________
14. cannot - ____________________
15. we are - ____________________
16. is not - ____________________
17. who is - ____________________
18. does not - ____________________
19. here is - ____________________
20. I have - ____________________
21. are not - ____________________
22. we are - ____________________

B. Directions: Circle the correct verb.

1. Juan has (saw, seen) the Hope Diamond.
2. She (teached, taught) us how to dive properly.
3. The balls were (thrown, threw) into the center of the ring.
4. This mop has been (shook, shaken) several times.
5. Her mother must have (come, came) by to see her today.
6. Herbs were (grown, grew) in a box on the window sill.
7. The Harrison family may have (went, gone) water skiing.
8. They should have (rode, ridden) their bikes in the rain.
9. Jenny has (swam, swum) since her first birthday.
10. Have you ever (broke, broken) a bone?

C. Circle the correct verb.
Answers are in boldfaced print.

1. Have you (laid, **lain**) on the bed very long?
2. If you would have asked, I would have (gave, **given**) you a key.
3. Each of the choir members has (**sung**, sang) a solo this year.
4. Was the fireman (took, **taken**) to the hospital for smoke inhalation?
5. Several of the bubbles had (**burst**, bursted) on the wand.
6. His answers were (**written**, wrote) in black ink.
7. The welder has (brung, **brought**) two torches with him.
8. His mother may have (spoke, **spoken**) to the coach about his injury.
9. Many hot dogs were (ate, **eaten**) by the hungry hikers.
10. The candle must have been (blew, **blown**) out.
11. I should have (**risen**, rose) earlier than nine o'clock.
12. Sandy could not have (**drunk**, drank) another ounce of soda.
13. That racer has (ran, **run**) the mile faster than his opponents.
14. That traveler will have (**driven**, drove) a thousand miles by the end of her trip.
15. All of the towels were (shook, **shaken**) and placed on the line to dry.
16. Have the boys and girls (**done**, did) the scenery for the play?
17. George Washington was (swore, **sworn**) into office in New York City.
18. This jacket must have (fell, **fallen**) on the dirty cement.
19. Many pizzas had been (froze, **frozen**) for the victory celebration.
20. Octopi are (**known**, knew) by their long, slender tentacles.
21. The baseball player had (stole, **stolen**) home during the last inning.
22. The Eastern team had (beat, **beaten**) the Western one in the playoffs.
23. Her jacket had been (**torn**, tore) by a bush with large thorns.
24. A lady has (**bought**, boughten) several ceramic giraffes.
25. Their family has (went, **gone**) to a circus.

C. Directions: Circle the correct verb.

1. Have you (laid, lain) on the bed very long?
2. If you would have asked, I would have (gave, given) you a key.
3. Each of the choir members has (sung, sang) a solo this year.
4. Was the fireman (took, taken) to the hospital for smoke inhalation?
5. Several of the bubbles had (burst, bursted) on the wand.
6. His answers were (written, wrote) in black ink.
7. The welder has (brung, brought) two torches with him.
8. His mother may have (spoke, spoken) to the coach about his injury.
9. Many hot dogs were (ate, eaten) by the hungry hikers.
10. The candle must have been (blew, blown) out.
11. I should have (risen, rose) earlier than nine o'clock.
12. Sandy could not have (drunk, drank) another ounce of soda.
13. That racer has (ran, run) the mile faster than his opponents.
14. That traveler will have (driven, drove) a thousand miles by the end of her trip.
15. All of the towels were (shook, shaken) and placed on the line to dry.
16. Have the boys and girls (done, did) the scenery for the play?
17. George Washington was (swore, sworn) into office in New York City.
18. This jacket must have (fell, fallen) on the dirty cement.
19. Many pizzas had been (froze, frozen) for the victory celebration.
20. Octopi are (known, knew) by their long, slender tentacles.
21. The baseball player had (stole, stolen) home during the last inning.
22. The Eastern team had (beat, beaten) the Western one in the playoffs.
23. Her jacket had been (torn, tore) by a bush with large thorns.
24. A lady has (bought, boughten) several ceramic giraffes.
25. Their family has (went, gone) to the circus.

D. Directions: Circle the verb that agrees with the subject.

Answers are in boldfaced print.

1. Sponges (is, **are**) a type of invertebrates.
2. A few loons (**swim**, swims) on that lake each day.
3. A kindergartner (walk, **walks**) with her father to school each day.
4. Each of the divers (perform, **performs**) three dives in the competition.
5. Several ranchers (meets, **meet**) each week to discuss plans for a town barbecue.
6. A woman with a pretty smile (greet, **greets**) us at church each week.
7. Pam's grandfathers (builds, **build**) vacation cabins in the mountains.
8. Everyone of the club members (attend, **attends**) at least three meetings a year.
9. Freda or her mother (take, **takes**) the dog for a walk each morning.

E. Directions: Cross out any prepositional phrases. Underline the subject once and the verb/verb phrase twice. In the space provided, write the tense: *present, past, future, present perfect, past perfect, future perfect, present progressive,* or *future progressive.*

1. past progressive — The boys were yelling ~~to their friends~~.
2. past — Patrick hit the baseball ~~past second base~~.
3. past perfect — One carpenter had forgotten his tools.
4. future perfect — ~~By March~~, she will have saved twenty dollars.
5. present perfect — Has anyone brought a drink ~~for the picnic~~?
6. present progressive — A dance student is buying new ballet shoes.
7. present — Their brother plays ~~in a sandbox~~ daily.
8. future progressive — Will those senators be meeting next week?
9. future — Miss Lee will make a decision ~~about moving~~.

D. Directions: Circle the verb that agrees with the subject.

1. Sponges (is, are) a type of invertebrates.
2. A few loons (swim, swims) on that lake each day.
3. A kindergartner (walk, walks) with her father to school each day.
4. Each of the divers (perform, performs) three dives in the competition.
5. Several ranchers (meets, meet) each week to discuss plans for a town barbecue.
6. A woman with a pretty smile (greet, greets) us at church each week.
7. Pam's grandfathers (builds, build) vacation cabins in the mountains.
8. Everyone of the club members (attend, attends) at least three meetings a year.
9. Freda or her mother (take, takes) the dog for a walk each morning.

E. Directions: Cross out any prepositional phrases. Underline the subject once the verb/verb phrase twice. In the space provided, write the tense: *present, past, future, present perfect, past perfect, future perfect, present progressive, past progressive,* or *future progressive.*

1. ______________________________ The boys were yelling to their friends.
2. ______________________________ Patrick hit the baseball past second base.
3. ______________________________ One carpenter had forgotten his tools.
4. ______________________________ By March, she will have saved twenty dollars.
5. ______________________________ Has anyone brought a drink for the picnic?
6. ______________________________ A dance student is buying new ballet shoes.
7. ______________________________ Their brother plays in a sandbox daily.
8. ______________________________ Will those senators be meeting next week?
9. ______________________________ Miss Lee will make a decision about moving.

F. Directions: Cross out any prepositional phrases. Underline the subject once and the verb/verb phrase twice. Label any direct object - D.O.

1. Her dog is (sitting, setting) ~~by her mother~~.

D.O.

2. Have you (laid, lain) this blanket here?

D.O.

3. Each person (rose, raised) his hand (to vote).

4. Is the cat (lying, laying) ~~near the litter box~~?

5. A toddler (lay, laid) down ~~on a couch~~ (to sleep).

6. Miss Lasko (raises, rises) late ~~on Saturdays~~.

D.O.

7. (You) (Sit, Set) this plate ~~on the table~~.

8. Everyone ~~in the arena~~ (rose, raised) (to sing) the national anthem.

9. (You) (Sit, Set) ~~in the last row~~.

G. Directions: Cross out any prepositional phrases. Underline the subject once and the verb/verb phrase twice. In the space provided, write L if the verb is linking and A if the verb shows action.

1. A Jonas's hamster eats special food.
2. A Dino tasted some cheesy Greek pie.
3. A Kami bowled a nearly perfect game.
4. L This bun became hard ~~after three days~~.
5. L Your fresh fudge seems too soft (to cut).
6. A Several children skated ~~on a pond~~.
7. L Yancy became an engineer.
8. A Mrs. Korb is staying ~~with her mother~~.
9. L The child seemed eager (to learn) (to skate).

F. Directions: Cross out any prepositional phrases. Underline the subject once and the verb/verb phrase twice. Label any direct object-D.O.

1. Her dog is (sitting, setting) by her mother.

2. Have you (laid, lain) this blanket here?

3. Each person (rose, raised) his hand to vote.

4. Is the cat (lying, laying) near the litter box?

5. A toddler (lay, laid) down on a couch to sleep.

6. Miss Lasko (raises, rises) late on Saturdays.

7. (Sit, Set) this plate on the table.

8. Everyone in the arena (rose, raised) to sing the national anthem.

9. (Sit, Set) in the last row.

G. Directions: Cross out any prepositional phrases. Underline the subject once and the verb/verb phrase twice. In the space provided, write L if the verb is linking and A if the verb shows action.

1. _____ Jonas's hamster eats special food.

2. _____ Dino tasted some cheesy Greek pie.

3. _____ Kami bowled a nearly perfect game.

4. _____ This bun became hard after three days.

5. _____ Your fresh fudge seems too soft to cut.

6. _____ Several children skated on a pond.

7. _____ Yancy became an engineer.

8. _____ Mrs. Korb is staying with her mother.

9. _____ The child seemed eager to learn to skate.

H. Directions: Cross out any prepositional phrases. Underline the subject once and the verb/verb phrase twice. Write the helping (auxiliary) verb(s) in the first column and the main verb in the second column.

	HELPING VERB(S)	**MAIN VERB**
1. I shall find a way.	shall	find
2. Should Bo come ~~with us~~?	should	come
3. He may have gone ~~to a baseball game~~.	may have	gone
4. Several watermelons are lying ~~near the fence~~ ~~in the garden~~.	are	lying
5. That booth was constructed ~~by high school seniors~~.	was	constructed
6. Someone ~~in that city~~ can win a trip ~~to Alaska~~.	can	win

I. Directions: Cross out any prepositional phrases. Underline the subject once and the verb/verb phrase twice.

1. Mr. Swanson might be going ~~to Canada~~ soon.
2. Have you taken your guitar ~~to the music store~~ ~~for repair~~?
3. Several rare birds had been seen ~~within a few hours~~.
4. ~~Before the wedding~~, the groom must have become very nervous.
5. One ~~of the robins~~ has built a nest ~~in the pine tree~~.
6. Connie will **not** be driving ~~to her grandmother's house~~ alone.
7. Can you understand the problem ~~between the two boys~~?
8. Would you be interested ~~in a ticket~~ ~~to an amusement park~~?

H. Directions: Cross out any prepositional phrases. Underline the subject once and the verb/verb phrase twice. Write the helping (auxiliary) verb(s) in the first column and the main verb in the second column.

	HELPING VERB(S)	MAIN VERB
1. I shall find a way.	__________	__________
2. Should Bo come with us?	__________	__________
3. He may have gone to a baseball game.	__________	__________
4. Several watermelons are lying near the fence in the garden.	__________	__________
5. That booth was constructed by high school seniors.	__________	__________
6. Someone in that city can win a trip to Alaska.	__________	__________

I. Directions: Cross out any prepositional phrases. Underline the subject once and the verb/verb phrase twice.

1. Mr. Swanson might be going to Canada soon.
2. Have you taken your guitar to the music store for repair?
3. Several rare birds had been seen within a few hours.
4. Before the wedding, the groom must have become very nervous.
5. One of the robins has built a nest in the pine tree.
6. Connie will not be driving to her grandmother's house alone.
7. Can you understand the problem between the two boys?
8. Would you be interested in a ticket to an amusement park?

Name________________________________
WORKBOOK PAGE 111
Date________________________________

CUMULATIVE REVIEW
Verb Unit

A. **Prepositions:**

Directions: Write fifty prepositions.

1. about
2. above
3. across
4. after
5. against
6. along
7. amid
8. among
9. around
10. at
11. atop
12. before
13. behind
14. below
15. beneath
16. beside
17. between
18. beyond
19. but (meaning except)
20. by
21. concerning
22. down
23. during
24. except
25. for
26. from
27. in
28. inside
29. into
30. like
31. near
32. of
33. off
34. on
35. onto
36. out
37. outside
38. over
39. past
40. regarding
41. since
42. through
43. throughout
44. to
45. toward
46. under
47. underneath
48. until
49. up
50. upon
51. with
52. within
53. without

B. Directions: Cross out any prepositional phrases. Underline the subject once and the verb/verb phrase twice.

1. ~~After a long day~~ ~~with many clients~~, the lawyer left her office ~~for another meeting~~.

2. One ~~of the professors~~ spoke ~~about his studies~~ ~~at a French university~~.

3. (You) Take the bus ~~along Hearn Road~~ (to arrive) ~~near a shopping center~~.

Name________________________________

Date________________________________

CUMULATIVE REVIEW
Verb Unit

A. **Prepositions:**

Directions: Write fifty prepositions.

1.	____________	14.	____________	27.	____________	40.	____________
2.	____________	15.	____________	28.	____________	41.	____________
3.	____________	16.	____________	29.	____________	42.	____________
4.	____________	17.	____________	30.	____________	43.	____________
5.	____________	18.	____________	31.	____________	44.	____________
6.	____________	19.	____________	32.	____________	45.	____________
7.	____________	20.	____________	33.	____________	46.	____________
8.	____________	21.	____________	34.	____________	47.	____________
9.	____________	22.	____________	35.	____________	48.	____________
10.	____________	23.	____________	36.	____________	49.	____________
11.	____________	24.	____________	37.	____________	50.	____________
12.	____________	25.	____________	38.	____________		
13.	____________	26.	____________	39.	____________		

B. **Prepositions in sentences:**

Directions: Cross out any prepositional phrases. Underline the subject once and the verb/verb phrase twice.

1. After a long day with many clients, the lawyer left her office for another meeting.

2. One of the professors spoke about his studies at a French university.

3. Take the bus along Hearn Road to arrive near a shopping center.

Name_______________________________

Date_______________________________

CUMULATIVE TEST
Verb Unit

Directions: Cross out any prepositional phrases. Underline the subject once and the verb/verb phrase twice.

1. ~~During the game's final seconds~~, a basketball player made a basket ~~from mid-court~~.
2. Everyone ~~of the hot air balloons~~ rose early ~~in the moist morning~~.
3. The horse and its rider continued (to meander) ~~down the dusty road~~.
4. Many bats had flown out ~~of the cave~~ ~~after the storm~~ ~~at sundown~~.
5. ~~Beyond that mountain~~ is a lush green valley ~~about ten square miles~~ ~~in area~~.
6. All calves ~~but the one~~ ~~near its mother~~ ambled over ~~to the fence~~.
7. Kathryn can**not** go ~~to the beach~~ ~~without sunblock and her beach umbrella~~.
8. Clay's paper ~~concerning rabies~~ has been placed ~~underneath some books~~ ~~on his desk~~.
9. ~~Toward the end~~ ~~of the tour~~, the choir will be traveling ~~through small Swiss villages~~.
10. Mrs. Kempler and her son ski ~~before dinner~~ nearly every day ~~except Sunday~~.
11. ~~In the lot~~ ~~across from the park~~, several volunteers planted flowers ~~among some tall trees~~.
12. (You) Please place these ~~within the manila envelopes~~ and address them, too.
13. ~~Throughout the game~~, the goalie does**n't** play ~~beyond that point~~.
14. The statue ~~inside the new history museum~~ looks ~~like their Uncle Anthony~~.
15. The small jet took off ~~within ten minutes~~ ~~of its arrival~~ ~~at Scottsdale Airport~~.

Name______________________________

Date_______________________________

CUMULATIVE TEST
Verb Unit

Directions: Cross out any prepositional phrases. Underline the subject once and the verb/verb phrase twice.

1. During the game's final seconds, a basketball player made a basket from mid-court.
2. Everyone of the hot air balloons rose early in the moist morning.
3. The horse and its rider continued to meander down the dusty road.
4. Many bats had flown out of the cave after the storm at sundown.
5. Beyond that mountain is a lush green valley about ten square miles in area.
6. All calves but the one near its mother ambled over to the fence.
7. Kathryn cannot go to the beach without sunblock and her beach umbrella.
8. Clay's paper concerning rabies has been placed underneath some books on his desk.
9. Toward the end of the tour, the choir will be traveling through small Swiss villages.
10. Mrs. Kempler and her son ski before dinner nearly every day except Sunday.
11. In the lot across from the park, several volunteers planted flowers among some tall trees.
12. Please place these within the manila envelopes and address them, too.
13. Throughout the game, the goalie does not play beyond that point.
14. The statue inside the new history museum looks like their Uncle Anthony.
15. The small jet took off within ten minutes of its arrival at Scottsdale Airport.

PAGE 227 = WORKBOOK PAGE 112

CONCRETE AND ABSTRACT NOUNS*

A noun names a person, a place, or a thing.

Concrete nouns usually can be seen: book, car, chair, hammer, towel, store

Some concrete nouns you technically won't be able to see unless they are examined in very small parts (atoms). Examples: air, wind, breath

Abstract nouns are those that cannot be seen: love, liberty, grace, sadness

To test if a word might be an abstract noun, do the following:

A. Check to see that the possible noun doesn't describe any word in the sentence. If it does, STOP. It's a describing word called an adjective.

Example: A <u>love</u> gift was collected for the needy.

In this sentence, <u>love</u> is an adjective that describes gift. Thus <u>love</u> is an adjective and not a noun in this sentence.

B. If the possible noun does not qualify as an adjective, try placing "the" in front of it. If you can put "the" in front of the possible noun, the word is probably a noun.

Example: A very special moment is sharing <u>love</u> with a pet.

You can say "the love" in this sentence, so love is a noun.

*Review the concept that nouns name persons, places or things. Students usually remember this concept from the previous grade level.

Name________________________________

WORKBOOK PAGE 113

Date________________________________

NOUNS

Concrete or Abstract?

Directions: In the space provided, place C if the noun is concrete and A if the noun is abstract.

1. ____A____ loyalty
2. ____C____ guitar
3. ____C____ spoon
4. ____A____ kindness
5. ____A____ joy
6. ____C____ cereal
7. ____A____ patience
8. ____C____ clock
9. ____A____ friendship
10. ____C____ boots
11. ____A____ hatred
12. ____C____ smoke
13. ____A____ gentleness
14. ____C____ door
15. ____C____ ears
16. ____A____ peace
17. ____C____ forest
18. ____A____ liberty
19. ____A____ anger
20. ____C____ rabbit
21. ____A____ fear
22. ____C____ pie
23. ____A____ wisdom
24. ____C____ cream
25. ____A____ beauty

Name________________________________

Date________________________________

NOUNS
Concrete or Abstract?

Directions: In the space provided, place C if the noun is concrete and A if the noun is abstract.

1. ________ loyalty
2. ________ guitar
3. ________ spoon
4. ________ kindness
5. ________ joy
6. ________ cereal
7. ________ patience
8. ________ clock
9. ________ friendship
10. ________ boots
11. ________ hatred
12. ________ smoke
13. ________ gentleness
14. ________ door
15. ________ ears
16. ________ peace
17. ________ forest
18. ________ liberty
19. ________ anger
20. ________ rabbit
21. ________ fear
22. ________ pie
23. ________ wisdom
24. ________ cream
25. ________ beauty

PAGE 231 = WORKBOOK PAGE 114

NOUNS

Nouns name persons, places, things, or ideas.

Sometimes the same word will be a noun in one sentence and an adjective (describing word) in another sentence.

Examples: A. The candle was blown out by the wind.

(*Candle* is a noun in this sentence.)

The candle holder was broken.

(*Candle* is an adjective because it describes holder in this sentence.)

B. Our desk is a mess.

(*Desk* is a noun in this sentence. It names a thing.)

This desk lamp is in need of repair.

(*Desk* is an adjective because it describes lamp in this sentence.)

Sometimes the same word will be a noun in one sentence and a verb in another sentence.

Examples: The park is nearby.

(*Park* is a noun in this sentence.)

Park the car.

(*Park* is a verb in this sentence.)

Name________________________________ **NOUNS**

WORKBOOK PAGE 115 Noun or Adjective?

Date________________________________

Directions: On the line provided, write N. if the underlined word is a noun or ADJ. if the word is an adjective (describing word).

1. __N.__ Don't break that glass.
2. __ADJ.__ Your glass vase is very expensive.
3. __ADJ.__ Her flower garden is in full bloom.
4. __N.__ My mother gave me a flower for my birthday.
5. __N.__ We often take pictures on vacation.
6. __ADJ.__ Do you have a picture compartment in your wallet?
7. __N.__ Those children are filing their nails.
8. __ADJ.__ A nail file was lying on the floor.
9. __ADJ.__ John made a great paper airplane.
10. __N.__ The papers were passed to the ones in the last row.
11. __N.__ An assortment of baskets hung on the wall.
12. __ADJ.__ Basket weaving is an enjoyable activity.
13. __N.__ Have you read this book?
14. __ADJ.__ New book mobile units were purchased by the library.
15. __N.__ Jimmy has a new wagon.
16. __ADJ.__ A wagon load of hay was pulled by the oxen.
17. __N.__ The group listened to many tapes about life.
18. __ADJ.__ Several tape players were on sale.
19. __ADJ.__ Peanut shells lay all over the floor.
20. __N.__ A peanut is high in protein.

Name_______________________________ **NOUNS**

Noun or Adjective?

Date_______________________________

Directions: On the line provided, write N. if the underlined word is a noun or ADJ. if the word is an adjective (describing word).

1. ___________ Don't break that glass.

2. ___________ Your glass vase is very expensive.

3. ___________ Her flower garden is in full bloom.

4. ___________ My mother gave me a flower for my birthday.

5. ___________ We often take pictures on vacation.

6. ___________ Do you have a picture compartment in your wallet?

7. ___________ Those children are filing their nails.

8. ___________ A nail file was lying on the floor.

9. ___________ John made a great paper airplane.

10. ___________ The papers were passed to the ones in the last row.

11. ___________ An assortment of baskets hung on the wall.

12. ___________ Basket weaving is an enjoyable activity.

13. ___________ Have you read this book?

14. ___________ New book mobile units were purchased by the library.

15. ___________ Jimmy has a new wagon.

16. ___________ A wagon load of hay was pulled by the oxen.

17. ___________ The group listened to many tapes about life.

18. ___________ Several tape players were on sale.

19. ___________ Peanut shells lay all over the floor.

20. ___________ A peanut is high in protein.

PAGE 234 = WORKBOOK PAGE 114
PAGE 235 = WORKBOOK PAGE 116
PAGE 236 = WORKBOOK PAGE 117

NOUNS

Nouns name persons, places, and things.

Sometimes the same word will be a noun in one sentence and a verb in another sentence. This is a difficulty for students.

Example: An old ring was found in the gutter.

Ring is a noun in this sentence.

Example: The phones ring very often.

Ring is the verb in this sentence.

Example: Our talk was interrupted by the little ones.

Talk is a noun in this sentence.

Example: Some people talk too loudly.

Talk is a verb in this sentence.

NOUNS

Classification of Determiners:

A. Articles: **a, an, the**

B. Demonstratives: **this, that, those, these**

C. Numbers

D. Possessive Adjectives (also called possessive pronouns used as adjectives)

E. Possessive Nouns (used as adjectives)

F. Indefinites: **some, few, many, several, no, any***

A. **A, an,** and **the** will come before a noun and sometimes a pronoun. The noun may have another word in front of it, but a noun will be in the vicinity of **a, an,** and **the**.

Examples: **a** book **the** movie **an** orange **a** lovely scene

B. The demonstratives, **this, that, those, these,** MAY be signals for a noun to follow. However, sometimes they stand alone.

Examples: **this** book **that** light **those** buttons **these** cars

NOTE: If any demonstrative does NOT have a person, place, or thing closely following it, that particular demonstrative will not be a determiner.

Examples: This is fun. (This stands alone; this is NOT a determiner.)

I like those. (Those stands alone; those is NOT a determiner.)

C. Numbers may signal a noun. STOP and check if a person, place, or thing follows the number(s). Describing words often come between the number and the noun.

Examples: **Fifty-one** people **seven** white ducklings

NOTE: If a number does NOT have a person, place, or thing after it, the number will NOT serve as a determiner for a noun.

Example: Three stayed behind. (Three stands alone; three is not a determiner.)

*This list is incomplete.

D. Possessive Pronouns (used as adjective determiners):

my, his, her, our, their, its, your

These often signal a noun. When you see one of these determiners, STOP! Check if a word naming a person, place, or thing is following. **My, its, your, our,** and **their** will be followed by a noun.

Examples: **my** hair **your** key **our** new radio

its tail **their** short trip

Examples:

Her ankle was broken. (Ankle is a noun signaled by **her**.)

Did you go with her? (Her does not go to a word naming a person, place, or thing.)

E. Possessive nouns often signal other nouns. Look for a word naming a person, place, or thing after any posssessive noun.

Examples: **Craig's** canoe **bank's** hours **visitor's** parking

F. Indefinites:

some, any, no, many, few, several

Indefinites are determiners when a noun follows. Upon seeing an indefinite, check to determine if a noun follows it. A describing word may fall between an indefinite and the noun.

Example: **Some** putty knives were lying on the counter.

(Knives is a noun signaled by **some**.)

Example: Some of the newspapers were thrown away.

(Cross out the prepositional phrase ~~of the newspapers~~. You have left: Some were thrown away. There is no noun after some.)

NOUN DETERMINERS

WORKBOOK PAGE 118

Although noun determiners are actually adjectives, it is better to simply call them determiners. Determiners are stop signals. When a student sees a determiner, he/she must stop! Determiners signal that a noun or pronoun may follow. The student must closely examine the sentence and decide if a noun (or pronoun) is following the determiner.

Classification of Determiners:

A. Articles: **a, an, the**

B. Demonstratives: **this, that, those, these**

C. Numbers (**ten** ducks)

D. Possessive adjectives (also called possessive pronouns used as adjectives)
my, his, her, your, its, our, their

E. Possessive nouns (used as adjectives): (**Jack's** net) (**fly's** wing)

F. Indefinites: **some, few, many, several, no, any***

Examples:

NOUN NOUN
My kite sailed high above **the** roof tops. — my kite / the tops

NOUN NOUN
Lori's suede shoes have **many** holes. — Lori's shoes / many holes

NOUN NOUN
Two chipmunks are playing under **that** bush. — two chipmunks / that bush

NOUN
A tourist's camera is usually important. — a camera / tourist's camera

*There are other indefinites.

Name________________________________ **NOUNS**
WORKBOOK PAGE 119 Determiners
Date________________________________

Directions: In the space provided, write the underlined determiner with the noun that it modifies.

Example: I swam in the lake today. ______the lake______

1. My family has gone fishing. ______My family______
2. Have you received Ann's letter? ______Ann's letter______
3. Several small squirrels played. ______Several squirrels______
4. I like these posters on your wall. ______these posters______
5. A snow cone is refreshing. ______A cone______
6. His old, black hat is a favorite. ______His hat______
7. Do you have any peppermint candy? ______any candy______
8. No mail has arrived. ______No mail______
9. Are ladies' shoes on display there? ______ladies' shoes______
10. Checkers is our most colorful game. ______our game______
11. He owns twenty-two rare coins. ______twenty-two coins______
12. Does this art class appeal to you? ______this class______
13. The cabinet makers met in New York. ______The makers______
14. They visited their old meeting place. ______their place______
15. Father's uncle once lived in a ghost town. ______Father's uncle______

Name______________________________ **NOUNS**

Determiners

Date______________________________

Directions: In the space provided, write the underlined determiner with the noun that it modifies.

Example: I swam in the lake today. ______the lake______

1. My family has gone fishing. ____________________
2. Have you received Ann's letter? ____________________
3. Several small squirrels played. ____________________
4. I like these posters on your wall. ____________________
5. A snow cone is refreshing. ____________________
6. His old, black hat is a favorite. ____________________
7. Do you have any peppermint candy? ____________________
8. No mail has arrived. ____________________
9. Are ladies' shoes on display there? ____________________
10. Checkers is our most colorful game. ____________________
11. He owns twenty-two rare coins. ____________________
12. Does this art class appeal to you? ____________________
13. The cabinet makers met in New York. ____________________
14. They visited their old meeting place. ____________________
15. Father's uncle once lived in a ghost town. ____________________

Name________________________________ **NOUNS**

WORKBOOK PAGE 120 Determiners

Date________________________________

Directions: Place D in the provided space if the underlined word serves as a determiner. Then circle the noun it modifies in the sentence. Place N in the space provided if the underlined word does not serve as a determiner. (Nouns will appear in bold print.)

Example: __D__ My alarm **clock** didn't go off.

__D__ 1. Those book **ends** are made of brass.

__N__ 2. Are you taking those with you?

__N__ 3. Fifty will be admitted.

__D__ 4. Charles earned fifty **dollars** by mowing lawns.

__D__ 5. Some **clay** lay on the table.

__N__ 6. We chose some of the latest tapes.*

__D__ 7. Was her **lecture** easy to follow?

__N__ 8. Go with her.

__N__ 9. What are these?

__D__ 10. Our baker likes these old **types** of pans.

__D__ 11. Were there fourteen **candles** on the cake?

__N__ 12. My brother purchased fourteen of the denim shirts.*

__N__ 13. Many of the streets were flooded.

__D__ 14. Do you have many **relatives** in this city?

__D__ 15. The cactus's **flowers** were in bloom.

*Crossing out prepositional phrase(s) may help.

Name________________________________ **NOUNS**

Determiners

Date________________________________

Directions: Place D in the provided space if the underlined word serves as a determiner. Then circle the noun it modifies in the sentence. Place N in the space provided if the underlined word does not serve as a determiner.

Example: __D__ My alarm clock didn't go off.

_______ 1. Those book ends are made of brass.

_______ 2. Are you taking those with you?

_______ 3. Fifty will be admitted.

_______ 4. Charles earned fifty dollars by mowing lawns.

_______ 5. Some clay lay on the table.

_______ 6. We chose some of the latest tapes.*

_______ 7. Was her lecture easy to follow?

_______ 8. Go with her.

_______ 9. What are these?

_______ 10. Our baker likes these old types of pans.

_______ 11. Were there fourteen candles on the cake?

_______ 12. My brother purchased fourteen of the denim shirts.*

_______ 13. Many of the streets were flooded.

_______ 14. Do you have many relatives in this city?

_______ 15. The cactus's flowers were in bloom.

*Crossing out prepositional phrase(s) may help.

PAGE 243 = WORKBOOK PAGE 121

COMMON AND PROPER NOUNS

By definition, common nouns do not name specific persons, places, or things. Most nouns are common nouns.

By definition, proper nouns name specific persons, places, or things. Proper nouns are capitalized.

common noun: cat

proper noun: Miss Kitty

common noun: bank

proper noun: People's Trust Bank

Problem: Although most students find common and proper nouns very easy, you may have a few who become confused. These few want to put classifications of nouns (example: dogs-spaniels) as proper nouns. In the example of *spaniels*, students will say that *spaniels* names a specific dog. You will need to explain that "spaniels" names a specific TYPE of dog, not a specific dog. Therefore, "spaniels" is still a common noun and is not capitalized.

Examples of common and proper nouns:

common noun	type (still a common noun)	proper noun
building	bank	Freestone Bank
bird	canary	Bugle Bird
horse	palomino	Thunder

Name________________________________ **NOUNS**

WORKBOOK PAGE 122 Common and Proper

Date________________________________

Directions: In the space provided, write a proper noun for each common noun.

Example: person: ____George Washington____

1. river: ____ANSWERS WILL VARY____
2. actor: ____________________
3. club: ____________________
4. street: ____________________
5. country: ____________________
6. athlete: ____________________
7. city: ____________________
8. school: ____________________
9. lake: ____________________
10. building: ____________________
11. company: ____________________
12. singer: ____________________
13. mountain: ____________________
14. store: ____________________
15. ocean: ____________________

Name________________________________

Date________________________________

NOUNS
Common and Proper

Directions: In the space provided, write a proper noun for each common noun.

Example: person: ________George Washington________

1. river: ________________________________
2. actor: ________________________________
3. club: ________________________________
4. street: ________________________________
5. country: ________________________________
6. athlete: ________________________________
7. city: ________________________________
8. school: ________________________________
9. lake: ________________________________
10. building: ________________________________
11. company: ________________________________
12. singer: ________________________________
13. mountain: ________________________________
14. store: ________________________________
15. ocean: ________________________________

Name________________________________

WORKBOOK PAGE 123

Date________________________________

NOUNS

Common or Proper?

Directions: In the space provided, write C if the word is a common noun and a P if the word is a proper noun.

1. C dictionary
2. P Lake Mead
3. P U.S.S. Arizona
4. C plans
5. P Bible
6. C strawberries
7. C spas
8. C parents
9. P Florida
10. C stereo
11. P Empire State Building
12. P Red Cross
13. P Mason & Dixon Line
14. C van
15. P Edgewater Church
16. P Girl Scouts
17. C roses
18. P Third Avenue
19. P Lamplighter Diner
20. P Mars
21. C comedy
22. P Gulf of Mexico
23. P Eagle Electric Co.
24. P Wayside Inn
25. C career
26. C clerk
27. P Dr. Billings
28. C magazine
29. P Camelback Mountain
30. C restaurant
31. P United States
32. P Dream Island
33. C island
34. P Yosemite National Park
35. C church
36. P Meteor Crater
37. C zoo
38. C hotel
39. P Fourth of July
40. C parrot

Name________________________________

Date________________________________

NOUNS

Common or Proper?

Directions: In the space provided, write C if the word is a common noun and a P if the word is a proper noun.

1. ____ dictionary
2. ____ Lake Mead
3. ____ U.S.S. Arizona
4. ____ plans
5. ____ Bible
6. ____ strawberries
7. ____ spas
8. ____ parents
9. ____ Florida
10. ____ stereo
11. ____ Empire State Building
12. ____ Red Cross
13. ____ Mason & Dixon Line
14. ____ van
15. ____ Edgewater Church
16. ____ Girl Scouts
17. ____ roses
18. ____ Third Avenue
19. ____ Lamplighter Diner
20. ____ Mars
21. ____ comedy
22. ____ Gulf of Mexico
23. ____ Eagle Electric Co.
24. ____ Wayside Inn
25. ____ career
26. ____ clerk
27. ____ Dr. Billings
28. ____ magazine
29. ____ Camelback Mountain
30. ____ restaurant
31. ____ United States
32. ____ Dream Island
33. ____ island
34. ____ Yosemite National Park
35. ____ church
36. ____ Meteor Crater
37. ____ zoo
38. ____ hotel
39. ____ Fourth of July
40. ____ parrot

Name________________________________ **NOUNS**

WORKBOOK PAGE 124

Date________________________________

Directions: Underline any noun(s) in the following sentences.

Example: Some motorcycles were parked in the front.

1. Remove the pencils, papers, and rulers from your desk.
2. Our total bill for the delightful lunch was twelve dollars.
3. On the farm we saw pigs, cows, chickens, and several horses.
4. Her last game of the season was played at a local stadium.
5. That gold cup was given to my grandmother by some famous actress.
6. We enjoy many freedoms such as liberty and justice.
7. An elm tree grew in their yard for forty-seven years.
8. Those bruises from the accident should be checked by a doctor.
9. No grass will grow on the side of that stony hill.
10. Your wallet, credit cards, and loose change are on the bed.
11. During our break, Stephanie's* mother brought in drinks and cookies.
12. In Bert's* report, he wrote about zoo animals.
13. A slithering snake crawled out of those woods this morning.
14. Were their street lights repaired after the dangerous storm?
15. Some things, like love and truth, are not purchased with any money.
16. A table with six chairs was delivered in several large cartons.
17. The miners searched for gold in the hills of North Dakota.
18. Dad's* gift was a beautiful bouquet of roses, carnations, and ferns.
19. Trucks, puzzles, and coloring books lay on the child's* floor.
20. Two classmates sent some invitations to members of their group.

*Possessive noun used as an adjective. Accept as an answer.

Name________________________________ **NOUNS**

Date________________________________

Directions: Underline any noun(s) in the following sentences.

Example: Some motorcycles were parked in the front.

1. Remove the pencils, papers, and rulers from your desk.
2. Our total bill for the delightful lunch was twelve dollars.
3. On the farm we saw pigs, cows, chickens, and several horses.
4. Her last game of the season was played at a local stadium.
5. That gold cup was given to my grandmother by some famous actress.
6. We enjoy many freedoms such as liberty and justice.
7. An elm tree grew in their yard for forty-seven years.
8. Those bruises from the accident should be checked by a doctor.
9. No grass will grow on the side of that stony hill.
10. Your wallet, credit cards, and loose change are on the bed.
11. During our break, Stephanie's mother brought in drinks and cookies.
12. In Bert's report, he wrote about zoo animals.
13. A slithering snake crawled out of those woods this morning.
14. Were their street lights repaired after the dangerous storm?
15. Some things, like love and truth, are not purchased with any money.
16. A table with six chairs was delivered in several large cartons.
17. The miners searched for gold in the hills of North Dakota.
18. Dad's gift was a beautiful bouquet of roses, carnations, and ferns.
19. Trucks, puzzles, and coloring books lay on the child's floor.
20. Two classmates sent some invitations to members of their group.

PAGE 251 = WORKBOOK PAGE 125
PAGE 252 = WORKBOOK PAGE 126
PAGE 253 = WORKBOOK PAGE 127

SINGULAR AND PLURAL NOUNS

It is suggested that the rules on the next three pages be duplicated for student use.

Simply fold back the notes directed to the teacher when making copies.

SINGULAR AND PLURAL NOUNS

Singular means one.

Plural means more than one.

Rule AA: **The plural of most words is made by adding s to the singular form.**

map	dent	basket
maps	dents	baskets

Rule A: **When a singular word ends in s, sh, ch, x, or z, es will be added to form the plural.**

class	wish	church	box	buzz
classes	wishes	churches	boxes	buzzes

Rule B: **When a singular word ends in ay, ey, oy, or uy, s will be added to form the plural.**

bay	key	boy	guy
bays	keys	boys	guys

Rule C: **When a word ends in consonant + y, the y is changed to i, and es will be added to form the plural.**

baby	candy	battery	cry
babies	candies	batteries	cries

Notes:

1. Don't ever assume that a student understands a concept. Explain the concept of singular and plural thoroughly.

2. Rules A, B, and C need to be memorized and learned. Students must be able to write each rule and give examples. Mastery should be required.

3. Because no words could be found ending in iy, the latter was deleted from the rule.

SINGULAR AND PLURAL NOUNS

Rule D: **Some words totally change in the plural form.**

man	woman	child	goose
men	women	children	geese

Use a dictionary to check the plural forms of nouns.

If the word totally changes to form the plural, the dictionary will spell out the plural.

Example: child (child) n., pl. children. 1. baby or infant
(pl. = plural)

Rule E: **Some words are the same in the singular and plural forms.**

sheep	deer	moose
sheep	deer	moose

Use a dictionary to check the plural forms of nouns.

If the word does not change from singular to plural, the dictionary will show it.

Example: moose (moos) n., pl. moose. 1. a large animal...
(pl. = plural)

Rule F: **Some words ending in f, change the f to v and add es to form the plural.**

calf	thief	leaf
calves	thieves	leaves

Use a dictionary to check the plural forms of nouns.

If the word changes f to v, the dictionary will show it.

Example: calf (kaf) , n., pl. calves. 1. a baby cow
(pl. = plural)

Rule G: **Some words ending in f do not change f to v. These words simply add s to form the plural.**

puff	whiff	grief
puffs	whiffs	griefs

Be sure to teach students to use the dictionary for plural forms. Dictionaries are their best tools. Indicate that if s is added to form the plural, the dictionary does not write out the plural form. In Rule G, grieves is a word, but grieves is a verb, not a noun.

SINGULAR AND PLURAL NOUNS

Rule H: **Some words ending in o, add s to form the plural.**

Some words ending in o, add es to form the plural.

Some words ending in o, add s or es to form the plural.

Use your dictionary to check for the correct plural form.

Examples: photo (fo to), n., pl. tos.
(plural = photos)

hero (hir o), n., pl. heroes.

zero (zir o), n., pl. ros, roes.
(plural = zeros, zeroes)

Rule I: **Some hyphenated words add s to the first part when forming the plural.**

The same applies to non-hyphenated words.

Check your dictionary for the correct plural form.

Examples: sister-in-law
sisters-in-law

commander in chief
commanders in chief

NOTE: In a dictionary, if two plural forms are given, the first listed is preferred and should be used.

Example: cactus: cacti, cactuses

Cacti should be used.

Name________________________________ **NOUNS**
WORKBOOK PAGE 128 Plurals
Date________________________________

Directions: Write the plural form in the space provided. In the space before the number, write the rule which applies.

Example: B 1. monkey monkeys

AA	1.	pencil	pencils
G	2.	gulf	gulfs
H	3.	dodo	dodos or dodoes
I	4.	mother-in-law	mothers-in-law
AA	5.	shirt	shirts
H	6.	potato	potatoes
D	7.	mouse	mice
B	8.	toy	toys
C	9.	entry	entries
AA	10.	idea	ideas
H	11.	hobo	hobo or hoboes
D	12.	foot	feet
F	13.	life	lives
D	14.	louse	lice
C	15.	reply	replies
AA	16.	customer	customers
A	17.	slush	slushes
D	18.	tooth	teeth
G/AA	19.	spoof	spoofs
B	20.	tray	trays
A	21.	bunch	bunches
A	22.	fox	foxes
C	23.	century	centuries
AA	24.	generation	generations
AA	25.	pet	pets

Name________________________________

Date________________________________

NOUNS

Plurals

Directions: Write the plural form in the space provided. In the space before the number, write the rule which applies.

Example: _B_ 1. monkey ____monkeys____

_____ 1. pencil________________________________
_____ 2. gulf________________________________
_____ 3. dodo________________________________
_____ 4. mother-in-law________________________________
_____ 5. shirt________________________________
_____ 6. potato________________________________
_____ 7. mouse________________________________
_____ 8. toy________________________________
_____ 9. entry________________________________
_____ 10. idea________________________________
_____ 11. hobo________________________________
_____ 12. foot________________________________
_____ 13. life________________________________
_____ 14. louse________________________________
_____ 15. reply________________________________
_____ 16. customer________________________________
_____ 17. slush________________________________
_____ 18. tooth________________________________
_____ 19. spoof________________________________
_____ 20. tray________________________________
_____ 21. bunch________________________________
_____ 22. fox________________________________
_____ 23. century________________________________
_____ 24. generation________________________________
_____ 25. pet________________________________

Name______________________________ **NOUNS**
WORKBOOK PAGE 129 Plurals
Date______________________________

Directions: Write the plural form in the space provided. In the space before the number, write the rule which applies.

Example: AA 1. star stars

B	1.	replay	replays
A	2.	box	boxes
C	3.	symphony	symphonies
F	4.	loaf	loaves
A	5.	mantis	mantises
AA	6.	soda	sodas
A	7.	ax	axes
H	8.	stereo	stereos
D	9.	ox	oxen
A	10.	push	pushes
AA	11.	funnel	funnels
H	12.	rodeo	rodeos
F	13.	calf	calves
B	14.	honey	honeys
A	15.	witch	witches
A	16.	press	presses
A	17.	hex	hexes
AA	18.	computer	computers
E/AA	19.	trout	trout/trouts
F	20.	leaf	leaves
A	21.	latch	latches
E/AA	22.	elk	elk/elks
C	23.	country	countries
B	24.	essay	essays
I	25.	father-in-law	fathers-in-law

Name________________________________ **NOUNS**

Plurals

Date________________________________

Directions: Write the plural form in the space provided. In the space before the number, write the rule which applies.

Example: _A A_ 1. star_____stars_____

___ 1. replay____________________

___ 2. box____________________

___ 3. symphony____________________

___ 4. loaf____________________

___ 5. mantis____________________

___ 6. soda____________________

___ 7. ax____________________

___ 8. stereo____________________

___ 9. ox____________________

___ 10. push____________________

___ 11. funnel____________________

___ 12. rodeo____________________

___ 13. calf____________________

___ 14. honey____________________

___ 15. witch____________________

___ 16. press____________________

___ 17. hex____________________

___ 18. computer____________________

___ 19. trout____________________

___ 20. leaf____________________

___ 21. latch____________________

___ 22. elk____________________

___ 23. country____________________

___ 24. essay____________________

___ 25. father-in-law____________________

____

PAGE 259 = WORKBOOK PAGE 130

POSSESSIVE NOUNS

' = apostrophe. Instruct students to make proper marks and not "chicken scratches" for apostrophes.

Students must understand that possessive indicates ownership. Have students name items that they own (their name + the item). You will get answers such as *Bill's bike, Mary's book, Terry's jacket.* Then go to other items that may "own" something. You will need to give a few examples: *book's cover, desk's top, flag's stripes, shoe's soles, shirt's collar.* This is a more difficult task; you may want to have students make lists on paper. The entire purpose of this approach is to understand the concept of possessives.

Be sure that students understand the difference between plurals and possessives. Some students get the two concepts confused.

POSSESSIVE NOUNS

Rule A: **To form the possessive of a singular noun, add 's to the word.**

Examples: truck + tires — man + wallet

truck's tires — man's wallet

The 's is added to all singular words, no matter in what letter the word ends.

Examples: waitress + apron — Jones + house

waitress's apron — Jones's house

Rule B: **To form the possessive of a plural noun that ends in s, simply add ' after the s (at the end of the word).**

Examples: ladies + club — cats + dish

ladies' club — cats' dish

teachers + workroom

teachers' workroom

Rule C: **To form the possessive of a plural noun that does NOT end in s, add 's to the word.**

Examples: children + playground — geese + formation

children's playground — geese's formation

Name________________________________ **NOUNS**
WORKBOOK PAGE 131 Possessives
Date________________________________

Directions: Write the possessive noun and what it possesses in the space provided.

Example: the club that belongs to three boys

boys' club

1. stickers that belong to one child

   one child's stickers

2. a ring that belongs to a boy

   a boy's ring

3. a restroom that belongs to all of the ladies

   the ladies' restroom

4. a car that belongs to James

   James' s car

5. a game that belongs to all of the children

   the children's game

6. tools that belong to two carpenters

   two carpenters' tools

7. a whistle that belongs to Sam

   Sam's whistle

8. a cup that belongs to an architect

   an architect's cup

9. a barn that is shared by all of the horses

   the horses' barn

10. a tail that a mouse has

    a mouse's tail

Name_______________________________ **NOUNS**

Possessives

Date_______________________________

Directions: Write the possessive noun and what it possesses in the space provided.

Example: the club that belongs to three boys

boys' club

1. stickers that belong to one child

____

2. a ring that belongs to a boy

____

3. a restroom that belongs to all of the ladies

____

4. a car that belongs to James

____

5. a game that belongs to all of the children

____

6. tools that belong to two carpenters

____

7. a whistle that belongs to Sam

____

8. a cup that belongs to an architect

____

9. a barn that is shared by all of the horses

____

10. a tail that a mouse has

____

Name________________________________ **NOUNS**

WORKBOOK PAGE 132 Possessives

Date________________________________

Directions: Write the possessive noun and what it possesses in the space provided.

Example: some pennies that belong to my brother

my brother's pennies

1. prizes that belong to two contestants

   two contestants' prizes

2. a horse that my friend owns

   my friend's horse

3. a room that two brothers share

   two brothers' room

4. gifts that were given to Dad

   Dad's gifts

5. a sandbox belonging to four children

   four children's sandbox

6. a field where two deer stay

   two deer's field

7. a toothbrush that belongs to Bess

   Bess's toothbrush

8. an organization belonging to all of the men

   the men's organization

9. luggage that belongs to a traveler

   a traveler's luggage

10. prayer that belongs to a child

    a child's prayer

Name________________________________ **NOUNS**

Possessives

Date________________________________

Directions: Write the possessive noun and what it possesses in the space provided.

Example: some pennies that belong to my brother

______my brother's pennies__________

1. prizes that belong to two contestants

____

2. a horse that my friend owns

____

3. a room that two brothers share

____

4. gifts that were given to Dad

____

5. a sandbox belonging to four children

____

6. a field where two deer stay

____

7. a toothbrush that belongs to Bess

____

8. an organization belonging to all of the men

____

9. luggage that belongs to a traveler

____

10. prayer that belongs to a child

____

Name______________________________ **NOUNS**

WORKBOOK PAGE 133 Possessives

Date______________________________

Directions: Write the possessive noun and what it possesses in the space provided.

Example: a foot belonging to an ox

an ox's foot

1. a routine belonging to three dancers

   three dancers' routine

2. some paintings belonging to a museum

   a museum's paintings

3. a gift belonging to Dennis

   Dennis's gift

4. a party given by five neighbors

   five neighbors' party

5. a pathway for bikers

   bikers' pathway

6. a desk belonging to a boss

   boss's desk

7. the voice of an announcer

   an announcer's voice

8. a luncheon attended by women

   a women's luncheon

9. a convention attended by cooks

   a cooks' convention

10. a store belonging to several owners

    several owners' store

Name________________________________ **NOUNS**

Possessives

Date________________________________

Directions: Write the possessive noun and what it possesses in the space provided.

Example: a foot belonging to an ox

an ox's foot

1. a routine belonging to three dancers

 ____

2. some paintings belonging to a museum

 ____

3. a gift belonging to Dennis

 ____

4. a party given by five neighbors

 ____

5. a pathway for bikers

 ____

6. a desk belonging to a boss

 ____

7. the voice of an announcer

 ____

8. a luncheon attended by women

 ____

9. a convention attended by cooks

 ____

10. a store belonging to several owners

 ____

Name________________________________ **NOUNS**
WORKBOOK PAGE 134 Possessives
Date________________________________

Directions: Write the possessive noun and what it possesses in the space provided.

Example: an apartment shared by sisters

sisters' apartment

1. cavities that are in the teeth

   the teeth's cavities

2. dishes that my grandmother owns

   my grandmother's dishes

3. a business owned by two women

   two women's business

4. a book belonging to that person

   that person's book

5. a play area belonging to several babies

   several babies' play area

6. an airplane owned by a company

   a company's airplane

7. a hot air balloon owned by several couples

   several couples' hot air balloon

8. a field belonging to one sheep

   one sheep's field

9. a field belonging to many sheep

   many sheep's field

10. a teacher that belongs to a class

    a class's teacher

Name________________________________ **NOUNS**

Possessives

Date________________________________

Directions: Write the possessive noun and what it possesses in the space provided.

Example: an apartment shared by sisters

sisters' apartment

1. cavities that are in the teeth

____

2. dishes that my grandmother owns

____

3. a business owned by two women

____

4. a book belonging to that person

____

5. a play area belonging to several babies

____

6. an airplane owned by a company

____

7. a hot air balloon owned by several couples

____

8. a field belonging to one sheep

____

9. a field belonging to many sheep

____

10. a teacher that belongs to a class

____

Name________________________________ **NOUNS**
WORKBOOK PAGE 135 Predicate Nominatives
Date________________________________

A predicate nominative is a noun (or pronoun) that occurs after a linking verb and means the same as the subject.

Linking verbs:	to feel	to become	to remain
	to taste	to seem	to appear
	to look	to sound	to stay
	to smell	to grow	to be (is, am, are, was, were, be, being, been)

P.N.
Example: Marilyn was her best friend ~~in college~~.
Proof: Her best friend was Marilyn.

Remember: To prove the predicate nominative, invert the sentence. Begin with the word(s) after the verb, include the predicate nominative, and, then, go to the beginning of the sentence. This is called inverting the sentence.

Directions: Cross out any prepositional phrases. Underline the subject once and the verb/verb phrase twice. Label any predicate nominative-P.N. Write the proof for the predicate nominative on the line provided.

P.N.
1. Mr. Harrison is Charlie's tennis coach.

Proof: Charlie's tennis coach is Mr. Harrison.

P.N.
2. Chess is their favorite pastime.

Proof: Their favorite pastime is chess.

P.N.
3. Guam is a tropical island ~~in the Pacific Ocean~~.

Proof: A tropical island is Guam.

P.N.
4. Dr. Jones has been the head physician ~~at that clinic~~ ~~for several years~~.

Proof: The head physician is (has been) Dr. Jones.

P.N.
5. ~~During her stay~~ ~~with the Wings~~, buttered popcorn became her favorite food.

Proof: Her favorite food became buttered popcorn.

Name________________________________

Date________________________________

NOUNS
Predicate Nominatives

A predicate nominative is a noun (or pronoun) that occurs after a linking verb and means the same as the subject.

Linking verbs:	to feel	to become	to remain
	to taste	to seem	to appear
	to look	to sound	to stay
	to smell	to grow	to be (is, am, are, was, were, be, being, been)

P.N.

Example: Marilyn was her best friend ~~in college~~.

Proof: Her best friend was Marilyn.

Remember: To prove the predicate nominative, invert the sentence. Begin with the word(s) after the verb, include the predicate nominative, and, then, go to the beginning of the sentence. This is called inverting the sentence.

Directions: Cross out any prepositional phrases. Underline the subject once and the verb/verb phrase twice. Label any predicate nominative-P.N. Write the proof for the predicate nominative on the line provided.

1. Mr. Harrison is Charlie's tennis coach.

   Proof: ____

2. Chess is their favorite pastime.

   Proof: ____

3. Guam is a tropical island in the Pacific Ocean.

   Proof: ____

4. Dr. Jones has been the head physician at that clinic for several years.

   Proof: ____

5. During her stay with the Wings, buttered popcorn became her favorite food.

   Proof: ____

Name________________________________ **NOUNS**

WORKBOOK PAGE 136 Predicate Nominatives

Date_________________________________

A predicate nominative is a noun (or pronoun) that occurs after a linking verb and means the same as the subject.

Directions: Cross out any prepositional phrases. Underline the subject once and the verb/verb phrase twice. Label any predicate nominative-P.N. Write the proof for the predicate nominative on the line provided.

P.N.

1. Thomas Jefferson was the author ~~of the Declaration of Independence~~.

   Proof: The author was Thomas Jefferson.

P.N.

2. A thick-bodied, gnawing rodent is a marmot.

   Proof: A marmot is a thick-bodied, gnawing rodent.

P.N.

3. ~~During Zack's childhood~~, his favorite hobby was stamp collecting.

   Proof: Stamp collecting was his favorite hobby.

P.N.

4. A partridge is a European game bird.

   Proof: A European game bird is a partridge.

P.N.

5. Thomas Edison was the inventor ~~of the phonograph~~.

   Proof: The inventor was Thomas Edison.

P.N.

6. Jonah became the editor ~~of a local newspaper~~.

   Proof: The editor was (became) Jonah.

P.N.

7. The helpful woman ~~with the Lewis and Clark expedition~~ was Sacajawea.

   Proof: Sacajawea was the helpful woman.

P.N. P.N.

8. The candidates ~~for President in 1992~~ were Bill Clinton and George Bush.

   Proof: Bill Clinton and George Bush were candidates for President.

Name_______________________________ **NOUNS**

Predicate Nominatives

Date_______________________________

A predicate nominative is a noun (or pronoun) that occurs after a linking verb and means the same as the subject.

Directions: Cross out any prepositional phrases. Underline the subject once and the verb/verb phrase twice. Label any predicate nominative-P.N. Write the proof for the predicate nominative on the line provided.

1. Thomas Jefferson was the author of the Declaration of Independence.

   Proof: _______________________________

2. A thick-bodied, gnawing rodent is a marmot.

   Proof: _______________________________

3. During Zack's childhood, his favorite hobby was stamp collecting.

   Proof: _______________________________

4. A partridge is a European game bird.

   Proof: _______________________________

5. Thomas Edison was the inventor of the phonograph.

   Proof: _______________________________

6. Jonah became the editor of a local newspaper.

   Proof: _______________________________

7. The helpful woman with the Lewis and Clark expedition was Sacajawea.

   Proof: _______________________________

8. The candidates for President in 1992 were Bill Clinton and George Bush.

   Proof: _______________________________

PAGE 273 = WORKBOOK PAGE 137

APPOSITIVES

An appositive is a word or group of words (phrase or clause) that stands next to a noun. An appositive adds additional information.

An appositive is set off by a comma or commas.

Examples: Love Bug, my pet canary, is fed daily. (phrase)

Ms. Tate, the lady who is by the pool, once won our local golf tournament. (clause)

Your bracelet is made of my favorite jewel, emeralds.

Dunn and Denver, our goldfish, eagerly gulp their food. (phrase)

More than one appositive may appear in a sentence.

Examples: Lady Gray, my horse, and Duke, my cousin's pony, won first place ribbons at the fair.

Desserts, peach cobbler and strawberry pie, were served to fifty guests, members of a wildlife club.

Sometimes appositives are joined by a conjunction.

Examples: These televisions, the color one and the portable one, will be sold at an auction.

The gathering was attended by two special guests, a cousin from Denmark and an uncle from France.

Name________________________________ **APPOSITIVES**

WORKBOOK PAGE 138

Date________________________________

Directions: Underline the appositive(s) in the following sentences.

Example: This flower, an African daisy, needs much water.

1. We visited Philadelphia, a city in Pennsylvania.
2. Popcorn, my favorite food, is prepared in many different ways.
3. Snoopy, a famous cartoon character, makes many people laugh.
4. Take my lunch, the one in the blue and orange bag.
5. Several students, Ron, Tammy, and Dirk, have been selected to go to a convention.
6. I spoke with Jacob L. Tompson, chief engineer for that company.
7. I like this portrait, the side view one, better.
8. Our meal, hot dogs and French fries, was delivered by a deli.
9. He chose his sister, Roberta Ann, as his running mate.
10. Water, a most refreshing drink, is very good for you.
11. Watch out for those golfers, those in red sweaters.
12. My father, the mayor of this town, is a great fisherman.
13. This ice cream, Parker's specialty, is extremely expensive.
14. Give this to her, the young lady in the back row.
15. Brian, their father-in-law, drives a truck for a major moving company.
16. The decorations, red and yellow streamers, had been placed on the walls before the dance had begun.
17. These glasses, some deep red goblets, belonged to Mrs. Trunman.
18. Mike, my oldest brother, has given an engagement ring to Viola, the clerk at Minton's Pharmacy.
19. Holland, a lovely country, is famous for its tulips.
20. Jim Thorpe, a famous native American, went to school in Carlisle, Pennsylvania.

Name________________________________ **APPOSITIVES**

Date________________________________

Directions: Underline the appositive(s) in the following sentences.

Example: This flower, an African daisy, needs much water.

1. We visited Philadelphia, a city in Pennsylvania.
2. Popcorn, my favorite food, is prepared in many different ways.
3. Snoopy, a famous cartoon character, makes many people laugh.
4. Take my lunch, the one in the blue and orange bag.
5. Several students, Ron, Tammy, and Dirk, have been selected to go to a convention.
6. I spoke with Jacob L. Tompson, chief engineer for that company.
7. I like this portrait, the side view one, better.
8. Our meal, hot dogs and French fries, was delivered by a deli.
9. He chose his sister, Roberta Ann, as his running mate.
10. Water, a most refreshing drink, is very good for you.
11. Watch out for those golfers, those in red sweaters.
12. My father, the mayor of this town, is a great fisherman.
13. This ice cream, Parker's specialty, is extremely expensive.
14. Give this to her, the young lady in the back row.
15. Brian, their father-in-law, drives a truck for a major moving company.
16. The decorations, red and yellow streamers, had been placed on the walls before the dance had begun.
17. These glasses, some deep red goblets, belonged to Mrs. Trunman.
18. Mike, my oldest brother, has given an engagement ring to Viola, the clerk at Minton's Pharmacy.
19. Holland, a lovely country, is famous for its tulips.
20. Jim Thorpe, a famous native American, went to school in Carlisle, Pennsylvania.

Name________________________________ **NOUNS**
WORKBOOK PAGE 139 Gerunds
Date________________________________

A gerund is a word formed by adding ing to a verb. This is called a verbal. A gerund serves as a noun in a sentence.

Example: to skate = skating

Skating is my favorite pastime.

In this sentence, skating is the subject.

Example: to play = playing

We like playing in the sand.

In this sentence, playing is a gerund that serves as a direct object. We can delete ~~in the sand~~ as a prepositional phrase. However, we can also call playing in the sand a gerund phrase. A gerund phrase is made by adding a word or words to a gerund.

Directions: Cross out any prepositional phrases. Underline the subject once and the verb/verb phrase twice. Label any direct object - D.O. Then, circle any gerund.

Gerunds are in boldfaced print.

1. **Cooking** is his favorite.

D.O.

2. Jim loves **skiing** ~~with his brother~~.

3. **Standing** ~~in line~~ is not fun ~~for my grandmother~~.

4. **Biking** has become very popular.

D.O.

5. Mr. and Mrs. Harris enjoy **looking** ~~for sea shells~~ ~~at the beach~~.

6. ~~During the summer~~, **fishing** is their most enjoyable pastime.

7. **Exercising** is great ~~for your body~~.

D.O.

8. Jack has started **practicing** ~~for a part~~ ~~in the play~~.

Name________________________________

Date________________________________

NOUNS
Gerunds

A gerund is a word formed by adding ing to a verb. This is called a verbal. A gerund serves as a noun in a sentence.

Example: to skate = skating

Skating is my favorite pastime.

In this sentence, skating is the subject.

Example: to play = playing

We like playing in the sand.

In this sentence, playing is a gerund that serves as a direct object. We can delete ~~in the sand~~ as a prepositional phrase. However, we can also call playing in the sand a gerund phrase. A gerund phrase is made by adding a word or words to a gerund.

Directions: Cross out any prepositional phrases. Underline the subject once and the verb/verb phrase twice. Label any direct object - D.O. Then, circle any gerund.

1. Cooking is his favorite.

2. Jim loves skiing with his brother.

3. Standing in line is not fun for my grandmother.

4. Biking has become very popular.

5. Mr. and Mrs. Harris enjoy looking for sea shells at the beach.

6. During the summer, fishing is their most enjoyable pastime.

7. Exercising is great for your body.

8. Jack has started practicing for a part in the play.

Name________________________________ **NOUN REVIEW**
WORKBOOK PAGE 140
Date________________________________

A. **Concrete or Abstract?:**

Directions: Write C if the word is a concrete noun; write A if the word is an abstract noun.

1. __C__ cloth
2. __C__ missile
3. __A__ truth
4. __C__ stomach
5. __A__ cheerfulness
6. __C__ butter
7. __A__ misunderstanding
8. __C__ gorilla
9. __A__ love
10. __C__ slipper
11. __A__ feeling
12. __C__ feather

B. **Common or Proper?:**

Directions: Write C if the noun is common; write P if the noun is proper.

1. __C__ CANYON
2. __C__ CRANE
3. __P__ PRATT PARK
4. __P__ THOMAS
5. __P__ BRYCE CANYON
6. __C__ CLUB
7. __P__ CONNECTICUT RIVER
8. __P__ ADAMS COUNTY FAIR
9. __C__ ELEMENTARY SCHOOL
10. __C__ GRANDSTAND

C. **Adjective or Noun?:**

Directions: Write N if the underlined word serves as a noun; write A if the underlined word serves as an adjective.

1. __N__ Put this shoe box in the closet, please.
2. __A__ A box lunch was served at the Valentine party.
3. __A__ This camera cover is made of leather.
4. __N__ Do you have film for the camera?
5. __A__ Georgette has a tea server in her new apartment.
6. __N__ Set the cup of steaming tea on the counter top.

Name________________________________ **NOUN REVIEW**

Date________________________________

A. **Concrete or Abstract?:**

Directions: Write C if the word is a concrete noun; write A if the word is an abstract noun.

1.	_____	cloth	5.	_____	cheerfulness	9.	_____	love
2.	_____	missile	6.	_____	butter	10.	_____	slipper
3.	_____	truth	7.	_____	misunderstanding	11.	_____	feeling
4.	_____	stomach	8.	_____	gorilla	12.	_____	feather

B. **Common or Proper?:**

Directions: Write C if the noun is common; write P if the noun is proper.

1.	_____	CANYON	6.	_____	CLUB
2.	_____	CRANE	7.	_____	CONNECTICUTT RIVER
3.	_____	PRATT PARK	8.	_____	ADAMS COUNTY FAIR
4.	_____	THOMAS	9.	_____	ELEMENTARY SCHOOL
5.	_____	BRYCE CANYON	10.	_____	GRANDSTAND

C. **Adjective or Noun?:**

Directions: Write N if the underlined word serves as a noun; write A if the underlined word serves as an adjective.

1. _____ Put this shoe box in the closet, please.
2. _____ A box lunch was served at the Valentine party.
3. _____ This camera cover is made of leather.
4. _____ Do you have film for the camera?
5. _____ Georgette has a tea server in her new apartment.
6. _____ Set the cup of steaming tea on the counter top.

Name________________________________ **NOUN REVIEW**

WORKBOOK PAGE 141

Date________________________________

D. **Noun or Verb?:**

Directions: Write N if the underlined word serves as a noun; write V if the underlined word serves as a verb.

1. N They keep a grocery list on the side of the refrigerator.
2. V You must list all of your prepositions, Sherry.
3. V Slip this envelope under the back door.
4. N The students wrote an answer on a slip of paper.
5. V The river may flood during the spring.
6. N During the flood, some folks were airlifted from their homes.

E. **Plurals:**

Directions: Write the plural of each noun.

1. tooth - teeth
2. photo - photos
3. wish - wishes
4. moose - moose
5. telephone - telephones
6. library - libraries
7. bunch - bunches
8. prayer - prayers
9. decoy - decoys
10. die - dice

F. **Possessives:**

Directions: Write the possessive noun with the the word it owns.

1. a rubber duck belonging to a toddler - toddler's rubber duck
2. a statement belonging to the witness - witness's statement
3. a nursery belonging to many babies - babies' nursery
4. popsicles belonging to their sister - sister's popsicles
5. a room belonging to more than one fireman - firemen's room

Name________________________________ **NOUN REVIEW**

Date________________________________

D. **Noun or Verb?:**

Directions: Write N if the underlined word serves as a noun; write V if the underlined word serves as a verb.

1. _____ They keep a grocery list on the side of the refrigerator.
2. _____ You must list all of your prepositions, Sherry.
3. _____ Slip this envelope under the back door.
4. _____ The students wrote an answer on a slip of paper.
5. _____ The river may flood during the spring.
6. _____ During the flood, some folks were airlifted from their homes.

E. **Plurals:**

Directions: Write the plural of each noun.

1. tooth -________________________
2. photo - ________________________
3. wish - ________________________
4. moose - ________________________
5. telephone - ________________________
6. library - ________________________
7. bunch - ________________________
8. prayer - ________________________
9. decoy - ________________________
10. die - ________________________

F. **Possessives:**

Directions: Write the possessive noun with the the word it owns.

1. a rubber duck belonging to a toddler - ________________________
2. a statement belonging to the witness - ________________________
3. a nursery belonging to many babies - ________________________
4. popsicles belonging to their sister - ________________________
5. a room belonging to more than one fireman - ________________________

Name________________________________ **NOUN REVIEW**
WORKBOOK PAGE 142
Date________________________________

G. **Determiners and Nouns:**

Directions: Write any determiner and the noun it modifies.

1. Mark's little brother makes his own pancakes. Mark's brother
his pancakes
2. This book contains many colorful pictures. This book
many pictures
3. Your tires need some air. Your tires
some air
4. A student purchased two pieces of pizza. A student
two pieces
5. Do they need these nails for their tree house? these nails
their (tree) house

H. **Nouns Serving as Direct Objects and Indirect Objects:**

Directions: Cross out any prepositional phrases. Underline the subject once and the verb/verb phrase twice. Label any direct object-D.O. Label any indirect object-I.O.

1. Miss Hanes handed the smiling bellman (**I.O.**) her luggage (**D.O.**).
2. An excited pep squad made the team (**I.O.**) a winning banner (**D.O.**) ~~for the pep rally~~.
3. The new nurse gave his patient (**I.O.**) a brochure (**D.O.**) ~~about diabetes~~.
4. A seamstress sewed the bride (**I.O.**) a beautiful, satin gown (**D.O.**) ~~with pearls and lace~~.
5. My grandfather tells everyone (**I.O.**) stories (**D.O.**) ~~about his high school days in Iowa~~.

Name________________________________ **NOUN REVIEW**

Date________________________________

G. **Determiners and Nouns:**

Directions: Write any determiner and the noun it modifies.

1. Mark's little brother makes his own pancakes. ______________________

____

2. This book contains many colorful pictures. ______________________

____

3. Your tires need some air. ______________________

____

4. A student purchased two pieces of pizza. ______________________

____

5. Do they need these nails for their tree house? ______________________

____

H. **Nouns Serving as Direct Objects and Indirect Objects:**

Directions: Cross out any prepositional phrases. Underline the subject once and the verb/verb phrase twice. Label any direct object-<u>D.O.</u> Label any indirect object-<u>I.O.</u>

1. Miss Hanes handed the smiling bellman her luggage.
2. An excited pep squad made the team a winning banner for the pep rally.
3. The new nurse gave his patient a brochure about diabetes.
4. A seamstress sewed the bride a beautiful, satin gown with pearls and lace.
5. My grandfather tells everyone stories about his high school days in Iowa.

Name________________________________ **NOUN REVIEW**

WORKBOOK PAGE 143

Date________________________________

I. **Nouns Serving as Appositives:**

Directions: Write the appositive in the space provided.

1. friend — Bridgette, my friend, plays the guitar.
2. dog — We called Fifi, our dog, several times.
3. subject — Sally completed her work in math, her favorite subject.
4. gentleman — A security officer, the gentleman in the blue uniform, checked various doors.

J. **Nouns Serving as Predicate Nominatives:**

Directions: Cross out any prepositional phrases. Underline the subject once and the verb/verb phrase twice. Label any predicate nominative-PN. Write the proof on the line provided.

1. A neon tetra is a colorful fish. (PN: fish)

   Proof: A colorful fish is a neon tetra.

2. The first wrestler ~~in the meet~~ was Adam. (PN: Adam)

   Proof: Adam was the first wrestler.

3. Baby Myra was the winner ~~of the pretty baby contest~~. (PN: winner)

   Proof: The winner was Baby Myra.

4. Tom Watson had become their friend ~~after college~~. (PN: friend)

   Proof: Their friend (had become) was Tom Watson.

K. **Noun Identification:** **Nouns are in boldfaced print.**

Directions: Box any noun(s).

1. Few **spectators** remained after the final **event** of the **Olympics**.
2. A **pianist** performed many famous **songs** for the delighted **crowd**.
3. My **uncle** and his two **sons** were playing **tennis** at a local tennis **club**.
4. The **student**, with **Linda's tutoring**, passed his **exams** with excellent **grades**.
5. An **elephant** lifted its **trunk** toward the tall **trees** and trumpeted several **times**.

Name________________________________ **NOUN REVIEW**

Date________________________________

I. **Nouns Serving as Appositives:**

Directions: Write the appositive in the space provided.

1. ______________________ Bridgette, my friend, plays the guitar.
2. ______________________ We called Fifi, our dog, several times.
3. ______________________ Sally completed her work in math, her favorite subject.
4. ______________________ A security officer, the gentleman in the blue uniform, checked various doors.

J. **Nouns Serving as Predicate Nominatives:**

Directions: Cross out any prepositional phrases. Underline the subject once and the verb/verb phrase twice. Label any predicate nominative-PN. Write the proof on the line provided.

1. A neon tetra is a colorful fish.

   Proof:____

2. The first wrestler in the meet was Adam.

   Proof:____

3. Baby Myra was the winner of the pretty baby contest.

   Proof:____

4. Tom Watson had become their friend after college.

   Proof:____

K. **Noun Identification:**

Directions: Box any noun(s).

1. Few spectators remained after the final event of the Olympics.
2. A pianist performed many famous songs for the delighted crowd.
3. My uncle and his two sons were playing tennis at a local tennis club.
4. The student, with Linda's tutoring, passed his exams with excellent grades.
5. An elephant lifted its trunk toward the tall trees and trumpeted several times.

Name________________________________ **NOUN TEST**

Date________________________________

A. Directions: Write C if the word is a concrete noun; write A if the word is an abstract noun.

1. __A__ wisdom 3. __C__ air 5. __A__ happiness
2. __C__ lion 4. __C__ shutter 6. __C__ microscope

B. Directions: Write **C** for common; write **P** for proper.

1. __C__ AIRPLANE
2. __C__ JET
3. __P__ FUNDWAY AIRLINES
4. __P__ ADAMS COUNTY
5. __P__ WASHINGTON, D.C.
6. __C__ SKATER

C. Directions: Write **N** if the boldfaced word serves as a noun; write **A** if the boldfaced word serves as an adjective. Write **V** if the boldfaced word serves as a verb.

1. __V__ Does she **park** her car there every night?
2. __N__ In the spring, the residents enjoy the **park**.
3. __A__ Those **park** lights are too bright.
4. __N__ "I'd like **cream** for my coffee," said Mr. Post.
5. __V__ To make these cookies, **cream** butter and sugar together first.
6. __A__ A white **cream** sauce is used as a base for this soup.

D. Directions: Write the possessive and the word it owns.

1. a computer belonging to Tate: Tate's computer
2. skis belonging to three girls: girls' skis
3. a restroom for more than one man: men's restroom
4. brushes belonging to James: James's brushes
5. a project belonging to two students: students' project

Name________________________________ **NOUN TEST**

Date________________________________

A. Directions: Write C if the word is a concrete noun; write A if the word is an abstract noun.

1. _____ wisdom 3. _____ air 5. _____ happiness
2. _____ lion 4. _____ shutter 6. _____ microscope

B. Write C for common; write P for proper.

1. _____ AIRPLANE 4. _____ ADAMS COUNTY
2. _____ JET 5. _____ WASHINGTON, D.C.
3. _____ FUNDWAY AIRLINES 6. _____ SKATER

C. Directions: Write N if the boldfaced word serves as a noun; write A if the boldfaced word serves as an adjective. Write V if the boldfaced word serves as a verb.

1. _____ Does she **park** her car there every night?
2. _____ In the spring, the residents enjoy the **park**.
3. _____ Those **park** lights are too bright.
4. _____ "I'd like **cream** for my coffee," said Mr. Barnet.
5. _____ To make these cookies, **cream** butter and sugar together first.
6. _____ A white **cream** sauce is used as a base for this soup.

D. Directions: Write the possessive and the word it owns.

1. a computer belonging to Tate: ________________________________
2. skis belonging to three girls: ________________________________
3. a restroom for more than one man: ________________________________
4. brushes belonging to James: ________________________________
5. a project belonging to two students: ________________________________

E. Directions: In the space provided, write PN if the boldfaced noun serves as a predicate nominative, D.O. if the boldfaced noun serves as a direct object, and I.O. if the boldfaced noun serves as an indirect object. If the noun serves as an appositive, write APP. in the space.

1. PN The first shape on the page is a **triangle**.
2. APP. Mr. Carlson, his soccer **coach**, talked to the team about sportsmanship.
3. D.O. Marge always sends post **cards** to her cousin.
4. I.O. The tailor made **Fred** a pin-striped suit.
5. PN The third United States President was **Jefferson**.
6. D.O. Please take your **belongings** with you.
7. I.O. Trish handed the mail **lady** a large envelope.

F. Directions: Write the plural of each noun.

1. crepe - **crepes**
2. octopus - **octopi**
3. crash - **crashes**
4. fez - **fezes**
5. decoy - **decoys**
6. berry - **berries**
7. cross - **crosses**
8. branch - **branches**

G. Directions: First, circle any determiner in the sentence. Then, box any noun following a determiner. Next, reread the sentence and box any other noun(s) in the sentence.

Determiners will be italicized; nouns will be in boldface.

1. *Some* **bats** will be flying from *that* **cave** after **sundown**.
2. Has ***Earl's*** **cousin** purchased *a* brick **home** across from *the* new **library**?
3. The ***ladies'*** **club** gave *two* **scholarships** to *those* **women** returning for *a* college **degree**.
4. *No* **money** was given to *my* **sister** for *an* **expedition** to **Africa** in *the* **spring**.
5. *Our* **grandmother** is known for *her* **wisdom** about *many* **matters**.
6. *Their* **family** went to **Lake Powell**, *a* beautiful **body** of **water** in northern **Arizona**.
7. **Todd** and I watched *an* energetic **monkey** chase *its* **partner**.

E. Directions: In the space provided, write PN if the boldfaced noun serves as a predicate nominative, D.O. if the boldfaced noun serves as a direct object, and I.O. if the boldfaced noun serves as an indirect object. If the noun serves as an appositive, write APP. in the space.

1. _____ The first shape on the page is a **triangle**.
2. _____ Mr. Carlson, his soccer **coach**, talked to the team about sportsmanship.
3. _____ Marge always sends post **cards** to her cousin.
4. _____ The tailor made **Fred** a pin-striped suit.
5. _____ The third United States President was **Jefferson**.
6. _____ Please take your **belongings** with you.
7. _____ Trish handed the mail **lady** a large envelope.

F. Directions: Write the plural of each noun.

1. crepe - ______________________
2. octopus - ______________________
3. crash - ______________________
4. fez - ______________________
5. decoy - ______________________
6. berry - ______________________
7. cross - ______________________
8. branch - ______________________

G. Directions: First, circle any determiner in the sentence. Then, box any noun following a determiner. Next, reread the sentence and box any other noun(s) in the sentence.

1. Some bats will be flying from that cave after sundown.
2. Has Earl's cousin purchased a brick home across from the new library?
3. The ladies' club gave two scholarships to those women returning for a college degree.
4. No money was given to my sister for an expedition to Africa in the spring.
5. Our grandmother is known for her wisdom concerning many matters.
6. Their family went to Lake Powell, a beautiful body of water in northern Arizona.
7. Todd and I watched a monkey chase its partner.

Name_______________________________ **CUMULATIVE REVIEW**

WORKBOOK PAGE 144 Noun Unit

Date_______________________________

A. Directions: Write fifty prepositions.

1. about
2. above
3. across
4. after
5. against
6. along
7. amid
8. among
9. around
10. at
11. atop
12. before
13. behind
14. below
15. beneath
16. beside
17. between
18. beyond
19. but (meaning except)
20. by
21. concerning
22. down
23. during
24. except
25. for
26. from
27. in
28. inside
29. into
30. like
31. near
32. of
33. off
34. on
35. onto
36. out
37. outside
38. over
39. past
40. regarding
41. since
42. through
43. throughout
44. to
45. toward
46. under
47. underneath
48. until
49. up
50. upon
51. with
52. within
53. without

B. Directions: Cross out any prepositional phrases. Underline the subject once and the verb/verb phrase twice.

1. ~~In the middle of the tournament~~, one chess player asked ~~for a short break~~.

2. The man ~~with Beth and Bill~~ has moved here ~~from the South~~.

3. ~~During the Thanksgiving holiday~~, we will be going ~~to Wisconsin~~.

4. Pigeons sit ~~above the eaves of that house on the corner~~.

5. ~~During Easter~~, Clyde and she will help ~~at their church~~.

Name________________________________

Date________________________________

CUMULATIVE REVIEW
Noun Unit

A. Directions: Write fifty prepositions.

1.	____________	14.	____________	27.	____________	40.	____________
2.	____________	15.	____________	28.	____________	41.	____________
3.	____________	16.	____________	29.	____________	42.	____________
4.	____________	17.	____________	30.	____________	43.	____________
5.	____________	18.	____________	31.	____________	44.	____________
6.	____________	19.	____________	32.	____________	45.	____________
7.	____________	20.	____________	33.	____________	46.	____________
8.	____________	21.	____________	34.	____________	47.	____________
9.	____________	22.	____________	35.	____________	48.	____________
10.	____________	23.	____________	36.	____________	49.	____________
11.	____________	24.	____________	37.	____________	50.	____________
12.	____________	25.	____________	38.	____________		
13.	____________	26.	____________	39.	____________		

B. Directions: Cross out any prepositional phrases. Underline the subject once and the verb/verb phrase twice.

1. In the middle of the tournament, one chess player asked for a short break.

2. The man with Beth and Bill has moved here from the South.

3. During the Thanksgiving holiday, we will be going to Wisconsin.

4. Pigeons sit above the eaves of that house on the corner.

5. During Easter, Clyde and she will help at their church.

C. Directions: Write the 23 auxiliary (helping) verbs:

WORKBOOK PAGE 145

has, have, had, do, does, did, may, must, might, should, would, could, shall, will, can,

is, am, are, was, were, be, being, been

D. Write the past participle form of the following infinitives: (Write *has, have,* or *had* with it.)

1. had ridden
2. had come
3. had fallen
4. had swum
5. had stolen
6. had taken
7. had drunk
8. had written
9. had gone
10. had bought
11. had taught
12. had worn
13. had burst
14. had eaten
15. had flown
16. had been
17. had sworn
18. had brought
19. had done
20. had known

E. Directions: Cross out any prepositional phrases. Underline the subject once and the verb/verb phrase twice. Label any direct object - **D.O.**

D.O.

1. The speaker (rose, raised) his voice (to make) a point.
2. Have you (sat, set) there ~~for a long time~~?
3. A calendar is (lying, laying) ~~on the desk~~.

D.O.

4. The artist (lay, laid) two oil paintings ~~on the oak desk~~.

D.O.

5. (You) (Sit, Set) these ceramic planters out ~~on the patio~~.
6. Water had (risen, raised) ~~in the lake~~ ~~after the constant rain~~.

C. Directions: Write the 23 auxiliary (helping) verbs:______________________

____

____

D. Write the past participle form of the following infinitives: (Write *has*, *have*, or *had* with it.)

1. to ride - ____________________
2. to come - ____________________
3. to fall - ____________________
4. to swim - ____________________
5. to steal - ____________________
6. to take - ____________________
7. to drink - ____________________
8. to write - ____________________
9. to go - ____________________
10. to buy - ____________________
11. to teach - ____________________
12. to wear - ____________________
13. to burst - ____________________
14. to eat - ____________________
15. to fly - ____________________
16. to be - ____________________
17. to swear - ____________________
18. to bring - ____________________
19. to do - ____________________
20. to know - ____________________

E. Directions: Cross out any prepositional phrases. Underline the subject once and the verb/verb phrase twice. Label any direct object-<u>D.O.</u>

1. The speaker (rose, raised) his voice to make a point.
2. Have you (sat, set) there for a long time?
3. A calendar is (lying, laying) on the desk.
4. The artist (lay, laid) two oil paintings on the oak desk.
5. (Sit, Set) these ceramic planters out on the patio.
6. Water had (risen, raised) in the lake after the constant rain.

F. Directions: List the 20 linking verbs (12 infinitives + 8)
WORKBOOK PAGE 146

to feel, to taste, to look, to smell, to appear, to become, to grow, to remain, to seem, to sound, to stay, to be (is, am, are, was, were, be, being, been)

G. Directions: Cross out any prepositional phrases. Underline the subject once and the verb twice. In the space provided, write A if the verb is action; write L if the verb is linking.

Remember: **Write *is, am, are, was,* or *were* above the verb. If the sentence makes sense, check to see if a word in the predicate goes back to describe the subject.**

is

1. L The toast smells burned.
2. A Kristina scraped the burned part ~~from the toast~~.

was

3. L This stale toast tasted terrible.
4. A Reluctantly, Chad tasted the toast.

H. Directions: Write the contraction.

1. won't	3. we're	5. that's
2. they're	4. can't	6. wasn't

I. Directions: Cross out any prepositional phrases. Underline the subject once and the verb/verb phrase twice. In the space provided, write the tense: *present, past, future, present perfect, past perfect, future perfect, present progressive, past progressive,* or *future progressive.*

1. past perfect — Several shoppers had stopped ~~at a pet store~~.
2. present — William's brother makes great pasta.
3. past — The graphic artist left sketches ~~with the owner~~.
4. past progressive — Many ~~workers~~ were ordering salads ~~for lunch~~.

J. Directions: Circle the correct verb.

1. are 2. ride 3. limps 4. yells

F. Directions: List the 20 linking verbs (12 infinitives + 8): ____________________

____

____

G. Directions: Cross out any prepositional phrases. Underline the subject once and the verb twice. In the space provided, write A if the verb is action; write L if the verb is linking.

Remember: **Write *is*, *am*, *are*, *was*, or *were* above the verb. If the sentence makes sense, check to see if a word in the predicate goes back to describe the subject.**

1. ______ The toast smells burned.
2. ______ Kristina scraped the burned part from the toast.
3. ______ This stale toast tasted terrible.
4. ______ Reluctantly, Chad tasted the toast.

H. Directions: Write the contraction.

1. will not - ____________	3. we are - ____________	5. that is - __________
2. they are - ___________	4. cannot - ____________	6. was not - ________

I. Directions: Cross out any prepositional phrases. Underline the subject once and the verb/verb phrase twice. In the space provided, write the tense: *present, past, future, present perfect, past perfect, future perfect, present progressive, past progressive,* or *future progressive.*

1. ________________________ Several shoppers had stopped at a pet store.
2. ________________________ William's brother makes great pasta.
3. ________________________ The graphic artist left sketches with the owner.
4. ________________________ Many workers were ordering salads for lunch.

J. Directions: Circle the correct verb.

1. Several summer jobs (is, are) available.
2. Brent and Annie (ride, rides) their bikes every day.
3. One deer (limps, limp) badly.
4. Everyone of the cheerleaders (yell, yells) loudly.

Name________________________________

Date_________________________________

CUMULATIVE TEST
Noun Unit

A. Directions: Cross out any prepositional phrases. Underline the subject once and the verb/verb phrase twice.

1. All band members, ~~but William and Iva~~, will be playing ~~in the concert~~.
2. A huge basket ~~of flowers~~ has been placed ~~upon the dining room table~~.
3. (You) Keep your shoes ~~with the rubber soles~~ ~~in the laundry room~~.
4. ~~During the storm~~, a group ~~of children~~ stayed inside (to play).
5. Gregg and I planted flowers ~~between a low wall and our house~~.

B. Directions: Write the contraction.

1. I have - I've
2. could not - couldn't
3. what is - what's
4. they are - they're
5. I would - I'd
6. will not - won't

C. Directions: Write L if the verb is linking; write A if the verb is action.

1. A The cook tastes all of her soups.
2. A After the lights went out, we felt our way down the hallway.
3. L Mrs. Fox has become a business owner.
4. L In January, the weather is usually very cold.

D. Directions: Write the correct form of the verb in the space provided.

1. Her wrist had been **broken** in the fall.
2. Lasagna **takes** much time to prepare.
3. Several trousers were **hung** (or **hanging**) in the closet.
4. He has **ridden** his horse for an hour.

Name________________________________

Date________________________________

CUMULATIVE TEST
Noun Unit

A. Directions: Cross out any prepositional phrases. Underline the subject once and the verb/verb phrase twice.

1. All band members, but William and Iva, will be playing in the concert.

2. A huge basket of flowers has been placed upon the dining room table.

3. Keep your shoes with the rubber soles in the laundry room.

4. During the storm, a group of children stayed inside to play.

5. Gregg and I planted flowers between a low wall and our house.

B. Directions: Write the contraction.

1.	I have - ____________	3.	what is - ____________	5.	I would - ____________
2.	could not - __________	4.	they are - __________	6.	will not - ____________

C. Directions: Write L if the verb is linking; write A if the verb is action.

1. _____ The cook tastes all of her soups.

2. _____ After the lights went out, we felt our way down the hallway.

3. _____ Mrs. Fox has become a business owner.

4. _____ In January, the weather is usually very cold.

D. Directions: Write the correct form of the verb in the space provided.

(to break) 1. Her wrist had been ________________ in the fall.

(to take) 2. Lasagna ________________ much time to prepare.

(to hang) 3. Several trousers were ________________ in the closet.

(to ride) 4. He has ________________ his horse for an hour.

5. The athlete had **swum** the English Channel.
6. Your behavior has **been** outstanding.
7. Several gallons of water had been **drunk** by the thirsty workers.
8. Both the coach and her assistant often **talk** with the team.
9. Several surfers had **come** to the beach before dawn.
10. Jim and Annie had **gone** to a car derby.
11. That company **sends** catalogs to its customers.
12. Many beach visitors had **lain** quietly watching the ocean.

E. Directions: Cross out any prepositional phrases. Underline the subject once and the verb/verb phrase twice. On the space provided, write the tense: *present, past, future, present perfect, past perfect, future perfect, present progressive, past progressive, or future progressive.*

1. present progressive — I am waiting ~~for the next bus~~.
2. past — The letter ~~from Aunt Sue~~ arrived ~~before noon~~.
3. present — Those boots are ~~in great shape~~.
4. future perfect — ~~By the end of the month~~, he will have written forty checks.

F. Directions: Cross out any prepositional phrases. Underline the subject once and the verb/verb phrase twice.

1. A petition ~~concerning zoning~~ was passed ~~around the neighborhood~~.
2. I shall **not** have (to leave) ~~until Wednesday~~.
3. (You) Go ~~toward your opponent~~ but move ~~outside his reach~~.
4. This plate should have been placed ~~under the fancy saucers~~.
5. Are the travelers going ~~through many tunnels~~ ~~during their time~~ ~~in Switzerland~~?

(to swim) 5. The athlete had _______________ the English Channel.

(to be) 6. Your behavior has _______________ outstanding.

(to drink) 7. Several gallons of water had been _____________ by the thirsty workers.

(to talk) 8. Both the coach and her assistant often ____________ with the team.

(to come) 9. Several surfers had ______________ to the beach before dawn.

(to go) 10. Jim and Annie had ___________ to a car derby.

(to send) 11. That company _______________ catalogs to its customers.

(to lie) 12. Many beach visitors had ___________ quietly watching the ocean.

E. Directions: Cross out any prepositional phrases. Underline the subject once and the verb/verb phrase twice. On the space provided, write the tense: *present*, *past*, *future*, *present perfect*, *past perfect*, *future perfect*, *present progressive*, *past progressive*, or *future progressive*.

1. _____________________ I am waiting for the next bus.

2. _____________________ The letter from Aunt Sue arrived before noon.

3. _____________________ Those boots are in great shape.

4. _____________________ By the end of the month, he will have written forty checks.

F. Directions: Cross out any prepositional phrases. Underline the subject once and the verb/verb phrase twice.

1. A petition concerning zoning was passed around the neighborhood.

2. I shall not have to leave until Wednesday.

3. Go toward your opponent but move outside his reach.

4. This plate should have been placed under the fancy saucers.

5. Are the travelers going through many tunnels during their time in Switzerland?

PAGE 301 = WORKBOOK PAGE 147

INTERJECTIONS

Interjections are words or phrases that express strong emotion.

Interjections have an exclamation point (!) after them.

Examples: A. **Wow!** We won!

B. **Good grief!** Is this my baby picture?

Reminder: Interjections are an easy concept, but they are easily forgotten. In order to insure mastery learning, review is needed throughout the school year. It is suggested that at least once a week students be given examples.

Name________________________________ **INTERJECTIONS**
WORKBOOK PAGE 148
Date________________________________

Directions: Underline the subject once and the verb/verb phrase twice. Circle any interjection(s).
Answers are in boldfaced print.

Example: **Whew**! That was a close call!

1. **Good grief**! Is that picture really included in our family album?

2. We won the tournament! **Wow**!

3. **Yikes**! There is a snake or a turtle in the water!

4. **Oh! No**! I forgot my homework!

5. The Italian stew has too much oregano! **Yuck**!

6. **Boy**! Are you in trouble!

7. **Yippee**! A parade is coming to our town!

8. **Far out**! John and I have been chosen for the debating team!

(You)
9. **No**! Don't go!

10. Someone has broken my favorite porcelain doll! **Boo**!

11. **Shhh**! We must not wake the sleeping baby!

12. A group of us had nearly drowned! **Whew**!

(You)
13. **Man**! Look at those performing acrobats!

14. **Drat**! Our aunt and uncle cannot take us water skiing today!

(You)
15. **Oh**! Stop a minute and listen to the lovely chimes!

Name_________________________________ **INTERJECTIONS**

Date_________________________________

Directions: Underline the subject once and the verb/verb phrase twice. Circle any interjection(s).

Example: **Whew**! That was a close call!

1. Good grief! Is that picture really included in our family album?
2. We won the tournament! Wow!
3. Yikes! There is a snake or a turtle in the water!
4. Oh! No! I forgot my homework!
5. The Italian stew has too much oregano! Yuck!
6. Boy! Are you in trouble!
7. Yippee! A parade is coming to our town!
8. Far out! John and I have been chosen for the debating team!
9. No! Don't go!
10. Someone has broken my favorite porcelain doll! Boo!
11. Shhh! We must not wake the sleeping baby!
12. A group of us had nearly drowned! Whew!
13. Man! Look at those performing acrobats!
14. Drat! Our aunt and uncle cannot take us water skiing today!
15. Oh! Stop a minute and listen to the lovely chimes!

PAGE 305 = WORKBOOK PAGE 149

CONJUNCTIONS

Conjunctions are connecting words.

The most common conjunctions are: **and, but, or.**

Conjunctions connect nouns:	Blueberries **and** cream taste good.
Conjunctions connect pronouns:	She **or** I will go tonight.
Conjunctions connect adjectives:	A blue **and** red helicopter landed.
Conjunctions connect adverbs:	We wrote quickly **but** neatly.
Conjunctions connect prepositions: (prepositional phrases)	The ball bounced into the living room **and** down the hallway.
Conjunctions connect verbs:	You may swim, hike, **or** rest today.
Conjunctions connect interjections:	Yippee **and** yeah! We won!
Conjunctions even connect other conjunctions:	Don't use but **or** and in that sentence.
Conjunctions connect phrases:	Do you like living in the woods **and** wandering in the meadows?

Correlative Conjunctions:

Correlative conjunctions are a special type of conjunction.

A. Correlative conjunctions occur in pairs.

B. The most common correlative conjunctions are:

1. **Both/And**	**Both** Ava **and** Robert are here.
2. **Either/Or**	You may **either** wait here **or** go on alone.
3. **Neither/Nor**	I want **neither** the blue **nor** the gray.
4. **Not only/ But also**	**Not only** was the dog taken to a veterinarian, **but also** he was given a shot.

Note: There are other words that will serve as connecting words or conjunctions.

Example: Your racing bike is faster than mine.

Name________________________________ **CONJUNCTIONS**

WORKBOOK PAGE 150

Date________________________________

Directions: Circle any conjunction(s) in the following sentences.
Answers are in boldfaced print.

Example: Jan **or** Libby won the race.

1. We swept **and** washed the floors, **but** they were still a mess.
2. Many trinkets **and** charms were for sale, **but** we bought none.
3. Sit beside me **or** across the table from me.
4. We left the skating rink, went home, **and** drank a soda.
5. I like you, **but** I do not agree with your idea.
6. Is your decision due tomorrow **or** the next day?
7. Judy enjoys eating hot dogs **and** French fries **but** dislikes carrots.
8. Will you practice your guitar now **or** wait until later?
9. He came to the meeting **but** would not participate in discussion.
10. Does Faith want salt **and** pepper **or** hollandaise sauce on her eggs?

Directions: Circle any conjunction(s) in the following sentences.

Example: **Neither** William **nor** my teacher arrived on time.

1. **Either** you must finish **or** take it home with you.
2. **Both** the men's **and** women's groups meet on Monday.
3. The prince had **either** to choose to be king **or** to leave the kingdom.
4. **Neither** the turnips **nor** the spinach pleased him.
5. **Not only** had we accepted the package **but also** had paid the postage.
6. The coach had chosen **both** the last **and** second string players.
7. Your choice of **either** tacos **or** tostadas is a good one.
8. **Neither** rain **nor** hail will keep us from going camping.
9. That person was **not only** a finalist **but also** a medal winner.
10. They have seen **both** the movie **and** the play of The Odd Couple.
11. Someone said they had **neither** seen him **nor** knew his location.
12. The symphony **either** must begin immediately **or** continue past midnight.

Name________________________________ **CONJUNCTIONS**

Date________________________________

Directions: Circle any conjunction(s) in the following sentences.

Example: Jan **or** Libby won the race.

1. We swept and washed the floors, but they were still a mess.
2. Many trinkets and charms were for sale, but we bought none.
3. Sit beside me or across the table from me.
4. We left the skating rink, went home, and drank a soda.
5. I like you, but I do not agree with your idea.
6. Is your decision due tomorrow or the next day?
7. Judy enjoys eating hot dogs and French fries but dislikes carrots.
8. Will you practice your guitar now or wait until later?
9. He came to the meeting but would not participate in discussion.
10. Does Faith want salt and pepper or hollandaise sauce on her eggs?

Directions: Circle any conjunction(s) in the following sentences.

Example: **Neither** William **nor** my teacher arrived on time.

1. Either you must finish or take it home with you.
2. Both the men's and women's groups meet on Monday.
3. The prince had either to choose to be king or to leave the kingdom.
4. Neither the turnips nor the spinach pleased him.
5. Not only had we accepted the package but also had paid the postage.
6. The coach had chosen both the last and second string players.
7. Your choice of either tacos or tostadas is a good one.
8. Neither rain nor hail will keep us from going camping.
9. That person was not only a finalist but also a medal winner.
10. They have seen both the movie and the play of The Odd Couple.
11. Someone said they had neither seen him nor knew his location.
12. The symphony either must begin immediately or continue past midnight.

PAGE 309 = WORKBOOK PAGE 151

ADJECTIVES

There are two general types of adjectives: limiting adjectives and descriptive adjectives.

A. Limiting Adjectives

1. **"Determiners"** are actually determining adjectives.

    a. Articles: **a, an,** and **the**

    b. Demonstratives: **this, that, those,** and **these**

    c. Numbers

    d. Possessives: **his, her, their, our, its, your, my**

    e. Possessive noun (used as adjectives): **Tom's** car

    f. Indefinites: **some, few, many, several, no, any** *

2. Any of these "determiners" must appear before a noun or pronoun in order to function as an adjective. If any of the above words stand alone, they function as pronouns.

    Examples: This cord is frayed. (This is an adjective because it modifies or goes over to cord.)

    This must be changed. (This is not an adjective because there is not a noun or pronoun following it. This is a pronoun.)

    Some onions lay on the table. (Some is an adjective because it modifies or goes over to onions.)

    Some were not invited. (Some is not an adjective because there is not a noun or pronoun following it. Some is a pronoun.)

* There are others.

Name________________________________ **ADJECTIVES**

WORKBOOK PAGE 152 Limiting Adjectives

Date________________________________

Directions: In the space provided, write the underlined, limiting adjective with the noun or pronoun that it modifies.

Example: My belt is a leather one. ___My belt___

1. Some practical jokes can be funny. ___Some jokes___
2. Are you in his jazz band? ___his band___
3. We saw an elephant in the parade. ___an elephant___
4. No cars may be parked here. ___No cars___
5. Did you bring your license? ___your license___
6. Few earthquakes occur there. ___Few earthquakes___
7. Is our picnic basket in the jeep? ___our basket___
8. Naps were taken several times daily. ___several times___
9. In fall some trees shed their leaves. ___their leaves___
10. There are three red jackets. ___three jackets___
11. Did Mr. Weber like these cards? ___these cards___
12. The chair's back is carved oak. ___chair's back___
13. That pebble was collected for Tim. ___That pebble___
14. There were twenty-one pink bikes. ___twenty-one bikes___
15. Sonny's service station succeeded. ___Sonny's station___

Name________________________________

Date________________________________

ADJECTIVES

Limiting Adjectives

Directions: In the space provided, write the underlined, limiting adjective with the noun or pronoun that it modifies.

Example: My belt is a leather one. My belt

1. Some practical jokes can be funny. ____________________
2. Are you in his jazz band? ____________________
3. We saw an elephant in the parade. ____________________
4. No cars may be parked here. ____________________
5. Did you bring your license? ____________________
6. Few earthquakes occur there. ____________________
7. Is our picnic basket in the jeep? ____________________
8. Naps were taken several times daily. ____________________
9. In fall some trees shed their leaves. ____________________
10. There are three red jackets. ____________________
11. Did Mr. Weber like these cards? ____________________
12. The chair's back is carved oak. ____________________
13. That pebble was collected for Tim. ____________________
14. There were twenty-one pink bikes. ____________________
15. Sonny's service station succeeded. ____________________

Name_______________________________ **ADJECTIVES**
WORKBOOK PAGE 153 Limiting Adjectives
Date_______________________________

Directions: Underline any article in the following sentences.

1. The receptionist wore an orange dress and a lavender pair of shoes to the office today.
2. The book club gave an exercise book as a free gift.
3. Going to Tahiti was an experience of a lifetime.

Directions: Underline any numbers that serve as adjectives in the following sentences.

1. We waited fifteen years to start this company.
2. Has Grace been given five or six toasters for wedding gifts?
3. Nearly forty players were aboard our flight to St. Paul.
4. One Broadway show was attended by five members of our family.
5. She saved two dollars by purchasing three products.

Directions: Underline any possessive nouns that serve as adjectives in the following sentences.

1. Jessica's new pen doesn't work properly.
2. Have you ever seen any of Tarzan's movies?
3. The birds' nest had been thrown from the tree during the storm.
4. Last night's paper reported that the women's club would meet on Tuesday.
5. Wendy's new shoes came from McMurray's Shoe Store.

Directions: Underline any adjective in the following sentences.

1. Her uncle is leaving that town in my brother's airplane.
2. Your three baseball cards are on the floor.
3. The anxious and weepy starlet had lost her emerald ring.
4. Many autograph books were passed out at a special celebration.
5. Her bright, straight teeth are beautiful.

Name________________________________

Date________________________________

ADJECTIVES
Limiting Adjectives

Directions: Underline any article in the following sentences.

1. The receptionist wore an orange dress and a lavender pair of shoes to the office today.
2. The book club gave an exercise book as a free gift.
3. Going to Tahiti was an experience of a lifetime.

Directions: Underline any numbers that serve as adjectives in the following sentences.

1. We waited fifteen years to start this company.
2. Has Grace been given five or six toasters for wedding gifts?
3. Nearly forty players were aboard our flight to St. Paul.
4. One Broadway show was attended by five members of our family.
5. She saved two dollars by purchasing three products.

Directions: Underline any possessive nouns that serve as adjectives in the following sentences.

1. Jessica's new pen doesn't work properly.
2. Have you ever seen any of Tarzan's movies?
3. The birds' nest had been thrown from the tree during the storm.
4. Last night's paper reported that the women's club would meet on Tuesday.
5. Wendy's new shoes came from McMurray's Shoe Store.

Directions: Underline any adjective in the following sentences.

1. Her uncle is leaving that town in my brother's airplane.
2. Your three baseball cards are on the floor.
3. The anxious and weepy starlet had lost her emerald ring.
4. Many autograph books were passed out at a special celebration.
5. Her bright, straight teeth are beautiful.

Name________________________________

WORKBOOK PAGE 154

Date________________________________

ADJECTIVES

Limiting Adjectives

Directions: Choose any demonstrative adjectives in the following sentences. **Answers are in boldfaced print for all the sections on this page.**

1. **Those** potatoes need to be peeled.
2. Did you buy **that** game yesterday?
3. Have you read **these** magazines?
4. **This** year has been fun.

Directions: Choose any indefinite adjectives in the following sentences.

1. Has the agent purchased **many** houses this year?
2. I have **no** coins for the machine.
3. Will we serve **several** vegetables for dinner?
4. **Few** shampoos were on sale today.
5. Do you have **any** money?
6. **Some** doughnuts will be served with breakfast.

Directions: Choose any possessive pronouns used as adjectives: my, her, his, your, its, our, their.

1. **Your** ticket is on the desk.
2. Did **her** pamphlet sell?
3. Some composers left **their** works behind.
4. What is **our** job?
5. **Their** train is leaving in an hour.
6. The monkey chased **its** tail and waved.
7. Do **your** parents know **his** father?

Name________________________________

Date________________________________

ADJECTIVES

Limiting Adjectives

Directions: Choose any demonstrative adjectives in the following sentences.

1. Those potatoes need to be peeled.
2. Did you buy that game yesterday?
3. Have you read these magazines?
4. This year has been fun.

Directions: Choose any indefinite adjectives in the following sentences.

1. Has the agent purchased many houses this year?
2. I have no coins for the machine.
3. Will we serve several vegetables for dinner?
4. Few shampoos were on sale today.
5. Do you have any money?
6. Some doughnuts will be served with breakfast.

Directions: Choose any possessive pronouns used as adjectives: my, her, his, your, its, our, their.

1. Your ticket is on the desk.
2. Did her pamphlet sell?
3. Some composers left their works behind.
4. What is our job?
5. Their train is leaving in an hour.
6. The monkey chased its tail and waved.
7. Do your parents know his father?

Name_______________________________ **ADJECTIVES**

WORKBOOK PAGE 155 Function?

Date________________________________

Directions: Place A in the provided space if the underlined word serves as an adjective. Place N in the space provided if the underlined word does not serve as an adjective.

Example: __A__ 1. Some shirts were on sale.

Remember: The underlined word must have a noun or pronoun closely following it in order to serve as an adjective. Be sure to cross out any prepositional phrase(s) beside an underlined word.

Example: __N__ 2. Some ~~of the goats~~ stood outside the barn.

__A__ 1. Many sand buggies rode through the desert.

__N__ 2. Many had been invited.

__N__ 3. There were only a few on display.

__A__ 4. A few monkeys were swinging on the bars.

__A__ 5. His truck was in the garage.

__N__ 6. Is his broken?

__N__ 7. Several of the batteries don't work.

__A__ 8. I have been given several dollars for my birthday.

__N__ 9. The guides went with her for instruction.

__A__ 10. Does she know her coat of arms?

__N__ 11. Do any of your friends want an ice cream bar?

__A__ 12. Are there any tomatoes in the garden?

Name________________________________

Date________________________________

ADJECTIVES
Function?

Directions: Place A in the provided space if the underlined word serves as an adjective. Place N in the space provided if the underlined word does not serve as an adjective.

Example: ___A___ 1. Some shirts were on sale.

Remember: The underlined word must have a noun or pronoun closely following it in order to serve as an adjective. Be sure to cross out any prepositional phrase(s) beside an underlined word.

Example: ___N___ 2. Some ~~of the goats~~ stood outside the barn.

______ 1. Many sand buggies rode through the desert.

______ 2. Many had been invited.

______ 3. There were only a few on display.

______ 4. A few monkeys were swinging on the bars.

______ 5. His truck was in the garage.

______ 6. Is his broken?

______ 7. Several of the batteries don't work.

______ 8. I have been given several dollars for my birthday.

______ 9. The guides went with her for instruction.

______ 10. Does she know her coat of arms?

______ 11. Do any of your friends want an ice cream bar?

______ 12. Are there any tomatoes in the garden?

PAGE 319 = WORKBOOK PAGE 156

ADJECTIVES

There are two general types of adjectives: limiting adjectives and descriptive adjectives.

B. **Descriptive Adjectives**

1. **Describe**. Examples: red, dumb, high, fine
2. Answer the question **WHAT KIND**?
3. Some descriptive adjectives end in the following suffixes:
   a. **ous** Examples: dangerous, courageous, famous
   b. **ful** Examples: cheerful, beautiful, sorrowful
   c. **able** Examples: remarkable, capable, adorable
   d. **y** Examples: silly, watery, rainy
   e. **ible** Examples: incredible, irresistible, deductible
   f. **ive** Examples: creative, productive, secretive
   g. **less** Examples: priceless, penniless, sugarless
   h. **al** Examples: special, final, postal
4. Descriptive adjectives modify or go over to a noun or pronoun.
   a. Descriptive adjectives often come before the noun or pronoun.

      Example: **White** swans swam on *our* lake.

      (**White** describes swans.)
      (*Our* is a possessive going over to lake.)

      Example: *Tanya's* dog is the **playful** one.

      (*Tanya's* is a possessive that goes over to the noun dog.)
      (**Playful** goes over to the pronoun one.)

   b. Descriptive adjectives sometimes come after the noun or pronoun.

      Examples: A grapefruit, **round** and **juicy**, was picked.

      (**Round** and **juicy** describe a grapefruit.)

      This doll is **old**.

      (**Old** is a predicate adjective.)

Name________________________________ **ADJECTIVES**
WORKBOOK PAGE 157
Date________________________________

Directions: Choose any adjective(s) in the following sentences.
Answers are in boldfaced print.

Example: **Micah's black** hair is very **shiny**.

1. **Our new brick** home is **spacious**, but **the garden** area is **weedy**.
2. **Her talkative** mother uses **the blue** phone for **endless** conversations.
3. **Some slow** turtles moved under **a large green** bush.
4. **Nancy's interesting** trip to **the quiet** moors of **the English** countryside must have been **fascinating.**
5. **My** story about **our unusual** vacation was **funny**.
6. **Their favorite guest** speaker didn't require reservations.
7. **Our boys'** room is **an absolute** mess.
8. **A few pretty fall** hairdos were included in **an** article in **this fashion** magazine.
9. **Many outstanding** artists held **a** showing at **the new art** gallery.
10. Take **your twenty** pieces of **black** glass and place them in **the old cedar** chest.
11. **Our basic** concern was for **those thirty lost** children.
12. **The** victim, **rested** and **thankful**, returned to **his suburban** home.
13. **This lucky** winner gave **a joyful** but **tearful** scream of **complete** surprise.
14. **That little**, **black** puppy at **the pet** store is both **loveable** and **affordable**.
15. **My festive** dessert was **delicious** but very **sugary**.

Name________________________________ **ADJECTIVES**

Date________________________________

Directions: Choose any adjective(s) in the following sentences.

Example: **Micah's black** hair is very **shiny**.

1. Our new brick home is spacious, but the garden area is weedy.
2. Her talkative mother uses the blue phone for endless conversations.
3. Some slow turtles moved under a large green bush.
4. Nancy's interesting trip to the quiet moors of the English countryside must have been fascinating.
5. My story about our unusual vacation was funny.
6. Their favorite guest speaker didn't require reservations.
7. Our boys' room is an absolute mess.
8. A few pretty fall hairdos were included in an article in this fashion magazine.
9. Many outstanding artists held a showing at the new art gallery.
10. Take your twenty pieces of black glass and place them in the old cedar chest.
11. Our basic concern was for those thirty lost children.
12. The victim, rested and thankful, returned to his suburban home.
13. This lucky winner gave a joyful but tearful scream of complete surprise.
14. That little, black puppy at the pet store is both loveable and affordable.
15. My festive dessert was delicious but very sugary.

PAGE 323 = WORKBOOK PAGE 158

ADJECTIVES

Proper Adjectives

Proper adjectives are descriptive words derived from proper nouns. Since proper nouns are capitalized, we also capitalize proper adjectives.*

Proper Noun	Proper Adjectives	
Switzerland	Swiss	(cheese)
Mexico	Mexican	(culture)
China	Chinese	(food)

Sometimes the proper adjective form does NOT change.

Phoenix	Phoenix	(police)
Edison	Edison	(invention)
Skyview	Skyview	(television)
San Francisco	San Francisco	(trolley)
Angel Face	Angel Face	(baby clothes)

*Check your dictionary for correct proper adjective forms.

Name__________________________________
WORKBOOK PAGE 159
Date__________________________________

ADJECTIVES
Proper Adjectives

Directions: Underline any proper adjective(s) in the following sentences. In the space provided, write the proper adjective and the noun(s) it modifies.

Example: I own an <u>american</u> flag. — American flag

1. Have you eaten <u>holloman</u> bread? — Holloman bread
2. I like <u>polish</u> dancing. — Polish dancing
3. Did Kammie order <u>dutch</u> tulips? — Dutch tulips
4. The <u>japanese</u> gardens are lovely. — Japanese gardens
5. When does the <u>jewish</u> new year begin? — Jewish new* year
6. The car was parked along a <u>san diego</u> freeway. — San Diego freeway
7. Several attended the <u>european</u> tour. — European tour
8. Those <u>mexican</u> jumping beans are very interesting. — Mexican jumping* beans
9. The <u>bencze</u> stereo is enjoyable. — Bencze stereo
10. Tara's salad was eaten first at the <u>easter</u> dinner. — Easter dinner
11. We ate <u>danish</u> sweet rolls for a snack. — Danish sweet* rolls
12. The <u>modacko</u> pictures were returned today. — Modacko pictures
13. His parents met in a <u>miami</u> store. — Miami store
14. Take me to a small, <u>swiss</u> village. — Swiss village
15. Jamilla owns a <u>german</u> shepherd and two <u>arabian</u> horses. — German shepherd; Arabian horses

*adjectives

Name________________________________

Date________________________________

ADJECTIVES
Proper Adjectives

Directions: Underline any proper adjective(s) in the following sentences. In the space provided, write the proper adjective and the noun(s) it modifies.

Example: I own an american flag. ______American flag______

1. Have you eaten holloman bread? ____________________
2. I like polish dancing. ____________________
3. Did Kammie order dutch tulips? ____________________
4. The japanese gardens are lovely. ____________________
5. When does the jewish new year begin? ____________________
6. The car was parked along a san diego freeway. ____________________
7. Several attended the european tour. ____________________
8. Those mexican jumping beans are very interesting. ____________________
9. The bencze stereo is enjoyable. ____________________
10. Tara's salad was eaten first at the easter dinner. ____________________
11. We ate danish sweet rolls for a snack. ____________________
12. The modacko pictures were returned today. ____________________
13. His parents met in a miami store. ____________________
14. Take me to a small, swiss village. ____________________
15. Jamilla owns a german shepherd and two arabian horses. ____________________

____

Name________________________________ **ADJECTIVES**
WORKBOOK PAGE 160
Date________________________________

Directions: Choose any adjective(s) in the following sentences.
Anwers are in boldfaced print.

Example: **The black** and **white** zebra lay in **an open** meadow.

1. **The Victorian** chair was covered in **bright green** velvet.

2. Have **the dirty** bandages been removed from **the large** cut **this** morning?

3. **Her** dress for **the** ball was **glamorous** and **dazzling** under **the shimmering, crystal** lights.

4. **An old, rustic** inn is **their** choice for **a romantic** vacation.

5. **Those** brownies are **moist** and **chewy,** but **these dozen** cookies are **hard** and **stale**.

6. **Our grandma's** kitchen has **pretty flowered** wallpaper and **an old Franklin** stove.

7. **Your neighbor's** cat had **seven tiny, furry** kittens **this** morning.

8. **The new Christmas** ornaments were **brilliant,** but **our few childhood** ones seemed **faded** and **cracked.**

9. **The** padding of **this** mattress is **thicker** and more **absorbent** for **your baby's** comfort.

10. For dinner we ate **fried chicken** legs, **mashed** potatoes, **onion** rings, **three bean** salad, **sour** pickles, **creamed** corn, **fruit** pies with **ice** cream, and **many** pitchers of **iced lemon** drink.

Name________________________________ **ADJECTIVES**

Date________________________________

Directions: Choose any adjective(s) in the following sentences.

Example: **The black** and **white** zebra lay in **an open** meadow.

1. The Victorian chair was covered in bright green velvet.
2. Have the dirty bandages been removed from the large cut this morning?
3. Her dress for the ball was glamorous and dazzling under the shimmering, crystal lights.
4. An old, rustic inn is their choice for a romantic vacation.
5. Those brownies are moist and chewy, but these dozen cookies are hard and stale.
6. Our grandma's kitchen has pretty flowered wallpaper and an old Franklin stove.
7. Your neighbor's cat had seven tiny, furry kittens this morning.
8. The new Christmas ornaments were brilliant, but our few childhood ones seemed faded and cracked.
9. The padding of this mattress is thicker and more absorbent for your baby's comfort.
10. For dinner we ate fried chicken legs, mashed potatoes, onion rings, three bean salad, sour pickles, creamed corn, fruit pies with ice cream, and many pitchers of iced lemon drink.

PAGE 329 = WORKBOOK PAGE 161
PAGE 336 = WORKBOOK PAGE 165
PAGE 337 = WORKBOOK PAGE 166

ADJECTIVES

Predicate Adjectives

1. A predicate adjective occurs after the verb in a statement (declarative sentence).

2. A predicate adjective always describes the subject of the sentence.

3. A sentence containing a predicate adjective must have a linking verb:

to feel	to become	to remain
to taste	to seem	to stay
to look	to sound	to be(is, am, are, was,
to smell	to grow	were, being, be,
to appear		been)

Remember: To check for a linking verb, try replacing the verb with a form of to be. If you can do this without altering the meaning of the sentence, the verb is linking.

Example: The milk smells sour.
The milk is sour.

4. A question (interrogative sentence) usually has the predicate adjective and the noun or pronoun after the verb.

Examples: Are your eyes **blue**? Does the cake seem **flat**?

Suggestion: Make a question into a statement and then find the predicate adjective.

Your eyes are **blue**. The cake does seem **flat**.

5. **When you believe there is a predicate adjective in the sentence, ask yourself these three questions.**

   A. Is there a linking verb?
   B. Does the adjective occur after the verb?
   C. Does the adjective go back and describe the subject?

If the answer to all three of these questions is YES, you have a predicate adjective.

Name______________________________
WORKBOOK PAGE 162
Date______________________________

ADJECTIVES
Predicate Adjectives

Directions: Underline the subject once and the verb/verb phrase twice. Circle any predicate adjective. Write the predicate adjective and the noun or pronoun it modifies (goes to) in the space provided.

Answers are in boldfaced print.

Example: You look **tired**. — tired you (person)

1. My bowling ball is **blue**. — blue ball
2. Do you feel **happy**? — happy (person) you
3. This book is **interesting**. — interesting book
4. Some apples tasted **tart**. — tart apples
5. My luggage is very **old**. — old luggage
6. The bread became **stale**. — stale bread
7. This lesson has been **difficult**. — difficult lesson
8. A few children felt **sick**. — sick children
9. My answer sounded **stupid**. — stupid answer
10. Many cups were **empty**. — empty cups
11. Those muffins smell **good**. — good muffins
12. My feelings remain **fond** for you. — fond feelings
13. Will your hair stay **short** for the summer months? — short hair
14. Some dolphins were **amusing**. — amusing dolphins
15. That silver appears **tarnished**. — tarnished silver

Name________________________________

Date________________________________

ADJECTIVES

Predicate Adjectives

Directions: Underline the subject once and the verb/verb phrase twice. Circle any predicate adjective. Write the predicate adjective and the noun or pronoun it modifies (goes to) in the space provided.

Example: You look tired. ______tired you (person)______

1. My bowling ball is blue. ____________________
2. Do you feel happy? ____________________
3. This book is interesting. ____________________
4. Some apples tasted tart. ____________________
5. My luggage is very old. ____________________
6. The bread became stale. ____________________
7. This lesson has been difficult. ____________________
8. A few children felt sick. ____________________
9. My answer sounded stupid. ____________________
10. Many cups were empty. ____________________
11. Those muffins smell good. ____________________
12. My feelings remain fond for you. ____________________
13. Will your hair stay short for the summer months? ____________________
14. Some dolphins were amusing. ____________________
15. That silver appears tarnished. ____________________

Name_______________________________ **ADJECTIVES**

WORKBOOK PAGE 163 Predicate Adjectives

Date_______________________________

Directions: Underline the subject once and the verb/verb phrase twice. Label any predicate adjective (P.A.). Write the predicate adjective and the noun or pronoun it modifies (goes to) in the space provided.

Example: The music is too loud. (P.A.) loud music

1. This paper feels rough. (P.A.) rough paper
2. That child seems restless. (P.A.) restless child
3. A crane's legs are too long. (P.A.) long legs
4. The onion smelled strong. (P.A.) strong onion
5. A siren sounded shrill. (P.A.) shrill siren
6. The fighter remained angry. (P.A.) angry fighter
7. Dinner smells delicious. (P.A.) delicious dinner
8. My vegetable soup tastes spicy. (P.A.) spicy soup
9. The contestant became excited. (P.A.) excited contestant
10. Our mother is very intelligent. (P.A.) intelligent mother
11. Your eyes appear swollen. (P.A.) swollen eyes
12. This room is cooler. (P.A.) cooler room
13. We grow impatient in crowds. (P.A.) impatient (people) we
14. The chocolate fudge was sticky. (P.A.) sticky fudge
15. Ted's sauce was too lemony. (P.A.) lemony sauce

Name________________________________

Date________________________________

ADJECTIVES
Predicate Adjectives

Directions: Underline the subject once and the verb/verb phrase twice. Label any predicate adjective (P.A.). Write the predicate adjective and the noun or pronoun it modifies (goes to) in the space provided.

Example: The music is too loud. (P.A.: loud) ______loud music______

1. This paper feels rough. ____________________
2. That child seems restless. ____________________
3. A crane's legs are too long. ____________________
4. The onion smelled strong. ____________________
5. A siren sounded shrill. ____________________
6. The fighter remained angry. ____________________
7. Dinner smells delicious. ____________________
8. My vegetable soup tastes spicy. ____________________
9. The contestant became excited. ____________________
10. Our mother is very intelligent. ____________________
11. Your eyes appear swollen. ____________________
12. This room is cooler. ____________________
13. We grow impatient in crowds. ____________________
14. The chocolate fudge was sticky. ____________________
15. Ted's sauce was too lemony. ____________________

Name_______________________________ **ADJECTIVES**

WORKBOOK PAGE 164 Predicate Adjectives

Date_______________________________

Directions: If the underlined word is a predicate adjective, place P.A. in the space provided. If the underlined word is NOT a predicate adjective, place NOT in the space provided.

Remember: When you believe there is a predicate adjective in the sentence, ask yourself these three questions:

A. Is there a linking verb?

B. Does the adjective occur after the verb (in a statement)?

C. Does the adjective go back and describe the subject?

If the answer is YES to all three questions, the word is a predicate adjective.

P.A. 1. Our balloons are red.

P.A. 2. Our car has become dirty.

NOT 3. We chose the purple toothbrush.

P.A. 4. The sky grew cloudy.

P.A. 5. These four books are great.

NOT 6. Their grandmother scrubbed clothes on a wooden scrub board.

P.A. 7. That house seems haunted.

NOT 8. Have you painted the yellow house?

NOT 9. Lance tasted several types of brick cheese.

P.A. 10. Fried shrimp tasted good.

NOT 11. Flowers grew three inches.

P.A. 12. After the long night, the nurse grew very weary.

Name________________________________ **ADJECTIVES**

Predicate Adjectives

Date________________________________

Directions: If the underlined word is a predicate adjective, place P.A. in the space provided. If the underlined word is NOT a predicate adjective, place NOT in the space provided.

Remember: When you believe there is a predicate adjective in the sentence, ask yourself these three questions:

A. Is there a linking verb?

B. Does the adjective occur after the verb (in a statement)?

C. Does the adjective go back and describe the subject?

If the answer is YES to all three questions, the word is a predicate adjective.

_________ 1. Our balloons are red.

_________ 2. Our car has become dirty.

_________ 3. We chose the purple toothbrush.

_________ 4. The sky grew cloudy.

_________ 5. These four books are great.

_________ 6. Their grandmother scrubbed clothes on a wooden scrub board.

_________ 7. That house seems haunted.

_________ 8. Have you painted the yellow house?

_________ 9. Lance tasted several types of brick cheese.

_________ 10. Fried shrimp tasted good.

_________ 11. Flowers grew three inches.

_________ 12. After the long night, the nurse grew very weary.

ADJECTIVES

Degrees of Adjectives

Adjectives often make comparisons.

A. The **comparative form** compares **two**.

B. The **superlative form** compares **three or more**.

Examples: This painting is **larger** than that one.
(Comparative form - comparing two)
Of the three, this painting is **largest**.
(Superlative form - comparing three or more)

There are several ways to form the comparative and superlative forms:

A. **Comparative:**

1. Add **er** to most one-syllable adjectives.
   high/high**er** big/bigg**er**

2. Add **er** to many two-syllable adjectives.
   lovely/loveli**er** happy/happi**er**

3. Place **more** (or **less**) before many two-syllable adjectives.
   partial/**more** partial loyal/**less** loyal

4. **Some adjectives totally change form.**
   good/better bad/worse

B. **Superlative:**

1. Add **est** to most one-syllable adjectives.
   high/high**est** big/bigg**est**

2. Add **est** to many two-syllable adjectives.
   lovely/loveli**est** happy/happi**est**

ADJECTIVES

Degrees of Adjectives

B. **Superlative** (cont.)

3. Place **most** (or **least**) before many two-syllable adjectives.

   partial/**most** partial   loyal/**least** loyal

   Suggestion: Use your dictionary to determine if est should be added to the adjective. If the dictionary does NOT give the est form, use most (or least) before the adjective.

4. Place **most** (or **least**) before three-syllable adjectives.

   wonderful/**most** wonderful

   beautiful/**most** beautiful

   expensive/**least** expensive

5. **Some adjectives totally change form.**

   good/best   bad/worst

Name________________________________ **ADJECTIVES**

WORKBOOK PAGE 167 Degrees of Adjectives

Date________________________________

Directions: Write the required comparative or superlative form of the given adjective in the space provided.

Example: superlative form of creative

most creative

1. comparative form of red

   redder

2. superlative form of special

   most special*

3. superlative form of sincere

   sincerest or most sincere*

4. comparative form of good

   better

5. comparative form of fast

   faster

6. comparative form of festive

   more festive*

7. superlative form of dirty

   dirtiest

8. superlative form of marvelous

   most marvelous*

9. comparative form of generous

   more generous*

10. superlative form of bad

    worst

*Less for comparative form and least for superlative form should also be accepted.

Name________________________________

Date________________________________

ADJECTIVES

Degrees of Adjectives

Directions: Write the required comparative or superlative form of the given adjective in the space provided.

Example: superlative form of creative

____most creative____________

1. comparative form of red

    ____

2. superlative form of special

    ____

3. superlative form of sincere

    ____

4. comparative form of good

    ____

5. comparative form of fast

    ____

6. comparative form of festive

    ____

7. superlative form of dirty

    ____

8. superlative form of marvelous

    ____

9. comparative form of generous

    ____

10. superlative form of bad

    ____

Name________________________________ **ADJECTIVES**
WORKBOOK PAGE 168 Degrees of Adjectives
Date________________________________

Directions: Choose the correct adjective in each sentence.
Answers are in boldfaced print.

Example: Rene is the (faster, **fastest**) runner in our class.

1. This sandwich is (**more delicious**, most delicious) than that one.
2. Of the triplets, Peter is (smaller, **smallest**).
3. Olivia's hair is (**curlier**, curliest) than when she was a baby.
4. This is the (more dangerous, **most dangerous**) road I have ever driven on.
5. Lois is a (gooder, **better**) mechanic than I.
6. That hill is the (taller, **tallest**) one of the three.
7. This is the (more fantastic, **most fantastic**) book of the twenty that I have read this year.
8. Of all the circus acts, the dog jumping was (sillier, **silliest**).
9. Both rings are lovely, but I think the larger one is (**more attractive**, most attractive).
10. My new car is (**more powerful**, most powerful) than my old one.
11. She is the (luckier, **luckiest**) person I know.
12. I think that this puppy is the (more loveable, **most loveable**) one of the entire litter.
13. The mush ball is (**softer**, softest) than the large, black ball.
14. This is the (baddest, **worst**) show I have ever seen.
15. Which one of the twins is (**more sensitive**, most sensitive)?

Name________________________________

Date________________________________

ADJECTIVES

Degrees of Adjectives

Directions: Choose the correct adjective in each sentence.

Example: Rene is the (faster, **fastest**) runner in our class.

1. This sandwich is (more delicious, most delicious) than that one.
2. Of the triplets, Peter is (smaller, smallest).
3. Olivia's hair is (curlier, curliest) than when she was a baby.
4. This is the (more dangerous, most dangerous) road I have ever driven on.
5. Lois is a (gooder, better) mechanic than I.
6. That hill is the (taller, tallest) one of the three.
7. This is the (more fantastic, most fantastic) book of the twenty that I have read this year.
8. Of all the circus acts, the dog jumping was (sillier, silliest).
9. Both rings are lovely, but I think the larger one is (more attractive, most attractive).
10. My new car is (more powerful, most powerful) than my old one.
11. She is the (luckier, luckiest) person I know.
12. I think that this puppy is the (more loveable, most loveable) one of the entire litter.
13. The mush ball is (softer, softest) than the large, black ball.
14. This is the (baddest, worst) show I have ever seen.
15. Which one of the twins is (more sensitive, most sensitive)?

Name________________________________

WORKBOOK PAGE 169

Date________________________________

ADJECTIVES

Degrees of Adjectives

Directions: Choose the correct adjective form in each sentence.
Answers are in boldfaced print.

1. This day is (funner, **more fun**) than yesterday.
2. Of the two paintings, I like this one (**better**, best).
3. Which train, the Slimton Express or the Apache Racer, is (**faster**, fastest)?
4. Our new house is (**larger**, largest) than our old one.
5. Of our three dogs, that one is (more gentle, **most gentle**).
6. I think that red is (brighter, **brightest**) of the colors in a rainbow.
7. This math problem is (**more difficult**, most difficult) than the one before it.
8. You are the (nicer, **nicest**) person I know.
9. Are the bananas or the grapes (**tastier**, tastiest)?
10. This is the (more interesting, **most interesting**) flower in the exotic flower show.
11. Chuck is (livelier, **liveliest**) of the four brothers.
12. Your photograph looks (**more natural**, most natural) than mine.
13. Of all the pancakes, this blueberry one is (rounder, **roundest**).
14. Your hair is (**curlier**, curliest) than Krista's.
15. This is the (taller, **tallest**) building in the city.

Name________________________________

Date________________________________

ADJECTIVES
Degrees of Adjectives

Directions: Choose the correct adjective form in each sentence.

1. This day is (funner, more fun) than yesterday.
2. Of the two paintings, I like this one (better, best).
3. Which train, the Slimton Express or the Apache Racer, is (faster, fastest)?
4. Our new house is (larger, largest) than our old one.
5. Of our three dogs, that one is (more gentle, most gentle).
6. I think that red is (brighter, brightest) of the colors in a rainbow.
7. This math problem is (more difficult, most difficult) than the one before it.
8. You are the (nicer, nicest) person I know.
9. Are the bananas or the grapes (tastier, tastiest)?
10. This is the (more interesting, most interesting) flower in the exotic flower show.
11. Chuck is (livelier, liveliest) of the four brothers.
12. Your photograph looks (more natural, most natural) than mine.
13. Of all the pancakes, this blueberry one is (rounder, roundest).
14. Your hair is (curlier, curliest) than Krista's.
15. This is the (taller, tallest) building in the city.

Name_______________________________ **ADJECTIVE REVIEW**

WORKBOOK PAGE 170

Date_______________________________

A. **Limiting Adjectives:**

Directions: Fill in the blank.

1. The three limiting adjectives that are also called articles are **a**, **an**, and **the**.
2. Four demonstrative words that may serve as limiting adjectives are **this**, **that**, **those**, and **these**.
3. The possessive pronouns that may serve as limiting adjectives are **my**, **his**, **her**, **your**, **its**, **our**, and **their**.
4. Four examples of indefinites that may serve as limiting adjectives are **no, any, some, few, many, several, etc.**
5. Write an example showing a number used as a limiting adjective: **one dog, etc.**
6. Write an example showing a possessive noun serving as a limiting adjective: **Answers will vary. Representative answers: Dee's bike / girls' room**

B. **Limiting Adjective or Pronoun?**

Directions: Write A in the space provided if the boldfaced word serves as an adjective; write P if the boldfaced word serves as a pronoun (stands alone). After the sentence, write the limiting adjective and the noun it modifies. (The line after any sentence marked P will be blank .)

Example: A **My** room is clean. My room

P I like **that**! ____________

1. A They spent **five** dollars for a ticket. five dollars
2. P **Five** must agree to help. ____________
3. P **Several** watched shoppers pass by. ____________
4. A **Several** babies began to cry. Several babies
5. P I would like **those** with bows. ____________
6. A Please hand me **those** magazines. those magazines

Name________________________________ **ADJECTIVE REVIEW**

Date________________________________

A. **Limiting Adjectives:**

Directions: Fill in the blank.

1. The three limiting adjectives that are also called articles are ____, ____, and ____.

2. Four demonstrative words that may serve as limiting adjectives are __________, __________, __________, and __________.

3. The possessive pronouns that may serve as limiting adjectives are ________, ________, ________, ________, ________, ________, and ________.

4. Four examples of indefinites that may serve as limiting adjectives are __________, __________, __________, and __________.

5. Write an example showing a number used as a limiting adjective:____________.

6. Write an example showing a possessive noun serving as a limiting adjective: ____
____

B. **Limiting Adjective or Pronoun?**

Directions: Write A in the space provided if the boldfaced word serves as an adjective; write P if the boldfaced word serves as a pronoun (stands alone). After the sentence, write the limiting adjective and the noun it modifies. (The line after any sentence marked P will be blank .)

Example: __A__ **My** room is clean. ____My room____________

__P__ I like **that**! ______________________

1. _____ They spent **five** dollars fór a ticket. ______________________
2. _____ **Five** must agree to help. ______________________
3. _____ **Several** watched shoppers pass by. ______________________
4. _____ **Several** babies began to cry. ______________________
5. _____ I would like **those** with bows. ______________________
6. _____ Please hand me **those** magazines. ______________________

Name________________________________ **ADJECTIVE REVIEW**

WORKBOOK PAGE 171

Date________________________________

C. **Descriptive Adjectives:**

Directions: Write three descriptive adjectives for each noun.

Answers will vary. Representative answers.

1. ball - round, red, spongy,
2. room - clean, messy, huge
3. woman - pretty, intelligent, happy
4. day - busy, gloomy, sensational

D. **Predicate Adjectives:**

Directions: Cross out any prepositional phrases. Underline the subject once and the verb/verb phrase twice. Label any predicate adjective-P.A. On the line, write the predicate adjective and the noun it modifies.

1. A few winter storms had been fierce. (P.A.) — fierce storms
2. A customer seemed angry ~~about the service~~. (P.A.) — angry customer
3. That fire drill bell sounds shrill. (P.A.) — shrill bell
4. The young lady is excited ~~about her new job~~. (P.A.) — excited lady
5. ~~At the end of the day~~, he grows very weary. (P.A.) — weary (man) he

E. **Proper Adjectives:**

Directions: Underline any proper adjective and capitalize it. In the space provided, write the proper adjective and the noun it modifies.

1. A spanish (S) village is very charming. — Spanish village
2. John was born in a chicago (C) suburb. — Chicago suburb
3. Do you have a sears (S) catalog? — Sears catalog
4. Kendra likes swedish (S) meatballs. — Swedish meatballs
5. Have you seen a franklin (F) stove? — Franklin stove

Name________________________________

Date________________________________

ADJECTIVE REVIEW

C. **Descriptive Adjectives:**

Directions: Write three descriptive adjectives for each noun.

1. ball - ____

2. room - ____

3. woman - ____

4. day - ____

D. **Predicate Adjectives:**

Directions: Cross out any prepositional phrases. Underline the subject once and the verb/verb phrase twice. Label any predicate adjective-P.A. On the line, write the predicate adjective and the noun it modifies.

1. A few winter storms had been fierce. ______________________

2. A customer seemed angry about the service. ______________________

3. That fire drill bell sounds shrill. ______________________

4. The young lady is excited about her new job. ______________________

5. At the end of the day, he grows very weary. ______________________

E. **Proper Adjectives:**

Directions: Underline any proper adjective and capitalize it. In the space provided, write the proper adjective and the noun it modifies.

1. A spanish village is very charming. ______________________________

2. John was born in a chicago suburb. ______________________________

3. Do you have a sears catalog? ______________________________

4. Kendra likes swedish meatballs. ______________________________

5. Have you seen a franklin stove? ______________________________

Name________________________________ **ADJECTIVE REVIEW**

WORKBOOK PAGE 172

Date________________________________

Answers are in boldface.

F. **Degrees:**

Directions: Circle the correct adjective form.

1. The red petunia is (**healthier**, healthiest) than the pink one.
2. This small yellow car is the (cheaper, **cheapest**) one on the entire lot.
3. The polka is a (**livelier**, liveliest) dance than the rumba.
4. Of all the days last week, Saturday was the (gloomier, **gloomiest**).
5. This glass vase looks (**more fragile**, most fragile) than the ceramic one.
6. Mrs. Jones's new car is (**longer**, longest) than her old one.
7. That man is (**friendliest**, friendlier) in the neighborhood.
8. Julio is the (more creative, **most creative**) triplet.

G. **Adjective Identification:**

Directions: Circle any adjectives.

Suggestion: First, look for limiting adjective(s). Then, reread the sentence and circle any adjective(s) that describe.

1. **Molly's** dress had **a plain** top and **a lovely flowered** skirt.
2. **The dental** technician gave **the happy** child **a funny** sticker and **a sugarless** candy.
3. **Several** cows grazed in **the lush green** meadow behind **a large** barn.
4. **His recent** speech discussed **the city's** plan for **crime** control.
5. Gloria spoke to **her younger** brother about **the three** snakes in **his** room.
6. **An** argument between **the two angry** boys was settled by **their wise** mother.
7. **Many** pioneers traveled by **covered** wagon on **these marked** trails.

Name________________________________ **ADJECTIVE REVIEW**

Date________________________________

F. **Degrees:**

Directions: Circle the correct adjective form.

1. The red petunia is (healthier, healthiest) than the pink one.
2. This small yellow car is the (cheaper, cheapest) one on the entire lot.
3. The polka is a (livelier, liveliest) dance than the rumba.
4. Of all the days last week, Saturday was the (gloomier, gloomiest).
5. This glass vase looks (more fragile, most fragile) than the ceramic one.
6. Mrs. Jones's new car is (longer, longest) than her old one.
7. That man is (friendliest, friendlier) in the neighborhood.
8. Julio is the (more creative, most creative) triplet.

G. **Adjective Identification:**

Directions: Circle any adjectives.

Suggestion: First, look for limiting adjective(s). Then, reread the sentence and circle any adjective(s) that describe.

1. Molly's dress had a plain top and a lovely flowered skirt.
2. The dental technician gave the happy child a funny sticker and a sugarless candy.
3. Several cows grazed in the lush green meadow behind a large barn.
4. His recent speech discussed the city's plan for crime control.
5. Gloria spoke to her younger brother about the three snakes in his room.
6. An argument between the two angry boys was settled by their wise mother.
7. Many pioneers traveled by covered wagon on these marked trails.

Name________________________________ **ADJECTIVE TEST**

Date________________________________

A. Directions: Write the proper adjective and the noun it modifies in the space provided.

1. Have you been to a maryland beach? — **Maryland** beach
2. Aren wants a horizon television. — **Horizon** television
3. Do you like mooby chocolate milk? — **Mooby** chocolate milk
4. A platter of french toast was served. — **French** toast
5. "I enjoy mexican food," said Miguel. — **Mexican** food
6. Cameo's choir is planning a European tour. — **European** tour
7. Some hawaiian sunsets are colorful. — **Hawaiian** sunsets

B. Directions: Write the predicate adjective and the noun it modifies in the space provided. If there is no predicate adjective in the sentence, write none on the line.

1. The head nurse appears upset. — **upset** nurse
2. Your antique quilt looks new. — **new** quilt
3. These stones feel sharp to my feet. — **sharp** stones
4. Her gift was a beautiful red shawl. — none
5. The girl remained calm during her speech. — **calm** girl
6. This lemon pie tastes quite tangy. — **tangy** pie
7. The picnickers remained in a quiet spot. — none
8. A worker grew tired in the midday heat. — **tired** worker

Name_______________________________ **ADJECTIVE TEST**

Date_______________________________

A. Directions: Write the proper adjective and the noun it modifies in the space provided.

1. Have you been to a maryland beach? _______________________________
2. Aren wants a horizon television. _______________________________
3. Do you like mooby chocolate milk? _______________________________
4. A platter of french toast was served. _______________________________
5. "I enjoy mexican food," said Miguel. _______________________________
6. Cameo's choir is planning a european tour._______________________________
7. Some hawaiian sunsets are colorful. _______________________________

B. Directions: Write the predicate adjective and the noun it modifies in the space provided. If there is no predicate adjective in the sentence, write <u>none</u> on the line.

1. The head nurse appears upset. _______________________________
2. Your antique quilt looks new. _______________________________
3. These stones feel sharp to my feet. _______________________________
4. Her gift was a beautiful red shawl. _______________________________
5. The girl remained calm during her speech. _______________________________
6. This lemon pie tastes quite tangy. _______________________________
7. The picnickers remained in a quiet spot. _______________________________
8. A worker grew tired in the midday heat. _______________________________

C. Choose the correct adjective form.

Answers are in boldfaced print.

1. Mt. Everest is (**taller**, tallest) than Mt. Fuji.
2. Is Lake Superior the (deeper, **deepest**) lake in the world?
3. Austrid is the (more intelligent, **most intelligent**) person I know.
4. Was your rafting trip the (more daring, **most daring**) one you've ever taken?
5. Mrs. Parks is the (**nicer**, nicest) of the two helpers.
6. Which of these three worms is (longer, **longest**)?
7. The wedding cake chosen by Cynthia was (**larger**, largest) than the one selected by her fiance.

D. Directions: Circle any adjectives. **Answers are in boldfaced print.**

Suggestion: Read each sentence carefully. Circle any limiting adjectives. Then, circle any descriptive adjectives.

1. **Two warm bran** muffins and **orange** juice were part of **the appetizing** breakfast.
2. **This tall street** light with **pink frosted** panes serves as **an easy** landmark.
3. Has **Jerome's great** uncle visited **the covered** bridges of **the New England** states?
4. **A cream-filled chocolate** eclair with **whipped cream** topping was **the main** dessert.
5. **Sarah's youngest** son had ridden **his mountain** bike on **that spring** outing.
6. **Several small** children were petting **a few comical, fluffy** puppies.
7. These were **the warmest leather** boots in **the entire shoe** store.
8. **An American** flag was flying at **their local post** office.
9. **Our favorite** restaurant is **a Chinese** one in **lower** Manhattan.
10. **Many flowering cherry** trees bloom **each** year in **our nation's** capital.

C. Directions: Choose the correct adjective form.

1. Mt. Everest is (taller, tallest) than Mt. Fuji.
2. Is Lake Superior the (deeper, deepest) lake in the world?
3. Austrid is the (more intelligent, most intelligent) person I know.
4. Was your rafting trip the (more daring, most daring) one you've ever taken?
5. Mrs. Parks is the (nicer, nicest) of the two helpers.
6. Which of these three worms is (longer, longest)?
7. The wedding cake chosen by Cynthia was (larger, largest) than the one selected by her fiance.

D. Directions: Circle any adjectives.

Suggestion: Read each sentence carefully. Circle any limiting adjectives. Then, circle any descriptive adjectives.

1. Two warm bran muffins and orange juice were part of the appetizing breakfast.
2. This tall street light with pink frosted panes serves as an easy landmark.
3. Has Jerome's great uncle visited the covered bridges of the New England states?
4. A cream-filled chocolate eclair with whipped cream topping was the main dessert.
5. Sarah's youngest son had ridden his mountain bike on that spring outing.
6. Several small children were petting a few comical, fluffy puppies.
7. These were the warmest leather boots in the entire shoe store.
8. An American flag was flying at their local post office.
9. Our favorite restaurant is a Chinese one in lower Manhattan.
10. Many flowering cherry trees bloom each year in our nation's capital.

Name________________________________

WORKBOOK PAGE 173

Date_________________________________

CUMULATIVE REVIEW

Adjective Unit

A. Directions: Cross out any prepositional phrases. Underline the subject once and the verb/verb phrase twice. Label any predicate nominative - P.N. Write the proof in the space provided.

P.N.

1. The admission price was one dollar ~~for children under twelve~~.

Proof: One dollar was the admission price.

P.N.

2. Janice's best friend is my sister.

Proof: My sister is Janice's best friend.

P.N.

3. Daffodils have become Miss Hine's favorite flowers.

Proof: Miss Hine's favorite flowers are (have become) daffodils.

B. Directions: Write N if the boldfaced word serves as a noun; write V if the boldfaced word serves as a verb.

1. V Does the toddler **dress** himself.
2. N The checkered **dress** has a red scarf.
3. V Farmer Mills **plows** his field each spring.
4. N Those antique **plows** are made of iron.

C. Directions: Write the past participle form.

1. to teach - (had) taught
2. to swim - (had) swum
3. to burst - (had) burst
4. to beat - (had) beaten
5. to freeze - (had) frozen
6. to be - (had) been
7. to ride - (had) ridden
8. to bring - (had) brought
9. to fly - (had) flown
10. to spring - (had) sprung

Name_______________________________

Date_______________________________

CUMULATIVE REVIEW
Adjective Unit

A. Directions: Cross out any prepositional phrases. Underline the subject once and the verb/verb phrase twice. Label any predicate nominative-PN Write the proof in the space provided.

1. The admission price was one dollar for children under twelve.

   Proof: _______________________________

2. Janice's best friend is my sister.

   Proof: _______________________________

3. Daffodils have become Miss Hine's favorite flowers.

   Proof: _______________________________

B. Directions: Write N if the boldfaced word serves as a noun; write V if the boldfaced word serves as a verb.

1. ______ Does the toddler **dress** himself?

2. ______ The checkered **dress** has a red scarf.

3. ______ Farmer Mills **plows** his field each spring.

4. ______ Those antique **plows** are made of iron.

C. Directions: Write the past participle form.

1. to teach - ____________________
2. to swim - ____________________
3. to burst - ____________________
4. to beat - ____________________
5. to freeze - ____________________
6. to be - ____________________
7. to ride - ____________________
8. to bring - ____________________
9. to fly - ____________________
10. to spring - ____________________

D. Directions: Write the possessive:

WORKBOOK PAGE 174

1. a comb belonging to Mary: **Mary's** comb
2. streets in a city: **city's** street
3. a trail for motor scooters: **scooters'** trail
4. a sandbox belonging to more than one child: **children's** sandbox

E. Directions: Write the contraction:

1. will not - won't
2. I would - I'd
3. I am - I'm
4. are not - aren't
5. does not - doesn't
6. we are - we're

F. Directions: Cross out any prepositional phrases. Underline the subject once and the verb twice. In the space provided, write **A** if the verb is action; write **L** if the verb is linking.

Suggestion: To help determine if the verb is linking, place *is, am, are, was,* or *were* above each verb.

1. A He always **tastes** his vegetables first.
2. A (You) Please **remain** ~~by the doors~~.
3. A Fertilizer has been **placed** ~~on the plants~~.
4. L Her eyes **grow** irritated ~~from pollen in the air~~.

G. Directions: Write the plural of the following nouns.

Students may have an occasional different spelling. Ask to see the dictionary used.

1. spoonful - spoonfuls
2. dairy - dairies
3. hero - heroes
4. elk - elk
5. flash - flashes
6. father-in-law - fathers-in-law
7. mouse - mice
8. leaf - leaves
9. spoof - spoofs
10. iris - irises

D. Directions: Write the possessive:

1. a comb belonging to Mary: ______________________________

2. streets in a city: ______________________________

3. a trail for motor scooters: ______________________________

4. a sandbox belonging to more than one child: ______________________

E. Directions: Write the contraction:

1. will not - ____________ 3. I am - ____________ 5. does not -____________

2. I would - ____________ 4. are not - ____________ 6. we are - ____________

F. Directions: Cross out any prepositional phrases. Underline the subject once and the verb/verb phrase twice. Write A if the boldfaced verb serves as an action verb; write L if the boldfaced verb serves as a linking verb.

Suggestion: To help determine if the verb is linking, place *is*, *am*, *are*, *was*, or *were* above each verb.

1. ______ He always **tastes** his vegetables first.

2. ______ Please **remain** by the doors.

3. ______ Fertilizer has been **placed** on the plants.

4. ______ Her eyes **grow** irritated from pollen in the air.

G. Directions: Write the plural of the following nouns. (Use a dictionary if necessary.)

1. spoonful - ____________________ 6. father-in-law - ____________________

2. dairy - ____________________ 7. mouse - ____________________

3. hero - ____________________ 8. leaf - ____________________

4. elk - ____________________ 9. spoof - ____________________

5. flash - ____________________ 10. iris - ____________________

H. Directions: Cross out any prepositional phrases. Underline the subject once and the verb/verb phrase twice.

WORKBOOK PAGE 175

1. The baby's rattle is (lying, laying) ~~beside the crib~~.
2. Bob (lay, laid) his head ~~on a pillow~~.
3. (You)(Rise, Raise) ~~for the singing of "The Star Spangled Banner"~~.
4. The fishermen are (sitting, setting) their tackle ~~along the river's banks~~.
5. Have you ever (set, sat) ~~among the pigeons in the park~~?

I. Directions: Write A if the boldfaced word serves as a limiting adjective and *No* if the boldfaced word does not serve as a limiting adjective.

1. __No__ **Several** have been spotted near the woods.
2. __A__ **Several** advertisements appeared in the newspaper.
3. __No__ You must try **those** sometime.
4. __A__ Have you ever tried **those** salads in bags?
5. __A__ Harriet has been given **twenty** bulbs to plant.
6. __A__ **Our** minister is also an author.
7. __No__ Is **this** yours?

J. Directions: Write any limiting adjective and the noun it modifies (goes to) in the space provided.

1. __Their duties__ Their duties include raising money for zoos.
2. __some fudge__ Were you planning on making some fudge?
3. __Karen's mother__ Last June, Karen's mother was ill.
4. __A game__ A final game was played on Saturday.

K. Directions: Write C if the word is concrete; write A if the word is abstract.

1. __A__ glory 2. __A__ sorrow 3. __C__ field 4. __C__ pole 5. __A__ fun

H. Directions: Cross out any prepositional phrases. Underline the subject once and the verb/verb phrase twice.

1. The baby's rattle is (lying, laying) beside the crib.

2. Bob (lay, laid) his head on a pillow.

3. (Rise, Raise) for the singing of "The Star-Spangled Banner".

4. The fishermen are (sitting, setting) their tackle along the river's banks.

5. Have you ever (set, sat) among the pigeons in the park?

I. Directions: Write A if the boldfaced word serves as a limiting adjective and *No* if the boldfaced word does not serve as a limiting adjective.

1. ______ **Several** have been spotted near the woods.

2. ______ **Several** advertisements appeared in the newspaper.

3. ______ You must try **those** sometime.

4. ______ Have you ever tried **those** salads in bags?

5. ______ Harriet has been given **twenty** bulbs to plant.

6. ______ **Our** minister is also an author.

7. ______ Is **this** yours?

J. Directions: Write any limiting adjective and the noun it modifies (goes to) in the space provided.

1. ______________________________ Their duties include raising money for zoos

2. ______________________________ Were you planning on making some fudge?

3. ______________________________ Last June, Karen's mother was ill.

4. ______________________________ A final game was played on Saturday.

K. Directions: Write C if the word is concrete; write A if the word is abstract.

1. _____ glory 2. _____ sorrow 3. _____ field 4. _____ pole 5. _____ fun

L. Directions: Circle any adjectives.
WORKBOOK PAGE 176
Answers are in boldfaced print.
Suggestion: First, identify limiting adjectives. Then, look for descriptive adjectives.

1. **An eager** girl jumped up and down with **great** enthusiasm.
2. **Few** deer live in **the wooded** area near **that frozen** lake.
3. Those are **his favorite chocolate chip** cookies.
4. **Our front** yard has **several** trees and **a** bed of **tiny purple** flowers.
5. **Small** brushes and **three** gallons of **dark latex** paint had been placed on **the** bench by **a house** painter.

M. Directions: Go back to part L. Write any noun(s) on the line provided.

Suggestion: Use limiting and descriptive adjectives to help locate nouns.

Sentence 1: girl, enthusiasm
Sentence 2: deer, area, lake
Sentence 3: cookies
Sentence 4: yard, trees, bed, flowers
Sentence 5: brushes, gallons, paint, bench, painter

N. Directions: Cross out any prepositional phrases. Underline the subject once and the verb/verb phrase twice. In the space provided, write the tense: *present, past, future, present perfect, past perfect, future perfect, present progressive, past progressive,* or *future progressive.*

1. present perfect — The mechanic has repaired the motorcycle.
2. present — Peter usually sleeps ~~under a fan~~.
3. past — ~~During a break~~, Kay went outside ~~for fresh air~~.
4. present progressive — A damp cloth is lying ~~by the washed car~~.
5. future — I shall put this ~~into my pocket~~.

L. Directions: Circle any adjectives.

Suggestion: First, identify limiting adjectives. Then, look for descriptive adjectives.

1. An eager girl jumped up and down with great enthusiasm.
2. Few deer live in the wooded area near that frozen lake.
3. Those are his favorite chocolate chip cookies.
4. Our front yard has several trees and a bed of tiny purple flowers.
5. Small brushes and three gallons of dark latex paint had been placed on the bench by a house painter.

M. Directions: Go back to part L. Write any noun(s) on the line provided.

Suggestion: Use limiting and descriptive adjectives to help locate nouns.

Sentence 1: ____

Sentence 2: ____

Sentence 3: ____

Sentence 4: ____

Sentence 5: ____

N. Directions: Cross out any prepositional phrases. Underline the subject once and the verb/verb phrase twice. In the space provided, write the tense: *present, past, future, present perfect, past perfect, future perfect, present progressive, past progressive*, or *future progressive*.

1. ______________________ The mechanic has repaired the motorcycle.
2. ______________________ Peter usually sleeps under a fan.
3. ______________________ During a break, Kay went outside for fresh air.
4. ______________________ A damp cloth is lying by the washed car.
5. ______________________ I shall put this into my pocket.

O. Directions: Write the correct form.
WORKBOOK PAGE 177

1. comparative of strong: **stronger**
2. superlative of fine: **finest**
3. comparative of horrible: **more horrible**
4. comparative of good: **better**
5. superlative of fantastic: **most fantastic**

P. Directions: Underline the entire noun appositive (phrase) in each sentence.
Remember: A phrase is a group of words.

1. We called to Corky, our dog.
2. Her friends, Martin and Beth, will be going to the fair.
3. Would you like this dessert, a hot fudge sundae?
4. The winner, the man in the blue sweater, smiled shyly.

Q. Directions: Circle the verb that agrees with the subject.
Answers are in boldfaced print.

1. Several plumbers (is, **are**) planning to work on that building.
2. One of the twirlers (bring, **brings**) her own music.
3. Mrs. Cole and her daughter (**buy**, buys) generic brands.
4. Mom and my brother (**go**, goes) hiking often.
5. Everyone of the boys (**was**, were) attentive.

R. Fill in the blank.

1. **A stomata is an opening in a plant.** The word, ***plant***, is a noun. It serves as the object of the preposition.
2. **His uncle is an Alaskan businessman.** The word, ***Alaskan***, is what type of an adjective? proper adjective
3. **You might be elected the next treasurer of the club.** The verb phrase of this sentence is might be elected. The main verb is elected.
4. **That bat is very old.** Is the word, ***old***, a predicate nominative or a predicate adjective? predicate adjective
5. An example of an interjection is (Answers will vary. Representative answers: Wow! Yeah! Good Grief!.
6. What are the three coordinating conjunctions? and, but, or.

O. Directions: Write the correct form.

1. comparative of strong: ________________________________

2. superlative of fine: ________________________________

3. comparative of horrible: ________________________________

4. comparative of good: ________________________________

5. superlative of fantastic: ________________________________

P. Directions: Underline the entire noun appositive (phrase) in each sentence.
Remember: A phrase is a group of words.

1. We called to Corky, our dog.
2. Her friends, Martin and Beth, will be going to the fair.
3. Would you like this dessert, a hot fudge sundae?
4. The winner, the man in the blue sweater, smiled shyly.

Q. Directions: Circle the verb that agrees with the subject.

1. Several plumbers (is, are) planning to work on that building.
2. One of the twirlers (bring, brings) her own music.
3. Mrs. Cole and her daughter (buy, buys) generic brands.
4. Mom and my brother (go, goes) hiking often.
5. Everyone of the boys (was, were) attentive.

R. Fill in the blank.

1. **A stomata is an opening in a plant.** The word, ***plant***, is a noun. It serves as the ________________ of the preposition.
2. **His uncle is an Alaskan businessman.** The word, ***Alaskan***, is what type of an adjective? ________________
3. **You might be elected the next treasurer of the club**. The verb phrase of this sentence is ________________. The main verb is ________________.
4. **That bat is very old.** Is the word, ***old***, a predicate nominative or a predicate adjective? ________________
5. An example of an interjection is ________________.
6. What are the three coordinating conjunctions?________, ________, ________.

Name________________________________

Date________________________________

CUMULATIVE TEST
Adjective Unit

A. Directions: Fill in the blank.
Answers may vary. Representative answers:

1. An example of an abstract noun is __truth, love, patience__.
2. An example of a common noun is __house, milk, bird__.
3. An example of an interjection is __Wow! Yeah! Good grief!__.
4. An example of a proper adjective is __Chinese (food), Ford (car)__.
5. A word that ends a prepositional phrase is called an __object__.

B. Directions: Write the plural of the following nouns.

1. cinch - **cinches**
2. fungus - **fungi***
3. paste - **pastes**
4. burglar - **burglars**
5. grocery - **groceries**
6. starfish - **starfish***
7. buoy - **buoys**
8. ox - **oxen**
9. sister-in-law - **sisters-in-law**

* This is the first plural listing in the dictionary.; therefore, it is the more acceptable plural form.

C. Directions: Write the contraction.

1. she is - __she's__
2. should not - __shouldn't__
3. cannot - __can't__
4. is not - __isn't__
5. you are - __you're__
6. had not - __hadn't__

D. Directions: Write A if the boldfaced word serves as an adjective; write N if the boldfaced word serves as a noun. Write V if the boldfaced word serves as a verb.

1. __A__ This **light** fixture is dirty.
2. __N__ Please turn on a **light**.
3. __V__ Please **light** the candles.
4. __V__ Janice **skates** on her neighbor's pond.
5. __N__ Place those **skates** in the closet.

Name________________________________

Date________________________________

CUMULATIVE TEST
Adjective Unit

A. Directions: Fill in the blank.

1. An example of an abstract noun is ____________________.

2. An example of a common noun is ________________________.

3. An example of an interjection is __________________________.

4. An example of a proper adjective is ________________________.

5. A word that ends a prepositional phrase is called an ____________________.

B. Directions: Write the plural of the following nouns.

1. cinch - __________ 4. burglar - __________ 7. buoy - ______________

2. fungus - _________ 5. grocery - __________ 8. ox - ________________

3. paste - __________ 6. starfish - __________ 9. sister-in-law - ________

C. Directions: Write the contraction.

1. she is - _____________ 3. cannot - ____________ 5. you are - __________

2. should not - _________ 4. is not - _____________ 6. had not - __________

D. Directions: Write A if the boldfaced word serves as an adjective; write N if the boldfaced word serves as a noun. Write V if the boldfaced word serves as a verb.

1. ______ This **light** fixture is dirty.
2. ______ Please turn on a **light**.
3. ______ Please **light** the candles.
4. ______ Janice **skates** on her neighbor's pond.
5. ______ Place those **skates** in the closet.

E. Directions: Write fifty prepositions.

1. about
2. above
3. across
4. after
5. against
6. along
7. amid
8. among
9. around
10. at
11. atop
12. before
13. behind
14. below
15. beneath
16. beside
17. between
18. beyond
19. but (meaning except)
20. by
21. concerning
22. down
23. during
24. except
25. for
26. from
27. in
28. inside
29. into
30. like
31. near
32. of
33. off
34. on
35. onto
36. out
37. outside
38. over
39. past
40. regarding
41. since
42. through
43. throughout
44. to
45. toward
46. under
47. underneath
48. until
49. up
50. upon
51. with
52. within
53. without

F. Directions: Cross out any prepositional phrases. Underline the subject once and the verb/verb phrase twice. Label any direct object - D.O.; label any indirect object - I.O.

D.O.

1. Everyone ~~of the girls on the softball team~~ must carry her own equipment.

2. Frank and his best friend will be going ~~to Baltimore and Annapolis in the spring~~.

I.O. **D.O.**

3. (You) Please give your mother this recipe ~~for hot cross buns~~.

4. ~~Throughout the year~~, several girls met ~~at Mrs. Polk's house~~ (to discuss) field day.

I.O. **D.O.**

5. Has your dentist given you information ~~about a new type of toothbrush~~?

E. Directions: Write fifty prepositions.

1. ____________	14. ____________	27. ____________	40. ____________
2. ____________	15. ____________	28. ____________	41. ____________
3. ____________	16. ____________	29. ____________	42. ____________
4. ____________	17. ____________	30. ____________	43. ____________
5. ____________	18. ____________	31. ____________	44. ____________
6. ____________	19. ____________	32. ____________	45. ____________
7. ____________	20. ____________	33. ____________	46. ____________
8. ____________	21. ____________	34. ____________	47. ____________
9. ____________	22. ____________	35. ____________	48. ____________
10. ____________	23. ____________	36. ____________	49. ____________
11. ____________	24. ____________	37. ____________	50. ____________
12. ____________	25. ____________	38. ____________	
13. ____________	26. ____________	39. ____________	

F. Directions: Cross out any prepositional phrases. Underline the subject once and the verb/verb phrase twice. Label any direct object - D.O.; label any indirect object - I.O.

1. Everyone of the girls on the softball team must carry her own equipment.
2. Frank and his best friend will be going to Baltimore and Annapolis in the spring.
3. Please give your mother this recipe for hot cross buns.
4. Throughout the year, several girls met at Mrs. Polk's house to discuss field day.
5. Has your dentist given you information about a new type of toothbrush?

G. Directions: Write the correct verb form in the space provided.

1. Has the group **chosen** its leader?
2. The dishes must be **done** soon.
3. Her toes have **sunk** into the mud.
4. The tardy bell had **rung**.
5. You should have **seen** the look on his face.
6. We were **given** several mush balls.
7. Have you ever **drunk** mineral water?
8. Campaign posters were **taken** down immediately after the election.
9. Jack has **brought** along his dog.
10. Whitney had **parted** her hair in the middle.

H. Directions: Circle the correct possessive:
Answers are in boldfaced print.

1. Several (lady's, **ladies'**) hats were on sale.
2. The (**children's**, childrens') playground is rather small.
3. One (**boy's**, boys') picture had been hung on the wall.
4. An award was presented to the (**city's**, citys') mayor.
5. Some (wasp's, **wasps'**) hives were in a palm tree.

I. Directions: Circle any adjectives.
Answers are in boldfaced print.

Suggestion: First, circle any limiting adjective(s) in a sentence. Then, circle any descriptive adjective(s).

1. **That** triangle has **three equal** sides.
2. **A few** dogs with **pretty** bows on **their** ears left **the groomer's work** area.
3. **Sixteen** tourists rode **a double-decker** bus through **several London** streets.
4. **A small, furry** animal darted in front of **their speeding** car.

G. Directions: Write the correct verb form in the space provided.

(to choose) 1. Has the group ______________ its leader?

(to do) 2. The dishes must be ______________ soon.

(to sink) 3. Her toes have ______________ into the mud.

(to ring) 4. The tardy bell had ______________.

(to see) 5. You should have ______________ the look on his face.

(to give) 6. We were ______________ several mush balls.

(to drink) 7. Have you ever ______________ mineral water?

(to take) 8. Campaign posters were ______________ down immediately after the election.

(to bring) 9. Jack has ______________ along his dog.

(to part) 10. Whitney had ______________ her hair in the middle.

H. Directions: Circle the correct possessive:

1. Several (lady's, ladies') hats were on sale.
2. The (children's, childrens') playground is rather small.
3. One (boy's, boys') picture had been hung on the wall.
4. An award was presented to the (city's, citys') mayor.
5. Some (wasp's, wasps') hives were in a palm tree.

I. Directions: Circle any adjectives.

Suggestion: First, circle any limiting adjective(s) in a sentence. Then, circle any descriptive adjective(s).

1. That triangle has three equal sides.
2. A few dogs with pretty bows on their ears left the groomer's work area.
3. Sixteen tourists rode a double-decker bus through several London streets.
4. A small, furry animal darted in front of their speeding car.

J. Directions: Write the tense of the verb in the space provided.
Answers are in boldfaced print.

1. This hamster **eats** very little.
2. We **will fly** a kite on a windy day.
3. Jonah **had learned** to crawl early.
4. Nelly **is going** to a gym.

K. Directions: Box any nouns.
Nouns will be in boldfaced print. (Limiting adjectives have been italicized.)
Suggestion: Identifying adjectives helps to locate most nouns.

1. *An* unusual **computer** is sitting on *a* card **table** in *the* **middle** of *their* **kitchen**.
2. In most **cases**, *that* **attorney** speaks to *his* new **client** in *a* private **office**.
3. In **Germany**, *my* **father** and I visited *one* **castle**, *several* **vineyards**, and *a* **lake**.
4. Will you help **Mr. Kirk** with *this* **bushel** of **apples** and *those* **sacks** of **potatoes**?

L. Directions: Write APP. if the boldfaced noun serves as an appositive, D.O. if the boldfaced word serves as a direct object, and PN if the boldfaced word serves as a predicate nominative.

1. APP. I have lost a coin, a **dime**.
2. PN The winner of a free basket of goodies is **Mrs. Larkins**.
3. D.O. Throughout the day, the dog chewed his new **bone**.
4. D.O. Give Jason a **copy** of that advertisement.

M. Directions: Circle the correct verb.
Answers are in boldfaced print.

1. Several chickens (**live**, lives) in that barn.
2. A customer (sat, **set**) her purse on the glass counter.
3. The child (**lay**, laid) on his stomach to watch television.
4. Benny's aunt and uncle (**work**, works) at a grocery store.
5. Neither my mother nor my sisters (**want**, wants) another cat.

J. Directions: Write the tense of the verb in the space provided.

(present of *to eat*) 1. This hamster _______________________ very little.

(future of *to fly*) 2. We _______________________ a kite on a windy day.

(past perfect of *to learn*) 3. Jonah _______________________ early.

(present progressive of *to go*) 4. Nelly _______________________ to a gym.

K. Directions: Box any nouns.

Suggestion: Identifying adjectives helps to locate most nouns.

1. An unusual computer is sitting on a card table in the middle of their kitchen.
2. In most cases, that attorney speaks to his new client in a private office.
3. In Germany, my father and I visited one castle, several vineyards, and a lake.
4. Will you help Mr. Kirk with this bushel of apples and those sacks of potatoes?

L. Directions: Write APP. if the boldfaced noun serves as an appositive, D.O. if the boldfaced word serves as a direct object, and PN if the boldfaced word serves as a predicate nominative.

1. ______ I have lost a coin, a **dime**.
2. ______ The winner of a free basket of goodies is **Mrs. Larkins**.
3. ______ Throughout the day, the dog chewed his new **bone**.
4. ______ Give Jason a **copy** of that advertisement.

M. Directions: Circle the correct verb.

1. Several chickens (live, lives) in that barn.
2. A customer (sat, set) her purse on the glass counter.
3. The child (lay, laid) on his stomach to watch television.
4. Benny's aunt and uncle (work, works) at a grocery store.
5. Neither my mother nor my sisters (want, wants) another cat.

PAGE 373 = WORKBOOK PAGE 178

TYPES OF SENTENCES

There are four types of sentences:

Declarative (statement):	That barn is rustic.
Interrogative (question):	Where's the mop?
Imperative (command):	Take this.
Exclamatory (strong feeling):	This tastes terrible!

Both the **declarative** and the **imperative** sentence end with a period.

Declarative: The high chair is yellow.

Imperative: Please pass the butter.

An **interrogative** sentence ends with a question mark.

Interrogative: How old are these brass beds?

An **exclamatory** sentence ends with an exclamation mark.

Exclamatory: What a good time we had!

Note: In an interrogative sentence, the entire clause is a question.

Example: Who has decided to be chairperson of this committee?

A sentence will be **declarative**, and not interrogative, even if part of the sentence infers a question.

Examples: Mother asked if we could stay longer.

Jacob wants to know how long to cook a hard-boiled egg.

Name________________________________ **TYPES OF SENTENCES**

WORKBOOK PAGE 179

Date________________________________

Directions: Write the sentence type: imperative, declarative, interrogative, or exclamatory.

1. interrogative — What did you do last night?
2. declarative — Our pencil sharpener is broken.
3. exclamatory — I want off!
4. imperative — Sit up, please.
5. interrogative — Has the pest control person sprayed this house?
6. declarative — I think that our exercise machine needs heavier weights.
7. interrogative — Have you seen Gone with the Wind?
8. imperative — Be quiet.
9. exclamatory — Yippee! They won the championship!
10. declarative — Shadows in the room made the atmosphere very scary.
11. exclamatory — I lost my wallet!
12. declarative — Those letters were addressed to a king.
13. interrogative — When are the flying instructions offered?
14. declarative — Brandon wants to know how you're feeling.
15. exclamatory — How lovely you look, Miss Jones!
16. declarative — Dad asked us to take out our trash.

Name______________________________ **TYPES OF SENTENCES**

Date______________________________

Directions: Write the sentence type: imperative, declarative, interrogative, or exclamatory.

1. ______________________________ What did you do last night?
2. ______________________________ Our pencil sharpener is broken.
3. ______________________________ I want off!
4. ______________________________ Sit up, please.
5. ______________________________ Has the pest control person sprayed this house?
6. ______________________________ I think that our exercise machine needs heavier weights.
7. ______________________________ Have you seen Gone with the Wind?
8. ______________________________ Be quiet.
9. ______________________________ Yippee! They won the championship!
10. ______________________________ Shadows in the room made the atmosphere very scary.
11. ______________________________ I lost my wallet!
12. ______________________________ Those letters were addressed to a king.
13. ______________________________ When are the flying instructions offered?
14. ______________________________ Brandon wants to know how you're feeling.
15. ______________________________ How lovely you look, Miss Jones!
16. ______________________________ Dad asked us to take out our trash.

Name________________________________ **TYPES OF SENTENCES**
WORKBOOK PAGE 180
Date________________________________

Directions: Write the sentence type: imperative, declarative, interrogative, or exclamatory. **Include end punctuation.**

1. exclamatory — Hurrah! I made it!
2. imperative — Fill out this card.
3. interrogative — Does stress actually cause cavities?
4. declarative — The public library opens at ten o'clock.
5. exclamatory — How terrific you look in red!
6. exclamatory — Yikes! I knew this would happen!
7. interrogative — Do you have any idea what this item costs?
8. declarative — Your sister asked us to visit.
9. declarative — His turn is next.
10. declarative — Sharon asks strange questions in science class.
11. imperative — Move to the end of the line.
12. interrogative — May James and I discuss this matter with you in your office?
13. declarative — A small brown dog chased some sheep.
14. declarative — Melinda wants to know if she may go for pizza with us.
15. imperative — Please park your car over there.
16. declarative — The child often asks questions when his mother is reading to him.

Note: Some sentences may be interpreted differently. For example, *sentence #9* may be exclamatory with an exclamation point at the end. Accept reasonable answers.

Name________________________________

Date________________________________

TYPES OF SENTENCES

Directions: Write the sentence type: imperative, declarative, interrogative, or exclamatory. **Include end punctuation.**

1. ____________________ Hurrah! I made it
2. ____________________ Fill out this card
3. ____________________ Does stress actually cause cavities
4. ____________________ The public library opens at ten o'clock
5. ____________________ How terrific you look in red
6. ____________________ Yikes! I knew this would happen
7. ____________________ Do you have any idea what this item costs
8. ____________________ Your sister asked us to visit
9. ____________________ His turn is next
10. ____________________ Sharon asks strange questions in science class
11. ____________________ Move to the end of the line
12. ____________________ May James and I discuss this matter with you in your office
13. ____________________ A small brown dog chased some sheep
14. ____________________ Melinda wants to know if she may go for pizza with us
15. ____________________ Please park your car over there
16. ____________________ The child often asks questions when his mother is reading to him

PAGE 379 = WORKBOOK PAGE 181
PAGE 380 = WORKBOOK PAGE 182

SENTENCES
FRAGMENTS
RUN-ONS

RUN-ONS:

A. **A run-on may consist of two independent clauses run together.**

S V S V
This cookie tastes good I like that one better.

B. **A run-on may consist of two independent clauses joined by a comma.**

S V S V
My friend is Amie, she lives next door.

C. **A run-on may consist of a group of sentences combined with too many conjunctions.**

We went to the store and we bought some bananas and we talked to our neighbor who just returned from his vacation but we still had time to return home and make our favorite cake and then we went jogging.

D. **A run-on may consist of a group of sentences combined with commas.**

With winter approaching, I become more anxious about skiing, sledding is going to be fun too, I mostly like to ice skate on a frozen lake.

CORRECTING RUN-ONS:

In a run-on containing two independent clauses, there are three methods of correction.

1. **Use a period between the independent clauses.**

   This cookie tastes good. I like that one better.

2. **Use a semicolon between the independent clauses.**

   This cookie tastes good; I like that one better.

3. **Use a comma and an appropriate conjunction between the independent clauses.**

   This cookie tastes good, but I like that one better.

In addition, one of the independent clauses may be changed to a dependent clause.

Although this cookie tastes good, I like that one better.

SENTENCES
FRAGMENTS
RUN-ONS

SENTENCES:

Clauses:

A. An independent clause contains a subject and verb.
An independent clause expresses a complete thought.
An independent clause can stand alone as a sentence.

Independent Clause: I have a record player.

B. A dependent clause contains subject and verb.
A dependent clause does not express a complete thought.
A dependent clause cannot stand alone as a sentence.
A dependent clause without an independent clause is a fragment.

Dependent Clause: When you return from the game.

Fragments:

A. An unattached dependent clause is a fragment.

Whenever I am lonely.

B. A fragment sometimes contains a subject or verb.

The conductor during the performance.

Drew several pictures for us.

C. A fragment may contain neither subject nor verb.

Tomorrow.

In the bottom drawer.

From this point to that one.

D. A command is NOT a fragment. Some commands may be only one word, but the subject is (You) meaning *You Understood.*

(You) Go!

(You) Do it now.

SENTENCES
FRAGMENTS
RUN-ONS

Sentences, fragments, and run-ons can best be taught by drawing from examples in students' writings. Reproduce the actual fragments and run-ons, giving students a line on which to write the corrected version. This can be done as a separate assignment or in a class discussion.

Examples: Went swimming last summer.

____

They ran out the door, I followed them.

____

Past Joan's house.

____

Name____

WORKBOOK PAGE 183

Date____

SENTENCES
FRAGMENTS
RUN-ONS

Directions: In the space provided, write S for sentence, F for fragment, and R-O for run-on.

Example: R-O The milk is old, it's sour.

S 1. Please call me later.

F 2. Fine.

S 3. Who has won?

F 4. Disturbing the peace.

R-O 5. The plant is wilting, water it.

S 6. A soccer ball was kicked to the far end of the field.

R-O 7. My firm answer is no, you may not go.

F 8. Copying the lesson from the book.

F 9. Matt up to me suspiciously.

S 10. A snake slithered under a rock.

R-O 11. My opinion is that you should keep the kitten, it definitely needs good care and you can give him a good home.

S 12. Our clothes were packed and ready for our trip.

F 13. At the end of the story.

S 14. Be prepared to make sudden stops on this road.

S 15. When Ann was little, she dreamed of becoming a doctor.

Name________________________________

Date________________________________

SENTENCES
FRAGMENTS
RUN-ONS

Directions: In the space provided, write S for sentence, F for fragment, and R-O for run-on.

Example: __R-O____ The milk is old, it's sour.

________ 1. Please call me later.

________ 2. Fine.

________ 3. Who has won?

________ 4. Disturbing the peace.

________ 5. The plant is wilting, water it.

________ 6. A soccer ball was kicked to the far end of the field.

________ 7. My firm answer is no, you may not go.

________ 8. Copying the lesson from the book.

________ 9. Matt up to me suspiciously.

________ 10. A snake slithered under a rock.

________ 11. My opinion is that you should keep the kitten, it definitely needs good care and you can give him a good home.

________ 12. Our clothes were packed and ready for our trip.

________ 13. At the end of the story.

________ 14. Be prepared to make sudden stops on this road.

________ 15. When Ann was little, she dreamed of becoming a doctor.

Name_______________________________

WORKBOOK PAGE 184

Date_______________________________

SENTENCES
FRAGMENTS
RUN-ONS

Directions: In the space provided, write S for sentence, F for fragment, and R-O for run-on.

Example: __F__ Down the street.

__S__ 1. Her jewelry had been appraised and insured.

__F__ 2. After your fine presentation.

__R-O__ 3. Mother drove the car Dad flew.

__F__ 4. Talking on the telephone at the end of the day.

__S__ 5. Can the roofer repair the damage?

__F__ 6. Unless Mrs. Farmington calls.

__S__ 7. Go!

__R-O__ 8. Look around, plan on buying at least one gift.

__S__ 9. This room is too dark and crowded.

__R-O__ 10. After beginning the day in a wonderful mood, he was rushed to the hospital for stitches in his left foot which he received when he broke a glass and stepped on a small fragment, and then the day became worse.

__S__ 11. This airplane is old.

__F__ 12. Walked and ran in his sleep last night.

__R-O__ 13. A computer class is offered, I'm taking it.

__F__ 14. If you need a ride.

__S__ 15. Send me your new address.

Name________________________________

Date________________________________

SENTENCES
FRAGMENTS
RUN-ONS

Directions: In the space provided, write S for sentence, F for fragment, and R-O for run-on.

Example: __F__ Down the street.

_________ 1. Her jewelry had been appraised and insured.

_________ 2. After your fine presentation.

_________ 3. Mother drove the car Dad flew.

_________ 4. Talking on the telephone at the end of the day.

_________ 5. Can the roofer repair the damage?

_________ 6. Unless Mrs. Farmington calls.

_________ 7. Go!

_________ 8. Look around, plan on buying at least one gift.

_________ 9. This room is too dark and crowded.

_________ 10. After beginning the day in a wonderful mood, he was rushed to the hospital for stitches in his left foot which he received when he broke a glass and stepped on a small fragment, and then the day became worse.

_________ 11. This airplane is old.

_________ 12. Walked and ran in his sleep last night.

_________ 13. A computer class is offered, I'm taking it.

_________ 14. If you need a ride.

_________ 15. Send me your new address.

PAGE 387 = WORKBOOK PAGE 185

PHRASE OR CLAUSE?

PHRASE: A phrase does not contain a subject and verb.

Examples: down the street

living in Atlanta

CLAUSE: A clause contains a subject and a verb.

A. A **dependent clause** contains a subject **and** verb, but it does not express a complete thought. A dependent clause cannot stand alone as a sentence.

Examples: When Todd was little

If you were right

Although school had ended

Whenever I hurry ~~through dinner~~ and eat fast

B. An **independent clause** contains subject **and** verb and expresses a complete thought. An independent clause can stand alone as a sentence.

Examples: The air deodorizer is gone.

The ten of hearts is missing from this deck.

The ten ~~of hearts~~ is missing ~~from this deck~~.

Both the man and his wife signed several legal papers.

Name________________________________ **PHRASE OR CLAUSE?**

WORKBOOK PAGE 186

Date________________________________

Directions: Write C on the line if the group of words is a clause. Write P on the line if the group of words is a phrase.

Suggestion: Cross out any prepositional phrases. Underline the subject once and the verb/verb phrase twice. If the sentence contains both a subject and a verb, it is a clause.

Example: ___C___ The fork was ~~on the floor~~.

___P___ 1. ~~Without supper~~.

___P___ 2. Danced ~~in the breeze~~.

___C___ 3. Our oven door is broken.

___C___ 4. After my homework was completed.

___P___ 5. Participating ~~in a game~~.

___P___ 6. The man ~~in the park~~.

___C___ 7. Even though I agreed.

___P___ 8. Hurried ~~down the lane~~.

___C___ 9. Leaves have fallen ~~from the trees~~.

___P___ 10. Hanging ~~on the wall~~ ~~over a fireplace~~.

___C___ 11. No one emptied the trash.

___P___ 12. Those large white eggs ~~on the table~~.

___C___ 13. Our basement is a storage area.

___C___ 14. If I could skate faster.

___P___ 15. Regardless ~~of the telephone's dial tone~~.

Name________________________________ **PHRASE OR CLAUSE?**

Date________________________________

Directions: Write C on the line if the group of words is a clause. Write P on the line if the group of words is a phrase.

Suggestion: Cross out any prepositional phrases. Underline the subject once and the verb/verb phrase twice. If the sentence contains both a subject and a verb, it is a clause.

Example: ___C___ The fork was ~~on the floor~~.

_________ 1. Without supper.

_________ 2. Danced in the breeze.

_________ 3. Our oven door is broken.

_________ 4. After my homework was completed.

_________ 5. Participating in a game.

_________ 6. The man in the park.

_________ 7. Even though I agreed.

_________ 8. Hurried down the lane.

_________ 9. Leaves have fallen from the trees.

_________ 10. Hanging on the wall over a fireplace.

_________ 11. No one emptied the trash.

_________ 12. Those large white eggs on the table.

_________ 13. Our basement is a storage area.

_________ 14. If I could skate faster.

_________ 15. Regardless of the telephone's dial tone.

Name_______________________________ **CLAUSES**

WORKBOOK PAGE 187 Dependent or Independent?

Date_______________________________

Directions: Write DC on the line if the clause is a dependent clause. Write IC on the line if the clause is an independent clause.

Example: ___IC___ The miniature horses are as small as dogs.

___IC___ 1. That store opens at nine o'clock.

___DC___ 2. Unless you plan on leaving.

___DC___ 3. Whatever the circumstances are.

___IC___ 4. Bottled water was delivered to their door.

___IC___ 5. Go away.*

___DC___ 6. If our ship arrives early.

___DC___ 7. Whenever we finish this task.

___IC___ 8. During the power failure, our lights went out.

___IC___ 9. Stop.*

___DC___ 10. Although the dam broke.

___IC___ 11. Laughing and splashing, the two boys played in the pool.

___DC___ 12. After I run these errands.

___IC___ 13. Mr. Dobbins loves chocolate chip cookies.

___DC___ 14. From the time I was three years old.

___IC___ 15. Harriet vowed never to do that again.

*Remember that (You), (called *you understood*), is often the subject of an imperative sentence (command).

Name________________________________

Date________________________________

CLAUSES
Dependent or Independent?

Directions: Write DC on the line if the clause is a dependent clause. Write IC on the line if the clause is an independent clause.

Example: ___IC___ The miniature horses are as small as dogs.

________ 1. That store opens at nine o'clock.

________ 2. Unless you plan on leaving.

________ 3. Whatever the circumstances are.

________ 4. Bottled water was delivered to their door.

________ 5. Go away.

________ 6. If our ship arrives early.

________ 7. Whenever we finish this task.

________ 8. During the power failure, our lights went out.

________ 9. Stop.

________ 10. Although the dam broke.

________ 11. Laughing and splashing, the two boys played in the pool.

________ 12. After I run these errands.

________ 13. Mr. Dobbins loves chocolate chip cookies.

________ 14. From the time I was three years old.

________ 15. Harriet vowed never to do that again.

*Remember that You, (called *you understood*), is often the subject of an imperative sentence (command).

PAGE 393 = WORKBOOK PAGE 188

ADVERBS

ADVERBS TELL HOW, WHERE, WHEN, AND TO WHAT EXTENT (HOW MUCH).

Adverbs that tell HOW:

An adverb that tells **how** usually modifies or goes back to the verb/verb phrase.

Example: The child speaks clearly. (*Clearly* tells **how** the child speaks.)

Example: Quickly he fell ~~to the ground~~. (*Quickly* tells **how** he fell.)

1. Give the students the sentence: " My mother (sister, dad, aunt....) drives ____________________________."

2. Instruct students to number 1-10 on their papers.

3. Instruct students to write ten adverbs that tell **HOW** Mother (or other choice) drives. Students must use one-word answers. "With care" is unacceptable because it's a two-word phrase.

4. Give students enough time to think and write.

5. As students share answers, write them on a chalkboard or overhead projector.

Representative answers:

carefully	crazily
carelessly	stupidly
slowly	excellently
recklessly	fast
patiently	

Most adverbs that tell *HOW* end in *ly*.

Name________________________________ **ADVERBS**
WORKBOOK PAGE 189 How?
Date________________________________

Directions: Cross out any prepositional phrases. Underline the subject once and the verb/verb phrase twice. Label any adverb (ADV.) that tells **HOW**. In the space provided, explain the use of the adverb in the sentence.

Example: Marta slowly explained ~~about the trip~~ ~~to Alaska~~. (ADV. = slowly)

Slowly tells HOW Marta explained.

1. The crowd cheered happily ~~for their team~~. (ADV. = happily)

   Happily tells HOW the crowd cheered.

2. Mary searched hurriedly ~~through the desk drawers~~. (ADV. = hurriedly)

   Hurriedly tells HOW Mary searched.

3. Carefully the packers arranged glassware ~~in strong boxes~~. (ADV. = Carefully)

   Carefully tells HOW the packers arranged glassware.

4. A typist quickly typed an office memo ~~for me~~. (ADV. = quickly)

   Quickly tells HOW a typist typed a memo.

5. Bart and Melody ran fast ~~in the fifty yard dash~~. (ADV. = fast)

   Fast tells HOW Bart and Melody ran.

6. That dog ~~under the table~~ does not feel well ~~in this heat~~. (ADV. = well)

   Well tells HOW the dog does (or doesn't) feel.

7. He sings weirdly ~~in the shower~~. (ADV. = weirdly)

   Weirdly tells HOW he sings.

8. Carelessly the car slid ~~around the corner~~. (ADV. = Carelessly)

   Carelessly tells HOW the car slid around the corner.

9. The child was dreadfully frightened ~~by the movie~~. (ADV. = dreadfully)

   Dreadfully tells HOW the child was frightened.

10. Do you work hard ~~on your lessons?~~ (ADV. = hard)

    Hard tells HOW you work on your lessons.

Name________________________________

Date________________________________

ADVERBS
How?

Directions: Cross out any prepositional phrases. Underline the subject once and the verb/verb phrase twice. Label any adverb (ADV.) that tells **HOW**. In the space provided, explain the use of the adverb in the sentence.

ADV.

Example: Marta slowly explained ~~about the trip to Alaska~~.

Slowly tells HOW Marta explained.

1. The crowd cheered happily for their team.

____

2. Mary searched hurriedly through the desk drawers.

____

3. Carefully the packers arranged glassware in strong boxes.

____

4. A typist quickly typed an office memo for me.

____

5. Bart and Melody ran fast in the fifty yard dash.

____

6. That dog under the table does not feel well in this heat.

____

7. He sings weirdly in the shower.

____

8. Carelessly the car slid around the corner.

____

9. The child was dreadfully frightened by the movie.

____

10. Do you work hard on your lessons?

____

ADVERBS

Adverbs that tell HOW:

At this point, a review of adjectives is needed. Keep it simple: red shirt, yellow pencil, long hair, blue eyes. (Use examples that students can see.)

On the chalkboard or overhead projector, place the terms adjective and adverb in this manner:

Adjective	**Adverb**

Have student give examples of adjectives and the adverb form for those given adjectives. You may want to start them. Be sure to include fast, hard, and slow.

Adjective	**Adverb**
beautiful	beautifully
terrific	terrifically
fast	fast
slow	slowly
hard	hard
lovely	-----------(no adverb form)

1. Instruct students that most adjectives add ly to form the adverb form.

2. Instruct students that a few words such as fast and hard are the same in both adjective and adverb forms.

3. Some adjectives such as lovely and red do not have adverb forms.

4. Write the sentence, "My mother drives __________." on the chalkboard or overhead projector. Look at the word slow in the adjective column. Because slow is an adjective, you cannot say, "My mother drives slow." The proper answer is "My mother drives slowly."

Name_________________________________ **ADVERBS**

WORKBOOK PAGE 190 Adjective or Adverb?

Date_________________________________

Directions: Underline the correct answer in the following sentences.

Example: The player ran (quick, quickly) to the end of the line.

1. This is an (easy, easily) test.
2. I can do that (easy, easily).
3. Penguins are (slow, slowly) runners.
4. They run (slow, slowly).
5. Some people drive (crazy, crazily) when it rains.
6. Does anyone think that my idea is a (crazy, crazily) one?
7. This truck makes (sudden, suddenly) stops.
8. It often stops (sudden, suddenly).
9. I go swimming quite (frequent, frequently).
10. I am a (frequent, frequently) visitor to the public pool.
11. That is an (unkind, unkindly) thing to say.
12. The angry person spoke (unkind, unkindly) to me.
13. You did that (careless, carelessly).
14. The riders went on a (peaceful, peacefully) trip in the mountains.
15. The toddler slept so (peaceful, peacefully).

Name________________________________

Date________________________________

ADVERBS

Adjective or Adverb?

Directions: Underline the correct answer in the following sentences.

Example: The player ran (quick, <u>quickly</u>) to the end of the line.

1. This is an (easy, easily) test.
2. I can do that (easy, easily).
3. Penguins are (slow, slowly) runners.
4. They run (slow, slowly).
5. Some people drive (crazy, crazily) when it rains.
6. Does anyone think that my idea is a (crazy, crazily) one?
7. This truck makes (sudden, suddenly) stops.
8. It often stops (sudden, suddenly).
9. I go swimming quite (frequent, frequently).
10. I am a (frequent, frequently) visitor to the public pool.
11. That is an (unkind, unkindly) thing to say.
12. The angry person spoke (unkind, unkindly) to me.
13. You did that (careless, carelessly).
14. The riders went on a (peaceful, peacefully) trip in the mountains.
15. The toddler slept so (peaceful, peacefully).

PAGE 401 = WORKBOOK PAGE 191

ADVERBS

Good or Well?

A. **Good is an adjective.**

They are ____**good**______ singers.

The forms of **good** are: **good, better, and best.**

They are **good** singers.

We are **better** singers than they.

Tracy is the **best** singer in the choir.

Because **good** is always an adjective, **good** will describe a noun or pronoun.

B. **Well is an adverb.**

They sing ____**well**____. (**Well** tells **HOW** they sing.)

The forms of **well** are: **well, better, best.**

They sing **well**.

We sing **better** than they.

Tracy sings **best** in our choir.

NOTE: Stress that **well** must be used to explain **how** one does something. Action verbs require **well** if an explanation of **how** is involved.

I advise asking each child to share with the class in sentence form something he does **well**!

Examples: I swim **well**.

I play basketball **well**.

Name________________________________ **ADVERBS**
WORKBOOK PAGE 192 Good or Well?
Date________________________________

Directions: Fill in the blank with **good** or **well**.

Example: I am a ___good___ ceramist.

1. Fred plays the violin very ___well___.
2. Marta is a ___good___ engineer.
3. ___Good___ scissors are hard to find.
4. Do you write ___well___?
5. The ringmaster at the circus did his job ___well___.
6. Are you feeling ___well*___ today?
7. Be a ___good___ listener.
8. Those windows were not washed ___well___.
9. Contractors worked together ___well___ to build that house.
10. You did a ___good___ job.
11. They were praised for their ___good___ behavior.
12. They behaved ___well___.
13. I like my steaks cooked ___well___.
14. Has your friend read two ___good___ books lately?
15. Wow! You do that so ___well___!

*Although good or well is supposedly acceptable here, I continue to require the adverb, well, to designate how one feels.

Name________________________________

Date________________________________

ADVERBS

Good or Well?

Directions: Fill in the blank with **good** or **well**.

Example: I am a ____good_______ ceramist.

1. Fred plays the violin very ______________________.
2. Marta is a ______________________engineer.
3. ______________________ scissors are hard to find.
4. Do you write ______________________?
5. The ringmaster at the circus did his job ______________________.
6. Are you feeling ______________________today?
7. Be a ______________________listener.
8. Those windows were not washed ______________________.
9. Contractors worked together ______________________ to build that house.
10. You did a ______________________ job.
11. They were praised for their ______________________behavior.
12. They behaved ______________________.
13. I like my steaks cooked ______________________.
14. Has your friend read two ______________________ books lately?
15. Wow! You do that so ______________________!

PAGE 405 = WORKBOOK PAGE 193

ADVERBS

Adverbs that tell WHERE:

An adverb that tells **where** usually modifies or goes over to the verb/verb phrase.

Example: He looked up. (Up tells where he looked.)

1. Give students the sentence, "My mother drives ________________."
2. Instruct students to number 1-10 on a paper.
3. Instruct students to write ten adverbs that tell WHERE mother drives. Students must use one-word answers. "To the store" is unacceptable because it is a three-word phrase.
4. Give students enough time to think and write.
5. As students share answers, write the answers on a chalkboard or on an overhead projector.

   Representative answers:

here	in*	inside
there	out	outside
everywhere	up	around
anywhere	down	far
nowhere	uptown	near
somewhere	downtown	
home	upstream	
where	downstream	

---

*Your very bright students will question in and a few other adverbs because they learned those words as prepositions. Praise your students. Then explain that when a word that is usually a preposition does not have an object (noun or pronoun) with it, that same word is an adverb.

Examples: Dad fell down. (Down is an adverb; there is no noun or pronoun following it.)

Dad fell down the steps. (Down is a preposition.)
(Down the steps is a prepositional phrase.)

Name________________________________ **ADVERBS**
WORKBOOK PAGE 194 Where?
Date________________________________

Directions: Cross out any prepositional phrases. Underline the subject once and the verb/verb phrase twice. Label any adverb (ADV.) that tells **WHERE**. In the space provided, explain the use of the adverb(s) in the sentence.

ADV.
Example: We went there ~~after school~~.

There tells WHERE we went.

ADV.
1. Have you gone anywhere ~~in a hurry~~?

Anywhere tells WHERE you have gone.

ADV.
2. I am going home ~~in an hour~~.

Home tells WHERE I am going.

ADV. ADV.
3. Marcia came in and sat down.

In tells WHERE Marcia came, and down tells WHERE she sat.

ADV.
4. They looked up ~~in the sky~~.

Up tells WHERE they looked.

ADV.
5. The boat floated downstream.

Downstream tells WHERE the boat floated.

ADV.
6. You may stay there ~~for the night~~.

There tells WHERE you may stay.

ADV.
7. Do you live far?

Far tells WHERE you live.

ADV.
8. Somewhere my friend hid my comb.

Somewhere tells WHERE my friend hid my comb.

Name_______________________________ **ADVERBS**
Where?

Date_______________________________

Directions: Cross out any prepositional phrases. Underline the subject once and the verb/verb phrase twice. Label any adverb (ADV.) that tells **WHERE**. In the space provided, explain the use of the adverb(s) in the sentence.

Example:
ADV.
We went there ~~after school~~.
There tells WHERE we went.

1. Have you gone anywhere in a hurry?

____

2. I am going home in an hour.

____

3. Marcia came in and sat down.

____

4. They looked up in the sky.

____

5. The boat floated downstream.

____

6. You may stay there for the night.

____

7. Do you live far?

____

8. Somewhere my friend hid my comb.

____

PAGE 409 = WORKBOOK PAGE 195

ADVERBS

Adverbs that tell WHEN:

An adverb that tells **when** usually modifies or goes back to the verb/verb phrase.

Example: John left early. (*Early* tells **when** John left.)

Example: Tonight we will eat ~~at a restaurant~~. (*Tonight* tells **when** we will eat.)

1. Give students the sentence, "My mother drives_________________."

2. Instruct students to number 1-10 on their papers.

3. Instruct students to write ten adverbs that tell **WHEN** Mother drives. Students must use one-word answers. "During the day" is unacceptable because it's a three-word phrase.

4. Give students enough time to think and write.

5. As students share answers, write them on a chalkboad or overhead projector.

Representative answers:

tonight	when	before
today	daily	after
tomorrow	yearly	
now	monthly	
then	nightly	
soon	hourly	
late	early	

Name________________________________

WORKBOOK PAGE 196

Date________________________________

ADVERBS

When?

Directions: Cross out any prepositional phrases. Underline the subject once and the verb/verb phrase twice. Label any adverb (ADV.) that tells **WHEN**. In the space provided, explain the use of the adverb(s) in the sentence.

Example: We will finish the task tonight ~~after dinner~~. (ADV. over tonight)

Tonight tells WHEN we will finish the task.

1. Yesterday we went ~~to the beach~~ ~~with my cousin~~. (ADV. over Yesterday)

   Yesterday tells WHEN we went to the beach.

2. The circus is coming ~~to town~~ soon. (ADV. over soon)

   Soon tells WHEN the circus is coming to town.

3. That person arrives late ~~for every meeting~~. (ADV. over late)

   Late tells WHEN that person arrives.

4. Mother purchased special pens ~~for us~~ today. (ADV. over today)

   Today tells WHEN Mother purchased pens.

5. Yearly the broker sends a stock report ~~to his customers~~. (ADV. over Yearly)

   Yearly tells WHEN the broker sends reports.

6. I never knew ~~about the proposed freeway~~. (ADV. over never)

   Never tells WHEN I knew about the freeway.

7. Is everyone leaving now? (ADV. over now)

   Now tells WHEN everyone is leaving.

8. Will the bus be transporting early ~~in the morning~~? (ADV. over early)

   Early tells WHEN the bus will be transporting.

9. They had been ~~on a television show~~ before. (ADV. over before)

   Before tells WHEN they had been on a show.

10. Tomorrow the carpenters will build a patio ~~in our yard~~. (ADV. over Tomorrow)

    Tomorrow tells WHEN the carpenters will build.

Name________________________________

Date________________________________

ADVERBS
When?

Directions: Cross out any prepositional phrases. Underline the subject once and the verb/verb phrase twice. Label any adverb (ADV.) that tells **WHEN**. In the space provided, explain the use of the adverb(s) in the sentence.

ADV.

Example: We will finish the task tonight ~~after dinner.~~

Tonight tells WHEN we will finish the task.

1. Yesterday we went to the beach with my cousin.

____

2. The circus is coming to town soon.

____

3. That person arrives late for every meeting.

____

4. Mother purchased special pens for us today.

____

5. Yearly the broker sends a stock report to his customers.

____

6. I never knew about the proposed freeway.

____

7. Is everyone leaving now?

____

8. Will the bus be transporting early in the morning?

____

9. They had been on a television show before.

____

10. Tomorrow the carpenters will build a patio in our yard.

____

PAGE 413 = WORKBOOK PAGE 197

ADVERBS

Adverbs that tell TO WHAT EXTENT:

An adverb that tells **to what extent (how much)** usually modifies or goes over to an adjective or another adverb.

ADJ.
Example: The rug is **extremely** dirty.

(*Extremely* tells **to what extent** the rug is dirty.)

ADV.
Example: The mountain climbers go **very** slowly.

(*Very* tells **to what extent** the climbers go slowly.)

You need to memorize and learn the following list. These words are adverbs.

not*	**quite**	**somewhat**
so	**rather**	
very	**too**	

Occasionally **so, very, too, rather**, and **quite** will be within a prepositional phrase.

Cross out the prepositional phrase and circle the adverb.

Example: We went ~~into a~~ **rather** ~~large estate~~.

Occasionally an adverb that tells **TO WHAT EXTENT** will modify or go to a verb.

Example: I would **rather** go to the store.

(*Rather* tells **to what extent** I would go.)

OTHER ADVERBS THAT TELL **TO WHAT EXTENT** USUALLY END IN **LY**.

*not = n't. Circle the n't as the ADVERB.

Name________________________________

WORKBOOK PAGE 198

Date________________________________

ADVERBS

To What Extent?

Directions: Underline any adverb(s) that tell **TO WHAT EXTENT**. Label any other adverbs ADV.

Example: I run extremely slowly. (ADV. above slowly)

1. The taxi arrived quite late. (ADV. above late)
2. I did the assignment rather carefully. (ADV. above carefully)
3. Often you are so hungry. (ADV. above Often)
4. Our pockets were absolutely empty.
5. Today you look really tired. (ADV. above Today)
6. A supersonic jet flies very fast. (ADV. above fast)
7. That outfit will be too wrinkled for the banquet tonight. (ADV. above tonight)
8. Our heifer is unusually thirsty lately. (ADV. above lately)
9. The lake is quite calm.
10. Bart walked with his very glamorous grandmother.
11. The repairman worked extremely hard yesterday. (ADV. above hard; ADV. above yesterday)
12. Mother and I worked well together. (ADV. above well; ADV. above together)
13. They arrived at the meeting too early. (ADV. above early)
14. Aunt Lisa built a rather lovely home here. (ADV. above here)
15. We searched the house rather frantically for the lost credit card. (ADV. above frantically)

Name________________________________

Date________________________________

ADVERBS
To What Extent?

Directions: Underline any adverb(s) that tell **TO WHAT EXTENT**. Label any other adverbs ADV.

Example: I run extremely slowly. (ADV. above "slowly"; "extremely" underlined)

1. The taxi arrived quite late.

2. I did the assignment rather carefully.

3. Often you are so hungry.

4. Our pockets were absolutely empty.

5. Today you look really tired.

6. A supersonic jet flies very fast.

7. That outfit will be too wrinkled for the banquet tonight.

8. Our heifer is unusually thirsty lately.

9. The lake is quite calm.

10. Bart walked with his very glamorous grandmother.

11. The repairman worked extremely hard yesterday.

12. Mother and I worked well together.

13. They arrived at the meeting too early.

14. Aunt Lisa built a rather lovely home here.

15. We searched the house rather frantically for the lost credit card.

PAGE 417 = WORKBOOK PAGE 199

ADVERBS

Adverb or Preposition?

Take out the original preposition list. Have students determine which words tell **WHERE**:

Representative Answers:

above	up
across	in
after	out
around	inside
before	outside
down	over

Any word on the preposition list that does not have a noun or pronoun following it will be an adverb.

Example: I fell ~~down the stairs~~. (Down the stairs is a prepositional phrase.)

I fell down. (Down is an adverb; there is no noun or pronoun following down.)

Instruct the students to cross out prepositional phrases in the sentence. Often an adverb will be beside a prepositional phrase.

Example: The guard entered in through the security door.

Wrong: The guard entered ~~in through the security door.~~

Right: The guard entered in ~~through the security door.~~

(In is an adverb telling where.)

Stress that a prepositional phrase begins with a single preposition.

Example: May you come over ~~to my house~~?

(Over is an adverb telling where.)

Name________________________________ **ADVERBS**
WORKBOOK PAGE 200 Adverb or Preposition?
Date________________________________

Directions: Place a P (Preposition) or A (Adverb) in the space provided. Be sure to think carefully about the underlined word.

Example: __P__ The lizard crawled over the mound of dirt.

__A__ 1. The portrait fell down.

__P__ 2. Someone fell down the steps.

__P__ 3. He tripped over the chair.

__A__ 4. A dried flower arrangement fell over in the wind.

__A__ 5. Don't jump off now!

__P__ 6. The one year old jumped off the diving board.

__P__ 7. Before lunch we shopped at a new mall.

__A__ 8. Have you tried this product before?

__A__ 9. Do you live near to me?

__P__ 10. The old miner lived near the train station.

__P__ 11. Go up the escalator and turn left.

__A__ 12. Tiles in our bathroom came up.

__A__ 13. We will not go outside today.

__P__ 14. Outside the barn is an ancient tractor.

__A__ 15. Come in please.

__P__ 16. In the middle of the night there was a storm.

Name______________________________

Date______________________________

ADVERBS

Adverb or Preposition?

Directions: Place a P (Preposition) or A (Adverb) in the space provided. Be sure to think carefully about the underlined word.

Example: ___P___ The lizard crawled over the mound of dirt.

_____ 1. The portrait fell down.

_____ 2. Someone fell down the steps.

_____ 3. He tripped over the chair.

_____ 4. A dried flower arrangement fell over in the wind.

_____ 5. Don't jump off now!

_____ 6. The one year old jumped off the diving board.

_____ 7. Before lunch we shopped at a new mall.

_____ 8. Have you tried this product before?

_____ 9. Do you live near to me?

_____ 10. The old miner lived near the train station.

_____ 11. Go up the escalator and turn left.

_____ 12. Tiles in our bathroom came up.

_____ 13. We will not go outside today.

_____ 14. Outside the barn is an ancient tractor.

_____ 15. Come in please.

_____ 16. In the middle of the night there was a storm.

Name________________________________ **ADVERBS**

WORKBOOK PAGE 201

Date________________________________

Directions: Circle any adverb(s) in the following sentences.

Adverbs are in boldfaced print.

1. Turn the pages **slowly**.
2. **Now** you may leave.
3. The steeple is **very** tall.
4. The jockey rode **well**.
5. **Today** my sister broke her ankle.
6. Go **away**.
7. Stand **up**.
8. Are we going **anywhere**?
9. These steaks are **so** tender.
10. Do **not** leave **yet**.
11. My boss pays me **hourly**.
12. **Sooner** or **later** you must know the truth.
13. **First** you must turn **right** at Darnmon Street.
14. **Then** take a bus **downtown**.
15. Your feelings are hurt **so easily**.
16. **There** are **not** any coins in this fountain.
17. **How** did you get **home**?
18. **When** did John start running **so fast**?
19. The chore was done **rather slowly**.
20. We will **not** have an answer **immediately**.

Name________________________________ **ADVERBS**

Date________________________________

Directions: Circle any adverb(s) in the following sentences.

1. Turn the pages slowly.
2. Now you may leave.
3. The steeple is very tall.
4. The jockey rode well.
5. Today my sister broke her ankle.
6. Go away.
7. Stand up.
8. Are we going anywhere?
9. These steaks are so tender.
10. Do not leave yet.
11. My boss pays me hourly.
12. Sooner or later you must know the truth.
13. First you must turn right at Darnmon Street.
14. Then take a bus downtown.
15. Your feelings are hurt so easily.
16. There are not any coins in this fountain.
17. How did you get home?
18. When did John start running so fast?
19. The chore was done rather slowly.
20. We will not have an answer immediately.

Name________________________________ **ADVERBS**
WORKBOOK PAGE 202
Date________________________________

Directions: Underline the subject once and the verb/verb phrase twice. Cross out any prepositional phrases. (Look for **too, very, so, quite,** and **rather** within a prepositional phrase.) Circle any adverbs.

Adverbs are in boldfaced print.

1. She looked **inside** and **outside** ~~for her umbrella~~.
2. ~~After the dance~~, everyone went **home**.
3. **Now** and **then** my **very** elderly uncle stays ~~with us~~.
4. **When** will you come **over** ~~to my house~~?
5. We jump **up** and **down** ~~in exercise class~~.
6. **Seldom** do the children go **in** and **out** ~~through that door~~.
7. **Unfortunately** this machine is **temporarily out** ~~of order~~.
8. The lump ~~on his arm~~ is **extremely** large.
9. **Often** we eat lunch **here** ~~on Saturdays~~.
10. Invitations were sent **out too early** ~~in the week~~.
11. The broom couldn**'t** be found **anywhere** ~~in the garage~~.
12. **There** are five lovely blooms ~~on the flowering plant.~~
13. Jill polished her new car **very gently**.
14. **Where** did the experts put the **rather** ugly trophy?
15. You did **so well** ~~in the softball game~~ **yesterday**.

Name_______________________________ **ADVERBS**

Date_______________________________

Directions: Underline the subject once and the verb/verb phrase twice. Cross out any prepositional phrases. (Look for **too**, **very**, **so**, **quite**, and **rather** within a prepositional phrase.) Circle any adverbs.

1. She looked inside and outside for her umbrella.
2. After the dance, everyone went home.
3. Now and then my very elderly uncle stays with us.
4. When will you come over to my house?
5. We jump up and down in exercise class.
6. Seldom do the children go in and out through that door.
7. Unfortunately this machine is temporarily out of order.
8. The lump on his arm is extremely large.
9. Often we eat lunch here on Saturdays.
10. Invitations were sent out too early in the week.
11. The broom couldn't be found anywhere in the garage.
12. There are five lovely blooms on the flowering plant.
13. Jill polished her new car very gently.
14. Where did the experts put the rather ugly trophy?
15. You did so well in the softball game yesterday.

PAGE 425 = WORKBOOK PAGE 203

ADVERBS

DEGREES OF ADVERBS

Adverbs often make comparisons.

A. The **comparative** form compares two *things.*

B. The **superlative** form compares three or more *things.*

Examples: Bill runs **faster** than I. (**COMPARATIVE** FORM: Bill and I are being compared - 2 people.)

Of the four, Bill runs **fastest**. (**SUPERLATIVE** FORM: four people are being compared.)

There are three ways to form the comparative and the superlative:

A. **Comparative:**

1. Add **er** to most one-syllable adverbs.

   fast/faster hard/harder

2. Place **more** before most two or more syllable adverbs.*

   slowly/more slowly favorably/more favorably

3. Some adverbs totally change form.

   well/better badly/worse

B. **Superlative:**

1. Add **est** to most one-syllable adverbs.

   fast/fastest hard/hardest

2. Place **most** before many two or more syllable adverbs.*

   slowly/most slowly favorably/most favorably

3. Some adverbs totally change form.

   well/best badly/worst

***Less** for the comparative and **least** for the superlative may also be used.

Adverb	Comparative	Superlative
well	better	best
badly	worse	worst
early	earlier	earliest
rapidly	more rapidly	most rapidly

Name________________________________ **ADVERBS**
WORKBOOK PAGE 204 Degrees
Date________________________________

Directions: Write the required comparative or superlative form in the space provided.

Example: comparative form of beautifully

more beautifully

1. comparative form of hesitantly

   more hesitantly*

2. superlative form of easily

   most easily*

3. comparative form of suddenly

   more suddenly*

4. comparative form of soon

   sooner

5. superlative form of badly

   worst

6. comparative form of weirdly

   more weirdly*

7. superlative form of late

   latest

8. superlative form of smoothly

   most smoothly*

9. comparative form of carefully

   more carefully*

10. superlative form of well

    best

*Less in comparative and least in superlative form should be accepted.

Name_______________________________ **ADVERBS**

Date_______________________________ Degrees

Directions: Write the required comparative or superlative form in the space provided.

Example: comparative form of beautifully

more beautifully

1. comparative form of hesitantly

____

2. superlative form of easily

____

3. comparative form of suddenly

____

4. comparative form of soon

____

5. superlative form of badly

____

6. comparative form of weirdly

____

7. superlative form of late

____

8. superlative form of smoothly

____

9. comparative form of carefully

____

10. superlative form of well

____

Name______________________________ **ADVERBS**
WORKBOOK PAGE 205 Degrees
Date______________________________

Directions: Select the correct adverb form in the following sentences.
Answers are in boldfaced print.

Example: My parents awake (**earlier**, earliest) than I do.

1. Of the triplets, Alonsa waits (more patiently, **most patiently**).
2. Van laughs (**more loudly**, most loudly) than his sister.
3. Leyla hiked (**farther**, farthest) than Lulu did.
4. When our group spotted a snake, Anton reacted (more fearfully, **most fearfully**).
5. The manicurist worked (**harder**, hardest) than the hair stylist.
6. Of the twins, he draws (**more artistically**, most artistically).
7. I feel (well, **better**) today than yesterday.
8. The third appraiser eyed the ring (more closely, **most closely**).
9. In our entire class, a left-handed student writes (more legibly, **most legibly**).
10. This plant grows (**more quickly**, most quickly) than that one.
11. I like this painting (better, **best**) of the entire display.
12. That maid cleans (**more thoroughly**, most thoroughly) than her friend.
13. This light shines (more brightly, **most brightly**) of all the lights in our home.
14. Miri plays tennis (badder, **worse**) than Joy.
15. He deals with us (honester, **more honestly**).

Name________________________________ **ADVERBS**

Degrees

Date________________________________

Directions: Select the correct adverb form in the following sentences.

Example: My parents awake (**earlier**, earliest) than I do.

1. Of the triplets, Alonsa waits (more patiently, most patiently).
2. Van laughs (more loudly, most loudly) than his sister.
3. Leyla hiked (farther, farthest) than Lulu did.
4. When our group spotted a snake, Anton reacted (more fearfully, most fearfully).
5. The manicurist worked (harder, hardest) than the hair stylist.
6. Of the twins, he draws (more artistically, most artistically).
7. I feel (well, better) today than yesterday.
8. The third appraiser eyed the ring (more closely, most closely).
9. In our entire class, a left-handed student writes (more legibly, most legibly).
10. This plant grows (more quickly, most quickly) than that one.
11. I like this painting (better, best) of the entire display.
12. That maid cleans (more thoroughly, most thoroughly) than her friend.
13. This light shines (more brightly, most brightly) of all the lights in our home.
14. Miri plays tennis (badder, worse) than Joy.
15. He deals with us (honester, more honestly).

Name________________________________ **ADVERBS**

WORKBOOK PAGE 206

Date________________________________

Directions: Underline the subject once and the verb/verb phrase twice. Cross out any prepositional phrases. (Be sure to look for the adverbs, **quite, too, so,** and **very**, within a prepositional phrase.) Circle any adverbs.

Adverbs are in boldfaced print.

1. **First** you must send money ~~to us~~.

2. ~~After breakfast~~ we went **outside** and played ~~in the snow.~~

3. Our puppy ran **around** ~~after its tail~~.

4. The cartoonist has been **very** busy **lately**.

5. The pottery ~~in the back~~ will be fired **soon**.

6. The business has **not** done **well** **recently**.

7. That apartment building will be **partially** completed **tomorrow**.

8. A group walked **in** and sat **down** **quietly**.

9. I have **already** decided to leave.

10. Some people become **rather** angry **quite** **easily**.

(You)

11. Turn **left** ~~at the first traffic signal~~.

12. The lady ~~in the~~ **very** ~~high heels~~ has visited us **often**.

13. **Now** and **then** I would like an **extremely** sweet dessert.

14. **Tonight** we will go **together** ~~to the carnival~~.

15. She looked **upward** ~~through the telescope~~ and smiled **slightly**.

Name________________________________ **ADVERBS**

Date________________________________

Directions: Underline the subject once and the verb/verb phrase twice. Cross out any prepositional phrases. (Be sure to look for the adverbs, **quite, too, so,** and **very**, within a prepositional phrase.) Circle any adverbs.

1. First you must send money to us.

2. After breakfast we went outside and played in the snow.

3. Our puppy ran around after its tail.

4. The cartoonist has been very busy lately.

5. The pottery in the back will be fired soon.

6. The business has not done well recently.

7. That apartment building will be partially completed tomorrow.

8. A group walked in and sat down quietly.

9. I have already decided to leave.

10. Some people become rather angry quite easily.

11. Turn left at the first traffic signal.

12. The lady in the very high heels has visited us often.

13. Now and then I would like an extremely sweet dessert.

14. Tonight we will go together to the carnival.

15. She looked upward through the telescope and smiled slightly.

PAGE 433 = WORKBOOK PAGE 207

DOUBLE NEGATIVES

No, **not**, **never**, **none**, **no one**, **nobody**, **nothing**, **scarcely**, **and hardly** are considered *negative words.** Do not use two of these in an independent clause.**

Example: Wrong: I do **not** want **nothing**.

Right: I do **not** want anything.

OR

I want **nothing**.

Wrong: I could**n't hardly** hear.

Right: I could**n't** hear.

OR

I could **hardly** hear.

Wrong: He **never** wants **none**.

Right: He **never** wants any.

OR

He wants **none**.

DO NOT "GO" BY SOUND. IF YOU ARE ACCUSTOMED TO HEARING OR USING DOUBLE NEGATIVES, THEY WILL SOUND CORRECT.

---

*Neither is also a negative word and should not be used in the same independent clause as the others in this list. However, it is fine to use it with the negative conjunction nor in an independent clause.

Wrong: **Neither** of them like **nobody**.

Right: **Neither** of them like anybody.

Exception: **Neither** plums **nor** apricots were in season.

**An independent clause contains a subject and verb and can stand alone as a complete thought (sentence).

Name________________________________ **ADVERBS**
WORKBOOK PAGE 208 Double Negatives
Date________________________________

Directions: Choose the correct answer.
Answers are in boldfaced print.

Example: Those guys don't give (**anyone**, no one) money.

1. I hadn't (never, **ever**) seen an alligator before today.
2. The dolphin did not do (no, **any**) tricks in the show.
3. Victor never tells (**anything**, nothing) that is told to him.
4. Our school scarcely has (no, **any**) water fountains.
5. I don't know (nothing, **anything**).
6. The divers (couldn't, **could**) hardly breathe.
7. He doesn't want (none, **any**).
8. There (**is**, isn't) scarcely any food in the pantry.
9. Don't do that (**ever**, never) again.
10. They don't want (**anybody**, nobody) to help them.
11. Those horses haven't (no, **any**) water.
12. I never do (nothing, **anything**) right.
13. Neither of the copiers do (**anything**, nothing) clearly.
14. Brett doesn't want (nobody, **anybody**) to tell him what to do.
15. I don't want (none, **any**)!

Name___________________________________

Date____________________________________

ADVERBS
Double Negatives

Directions: Choose the correct answer.

Example: Those guys don't give (**anyone**, no one) money.

1. I hadn't (never, ever) seen an alligator before today.
2. The dolphin did not do (no, any) tricks in the show.
3. Victor never tells (anything, nothing) that is told to him.
4. Our school scarcely has (no, any) water fountains.
5. I don't know (nothing, anything).
6. The divers (couldn't, could) hardly breathe.
7. He doesn't want (none, any).
8. There (is, isn't) scarcely any food in the pantry.
9. Don't do that (ever, never) again.
10. They don't want (anybody, nobody) to help them.
11. Those horses haven't (no, any) water.
12. I never do (nothing, anything) right.
13. Neither of the copiers do (anything, nothing) clearly.
14. Brett doesn't want (nobody, anybody) to tell him what to do.
15. I don't want (none, any)!

Name_______________________________ **ADVERBS**
WORKBOOK PAGE 209 Double Negatives
Date_______________________________

Directions: Choose the correct answer.

Answers are in boldfaced print.

Example: I haven't (never, **ever**) toured a prison.

1. Our cookies (weren't, **were**) hardly edible.
2. There wasn't (**anyone**, no one) in the store.
3. I don't want (nothing, **anything**).
4. Our mail person (hasn't, **has**) no helpers.
5. I couldn't take (**any**, none) with me.
6. There (weren't, **were**) scarcely any cookies in the jar.
7. They will not do it for (nothing, **anything**).
8. The patient can't have (**any**, no) visitors.
9. Neither of the voters spoke to (nobody, **anybody**).
10. I (can't, **can**) hardly see the board from here.
11. Some children haven't (never, **ever**) been to the zoo.
12. You may not go to (neither, **either**) place.
13. I'm doing (**nothing**, anything) for a whole week.
14. The photographer shouldn't have waited for (none, **any**) of the others in the group.
15. I couldn't find (**anything**, nothing) to read.

Name________________________________

Date________________________________

ADVERBS

Double Negatives

Directions: Choose the correct answer.

Example: I haven't (never, **ever**) toured a prison.

1. Our cookies (weren't, were) hardly edible.
2. There wasn't (anyone, no one) in the store.
3. I don't want (nothing, anything).
4. Our mail person (hasn't, has) no helpers.
5. I couldn't take (any, none) with me.
6. There (weren't, were) scarcely any cookies in the jar.
7. They will not do it for (nothing, anything).
8. The patient can't have (any, no) visitors.
9. Neither of the voters spoke to (nobody, anybody).
10. I (can't, can) hardly see the board from here.
11. Some children haven't (never, ever) been to the zoo.
12. You may not go to (neither, either) place.
13. I'm doing (nothing, anything) for a whole week.
14. The photographer shouldn't have waited for (none, any) of the others in the group.
15. I couldn't find (anything, nothing) to read.

Name_______________________________ **ADVERB REVIEW**
WORKBOOK PAGE 210
Date_______________________________

Answers are in boldfaced print.
A. **Adverb or Adjective?:**

Directions: Circle the adverb form.

1. crazy, **crazily**

2. **capably**, capable

3. courageous, **courageously**

4. good, **well**

5. **absolutely**, absolute

6. careful, **carefully**

7. safe, **safely**

B. **Adverbs - How:**

Directions: Cross out any prepositional phrases. Underline the subject once and verb/verb phrase twice. Label any adverb(s) telling HOW - ADV. In the space provided, explain the use of the adverb in the sentence.

ADV.
1. ~~For a beginning speaker~~, Horace speaks well.
Well tells HOW Horace speaks.

ADV.
2. She stopped abruptly ~~at the entrance to the gated community~~.
Abruptly tells HOW she stopped.

ADV. **ADV.**
3. The audience jumped wildly and cheered loudly.
Wildly tells HOW the audience jumped; loudly tells HOW the audience cheered.

ADV.
4. The child chuckled gleefully ~~at her reflection in the mirror~~.
Gleefully tells HOW the child chuckled.

Name________________________________ **ADVERB REVIEW**

Date________________________________

A. **Adverb or Adjective?:**

Directions: Circle the adverb form.

1. crazy, crazily
2. capably, capable
3. courageous, courageously
4. good, well
5. absolutely, absolute
6. careful, carefully
7. safe, safely

B. **Adverbs - How:**

Directions: Cross out any prepositional phrases. Underline the subject once and verb/verb phrase twice. Label any adverb(s) telling HOW - ADV. In the space provided, explain the use of any adverb in the sentence.

1. For a beginning speaker, Horace speaks well.

____

2. She stopped abruptly at the entrance to the gated community.

____

3. The audience jumped wildly and cheered loudly.

____

4. The child chuckled gleefully at her reflection in the mirror.

____

Name________________________________ **ADVERB REVIEW**
WORKBOOK PAGE 211
Date________________________________

C. **Adverbs - How:** **Adverbs are in boldfaced print.**

Directions: Cross out any prepositional phrases. Underline the subject once and the verb/verb phrase twice. Circle any adverb(s) telling HOW.

1. The criticism was accepted **graciously**.

2. Can you hit a ball **hard**?

3. ~~After the symphony~~, everyone left **cheerfully**.

D. **Adverbs - When:**

Directions: Cross out any prepositional phrases. Underline the subject once and the verb/verb phrase twice. Label any adverb(s) telling WHEN - ADV. In the space provided, explain the use of any adverb in the sentence.

1. ~~Since her fortieth birthday~~, Mother never (**ADV.**) has wanted a party.

Never tells WHEN Mother has wanted a party.

2. The travel agent will arrange bus service tomorrow (**ADV.**).

Tomorrow tells WHEN the travel agent will arrange bus service.

3. First (**ADV.**), plans ~~for a spring clean up~~ must be discussed.

First tells WHEN plans must be discussed.

E. Adverbs - When: **Answers are in boldfaced print.**

Directions: Cross out any prepositional phrases. Underline the subject once and the verb/verb phrase twice. Circle any adverb(s) telling WHEN.

1. This toothpaste ~~in a huge tube~~ lasts **forever**.

2. **Sooner** or **later**, someone will give us some help.

3. These awards are presented **annually**.

Name________________________________ **ADVERB REVIEW**

Date________________________________

C. **Adverbs - How:**

Directions: Cross out any prepositional phrases. Underline the subject once and the verb/verb phrase twice. Circle any adverb(s) telling HOW.

1. The criticism was accepted graciously.
2. Can you hit a ball hard?
3. After the symphony, everyone left cheerfully.

D. **Adverbs - When:**

Directions: Cross out any prepositional phrases. Underline the subject once and the verb/verb phrase twice. Label any adverb(s) telling WHEN - ADV. In the space provided, explain the use of any adverb in the sentence.

1. Since her fortieth birthday, Mother never has wanted a party.

   ____

2. The travel agent will arrange bus service tomorrow.

   ____

3. First, plans for a spring clean-up must be discussed.

   ____

E. Adverbs - When:

Directions: Cross out any prepositional phrases. Underline the subject once and the verb/verb phrase twice. Circle any adverb(s) telling WHEN.

1. This toothpaste in a huge tube lasts forever.
2. Sooner or later, someone will give us some help.
3. These awards are presented annually.

Name_______________________________ **ADVERB REVIEW**

WORKBOOK PAGE 212

Date_______________________________

F. **Adverbs - Where:**

Directions: Cross out any prepositional phrases. Underline the subject once and the verb/verb phrase twice. Label any adverb(s) telling WHERE - ADV. In the space provided, explain the use of any adverb(s) in the sentence.

1. That car is rolling backwards! (**ADV.**: backwards)

   Backwards tells WHERE the car is rolling.

2. ~~At the department store~~, he went upstairs ~~on an escalator~~. (**ADV.**: upstairs)

   Upstairs tells WHERE he went.

3. The couple fished downstream ~~before lunch~~. (**ADV.**: downstream)

   Downstream tells WHERE the couple fished.

G. **Adverbs - Where:** **Adverbs are in boldfaced print.**

Directions: Cross out any prepositional phrases. Underline the subject once and the verb/verb phrase twice. Circle any adverb(s) telling WHERE.

1. Would you like (to go) **somewhere** ~~in an hour~~?
2. (You) Please step **forward** and stop ~~by the sign~~.
3. Sherri walked **over there** ~~near the hot dog stand~~.
4. The stewardess drove **home** ~~from the airport~~.

H. **Adverbs - to What Extent:**

Directions: Write the seven adverbs that repeatedly tell *to what extent.*

not, so, very, too quite, rather, somewhat

Name______________________________ **ADVERB REVIEW**

Date______________________________

F. **Adverbs - Where:**

Directions: Cross out any prepositional phrases. Underline the subject once and the verb/verb phrase twice. Label any adverb(s) telling WHERE - ADV. In the space provided, explain the use of any adverb(s) in the sentence.

1. That car is rolling backwards!

____

2. At the department store, he rode upstairs in an escalator.

____

3. The couple fished downstream before lunch.

____

G. **Adverbs - Where:**

Directions: Cross out any prepositional phrases. Underline the subject once and the verb/verb phrase twice. Circle any adverb(s) telling WHERE.

1. Would you like to go somewhere in an hour?
2. Please step forward and stop by the sign.
3. Sherri walked over there near the hot dog stand.
4. The stewardess drove home from the airport.

H. **Adverbs - to What Extent:**

Directions: Write the seven adverbs that repeatedly tell *to what extent*.

____

Name________________________________ **ADVERB REVIEW**

WORKBOOK PAGE 213

Date________________________________

I. **Good or Well?**

Directions: Write **good** or **well** in the space provided.

1. Her grandmother paints ceramics ______**well**______.
2. You estimated that answer quite ______**well**______.
3. Dr. Barton is a ______**good**______ internist.
4. That city in the Midwest has an extremely______**good**______ water system.
5. The colonists governed themselves ______**well**______.
6. During the summer months, Charlie was hired by a ______**good**______ company.
7. Patricia and Mickey play golf ______**well**______ at the Troon course.
8. A ______**good**______ turkey dinner often makes us tired.

J. **Adverbs - Double Negatives:** **Adverbs are in boldfaced print.**

Directions: Circle the correct answer.

1. Janelle doesn't have (no, **any**) brothers.
2. His hair hardly ever has (**any**, no) curl.
3. I don't want (nobody, **anybody**) to come with me.
4. He hardly ever says (nothing, **anything**).
5. Herm can't order (**anything**, nothing).
6. Our friend doesn't (never, **ever**) go scuba diving.
7. I can't do (**anything**, nothing) with this!
8. My uncle can't go (nowhere, **anywhere**) without his camera.

Name________________________________

ADVERB REVIEW

Date________________________________

I. **Good or Well?**

Directions: Write **good** or **well** in the space provided.

1. Her grandmother paints ceramics ________________.
2. You estimated that answer quite ________________.
3. Dr. Barton is a ________________ internist.
4. That city in the Midwest has an extremely ________________ water system.
5. The colonists governed themselves ________________.
6. During the summer months, Charlie was hired by a ________________ company.
7. Patricia and Mickey play golf ________________ at the Troon course.
8. A ________________ turkey dinner often makes us tired.

J. **Adverbs - Double Negatives:**

Directions: Circle the correct answer.

1. Janelle doesn't have (no, any) brothers.
2. His hair hardly ever has (any, no) curl.
3. I don't want (nobody, anybody) to come with me.
4. He hardly ever says (nothing, anything).
5. Herm can't order (anything, nothing).
6. Our friend doesn't (never, ever) go scuba diving.
7. I can't do (anything, nothing) with this!
8. My uncle can't go (nowhere, anywhere) without his camera.

Name_______________________________ **ADVERB REVIEW**
WORKBOOK PAGE 214
Date________________________________

K. **Adverbs:** **Answers are in boldfaced print.**

Directions: Circle any adverbs.

Suggestion: Cross out any prepositional phrases. However, check to see if one of the 7 adverbs that tell to what extent may be in any prepositional phrase. If it is, circle it. Underline the subject once and verb/verb phrase twice. Next, go through the sentence looking specifically for any adverbs that tell **how**. Reread the sentence, searching for any adverbs that tell **when**. Next, look for any adverbs that tell **where**. Finally, look for any adverbs that tell **to what extent** and are not located in a prepositional phrase. Circle any adverb(s).This process may sound long, but once you do it step-by-step, it will become faster and will definitely help you to determine adverbs.

1. (You) **Now**, hang **on tightly** ~~to your seat~~.
2. That baby crawls **extremely fast** ~~across the bare floor~~.
3. We shall **probably** arrive **late** ~~in the evening~~.
4. Gail, upset ~~by the **very** loud noises~~, put her work **aside**.
5. **Today**, an eagle flew **briskly away** ~~from its nest~~.
6. **Sooner** or **later**, he must grow **rather** tired ~~from those exercises~~.
7. **Daily**, those roosters crow **so loudly**.

L. **Adverbs - Degrees:**

Directions: Circle the correct adverb form.

1. The winners shot (**more often**, oftener) than the losing team.
2. Marcus swam (**better**, gooder) today than yesterday.
3. This hula hoop spins (**more swiftly**, most swiftly) than the yellow one.
4. Of the entire team, she runs (more slowly, **most slowly**).
5. (You) Carry these eggs (**more carefully**, most carefully) than the jelly beans.
6. Kay acts (more courageous, **more courageously**) when she's frightened.

Name________________________________ **ADVERB REVIEW**

Date________________________________

K. **Adverbs:**

Directions: Circle any adverbs.

Suggestion: Cross out any prepositional phrases. However, check to see if one of the 7 adverbs that tell to what extent may be in any prepositional phrase. If it is, circle it. Underline the subject once and verb/verb phrase twice. Next, go through the sentence looking specifically for any adverbs that tell **how**. Reread the sentence, searching for any adverbs that tell **when**. Next, look for any adverbs that tell **where**. Finally, look for any adverbs that tell **to what extent** and are not located in a prepositional phrase. This process may sound long, but once you do it step-by-step, it will become faster and will definitely help you to determine adverbs.

1. Now, hang on tightly to your seat.
2. That baby crawls extremely fast across the bare floor.
3. We shall probably arrive late in the evening.
4. Gail, upset by the very loud noises, put her work aside.
5. Today, an eagle flew briskly away from its nest.
6. Sooner or later, he must grow rather tired from those exercises.
7. Daily, those roosters crow so loudly.

L. **Adverbs - Degrees:**

Directions: Circle the correct adverb form.

1. The winners shot (more often, oftener) than the losing team.
2. Marcus swam (better, gooder) today than yesterday.
3. This hula hoop spins (more swiftly, most swiftly) than the yellow one.
4. Of the entire team, she runs (more slowly, most slowly).
5. Carry these eggs (more carefully, most carefully) than jelly beans.
6. Kay acts (more courageous, more courageously) when she's frightened.

Name________________________________ **ADVERB TEST**

Date________________________________

A. Directions: Write the adverb form of each word.

1. easy - easily
2. foolish - foolishly
3. nervous - nervously
4. fast - fast
5. final - finally
6. sudden - suddenly
7. good - well
8. recent - recently

B. Directions: Cross out any prepositional phrases. Underline the subject once and the verb/verb phrase twice. Circle any adverbs.

Adverbs are in boldfaced print.

1. **Quickly**, he grabbed the fire extinguisher **from** ~~above the fireplace~~.
2. (You) Please remove the tiles ~~in the family room~~ **very carefully**.
3. Shanna hit the ball **hard** ~~during her first practice~~.
4. A waitress **usually** works **fast** ~~during dinner hour~~.
5. You can swim ~~underneath the water~~ **so well**.
6. He answered all questions **courteously** and **confidently**.
7. We need (to work) **together** ~~on this project~~ ~~concerning recycling~~.
8. A plumber could **not** come **immediately**.
9. You are **always quite** friendly and act **agreeably**.
10. One ~~of the penguins~~ padded **quite swiftly** ~~to the water's edge~~.

Name______________________________ **ADVERB TEST**

Date______________________________

A. Directions: Write the adverb form of each word.

1. easy - ______________________________
2. foolish - ______________________________
3. nervous - ______________________________
4. fast - ______________________________
5. final - ______________________________
6. sudden - ______________________________
7. good - ______________________________
8. recent - ______________________________

B. Directions: Cross out any prepositional phrases. Underline the subject once and verb/verb phrase twice. Circle any adverbs.

1. Quickly he grabbed the fire extinguisher from above the fireplace.
2. Please remove the tiles in the family room very carefully.
3. Shanna hit the ball hard during her first practice.
4. A waitress usually works fast during dinner hour.
5. You can swim underneath the water so well.
6. He answered all questions courteously and confidently.
7. We need to work together on this project concerning recycling.
8. A plumber could not come immediately.
9. You are always quite friendly and act agreeably.
10. One of the penguins padded quite swiftly to the water's edge.

C. Directions: Write **good** or **well** in the space provided.

1. His exams went ___well___.
2. This is a ___good___ way to tie a double knot.
3. You are doing ___well___; keep it up!
4. Miss Jansen doesn't feel ___well___ today.
5. Oprah swims very ___well___ for a beginner.

D. Directions: Circle the correct answer.
Answers are in boldfaced print.

1. This frisbee flies (gooder, **better**) than that one.
2. Of the triplets, Tiffany sings (more beautifully, **most beautifully**).
3. Sweeping the kitchen takes (longer, **longest**) of all the chores.
4. My sister walks (**more slowly**, most slowly) to school than from school.
5. Jana hits the ball (harder, **hardest**) of the entire team.
6. To avoid a collision, the first car stopped (more abruptly, **most abruptly**) of the four.

E. Directions: Circle the correct answer.
Answers are in boldfaced print.

1. Mark doesn't have (no, **any**) ride to the store.
2. I don't want (**any**, none).
3. Kenneth has (**no**, any) hobby.
4. She scarcely has (**any**, no) time to play.
5. The hamster hardly eats (**anything**, nothing).
6. You never want (**anybody**, nobody) to help you.

C. Directions: Write **good** or **well** in the space provided.

1. His exams went ____________________.
2. This is a ________________ way to tie a double knot.
3. You are doing ___________________ ; keep it up!
4. Miss Jansen doesn't feel ________________ today.
5. Oprah swims very ________________ for a beginner.

D. Directions: Circle the correct answer.

1. This frisbee flies (gooder, better) than that one.
2. Of the triplets, Tiffany sings (more beautifully, most beautifully).
3. Sweeping the kitchen takes (longer, longest) of all the chores.
4. My sister walks (more slowly, most slowly) to school than from school.
5. Jana hits the ball (harder, hardest) of the entire team.
6. To avoid a collision, the first car stopped (more abruptly, most abruptly) of the four.

E. Directions: Circle the correct answer.

1. Mark doesn't have (no, any) ride to the store.
2. I don't want (any, none).
3. Kenneth has (no, any) hobby.
4. She scarcely has (any, no) time to play.
5. The hamster hardly eats (anything, nothing).
6. You never want (anybody, nobody) to help you.

Name________________________________ **CUMULATIVE REVIEW**
WORKBOOK PAGE 215 Adverb Unit
Date________________________________

A. Directions: Cross out any prepositional phrases. Underline the subject once and the verb/verb phrase twice.

1. ~~Without Lana's help~~, we may have (to postpone) our bake sale.
2. (You) Place this wallpaper up ~~against those cupboards~~ ~~on the back wall~~.
3. The painter and several workers are **not** leaving ~~until noon~~.

B. Directions: Circle the correct adjective form.
Answers are in boldfaced print.

1. This speaker seems (**more nervous**, nervouser) than the preceding one.
2. Your left ankle is (**more swollen**, most swollen).
3. Of those four kittens, the tiniest is (more playful, **most playful**).

C. Directions: Write the contraction:

1. cannot - **can't** 3. it is - **it's** 5. I am - **I'm**
2. you are - **you're** 4. I have - **I've** 6. they will - **they'll**

D. Directions: Cross out any prepositional phrases. Underline the subject once and the verb/verb phrase twice. Write the tense in the blank provided.

1. future — I shall finish ~~within two hours~~.
2. present perfect — Have you been ~~to Vermont~~?
3. past — ~~Before the party~~, Allen made lemon chicken.
4. present — ~~Throughout the night~~, those two dogs bark.
5. future progressive — Heyward will be going ~~to camp~~ ~~during July~~.

E. Directions: Write A if the noun is abstract; write C if the noun is concrete.

1. A bravery 2. C garage 3. A sympathy 4. C steak 5. C smog

Name________________________________

Date________________________________

CUMULATIVE REVIEW
Adverb Unit

A. Directions: Cross out any prepositional phrases. Underline the subject once and verb/verb phrase twice.

1. Without Lana's help, we may have to postpone our bake sale.

2. Place this wallpaper up against those cupboards on the back wall.

3. The painter and several workers are not leaving until noon.

B. Directions: Circle the correct adjective form.

1. This speaker seems (more nervous, nervouser) than the preceding one.
2. Your left ankle is (more swollen, most swollen).
3. Of those four kittens, the tiniest is (more playful, most playful).

C. Directions: Write the contraction:

1. cannot - _______________ 3. it is - _______________ 5. I am - _______________

2. you are - _______________ 4. I have - _______________ 6. they will - _______________

D. Directions: Cross out any prepositional phrases. Underline the subject once and the verb/verb phrase twice. Write the tense in the blank provided.

1. ____________________________ I shall finish within two hours.

2. ____________________________ Have you been to Vermont?

3. ____________________________ Before the party, Allen made lemon chicken.

4. ____________________________ Throughout the night, those two dogs bark.

5. ____________________________ Heyward will be going to camp during July.

E. Directions: Write <u>A</u> if the noun is abstract; write <u>C</u> if the noun is concrete.

1. ___ bravery 2. ___ garage 3. ___ sympathy 4. ___ steak 5. ___ smog

F. Directions: Write the possessive form:

WORKBOOK PAGE 216

1. a basketball belonging to four girls: ___four girls' basketball___
2. a road through the park: ___the park's road___
3. a gift for a class: ___a class's gift___
4. a decision made by more than one woman: ___women's decision___

G. Directions: Write N if the boldfaced word is a noun. Write A if the boldfaced word serves as an adjective. Write V if the boldfaced word serves as a verb.

1. ___N___ Several runners darted around a **track** at the local high school.
2. ___A___ Holly set a **track** record yesterday.
3. ___V___ We must **track** a course for the car derby.
4. ___V___ Mia and Joel **star** in many shows.
5. ___N___ A **star** is fascinating!

H. Directions: Write the past participle form:

1. to shake - ___had shaken___
2. to leave - ___had left___
3. to give - ___had given___
4. to eat - ___had eaten___
5. to sit - ___had sat___
6. to rise - ___had risen___
7. to sink - ___had sunk___
8. to freeze - ___had frozen___

I. Directions: Write the plural of each noun.

1. rash - ___rashes___
2. ax - ___axes___
3. bass - ___bass___
4. fee - ___fees___
5. goose - ___geese___
6. cross - ___crosses___

J. Directions: Label any conjunction or interjection.

Intj. **conj.**
1. Great! I've won a new radio or some money.

Intj. **(both + and = correlative conj.)**
2. Good heavens! I've locked both my keys and purse in the car!

F. Directions: Write the possessive form:

1. a basketball belonging to four girls: ______________________________

2. a road through the park: ______________________________

3. a gift for a class: ______________________________

4. a decision made by more than one woman: ______________________________

G. Directions: Write N if the boldfaced word is a noun. Write A if the boldfaced word serves as an adjective. Write V if the boldfaced word serves as a verb.

1. _____ Several runners darted around a **track** at the local high school.
2. _____ Holly set a **track** record yesterday.
3. _____ We must **track** a course for the car derby.
4. _____ Mia and Joel **star** in many shows.
5. _____ A **star** is fascinating!

H. Directions: Write the past participle form:

1. to shake - ____________________
2. to leave - ____________________
3. to give - ____________________
4. to eat - ____________________
5. to sit - ____________________
6. to rise - ____________________
7. to sink - ____________________
8. to freeze - ____________________

I. Directions: Write the plural of each noun:

1. rash - ____________
2. ax - ____________
3. bass - ____________
4. fee - ____________
5. goose - ____________
6. cross - ____________

J. Directions: Label any conjunction or interjection.

1. Great! I've won a new radio or some money.

2. Good heavens! I've locked both my keys and purse in the car!

K. Directions: Cross out any prepositional phrases. Underline the subject once and the verb/verb phrase twice.

WORKBOOK PAGE 217

1. The child has (began, begun) (to swim).
2. Have you ever (drank, drunk) pink lemonade?
3. ~~By Friday~~, the student will have (ridden, rode) fifty miles back and forth ~~to college~~.
4. Mrs. Carlson has (gone, went) ~~to a yard sale~~.
5. Each ~~of the pamphlets~~ (has, have) been passed out.
6. (You) (Rise, Raise) the window shade ~~about four inches~~.
7. The member must have (brung, brought) a friend ~~with her~~.
8. (May, Can) I look ~~underneath the seat~~ ~~for the lost credit card~~?
9. Their newspaper is still (laying, lying) ~~in front~~ ~~of their door~~.
10. None ~~of the men~~ (has, have) a book ~~concerning French money~~.
11. Had you (flew, flown) ~~to Atlanta~~ ~~before lunch~~?
12. She must have (came, come) in very quietly.
13. I might have (broke, broken) this lock accidentally.
14. He could have (lain, laid) the saw ~~under the counter~~ ~~in the workroom~~.
15. You should have (taken, took) some money along ~~with you~~.
16. (You) Please, (sit, set) ~~beneath the ramada~~.

L. Directions: Cross out any prepositional phrases. Underline the subject once and the verb/verb phrase twice. Write A in the blank if the verb is action; write L if the verb is linking.

1. _L__ They feel sad ~~about their neighbor's sick dog~~.

2. _A__ Dave felt the lump ~~on his head~~.

3. _A__ ~~From June~~ ~~until August~~, the Garr family stays ~~in a cabin~~ ~~by a lake~~. (There is nothing left after the verb to which the subject can be linked.)

4. _L__ Her finger stayed red ~~for several days~~.

K. Directions: Cross out any prepositional phrases. Underline the subject once and the verb/verb phrase twice.

1. The child has (began, begun) to swim.
2. Have you ever (drank, drunk) pink lemonade?
3. By Friday, the student will have (ridden, rode) fifty miles back and forth to college.
4. Mrs. Carlson has (gone, went) to a yard sale.
5. Each of the pamphlets (has, have) been passed out.
6. (Rise, Raise) the window shade about four inches.
7. The member must have (brung, brought) a friend with her.
8. (May, Can) I look underneath the seat for the lost credit card?
9. Their newspaper is still (laying, lying) in front of their door.
10. None of the men (has, have) a book concerning French money.
11. Had you (flew, flown) to Atlanta before lunch?
12. She must have (came, come) in very quietly.
13. I might have (broke, broken) this lock accidentally.
14. He could have (lain, laid) the saw under the counter in the workroom.
15. You should have (taken, took) some money along with you.
16. Please, (sit, set) beneath the ramada.

L. Directions: Cross out any prepositional phrases. Underline the subject once and the verb/verb phrase twice. Write A in the blank if the verb is action, write L if the verb is linking.

Suggestion: Write *is*, *am*, *are*, *was*, or *were* above each verb to help.

1. _____ They feel sad about their neighbor's sick dog.
2. _____ Dave felt the lump on his head.
3. _____ From June to August, the Garr family stays in a cabin by a lake.
4. _____ Her finger stayed red for several days.

M. Directions: List the 23 auxiliary (helping) verbs:
WORKBOOK PAGE 218

has, have, had, do, does, did, may, must, might, should, would, could, shall, will, can, is, am, are, was, were, be, being, been

N. Directions: Cross out any prepositional phrases. Underline the subject once and the verb/verb phrase twice. Write the helping verb(s) in column one and the main verb in column 2.

	HELPING VERB(S)	MAIN VERB
1. I should not have given that away.	should have	given
2. Everyone ~~of the boys~~ is going.	is	going
3. He must have left his shoes here.	must have	left
4. Did Brad ask ~~for a new pack~~?	Did	ask
5. Could you move over ~~to the door~~?	Could	move

O. Directions: Write the 20 linking verbs (12 infinitives + 8):

to feel, to taste, to look, to smell, to appear, to become, to grow, to remain, to seem, to sound, to stay, to be (is, am, are, was, were, be, being, been)

P. Directions: List the limiting (determining) adjectives.

1. The three articles are **a**, **an**, and **the**.
2. The four demonstratives are **this**, **that**, **those**, and **these**.
3. Name the possessive pronouns that can serve as limiting adjectives: **my**, **his**, **her**, **its**, **your**, **our**, and **their**.
4. Give an example of a possessive noun used as a determiner:

   Answers will vary.

   Representative answers: Marge's coat, club's leader
5. Give an example of a number used as a determiner:

   Answers will vary.

   Representative answers: thirteen doughnuts, fifty swimmers
6. Five examples of indefinites used as determiners are:

   Answers will vary.

   Representative answers: no, any, some, few, several, many

M. Directions: List the 23 auxiliary (helping) verbs: ______________________

____

____

N. Directions: Cross out any prepositional phrases. Underline the subject once and the verb/verb phrase twice. Write the helping verb(s) in column one and the main verb in column 2.

	HELPING VERB(S)	MAIN VERB
1. I should not have given that away.	______________	______________
2. Everyone of the boys is going.	______________	______________
3. He must have left his shoes here.	______________	______________
4. Did Brad ask for a new pack?	______________	______________
5. Could you move over to the door?	______________	______________

O. Directions: Write the 20 linking verbs (12 linking verbs + 8): ______________

____

____

P. Directions: List the limiting (determining) adjectives.

1. The three articles are _____, _____, and _____.
2. The four demonstratives are ________, ________, ________, and ________.
3. Name the possessive pronouns that can serve as limiting adjectives: ________, ________, ________, ________, ________, ________, and ________.
4. Give an example of a possessive noun used as a determiner: ______________
5. Give an example of a number used as a determiner: ______________
6. Five examples of indefinites used as determiners are ______________, ______________, ______________, ______________, and ______________.

Q. Directions: If the boldfaced word serves as an adjective, write Adj. in the blank. If the boldfaced word does not serve as an adjective, write *No.*

WORKBOOK PAGE 219

1. Adj. **Several** new pots and pans were purchased.
2. No **Several** will be given awards at the luncheon.
3. No **Carl's** is the best!
4. Adj. Have you seen **Carl's** salt map?
5. Adj. She doesn't like **her** stewed tomatoes.
6. No Please give **those** to Maria and Jackson.

R. Directions: Circle any adjectives.

Adjectives are in boldfaced print.

1. **A** very **old brass** bed had been sold at **that antique** auction recently.
2. **Many lively** children are patiently waiting for **their talkative** parents.
3. **His aunt's** bathroom has **striped** wallpaper with **an unusual, orange floral** border.
4. Those are **two good** examples of **the disastrous** effects of **wind** erosion.

S. Directions: Box any nouns.

Nouns are in boldface. (Adjectives have been placed in italics.)

1. **Jake** studies *many* **insects** and **reptiles** in *his spare* **time**.
2. *This* **broom** and *that old* **rake** will be thrown in *the* **garbage** on **Monday**.
3. *A friendly* **dog** scampered across *the enormous* **room** and licked *my* **hand**.
4. *Several* **problems** were discussed by *the concerned* **parents** during *a* **meeting**.

Q. Directions: If the boldfaced word serves as an adjective, write Adj. in the blank. If the boldfaced word does not serve as an adjective, write *No.*

1. _____ **Several** new pots and pans were purchased.

2. _____ **Several** will be given awards at the luncheon.

3. _____ **Carl's** is the best!

4. _____ Have you seen **Carl's** salt map?

5. _____ She doesn't like **her** stewed tomatoes.

6. _____ Please give **those** to Maria and Jackson.

R. Directions: Circle any adjectives.

Suggestion: Read each sentence and circle limiting adjectives. Then, circle any descriptive adjectives.

1. A very old brass bed had been sold at that antique auction recently.

2. Many lively children are patiently waiting for their talkative parents.

3. His aunt's bathroom has striped wallpaper with an unusual, orange floral border.

4. Those are two good examples of the disastrous effects of wind erosion.

S. Directions: Box any nouns.

Suggestion: First, locate limiting and descriptive adjectives. Use these to help locate nouns. Then, reread the sentence looking for nouns that appear without an adjective.

1. Jake studies many insects and reptiles in his spare time.

2. This broom and that old rake will be thrown in the garbage on Monday.

3. A friendly dog scampered across the enormous room and licked my hand.

4. Several problems were discussed by the concerned parents during a meeting.

T. Fill in the blank:

WORKBOOK PAGE 220

1. **The winner is Frank.** Frank is a predicate nominative. Write a proof:
   Proof: __Frank is the winner.__
2. **Dad made Mom a wooden shelf.** Mom serves as the __indirect object__ of this sentence.
3. **Fred crushed the can with his foot.** The direct object of this sentence is __can__.
4. **A kite had become tangled among some branches.** Branches serves as the __object__ of the preposition in this sentence.
5. Name a set of correlative conjunctions. __both/and, neither/nor, either/or__

U. Directions: Write the sentence type in the space provided.

1. __exclamatory__ That's right!
2. __interrogative__ Is an olive a type of fruit?
3. __declarative__ A tomato is technically a fruit.
4. __imperative__ Finish this assignment.

V. Directions: Write P if the group of words is a phrase; write C if the group of words is a clause.

1. __P__ Under the bed.
2. __C__ Their house is on Dunbar Lane.
3. __C__ When she sings alone.
4. __P__ Taking the wrong road.

W. Directions: Write S if the group of words is a sentence. Write F if the group of words is a fragment. Write R-O if the group of words is a run-on.

1. __F__ Harold after the last speech.
2. __R-O__ They have a cat, it's a Siamese.
3. __S__ Has this floor been washed?

T. Fill in the blank:

1. **The winner is Frank.** Frank is a predicate nominative. Write a proof:
   Proof: ____

2. **Dad made Mom a wooden shelf.** Mom serves as the ____________________ ____________________ of this sentence.

3. **Fred crushed the can with his foot.** The direct object of this sentence is ________.

4. **A kite had become tangled among some branches.** Branches serves as the ____________ of the preposition in this sentence.

5. Name a set of correlative conjunctions. ______________________________

U. Directions: Write the sentence type in the space provided.

1. ______________________ That's right!
2. ______________________ Is an olive a type of fruit?
3. ______________________ A tomato is technically a fruit.
4. ______________________ Finish this assignment.

V. Directions: Write P if the group of words is a phrase; write C if the group of words is a clause.

1. _____ Under the bed.
2. _____ Their house is on Dunbar Lane.
3. _____ When she sings alone.
4. _____ Taking the wrong road.

W. Directions: Write S if the group of words is a sentence. Write F if the group of words is a fragment. Write R-O if the group of words is a run-on.

1. _____ Harold after the last speech.
2. _____ They have a cat, it's a Siamese.
3. _____ Has this floor been washed?

Name______________________________

Date______________________________

CUMULATIVE TEST
Adverb Unit

A. Directions: Circle any abstract noun.
Answers are in boldfaced print.

fin fan fist **fun** friend female fort fence **faith** **freedom**

B. Directions: Write the plural of each noun.

1. proof - **proofs**
2. ash - **ashes**
3. ploy - **ploys**
4. calf - **calves**
5. tissue - **tissues**
6. tooth - **teeth**
7. mother-in-law **mothers-in-law**
8. derby - **derbies**

C. Directions: Write the contraction.

1. should not - shouldn't
2. we will - we'll
3. it is - it's
4. you are - you're
5. they are - they're
6. I would - I'd

D. Directions: Write A if the boldfaced word serves as an adjective; write V if the boldfaced word serves as a verb. Write N if the boldfaced word serves as a noun.

1. A She attended a **flute** recital.
2. N Is the **flute** an expensive instrument?
3. V Did you **flute** the edges of the pie?

E. Directions: Cross out any prepositional phrases. Underline the subject once and the verb/verb phrase twice. Label any direct object - D.O. Label any indirect object - I.O.

1. Most ~~of the guests~~ signed the register. (register: **D.O.**)
2. ~~At the end of the seminar~~, books were sold ~~at various booths~~.
3. Kelly baked the class brownies ~~for her birthday~~. (class: **I.O.**; brownies: **D.O.**)

Name________________________________

Date________________________________

CUMULATIVE TEST
Adverb Unit

A. Directions: Circle any abstract noun.

fin fan fist fun friend female fort fence faith freedom

B. Directions: Write the plural of each noun.

1. proof - ____________ 4. calf - ____________ 7. mother-in-law______________
2. ash - ____________ 5. tissue - __________ 8. derby - ____________________
3. ploy - ____________ 6. tooth - ___________

C. Directions: Write the contraction.

1. should not - ____________ 3. it is - ______________ 5. they are - ___________
2. we will - ______________ 4. you are - ____________ 6. I would - ____________

D. Directions: Write A if the boldfaced word serves as an adjective; write V if the bold faced word serves as a verb. Write N if the boldfaced word serves as a noun.

1. _____ She attended a **flute** recital.
2. _____ Is the **flute** an expensive instrument?
3. _____ Did you **flute** the edges of the pie?

E. Directions: Cross out any prepositional phrases. Underline the subject once and the verb/verb phase twice. Label any direct object-D.O. Label any indirect object-I.O.

1. Most of the guests signed the register.
2. At the end of the seminar, books were sold at various booths.
3. Kelly baked the class brownies for her birthday.

F. Directions: Cross out any prepositional phrases. Underline the subject once and the verb/verb phrase twice.

1. Kimberly wouldn't ride her horse ~~in the rodeo parade~~.
2. ~~After sunrise~~, a group ~~of men~~ played golf ~~for several hours~~.
3. Those ladies and their sons will be attending a banquet ~~at our church~~.
4. (You) Take these along ~~with you~~, and wear them ~~after your shower~~.

G. Directions: If the boldfaced noun serves as an appositive, write APP. in the space. If the boldfaced noun serves as a direct object, write D.O. in the space. If the boldfaced noun serves as a predicate nominative, write PN in the space.

1. APP. Their cousin, **Ella**, attends a junior college.
2. PN Our new neighbor is **Adam Jones**.
3. D.O. The car door hit **Frankie** in the back.

H. Directions: Fill in the blank.

1. Write a proper noun. Answers will vary:

   Representative answers: Bond Lake, Susan, Sears Tower, Walmart

2. Write a proper adjective. Answers will vary:

   Representative answers: **German** food, **New York** subway

3. Write a phrase. Answers will vary:

   Representative answers: from my dad, looking for my brother

I. Directions: Write the sentence type.

1. interrogative Where have you put the stapler?
2. declarative My answer is final.
3. imperative Please stop that.
4. exclamatory The train is moving!

F. Directions: Cross out any prepositional phrases. Underline the subject once and the verb/verb phrase twice.

1. Kimberly wouldn't ride her horse in the rodeo parade.

2. After sunrise, a group of men played golf for several hours.

3. Those ladies and their sons will be attending a banquet at our church.

4. Take these along with you, and wear them after your shower.

G. Directions: If the boldfaced noun serves as an appositive, write APP. in the space. If the boldfaced noun serves as a direct object, write D.O. in the space. If the boldfaced noun serves as a predicate nominative, write PN in the space.

Remember: You need a proof for a predicate nominative.

1. _______ Their cousin, **Ella**, attends a junior college.

2. _______ Our new neighbor is **Adam Jones**.

3. _______ The car door hit **Frankie** in the back.

H. Directions: Fill in the blank.

1. Write a proper noun. ______________________________

2. Write a proper adjective. ______________________________

3. Write a phrase. ______________________________

I. Directions: Write the sentence type.

1. ______________________ Where have you put the stapler?

2. ______________________ My answer is final.

3. ______________________ Please stop that.

4. ______________________ The train is moving!

J. Directions: Circle the correct adjective form.
Answers are in boldfaced print.

1. This is the (funnier, **funniest**) show I have seen.
2. Jody's published copy was (**better**, best) than her rough draft.
3. Her reaction was (**more pleasant**, pleasanter) than I expected.
4. Of all the science projects, yours was the (more interesting, **most interesting**).
5. Of the triplets, Julie is (more creative, **most creative**).

K. Directions: Circle the correct verb.
Answers are in boldfaced print.

1. The policeman (rose, **raised**) his hand to tell the driver to stop.
2. One of the truckers (wear, **wears**) a blue uniform.
3. Have you (chose, **chosen**) a different route for the detour?
4. The baby may have (drank, **drunk**) a full six ounces of milk.
5. A bracelet is (laying, **lying**) on the floor.
6. Has the chemist (gave, **given**) us the test results?
7. Few workers (is, **are**) taking a break early.
8. We should have (**brought**, brang) our jackets.
9. The jurist must have (took, **taken**) a newspaper along.
10. One of the dogs (eat, **eats**) the other's food.
11. The key chain and an extra key (was, **were**) on the desk.
12. A visitor must have been (**sitting**, setting) in that empty seat.
13. Have you ever (wrote, **written**) your name backwards?
14. (Lie, **Lay**) your tiles for the board game on the table.
15. Mr. and Mrs. Dobson (leaves, **leave**) early each morning.

J. Directions: Circle the correct adjective form.

1. This is the (funnier, funniest) show I have seen.
2. Jody's published copy was (better, best) than her rough draft.
3. Her reaction was (more pleasant, pleasanter) than I expected.
4. Of all the science projects, yours was the (more interesting, most interesting).
5. Of the triplets, Julie is (more creative, most creative).

K. Directions: Circle the correct verb.

1. The policeman (rose, raised) his hand to tell the driver to stop.
2. One of the truckers (wear, wears) a blue uniform.
3. Have you (chose, chosen) a different route for the detour?
4. The baby may have (drank, drunk) a full six ounces of milk.
5. A bracelet is (laying, lying) on the floor.
6. Has the chemist (gave, given) us the test results?
7. Few workers (is, are) taking a break early.
8. We should have (brought, brang) our jackets.
9. The jurist must have (took, taken) a newspaper along.
10. One of the dogs (eat, eats) the other's food.
11. The key chain and an extra key (was, were) on the desk.
12. A visitor must have been (sitting, setting) in that empty seat.
13. Have you ever (wrote, written) your name backwards?
14. (Lie, Lay) your tiles for the board game on the table.
15. Mr. and Mrs. Dobson (leaves, leave) early each morning.

L. Directions: Write the possessive form.

1. a yard sale belonging to two families - **families' yard sale**
2. notes belonging to a speaker - **a speaker's notes**
3. a clothing store for more than one man - **a men's clothing store**

M. Directions: Circle any adjectives.
Adjectives are in boldfaced print.

1. **Several blue helium** balloons are attached to **that long metal** pole.

N. Directions: Box any nouns.
Nouns are in boldfaced print.

1. I must take two **boxes** of mystery **books** to the **library** during the **afternoon**.

O. Directions: Write P if the group of words is a phrase; write C if the group of words is a clause.

1. P Down the street.
2. C After James left.
3. P Running through the hall
4. C Claude has a new hamster.

P. Directions: Write the tense.

1. present His grandfather goes to bed early.
2. present perfect Have you washed your hair today?
3. present progressive Are you planning a surprise party?

Q. Directions: Write S if the group of words is a sentence. Write F if the group of words is a fragment. Write R-O if the group of words is a run-on.

1. S The batter struck out, but he ran to first base anyway.
2. R-O Melinda rides to the store, her friend always walks.
3. F Driving a truck to pick up a load of hay.

R. Directions: Fill in the blank.

1. **Wow! We almost won!** What part of speech is Wow!? interjection
2. **Are you chewing gum?** The verb phrase is are chewing. The main verb is chewing.
3. **The little boy and girl painted Peter a picture.** Peter is the indirect object.

L. Directions: Write the possessive form.

1. a yard sale belonging to two families - ______________________________

2. notes belonging to a speaker - ______________________________

3. a clothing store for more than one man - ______________________________

M. Directions: Circle any adjectives.

1. Several blue helium balloons are attached to that long metal pole.

N. Directions: Box any nouns.

1. I must take two boxes of mystery books to the library during the afternoon.

O. Directions: Write P if the group of words is a phrase; write C if the group of words is a clause.

1. _____ Down the street.

2. _____ After James left.

3. _____ Running through the hall.

4. _____ Claude has a new hamster.

P. Directions: Write the tense.

1. ____________________ His grandfather goes to bed early.

2. ____________________ Have you washed your hair today?

3. ____________________ Are you planning a surprise party?

Q. Directions: Write S if the group of words is a sentence. Write F if the group of words is a fragment. Write R-O if the group of words is a run-on.

1. _____ The batter struck out, but he ran to first base anyway.

2. _____ Melinda rides to the store, her friend always walks.

3. _____ Driving a truck to pick up a load of hay.

R. Directions: Fill in the blank.

1. **Wow! We almost won!** What part of speech is Wow!? ____________________

2. **Are you chewing gum?** The verb phrase is ____________________. The main verb is ____________________.

3. **The little boy and girl painted Peter a picture.** Peter is the ____________________

PAGE 474 = WORKBOOK PAGE 221
PAGE 475 = WORKBOOK PAGE 222

PRONOUNS

Pronouns are difficult for many students because pronouns are used incorrectly so often.

The "me and Bob" syndrome is rampant. Some students have heard "me and ______" from birth, and it SOUNDS correct to them. Again, the teacher needs to courteously correct mistakes.

If a student says, "May me and Tom go to the library?", try eliminating "and Tom" from the sentence.* In other words, you repeat back to the student, "May **me** go to the library?" The student will usually make the correction. If this does not occur, repeat the incorrect form again. There might be a few who either don't honestly understand the mistake or choose to ignore it. It then becomes your decision to proceed in a manner which is comfortable for you. (If it's a request, some teachers will not consider the proposition until it has been presented in proper grammatical form. There are some teachers who won't affirm a request unless it's asked properly the first time. Again, you must do that which is comfortable for *you.*)

Hopefully, by the time that the pronoun unit has been presented in a step-by-step manner, students will understand the reasons for their mistakes and develop techniques to help them speak and write properly using correct pronouns. Some helpful hints have been included here:

A. Be sure that students understand the proof method for determining predicate pronouns. This is one place where proof, not sound, must be applied.

B. In a sentence such as, "(We, Us) girls left," have students cross out, literally or mentally, the noun (girls) beside the pronoun. It is then easy to see that one says, "*We* left." Therefore, "We girls left," is correct.

C. Another frequent mistake is, "John is taller than *me.*" This error can easily be corrected by showing students that the sentence should actually read, "John is taller than __________am." Of course, the "am" is often omitted. Since "John is taller than *I* am (not *me* am)," is correct, "John is taller than I ," is the correct form.

D. Be sure that students understand the concept of using an objective pronoun with the preposition *between* . "The matter must remain *between* you and me."

E. If students have trouble discerning the correct pronoun in **compound formations**, teach placing one's finger over the first part of the formation. This is one area where you can teach students to determine the pronoun by sound.

Example: The award will be given to Shelley or (I, me).
The award will be given to me.

*Students will also correct each other.

PRONOUNS

Pronouns take the place of nouns. They agree in number and gender.

Number: **Sarah** and **John** missed **their** bus. (Two requires their.)

Gender: Use a female pronoun (she, her) when referring to a girl or woman. Use a male pronoun (he, him) when referring to a boy or man.

Examples: **Joan** likes to ride **her** bike.

He gives **his** dog a bath each week.

Note: If you aren't sure if the noun is female or male, you may use ***his/her.*** However, ***his*** has become acceptable in this situation.

Each **person** brought his/her own lunch.

or

Each **person** brought his own lunch.

PERSONAL PRONOUNS:

Nominative Pronouns (Subjective Pronouns)	**Objective Pronouns**	**Possessive Pronouns**
I	**me**	**my, mine**
he	**him**	**his**
she	**her**	**her, hers**
you	**you**	**your, yours**
it	**it**	**its**
we	**us**	**our, ours**
they	**them**	**their, theirs**
who	**whom**	**whose**
FUNCTION IN A SENTENCE:	**FUNCTION IN A SENTENCE:**	**FUNCTION IN A SENTENCE:**
1. SUBJECT **2. PREDICATE NOMINATIVE**	**1. OBJECT OF THE PREPOSITION** **2. DIRECT OBJECT** **3. INDIRECT OBJECT**	**SHOW OWNERSHIP**

PRONOUNS

Personal Pronouns / Nominative Pronouns:

The nominative pronouns are **I**, **he**, **she**, **you**, **it**, **we**, **they**, and **who**.

Look at your pronoun chart. There are only two pronouns that are in both the nominative and objective columns: **you** and **it**. These are called neutral pronouns and do not change from nominative to objective form.

NOMINATIVE PRONOUNS FUNCTION AS EITHER THE SUBJECT OR PREDICATE NOMINATIVE IN A SENTENCE.

A. Review of Subjects:

The subject of a sentence, in easiest terms, is who or what the sentence is about.

Examples: That handle is broken.

We have not begun a new project.

B. Review of Predicate Nominatives:

The predicate nominative is the same as the subject of the sentence. To check a predicate nominative, try inverting the sentence.

PN
Examples: That lady is my sister.

My sister is that lady.

PN
The winner was she.

She was the winner.

Note: Be sure to use the inverted form with pronouns. Perhaps you have heard someone say something like, "The winner was her." Her has to be wrong because the inverted form would read, "Her is the winner."

Name_______________________________ **PRONOUNS**
WORKBOOK PAGE 223 Subjects
Date_______________________________

Directions: Cross out any prepositional phrases. Underline the subject once and the verb/verb phrase twice.

Example: Bill and I have gone ~~with Uncle Fred~~.

1. May Clarene and I go ~~to the store~~?
2. We must have lost his phone number.
3. The hikers and we might try (to climb) that mountain.
4. Did she place the garden hose ~~by the fountain~~?
5. Jeremy, Joshua, Julie, and I should have prepared the meal.
6. ~~In the middle of the night~~, they left ~~for Baton Rouge, Louisiana~~.
7. Nancy and I can**not** carry this package.
8. Have you ever taken gymnastics?
9. ~~After the show~~, we went out ~~for pizza~~.
10. Did they ask ~~for more information~~.
11. Those leaders and we are ~~in charge of the social hour~~.
12. Either Mother or I will be attending the meeting.
13. It is a rather hot, muggy day.
14. You could have shined all ~~of the silver~~ ~~for me~~.
15. My father and I have**n't** ever camped ~~beside a river~~.

Name________________________________

Date________________________________

PRONOUNS
Subjects

Directions: Cross out any prepositional phrases. Underline the subject once and the verb/verb phrase twice.

Example: Bill and I have gone ~~with Uncle Fred~~.

1. May Clarene and I go to the store?
2. We must have lost his phone number.
3. The hikers and we might try to climb that mountain.
4. Did she place the garden hose by the fountain?
5. Jeremy, Joshua, Julie, and I should have prepared the meal.
6. In the middle of the night, they left for Baton Rouge, Louisiana.
7. Nancy and I cannot carry this package.
8. Have you ever taken gymnastics?
9. After the show, we went out for pizza.
10. Did they ask for more information.
11. Those leaders and we are in charge of the social hour.
12. Either Mother or I will be attending the meeting.
13. It is a rather hot, muggy day.
14. You could have shined all of the silver for me.
15. My father and I haven't ever camped beside a river.

Name________________________________ **PRONOUNS**

WORKBOOK PAGE 224 Predicate Nominatives

Date________________________________

Directions: Cross out any prepositional phrases. Underline the subject once and the verb/verb phrase twice. Label any predicate nominative(s) - PN. Then write the inverted form of the sentence on the line provided.

Example: The lady ~~in the red dress~~ is Flora's agent. (PN: Flora's agent)

Check: Flora's agent is the lady in the red dress.

1. Justin Harper is my friend. (PN: my friend)

   My friend is Justin Harper.

2. Justin Harper is he. (PN: he)

   He is Justin Harper.

3. The loser is Wanda. (PN: Wanda)

   Wanda is the loser.

4. The loser is she. (PN: she)

   She is the loser.

5. My lawyer is the man ~~in the brown suit~~. (PN: man)

   The man ~~in the brown suit~~ is my lawyer.

6. My lawyer is he ~~in the brown suit~~. (PN: he)

   He ~~in the brown suit~~ is my lawyer.

7. The runners ~~in that race~~ are the Hinkle twins. (PN: twins)

   The Hinkle twins are the runners ~~in that race~~.

8. The runners ~~in that race~~ are they. (PN: they)

   They are the runners ~~in that race~~.

9. The next person ~~in line~~ should be ________________________(your name). (PN)

   (Name) should be the next person ~~in line~~.

10. The next person ~~in line~~ should be I. (PN: I)

    I should be the next person ~~in line~~.

Name________________________________

Date________________________________

PRONOUNS
Predicate Nominatives

Directions: Cross out any prepositional phrases. Underline the subject once and the verb/verb phrase twice. Label any predicate nominative(s) - PN. Then write the inverted form of the sentence on the line provided.

PN

Example: The lady ~~in the red dress~~ is Flora's agent.

Check: Flora's agent is the lady in the red dress.

1. Justin Harper is my friend.

____

2. Justin Harper is he.

____

3. The loser is Wanda.

____

4. The loser is she.

____

5. My lawyer is the man in the brown suit.

____

6. My lawyer is he in the brown suit.

____

7. The runners in that race are the Hinkle twins.

____

8. The runners in that race are they.

____

9. The next person in line should be ______________________(your name).

____

10. The next person in line should be I.

____

Name________________________________ **PRONOUNS**
WORKBOOK PAGE 225 Subject or Predicate Nominative?
Date________________________________

Directions: Write S on the line if the underlined pronoun is the subject of the sentence. Write PN on the line provided if the underlined pronoun is the predicate nominative of the sentence.

Example: __S__ Do you want a bike?

__S__ 1. The security guard and I searched the building.

__S__ 2. They will not be fishing in that lake.

__PN__ 3. Our student council officers are those three and I.

__S__ 4. He was not in class this morning.

__PN__ 5. The last ones to finish were we.

__S__ 6. Have you lived in Miami long?

__S__ 7. We could not go to the computer center today.

__PN__ 8. The next debaters will be Fred and I.

__PN__ 9. The guest speaker was she in the second row.

__S__ 10. It might have worked out for all of us.

__PN__ 11. The members of the swimming team are they in the red.

__PN__ 12. Yesterday, the last person selected was I.

__S__ 13. Maybe we could ride the rollercoaster next.

__PN__ 14. The ones recommended for the job are he and she.

__S__ 15. Could it be possible?

Name________________________________

Date________________________________

PRONOUNS
Subject or Predicate Nominative?

Directions: Write S on the line if the underlined pronoun is the subject of the sentence. Write PN on the line provided if the underlined pronoun is the predicate nominative of the sentence.

Example: ___S___ Do you want a bike?

__________ 1. The security guard and I searched the building.

__________ 2. They will not be fishing in that lake.

__________ 3. Our student council officers are those three and I.

__________ 4. He was not in class this morning.

__________ 5. The last ones to finish were we.

__________ 6. Have you lived in Miami long?

__________ 7. We could not go to the computer center today.

__________ 8. The next debaters will be Fred and I.

__________ 9. The guest speaker was she in the second row.

__________ 10. It might have worked out for all of us.

__________ 11. The members of the swimming team are they in the red.

__________ 12. Yesterday, the last person selected was I.

__________ 13. Maybe we could ride the rollercoaster next.

__________ 14. The ones recommended for the job are he and she.

__________ 15. Could it be possible?

PAGE 483 = WORKBOOK PAGE 226

PRONOUNS

Personal Pronouns / Objective Case:

The objective pronouns are **me**, **him**, **her**, **you**, **it**, **us**, **them** and **whom**.

Look at your pronoun chart. There are only two pronouns that are in both the objective and nominative columns: **you** and **it**. These are called neutral pronouns and do not change forms.

OBJECTIVE PRONOUNS FUNCTION AS ONE OF THE FOLLOWING:

A. Object of the Preposition

B. Direct Object

C. Indirect Object

A. Review of Object of the Preposition:

The object of the preposition is the noun or pronoun that follows a preposition.

Examples: Stay *in your **room***.

Go *with **me***.

B. Review of Direct Object:

A direct object receives the action of the verb.

D.O.
Examples: I dropped the **eggs**.

D.O.
The dog licked **me.**

C. Review of Indirect Object:

The indirect object "indirectly" receives a direct object. "To" or "for" can be inserted mentally before an indirect object.

Examples: The baker made Mother a pie.
for **I.O.**
The baker made / **Mother** a pie.

Our grocer gave her coupons.
to **I.O.**
Our grocer gave / **her** coupons.

Name_______________________________ **PRONOUNS**
WORKBOOK PAGE 227 Object of Prepositions
Date_______________________________

Directions: Cross out any prepositional phrases. Label any object of the preposition - O.P. Underline the subject once and the verb/verb phrase twice in each sentence.

O.P.
Example: Everyone ~~except me~~ left immediately.

(You) **O.P.**
1. Please do that ~~for me.~~

O.P. **O.P.**
2. The wind blew ~~against him~~ ~~during the storm~~.

O.P.
3. Does the new teacher live ~~near you~~?

O.P.
4. Joshua ate lunch ~~beside me~~ today.

O.P.
5. The bus left ~~without her~~.

O.P.
6. A bullet whizzed ~~past them~~.

O.P.
7. The story was all ~~about us~~.

O.P.
8. Have you received a letter ~~from me~~?

O.P.
9. The crew docked the boat and went ~~inside it~~.

O.P.
10. The gift was sent ~~to them~~ yesterday.

O.P.
11. He often chases ~~after us~~.

O.P. **O.P.**
12. Their relatives go ~~with them~~ ~~on vacations~~.

O.P. **O.P.**
13. Bob sits ~~behind Ross and me~~.

O.P. **O.P.**
14. A bicycle was lying ~~along the side~~ ~~of the road~~.

O.P.
15. Do you want me (to go) ~~with you~~?

Name________________________________

Date________________________________

PRONOUNS

Object of Prepositions

Directions: Cross out any prepositional phrases. Label any object of the preposition - O.P. Underline the subject once and the verb/verb phrase twice in each sentence.

O.P.

Example: Everyone ~~except me~~ left immediately.

1. Please do that for me.
2. The wind blew against him during the storm.
3. Does the new teacher live near you?
4. Joshua ate lunch beside me today.
5. The bus left without her.
6. A bullet whizzed past them.
7. The story was all about us.
8. Have you received a letter from me?
9. The crew docked the boat and went inside it.
10. The gift was sent to them yesterday.
11. He often chases after us.
12. Their relatives go with them on vacations.
13. Bob sits behind Ross and me.
14. A bicycle was lying along the side of the road.
15. Do you want me to go with you?*

*To + verb = infinitive

To go is an infinitive (not a prepositional phrase).

Name________________________________ **PRONOUNS**

WORKBOOK PAGE 228 Direct Objects

Date________________________________

Directions: Cross out any prepositional phrases. Underline the subject once and the verb/verb phrase twice. Label any direct object - D.O.

Example: We picked flowers ~~in the meadow~~. (D.O.: flowers)

1. A chicken scratched the ground ~~for food~~. (**D.O.**: ground)
2. They baked the chicken ~~in the oven~~. (**D.O.**: chicken)
3. The pen pal wrote a long letter. (**D.O.**: letter)
4. Jeremy erased the marks ~~from his paper~~. (**D.O.**: marks)
5. Mother put all the tea bags ~~in a canister~~. (**D.O.**: bags)
6. The child hit the ball hard. (**D.O.**: ball)
7. The judge selected it as the best. (**D.O.**: it)
8. A bee stung me. (**D.O.**: me)
9. The mayor telephoned us ~~with his concerns~~. (**D.O.**: us)
10. Some art enthusiasts purchased them ~~for their homes~~. (**D.O.**: them)
11. Has the movie frightened you? (**D.O.**: you)
12. A fun-loving youngster threw her ~~into the pool~~. (**D.O.**: her)
13. That person followed William and me home. (**D.O.**: William; **D.O.**: me)
14. I sent it ~~to the wrong address~~. (**D.O.**: it)
15. Their parents sent the triplets and her ~~to Cypress Gardens~~. (**D.O.**: triplets; **D.O.**: her)

Name________________________________

Date________________________________

PRONOUNS
Direct Objects

Directions: Cross out any prepositional phrases. Underline the subject once and the verb/verb phrase twice. Label any direct object - D.O.

D.O.
Example: We picked flowers ~~in the meadow~~.

1. A chicken scratched the ground for food.

2. They baked the chicken in the oven.

3. The pen pal wrote a long letter.

4. Jeremy erased the marks from his paper.

5. Mother put all the tea bags in a canister.

6. The child hit the ball hard.

7. The judge selected it as the best.

8. A bee stung me.

9. The mayor telephoned us with his concerns.

10. Some art enthusiasts purchased them for their homes.

11. Has the movie frightened you?

12. A fun-loving youngster threw her into the pool.

13. That person followed William and me home.

14. I sent it to the wrong address.

15. Their parents sent the triplets and her to Cypress Gardens.

Name_______________________________ **PRONOUNS**
WORKBOOK PAGE 229 Indirect Objects
Date_______________________________

Directions: Underline the subject once and the verb/verb phrase twice. Label a direct object - D.O. Label an indirect object - I.O.

Example: Kirk sent the senator a letter. (I.O. senator; D.O. letter)

1. Mack gave the teacher a note from his father. (I.O. teacher; D.O. note)

2. Grace tossed me a cookie. (I.O. me; D.O. cookie)

3. The company sent them the wrong order. (I.O. them; D.O. order)

4. Mrs. Brewster gave us some peanut candy. (I.O. us; D.O. candy)

5. The nurse brought me a television to watch. (I.O. me; D.O. television)

6. (You) Send him the best recorder in your store. (I.O. him; D.O. recorder)

7. The bank offered Chuck and me a loan for our business. (I.O. Chuck; I.O. me; D.O. loan)

8. He left us a fifty dollar bill on the entryway table. (I.O. us; D.O. bill)

9. A tall waiter served us our dinner. (I.O. us; D.O. dinner)

10. The teacher gave the class a test. (I.O. class; D.O. test)

11. During the night, someone passed us two blankets. (I.O. us; D.O. blankets)

12. The person on the end passed Rachel and us some popcorn. (I.O. Rachel; I.O. us; D.O. popcorn)

Name________________________________

Date________________________________

PRONOUNS
Indirect Objects

Directions: Underline the subject once and the verb/verb phrase twice. Label a direct object - D.O. Label an indirect object - I.O.

I.O. D.O.
Example: Kirk sent the senator a letter.

1. Mack gave the teacher a note from his father.

2. Grace tossed me a cookie.

3. The company sent them the wrong order.

4. Mrs. Brewster gave us some peanut candy.

5. The nurse brought me a television to watch.

6. Send him the best recorder in your store.

7. The bank offered Chuck and me a loan for our business.

8. He left us a fifty dollar bill on the entryway table.

9. A tall waiter served us our dinner.

10. The teacher gave the class a test.

11. During the night, someone passed us two blankets.

12. The person on the end passed Rachel and us some popcorn.

Name_______________________________

WORKBOOK PAGE 230

Date_______________________________

PRONOUNS

Personal Pronouns

Directions: Select the correct pronoun.
Answers are in boldfaced print.

Example: (**They**, Them) surely are great slides.

1. Someone must sit near (I, **me**).
2. (**We**, Us) want a new kite.
3. The kitten followed (we, **us**).
4. Our principal presented Tom and (I, **me**) awards.
5. My father and (**I**, me) refinished an old cart.
6. The applicants for that job were Frank and (**I**, me).
7. Who bought (they, **them**) a magazine?
8. Rosa asked (they, **them**) a question.
9. My partner and (**I**, me) agreed to meet at six o'clock.
10. Our best actors are Cliff and (**she**, her).
11. Someone gave (we, **us**) a new picture.
12. The cat scratches (she, **her**) nearly every day.
13. Did anyone discuss the subject with (he, **him**)?
14. Great Grandpa sent (they, **them**) airplane tickets to Seattle.
15. Will you take (I, **me**) to Hong Kong?

Name________________________________

Date________________________________

PRONOUNS
Personal Pronouns

Directions: Select the correct pronoun.

Example: (**They**, Them) surely are great slides.

1. Someone must sit near (I, me).
2. (We, Us) want a new kite.
3. The kitten followed (we, us).
4. Our principal presented Tom and (I, me) awards.
5. My father and (I, me) refinished an old cart.
6. The applicants for that job were Frank and (I, me).
7. Who bought (they, them) a magazine?
8. Rosa asked (they, them) a question.
9. My partner and (I, me) agreed to meet at six o'clock.
10. Our best actors are Cliff and (she, her).
11. Someone gave (we, us) a new picture.
12. The cat scratches (she, her) nearly every day.
13. Did anyone discuss the subject with (he, him)?
14. Great Grandpa sent (they, them) airplane tickets to Seattle.
15. Will you take (I, me) to Hong Kong?

Name________________________________

WORKBOOK PAGE 231

Date________________________________

PRONOUNS

Personal Pronouns

Directions: Write the function of the underlined pronoun in the space provided. Use the following abbreviations:

D.O. = Direct Object
I. O. = Indirect Object
P. N. = Predicate Nominative
O. P. = Object of the Preposition
S. = Subject

Example: __I.O.__ The child made me a mud pie.

Remember: The pronouns **I, he, she, we, they,** and **who** function as either a subject or a predicate nominative.

The pronouns **me, him, her, us, them,** and **whom** function as either a direct object, an indirect object, or an object of the preposition.

The pronouns **you** and **it** can function as a subject, a predicate nominative, a direct object, an indirect object, or an object of the preposition.

__O.P.__ 1. Someone must sit near me.

__S.__ 2. We want a new kite.

__D.O.__ 3. The kitten followed us.

__I.O.__ 4. Our principal presented Tom and me awards.

__P.N.__ 5. The applicants for the job were Frank and I.

__I.O.__ 6. Who bought them a magazine?

__P.N.__ 7. Our best actors are Cliff and she.

__D.O.__ 8. The cat scratches her nearly every day.

__O.P.__ 9. Did anyone discuss the subject with him?

__D.O.__ 10. Will you take me to Hong Kong?

Name______________________________

Date______________________________

PRONOUNS
Personal Pronouns

Directions: Write the function of the underlined pronoun in the space provided. Use the following abbreviations:

D.O. = Direct Object
I. O. = Indirect Object
P. N. = Predicate Nominative
O. P. = Object of the Preposition
S. = Subject

Example: ___I.O.___ The child made me a mud pie.

Remember: The pronouns **I, he, she, we, they,** and **who** function as either a subject or a predicate nominative.

The pronouns **me, him, her, us, them,** and **whom** function as either a direct object, an indirect object, or an object of the preposition.

The pronouns **you** and **it** can function as a subject, a predicate nominative, a direct object, an indirect object, or an object of the preposition.

__________ 1. Someone must sit near me.

__________ 2. We want a new kite.

__________ 3. The kitten followed us.

__________ 4. Our principal presented Tom and me awards.

__________ 5. The applicants for the job were Frank and I.

__________ 6. Who bought them a magazine?

__________ 7. Our best actors are Cliff and she.

__________ 8. The cat scratches her nearly every day.

__________ 9. Did anyone discuss the subject with him?

__________ 10. Will you take me to Hong Kong?

PAGE 495 = WORKBOOK PAGE 232
PAGE 496 = WORKBOOK PAGE 233
PAGE 497 = WORKBOOK PAGE 234

PRONOUNS

Personal Pronouns / Possessives:

The possessive pronouns are: **my, mine**
his
her, hers
your, yours
its
our, ours
their, theirs
whose

A. **My, his, her, your, its, our, their**, and **whose** are used before nouns and other pronouns and are often called possessive adjectives.

Examples: Has **my** *book* been found?

His *house* is painted yearly.

Your *watch* is incorrect.

A lion licked **its** *paws*.

Has **our** *mail* been delivered?

Their *cars* weren't in the driveway.

B. **Mine, hers, yours, ours, and theirs** do not usually come before a noun or pronoun but refer back to it in the sentence.

Examples: Those *journals* are **mine**.

Is this *cup* **yours**?

A cream-colored *car* is **hers**.

That tree *house* is **ours**.

C. **The possessivie his occurs in the same form before and after a noun or pronoun.**

Example: **His** *plan* succeeded.

Those *models* are **his**.

PRONOUNS

Personal Pronouns / Possessives:

Possessive Pronouns do **NOT** have an apostrophe **(')**.

A. **It's** is not a possessive pronoun: **it's = it + is**

Its is a possessive pronoun. Example: The bird drank **its** water.

Suggestion: If you are unsure if its or it's should be used, read the sentence with the it's (it is) form. Trust SOUND to determine the correct form.

Example: It's hot.
Check: It is hot.

Example: The bird drank it's water.
Check: The bird drank it is water.
Correct: The bird drank its water.

B. **You're** is not a possessive pronoun: **you're = you + are**

Your is a possessive pronoun. Example: What is **your** name?

Suggestion: If you are unsure if you're or your should be used, read the sentence with the you're form. Trust SOUND to determine the correct form.

Example: You're the greatest.

Check: You are the greatest.

Example: You're shoe is untied.

Check: You are shoe is untied.

Correct: Your shoe is untied.

PRONOUNS

Personal Pronouns / Possessives:

Possessive Pronouns do **NOT** have an apostrophe **(')**.

C. **They're** is not a possessive pronoun: **They're = They + are**

Their is a possessive pronoun. Example: **Their** house is old.

Suggestion: If you are unsure if they're or their should be used, read the sentence with the they're (they are) form. Trust SOUND to determine the correct form.

Example: They're playing checkers.
Check: They are playing checkers.

Example: They're house is old.
Check: They are house is old.
Correct: Their house is old.

Name________________________________ **PRONOUNS**

WORKBOOK PAGE 235

Date________________________________

Answers are in boldfaced print.

Directions: Select the correct pronoun.

Example: (**It's**, Its) a rainy day.

1. (You're, **Your**) copies are ready.
2. Marcy wanted to know if (**they're**, their) coming.
3. A giraffe ate (it's, **its**) dinner.
4. Did they ask if (**you're**, your) going?
5. (They're, **Their**) house is the fourth one on Arbor Lane.
6. Do you think that (**it's**, its) possible?
7. (**Who's**, Whose) the new student?
8. I think that (they're, **their**) plans have changed.
9. (Who's, **Whose**) foot did I just step on?
10. Has the peacock lost some of (it's, **its**) feathers?
11. (**You're**, Your) not supposed to throw that.
12. Has anyone told them that (**they're**, their) allowed to go?
13. Our group hasn't decided (who's, **whose**) advice to follow.
14. Does Molly like (you're, **your**) choice of colors?
15. Give me that if (**it's**, its) dry.

Name________________________________ **PRONOUNS**

Date________________________________

Directions: Select the correct pronoun.

Example: (**It's**, Its) a rainy day.

1. (You're, Your) copies are ready.
2. Marcy wanted to know if (they're, their) coming.
3. A giraffe ate (it's, its) dinner.
4. Did they ask if (you're, your) going?
5. (They're, Their) house is the fourth one on Arbor Lane.
6. Do you think that (it's, its) possible?
7. (Who's, Whose) the new student?
8. I think that (they're, their) plans have changed.
9. (Who's, Whose) foot did I just step on?
10. Has the peacock lost some of (it's, its) feathers?
11. (You're, Your) not supposed to throw that.
12. Has anyone told them that (they're, their) allowed to go?
13. Our group hasn't decided (who's, whose) advice to follow.
14. Does Molly like (you're, your) choice of colors?
15. Give me that if (it's, its) dry.

PAGE 501 = WORKBOOK PAGE 236

PRONOUNS

Antecedents:

An antecedent is the noun or pronoun to which a possessive or a reflexive pronoun refers back in the sentence.

Example: That dog lost its collar.

A. The pronoun its refers back to **dog**.
(The dog lost the dog's collar.)

B. **Dog** is the noun its refers back to in the sentence.

C. **Dog** is the antecedent.

Example: Some ducklings waddled after their mother.

A. The pronoun their refers back to **ducklings**.
(Some ducklings waddled after the ducklings' mother.)

B. **Ducklings** is the noun their refers back to in the sentence.

C. **Ducklings** is the antecedent.

Example: Has anyone lost his comb?

A. The pronoun his refers back to **anyone**.
(Has anyone lost anyone's comb?)

B. **Anyone** is the pronoun his refers back to in the sentence.

C. **Anyone** is the antecedent.

Name________________________________

WORKBOOK PAGE 237

Date________________________________

PRONOUNS

Antecedents

Directions: In the space provided, write the antecedent for the boldfaced word.

Example: monkey A monkey hurt **its** arm.

1. girl — The little girl broke **her** foot on the slide.
2. movers — The furniture movers left **their** truck in the driveway.
3. Will / I — Will and I don't want **our** meals.
4. trucker — Has the trucker finished **his** trip?
5. students — A few students left **their** notebooks in the library.
6. spider — A large, black spider spun **its** web.
7. He — He finished **his** photo album today.
8. women — The women left **their** office.
9. They — They handed in **their** final exams.
10. lamb — A lamb lost **its** way back to the barn.

Name________________________________

Date________________________________

PRONOUNS
Antecedents

Directions: In the space provided, write the antecedent for the boldfaced word.

Example: ___monkey___ A monkey hurt **its** arm.

1. ____________________ The little girl broke **her** foot on the slide.

2. ____________________ The furniture movers left **their** truck in the driveway.

3. ____________________ Will and I don't want **our** meals.

4. ____________________ Has the trucker finished **his** trip?

5. ____________________ A few students left **their** notebooks in the library.

6. ____________________ A large, black spider spun **its** web.

7. ____________________ He finished **his** photo album today.

8. ____________________ The women left **their** office.

9. ____________________ They handed in **their** final exams.

10. ____________________ A lamb lost **its** way back to the barn.

Name______________________________ **PRONOUNS**

WORKBOOK PAGE 238 Antecedents

Date______________________________

Directions: In the space provided, write the antecedent for the boldfaced word.

Example: student A student cleaned out **her** desk.

club	1.	Our club held **its** annual car wash.
Dad	2.	Has Dad worn **his** new suit yet?
I	3.	I don't want **my** dinner.
clerks	4.	The clerks were on **their** break.
Stacy	5.	Stacy left **her** surfboard here.
Nobody	6.	Nobody has **his** radio tuned into that station.
You	7.	You must send **your** cards early.
squirrels	8.	Some squirrels were playing in **their** tree.
Susan / Zak	9.	Susan and Zak enjoy **their** karate lessons.
bird	10.	A bird fluttered **its** wings and flew off.
brother / I	11.	My brother and I want **our** own phone.
Antonio	12.	Antonio cooked **his** own breakfast.
plant	13.	A plant manufactures **its** own food.
Someone	14.	Someone has forgotten to do **her** chore.
pilots	15.	Three pilots purchased **their** own plane.

Name________________________________

PRONOUNS
Antecedents

Date________________________________

Directions: In the space provided, write the antecedent for the boldfaced word.

Example: ___student___ A student cleaned out **her** desk.

__________________ 1. Our club held **its** annual car wash.

__________________ 2. Has Dad worn **his** new suit yet?

__________________ 3. I don't want **my** dinner.

__________________ 4. The clerks were on **their** break.

__________________ 5. Stacy left **her** surfboard here.

__________________ 6. Nobody has **his** radio tuned into that station.

__________________ 7. You must send **your** cards early.

__________________ 8. Some squirrels were playing in **their** tree.

__________________ 9. Susan and Zak enjoy **their** karate lessons.

__________________ 10. A bird fluttered **its** wings and flew off.

__________________ 11. My brother and I want **our** own phone.

__________________ 12. Antonio cooked **his** own breakfast.

__________________ 13. A plant manufactures **its** own food.

__________________ 14. Someone has forgotten to do **her** chore.

__________________ 15. Three pilots purchased **their** own plane.

PAGE 507 = WORKBOOK PAGE 239

PRONOUNS

Reflexive Pronouns:

Reflexive pronouns are **myself, himself, herself, itself, yourself, ourselves,** and **themselves**.

Hisself and **theirselves** are incorrect. Never use them.

Reflexive pronouns reflect back to another noun or pronoun in the sentence. A reflexive pronoun will have an antecedent.

Examples:

A. The lady washed the car **herself.**

(Lady is the noun antecedent to which the reflexive pronoun, **herself**, refers.)

B. Can you fix the tire **yourself**?

(You is the pronoun antecedent to which the reflexive pronoun, **yourself**, refers.)

C. That machine automatically shuts **itself** off.

(Machine is the noun antecedent to which the reflexive pronoun, **itself**, refers.)

Name________________________________ **PRONOUNS**
WORKBOOK PAGE 240 Reflexive Pronouns
Date________________________________

Directions: Circle any reflexive pronoun(s) in each sentence.
Answers are in boldfaced print.

1. Do you prefer to handle that **yourself**?
2. The child remarked, "I will do this **myself**."
3. Did the carpenters enjoy building the cabin **themselves**?
4. The mower turns **itself** off automatically.
5. We, **ourselves**, must choose the goals.
6. Let Grant speak to Mr. Jones **himself**.
7. I want to tackle this task **myself.**
8. Janet and I have only **ourselves** to blame.
9. A yellow canary perched **itself** on the top rung.
10. Has anyone ever tried this **herself**?
11. Richard often talks to **himself**.
12. They patted **themselves** on the back for a job well done.
13. She would not allow **herself** to face defeat.
14. I refuse to do it **myself**.
15. Walter's dad built the cabinets **himself**.
16. The cat licked **itself**.
17. Do you want to do it **yourself**?
18. We enjoyed **ourselves** at the party.
19. The children made the cookies **themselves.**
20. That machine will not repeat **itself** during a power failure.

Name________________________________

Date________________________________

PRONOUNS
Reflexive Pronouns

Directions: Circle any reflexive pronoun(s) in each sentence.

1. Do you prefer to handle that yourself?
2. The child remarked, "I will do this myself."
3. Did the carpenters enjoy building the cabin themselves?
4. The mower turns itself off automatically.
5. We, ourselves, must choose the goals.
6. Let Grant speak to Mr. Jones himself.
7. I want to tackle this task myself.
8. Janet and I have only ourselves to blame.
9. A yellow canary perched itself on the top rung.
10. Has anyone ever tried this herself?
11. Richard often talks to himself.
12. They patted themselves on the back for a job well done.
13. She would not allow herself to face defeat.
14. I refuse to do it myself.
15. Walter's dad built the cabinets himself.
16. The cat licked itself.
17. Do you want to do it yourself?
18. We enjoyed ourselves at the party.
19. The children made the cookies themselves.
20. That machine will not repeat itself during a power failure.

PAGE 511 = WORKBOOK PAGE 241

PRONOUNS

Demonstrative Pronouns:

Demonstrative pronouns are **this, that, these,** and **those.**

Examples: I want **that.**

This is a pitted spoon.

Are **these** supposed to be here?

Those became ruined when washed in hot water.

If **this, that, these,** or **those** modify or go over to a noun or another pronoun, they are adjectives.

Examples: A. ***This*** trim is crooked. (**This** is an adjective: this trim.)

This is crooked. (**This** is a pronoun.)

B. Did you enjoy ***that*** play? (**That** is an adjective: that play.)

Did you enjoy **that**? (**That** is a pronoun.)

C. Give me ***those*** ornaments. (**Those** is an adjective: those ornaments.)

Give me **those**. (**Those** is a pronoun.)

D. Bring ***these*** bars with you. (**These** is an adjective: these bars.)

Bring **these** with you. (**These** is a pronoun.)

Name________________________________

WORKBOOK PAGE 242

Date_________________________________

PRONOUNS

Demonstrative Pronouns

Directions: Write P on the line provided if the underlined word serves as a pronoun in the sentence. Write A on the line provided if the underlined word serves as an adjective in the sentence.

Example: __P__ Do you want this on your sandwich?

__A__ 1. Those candles burn brightly.

__P__ 2. Give me that, please.

__A__ 3. Does this fence need to be repaired?

__A__ 4. In a few days these avocados will be ripe.

__A__ 5. That fly landed on my arm.

__P__ 6. Pull those down over your feet.

__A__ 7. I think that answer should be forty-four.

__P__ 8. Are these the ones you wanted?

__P__ 9. I will give you this for your sixteenth birthday.

__A__ 10. This one must have been lost for a long time.

__A__ 11. My brother gave me those four magnets.

__P__ 12. Carrie might be able to use those for the party.

__P__ 13. How did you know that, Irving?

__A__ 14. These onions are making me cry.

__P__ 15. Grandmother says she enjoys doing this for us.

Name_______________________________

Date_______________________________

PRONOUNS
Demonstrative
Pronouns

Directions: Write P on theline provided if the underlined word serves as a pronoun in the sentence. Write A on the line provided if the underlined word serves as an adjective in the sentence.

Example: __P__ Do you want this on your sandwich?

_________ 1. Those candles burn brightly.

_________ 2. Give me that, please.

_________ 3. Does this fence need to be repaired?

_________ 4. In a few days these avocados will be ripe.

_________ 5. That fly landed on my arm.

_________ 6. Pull those down over your feet.

_________ 7. I think that answer should be forty-four.

_________ 8. Are these the ones you wanted?

_________ 9. I will give you this for your sixteenth birthday.

_________ 10. This one must have been lost for a long time.

_________ 11. My brother gave me those four magnets.

_________ 12. Carrie might be able to use those for the party.

_________ 13. How did you know that, Irving?

_________ 14. These onions are making me cry.

_________ 15. Grandmother says she enjoys doing this for us.

PAGE 515 = WORKBOOK PAGE 243

PRONOUNS

Interrogative Pronouns:

Interrogative pronouns are **who**, **whom**, **whose**, **which**, and **what**.

Interrogative pronouns ask a question.

Examples: **Who** is your favorite singer?

To **whom** do I give my tray?

Whose is that?

Which will Samantha select?

What is your opinion?

Who is in the nominative case and will serve as either a subject or a predicate nominative.

Examples: **Who** won? (subject)

The winner is **who**? (predicate nominative)

Whom is in the objective case and will serve as a direct object, an indirect object, or an object of the preposition.

Examples: To **whom** did you reply? (object of the preposition)

The florist sent **whom** that corsage? (indirect object)

The teacher chose **whom**? (direct object)

Whose, **which**, and **what** are pronouns when they stand alone. However, if they modify (go over to) a noun or another pronoun, they function as adjectives.

Examples: **Whose** has been selected? (pronoun)

Whose *paper* is on the floor? (adjective: whose paper)

Which do we need? (pronoun)

Which *one* looks better? (adjective: which one)

Name_______________________________

WORKBOOK PAGE 244

Date_______________________________

PRONOUNS
Interrogative
Pronouns

Directions: Write P on the line if the boldfaced word serves as a pronoun. Write A on the line if the boldfaced word serves as an adjective.

Example: __P__ **Which** do you prefer?

__A__ 1. **Whose** coat is this?

__P__ 2. **What** is your answer?

__P__ 3. **Whose** are these?

__A__ 4. **Which** car are you buying?

__P__ 5. **What** are you doing?

__A__ 6. Do you know **whose** dog this is?

__P__ 7. **Which** does Maryanne want?

__A__ 8. **What** rock group do you like best?

__A__ 9. **Which** one have you decided upon?

__P__ 10. You said **what**?

Directions: Select the correct answer.
Answers are in boldfaced print.

Example: (**Who**, Whom) is your friend?

1. To (who, **whom**) do I give my money?

2. (**Who**, Whom) will be our next club president?

3. Dad gave the tickets to (who, **whom**)?

4. The winner was (**who**, whom)?

Name________________________________ **PRONOUNS**
Interrogative
Pronouns

Date________________________________

Directions: Write P on the line if the boldfaced word serves as a pronoun. Write A on the line if the boldfaced word serves as an adjective.

Example: __P__ **Which** do you prefer?

_________ 1. **Whose** coat is this?

_________ 2. **What** is your answer?

_________ 3. **Whose** are these?

_________ 4. **Which** car are you buying?

_________ 5. **What** are you doing?

_________ 6. Do you know **whose** dog this is?

_________ 7. **Which** does Maryanne want?

_________ 8. **What** rock group do you like best?

_________ 9. **Which** one have you decided upon?

_________ 10. You said **what**?

Directions: Select the correct answer.

Example: (**Who**, Whom) is your friend?

1. To (who, whom) do I give my money?
2. (Who, Whom) will be our next club president?
3. Dad gave the tickets to (who, whom)?
4. The winner was (who, whom)?

PAGE 519 = WORKBOOK PAGE 245
PAGE 524 = WORKBOOK PAGE 248
PAGE 525 = WORKBOOK PAGE 249

PRONOUNS

Indefinite Pronouns:

Indefinite pronouns are **some**, **many**, **few**, **several**, **each**, **both**, **either**, **neither**, **someone**, **somebody**, **anyone**, **anybody**, **nobody**, **everyone**, **everybody**, **any**, and **none**.

Examples: **Some** will be expected to participate.
Are there **many** in the ice chest?
A **few** said no.
Several have already received scholarships.
Each must learn a new step in that dance.
I'll take **both**.
We don't want **either**.
Neither has been eating much today.
Ask **someone** to drive you to school.
Did Mindy tell **somebody** about the incident?
Would **anyone** like to take a helicopter ride?
Anybody may join.
Nobody talks during a movie.
My neighbor seems to know **everyone**.
Everybody was having a good time.
They don't think that he has **any** left.
Although the baked beans smelled good, I wanted **none**.

Pronoun or Adjective:

If **some, many, few, several, each, both, either, neither, someone, somebody, anyone, anybody, nobody, everyone, everybody, and any** modify (go over to) a noun or pronoun, they function as adjectives instead of pronouns.

Examples: **Many** *ribbons* were given.
A **few** *pancakes* remained on the plate.
Everyone's *cars* were parked along the street.
Both *envelopes* were unopened.
Does he want **any** *juice* ?

Name________________________________ **PRONOUNS**
WORKBOOK PAGE 246 Indefinite
Date________________________________ Pronouns

Directions: Write P on the line if the boldfaced word serves as a pronoun. Write A on the line if the boldfaced word serves as an adjective.

Example: __A__ **Some** people never learn.

__A__ 1. **Both** dogs are German shepherds.

__P__ 2. Do you like **both**?

__P__ 3. I want one of **each** please.

__A__ 4. I think that **each** speaker was interesting.

__A__ 5. A **few** projects were on display.

__P__ 6. There were only a **few** left.

__A__ 7. **Everyone's** luggage was aboard the plane.

__P__ 8. The announcer told **everyone** about the change in schedule.

__P__ 9. Are there **several** who aren't coming with us?

__A__ 10. The visitors toured our city **several** times.

__A__ 11. **Many** ants were crawling on the ground.

__P__ 12. Had **many** fallen at the skating rink?

__P__ 13. Does **anyone** have the time?

__A__ 14. Is this **anyone's** pen?

__A__ 15. There are **some** hot dogs in the freezer.

__P__ 16. **Some** enjoy the harbor cruise at night.

Name________________________________

Date________________________________

PRONOUNS
Indefinite
Pronouns

Directions: Write P on the line if the boldfaced word serves as a pronoun. Write A on the line if the boldfaced word serves as an adjective.

Example: __A___ **Some** people never learn.

_________ 1. **Both** dogs are German shepherds.

_________ 2. Do you like **both**?

_________ 3. I want one of **each** please.

_________ 4. I think that **each** speaker was interesting.

_________ 5. A **few** projects were on display.

_________ 6. There were only a **few** left.

_________ 7. **Everyone's** luggage was aboard the plane.

_________ 8. The announcer told **everyone** about the change in schedule.

_________ 9. Are there **several** who aren't coming with us?

_________ 10. The visitors toured our city **several** times.

_________ 11. **Many** ants were crawling on the ground.

_________ 12. Had **many** fallen at the skating rink?

_________ 13. Does **anyone** have the time?

_________ 14. Is this **anyone's** pen?

_________ 15. There are **some** hot dogs in the freezer.

_________ 16. **Some** enjoy the harbor cruise at night.

Name________________________________ **PRONOUNS**
WORKBOOK PAGE 247 Indefinite
Date________________________________ Pronouns

Directions: Write P on the line if the boldfaced word serves as a pronoun. Write A on the line if the boldfaced word serves as an adjective.

Example: __A__ **Few** animals hang by their tails.

__P__ 1. Will you take **both** with you?

__P__ 2. **Several** have been sold recently.

__A__ 3. **Some** shrimp boats returned to shore.

__A__ 4. This may take **several** hours.

__P__ 5. Is **everyone** ready?

__A__ 6. That is **nobody's** idea of a joke.

__P__ 7. I'll take a **few** of those.

__P__ 8. How **many** do you want?

__P__ 9. I have **none**.

__A__ 10. The box didn't have **any** top.

__P__ 11. **Each** must take his turn at the swings.

__P__ 12. Has **anyone** seen my checkbook?

__A__ 13. That game was fun for **both** participants.

__P__ 14. **Neither** of them is allowed beyond this point.

__A__ 15. **Somebody's** shoe is under the couch.

Name________________________________

Date________________________________

PRONOUNS
Indefinite
Pronouns

Directions: Write P on the line if the boldfaced word serves as a pronoun. Write A on the line if the boldfaced word serves as an adjective.

Example: __A__ **Few** animals hang by their tails.

_______ 1. Will you take **both** with you?

_______ 2. **Several** have been sold recently.

_______ 3. **Some** shrimp boats returned to shore.

_______ 4. This may take **several** hours.

_______ 5. Is **everyone** ready?

_______ 6. That is **nobody's** idea of a joke.

_______ 7. I'll take a **few** of those.

_______ 8. How **many** do you want?

_______ 9. I have **none**.

_______ 10. The box didn't have **any** top.

_______ 11. **Each** must take his turn at the swings.

_______ 12. Has **anyone** seen my checkbook?

_______ 13. That game was fun for **both** participants.

_______ 14. **Neither** of them is allowed beyond this point.

_______ 15. **Somebody's** shoe is under the couch.

PRONOUNS

Indefinite Pronouns:

A. **Some, many, few, several,** and **both** are plural pronouns.

In making subject and verb agree, do not add **s** to the verb.

Examples: Both like the same styles. (present tense)

Several feel sorry for leaving early. (present tense)

Some liked the idea. (past tense)

The possessive pronoun **their** is used with **some, many, few,** and **several**.

B. **Each, either, neither, someone, somebody, anyone, anybody, nobody, everyone, everybody, one, no one, another, anything, and nothing** are singular pronouns.

In making subject and verb agree, add **s** to most verb forms in the present tense.

Examples: Each likes the new pony. (present tense)

Nobody writes to me. (present tense)

Everybody jogged a mile. (past tense)

The possessive pronouns **her, his,** or **its** are used with singular pronouns.

PRONOUNS

Indefinite Pronouns:

C. The possessive pronouns **his, her,** and **its** are used with singular indefinite pronouns: **each, either, neither, someone, somebody, anyone, anybody, nobody, no one,** and **another.**

Examples: **Each** chooses his own course of study.

Either of the clowns has his own popcorn stand.

Neither of the teams won its championship.

Someone shared her lunch with me.

Somebody left her wallet on the step.

One left its nest.

Everyone must leave his book on the desk.

Has **anyone** decided on her choice of desserts?

Everybody needs his pencil and pen.

No one brought her towel to the pool.

In making subject and verb agree, be sure to find the subject by crossing out prepositional phrases.

Examples: One of the girls speaks with an accent.

Either of the books is a good choice.

Each of the triplets wants *her* own room.

Name________________________________
WORKBOOK PAGE 250
Date________________________________

PRONOUNS
Indefinite Pronouns

Directions: Circle the correct answer.
Answers are in boldfaced print.

1. Few took (his, **their**) shoes to the beach.
2. Somebody must give (**his**, their) bread to the birds.
3. Each needs to bring (**her**, their) towel to the pool.
4. Someone has lost (**her**, their) purse.
5. Several should have sent (his, **their**) letters today.
6. Did either of the children share (**his**, their) toys?
7. Everybody should take (**his**, their) time.
8. Has either of the snakes shed (**its**, their) skin?
9. Many want to leave (her, **their**) cars in the parking garage.
10. Neither wants (**her**, their) boots on.
11. Nobody wanted to prepare (**his**, their) own lunch.
12. Did everyone remember to bring (**his,** their) jacket?
13. One of the girls has given (**her**, their) saxophone to a friend.
14. Marcia and Todd have not had (there, **their**) tetanus shots yet.
15. Neither of the doctors has (**his**, their) office downtown.

Name________________________________

Date________________________________

PRONOUNS
Indefinite Pronouns

Directions: Circle the correct answer.

1. Few took (his, their) shoes to the beach.
2. Somebody must give (his, their) bread to the birds.
3. Each needs to bring (her, their) towel to the pool.
4. Someone has lost (her, their) purse.
5. Several should have sent (his, their) letters today.
6. Did either of the children share (his, their) toys?
7. Everybody should take (his, their) time.
8. Has either of the snakes shed (its, their) skin?
9. Many want to leave (her, their) cars in the parking garage.
10. Neither wants (her, their) boots on.
11. Nobody wanted to prepare (his, their) own lunch.
12. Did everyone remember to bring (his, their) jacket?
13. One of the girls has given (her, their) saxophone to a friend.
14. Marcia and Todd have not had (there, their) tetanus shots yet.
15. Neither of the doctors has (his, their) office downtown.

Name________________________________ **PRONOUNS**
WORKBOOK PAGE 251 Indefinite Pronouns
Date________________________________

Directions: Circle the correct answer.
Answers are in boldfaced print.

1. Everyone could not bring (**his**, their) pet to the program.
2. Neither wants (**her**, their) statements published.
3. In the fall, a few trees shed (its, **their**) leaves.
4. In the dark of the night, nobody wants to leave (**his**, their) nice, warm bed.
5. Have many given you (her, **their**) dues?
6. Be sure that each does (**her**, their) required number of sit-ups.
7. Had either of the dogs had (**its**, their) tail clipped?
8. Several of the shoppers gave (his, **their**) opinions about the new product.
9. May everybody read (**his**, their) book for fifteen minutes?
10. Both are taking (her, **their**) tents in the small canoe.
11. We have a few who purchased (his, **their**) own clothes.
12. Will someone give me (**his**, their) pencil?
13. Did one of the books have (**its**, their) cover missing?
14. Some will want (his, **their**) way constantly.
15. Everybody must take (**his**, their) books.

Name________________________________

Date________________________________

PRONOUNS
Indefinite Pronouns

Directions: Circle the correct answer.

1. Everyone could not bring (his, their) pet to the program.
2. Neither wants (her, their) statements published.
3. In the fall, a few trees shed (its, their) leaves.
4. In the dark of the night, nobody wants to leave (his, their) nice, warm bed.
5. Have many given you (her, their) dues?
6. Be sure that each does (her, their) required number of sit-ups.
7. Had either of the dogs had (its, their) tail clipped?
8. Several of the shoppers gave (his, their) opinions about the new product.
9. May everybody read (his, their) book for fifteen minutes?
10. Both are taking (her, their) tents in the small canoe.
11. We have a few who purchased (his, their) own clothes.
12. Will someone give me (his, their) pencil?
13. Did one of the books have (its, their) cover missing?
14. Some will want (his, their) way constantly.
15. Everybody must take (his, their) books.

Name______________________________ **PRONOUNS**
WORKBOOK PAGE 252 Indefinite Pronouns
Date______________________________

Directions: Circle the correct answer.
Answers are in boldfaced print.

1. Each (know, **knows**) the correct answer.
2. Nobody (need, **needs**) to do that tonight.
3. Several (**guide**, guides) people through the historic park.
4. Everyone (bring, **brings**) his lunch on Fridays.
5. Few (**eat**, eats) there.
6. Either (ride, **rides**) a bus downtown.
7. One (crawl, **crawls**) , and the other baby walks.
8. Neither of the musicians (play, **plays**) the guitar.
9. Some (**walk**, walks) three miles every day.
10. During the day, many (**choose**, chooses) to stay indoors.
11. Someone (**has**, have) a new motorcycle.
12. Someone (read, **reads**) to the children nightly.
13. Both (**create**, creates) a problem.
14. After the game, no one (go, **goes**) there anymore.
15. Either of the fans (work, **works**).

Name________________________________

Date________________________________

PRONOUNS
Indefinite Pronouns

Directions: Circle the correct answer.

1. Each (know, knows) the correct answer.
2. Nobody (need, needs) to do that tonight.
3. Several (guide, guides) people through the historic park.
4. Everyone (bring, brings) his lunch on Fridays.
5. Few (eat, eats) there.
6. Either (ride, rides) a bus downtown.
7. One (crawl, crawls) , and the other baby walks.
8. Neither of the musicians (play, plays) the guitar.
9. Some (walk, walks) three miles every day.
10. During the day, many (choose, chooses) to stay indoors.
11. Someone (has, have) a new motorcycle.
12. Someone (read, reads) to the children nightly.
13. Both (create, creates) a problem.
14. After the game, no one (go, goes) there anymore.
15. Either of the fans (work, works).

Name_______________________________ **PRONOUN REVIEW**
WORKBOOK PAGE 253
Date_______________________________

A. **Subject or Predicate Nominative?**

Directions: Write S if the pronoun in boldfaced print functions as the subject; write PN if the pronoun in boldfaced print functions as a predicate nominative.

Suggestion: Cross out any prepositional phrase(s). Underline the subject once and the verb/verb phrase twice. Then, make your decision.

Remember: Invert the sentence to prove a predicate nominative.

1. S Ralph and **I** will be attending the governor's meeting.
2. PN The wisest church elder is **he** ~~in the dark blue suit~~. (PN)
3. PN Our guest ~~for the spring festival~~ will be **she**. (PN)
4. S Perhaps **you** should add a few more drops ~~of oil~~ ~~to the vinegar~~.

B. **Objective Pronouns:**

Directions: Choose the letter that tells how the pronoun in boldfaced print functions in the sentence.

1. b The soccer ball hit **her** in the head.
   a. object of the preposition
   b. direct object
   c. indirect object

2. c Please give **them** a copy of the report.
   a. object of the preposition
   b. direct object
   c. indirect object

3. a Sit beside **me**!
   a. object of the preposition
   b. direct object
   c. indirect object

Name________________________________ **PRONOUN REVIEW**

Date________________________________

A. Subject or Predicate Nominative?

Directions: Write S if the pronoun in boldfaced print functions as the subject; write PN if the pronoun in boldfaced print functions as a predicate nominative.

Suggestion: **Cross out any prepositional phrase(s). Underline the subject once and the verb/verb phrase twice. Then, make your decision.**

Remember: **Invert the sentence to prove a predicate nominative.**

1. _____ Ralph and **I** will be attending the governor's meeting.

2. _____ The wisest church elder is **he** in the dark blue suit.

3. _____ Our guest for the spring festival will be **she**.

4. _____ Perhaps **you** should add a few more drops of oil to the vinegar.

B. Objective Pronouns:

Directions: Choose the letter that tells how the pronoun in boldfaced print functions in the sentence.

1. _____ The soccer ball hit **her** in the head.
   a. object of the preposition
   b. direct object
   c. indirect object

2. _____ Please give **them** a copy of the report.
   a. object of the preposition
   b. direct object
   c. indirect object

3. _____ Sit beside **me**!
   a. object of the preposition
   b. direct object
   c. indirect object

Name________________________________ **PRONOUN REVIEW**

WORKBOOK PAGE 254

Date________________________________

C. **Using Nominative and Objective Pronouns:**

Directions: Choose the correct word. **Answers are in boldfaced print.**

1. Tell (I, **me**) your phone number.
2. Does (**she**, her) go to the library weekly?
3. His mother looked at (he, **him**) with a frown.
4. The lady gave (we, **us**) shoppers some coupons.
5. The forest ranger is (him, **he**) standing by the truck.
6. The pastor's wife is (**she**, her) in the flowered dress.
7. A paper airplane landed between Timothy and (I, **me**).
8. The chef prepared (we, **us**) a special salad without meat.
9. One of the greatest Cubs fans was (me, **I**).

D. **Pronouns in Compounds:**

Directions: Choose the correct word. **Answers are in boldfaced print.**

Suggestion: You may want to cover the first part of the compound.

1. Rick and (**I**, me) went to the zoo.
2. The clerk handed Mrs. Jones and (**them**, they) several bags.
3. Give Stan and (he, **him**) money for the tickets.
4. My cousins are Yvonne and (**she**, her).
5. Some children sat near the sunbathers and (we, **us**).
6. His mother and (**we**, us) watched an air show.
7. The coach patted Jason and (I, **me**) on the back.
8. Programs were handed to parents and (they, **them**).

Name________________________________ **PRONOUN REVIEW**

Date________________________________

C. **Using Nominative and Objective Pronouns:**
Directions: Choose the correct word.

1. Tell (I, me) your phone number.
2. Does (she, her) go to the library weekly?
3. His mother looked at (he, him) with a frown.
4. The lady gave (we, us) shoppers some coupons.
5. The forest ranger is (him, he) standing by the truck.
6. The pastor's wife is (she, her) in the flowered dress.
7. A paper airplane landed between Timothy and (I, me).
8. The chef prepared (we, us) a special salad without meat.
9. One of the greatest Cubs fans was (me, I).

D. **Pronouns in Compounds:**
Directions: Choose the correct word.
Suggestion: You may want to cover the first part of the compound.

1. Rick and (I, me) went to the zoo.
2. The clerk handed Mrs. Jones and (them, they) several bags.
3. Give Stan and (he, him) money for the tickets.
4. My cousins are Yvonne and (she, her).
5. Some children sat near the sunbathers and (we, us).
6. His mother and (we, us) watched an air show.
7. The coach patted Jason and (I, me) on the back.
8. Programs were handed to parents and (they, them).

Name________________________________ **PRONOUN REVIEW**

WORKBOOK PAGE 255

Date________________________________

E. **Possessives:**

Directions: Select the correct word. **Answers are in boldfaced print.**

1. (Your, **You're**) so funny.

2. I want to know if (their, **they're**) sincere about helping.

3. (**Its**, It's) foot was caught in a trap.

4. (**Your**, You're) hair needs to be cut.

F. **Antecedents:**

Directions: Write the antecedent of the boldfaced pronoun.

1. Bridgette ____________ Bridgette wants to bring **her** dog along.

2. I ____________ Must I carry these bags **myself**?

3. We ____________ We like **our** relatives.

4. boy ____________ The boy wants to do the puzzle **himself**.

5. Mrs. Elles/friend ____________ Mrs. Elles and her friend are taking **their** time.

G. **Pronouns:**

Directions: Fill in the blank.

1. Write two examples of demonstrative pronouns: **this, that, those, these**

2. Write two examples of interrogative pronouns: **who, what, which, whom, whose**

3. Write two examples of reflexive pronouns: **myself, himself, herself, itself, yourself, ourselves, themselves**

4. Write two examples of indefinite pronouns: **some, few, several, many, any, both, each, either, neither, someone, somebody, anyone, anybody, nobody, everyone, none**

5. Write two examples of possessive pronouns: **my, his, her, your, its, our, their, mine, etc.**

Name________________________________

Date________________________________

PRONOUN REVIEW

E. **Possessives:**

Directions: Select the correct word.

1. (Your, You're) so funny.
2. I want to know if (their, they're) sincere about helping.
3. (Its, It's) foot was caught in a trap.
4. (Your, You're) hair needs to be cut.

F. **Antecedents:**

Directions: Write the antecedent of the boldfaced pronoun.

1. ____________________ Bridgette wants to bring **her** dog along.
2. ____________________ Must I carry these bags **myself**?
3. ____________________ We like **our** relatives.
4. ____________________ The boy wants to do the puzzle **himself**.
5. ____________________ Mrs. Elles and her friend are taking **their** time.

G. **Pronouns:**

Directions: Fill in the blank.

1. Write two examples of demonstrative pronouns: ____________ and ____________.
2. Write two examples of interrogative pronouns: ____________ and ____________.
3. Write two examples of reflexive pronouns: ____________ and ____________.
4. Write two examples of indefinite pronouns: ____________ and ____________.
5. Write two examples of possessive pronouns: ____________ and ____________.

Name________________________________ **PRONOUN REVIEW**

WORKBOOK PAGE 256

Date________________________________

H. **Demonstrative, Interrogative, and Indefinite Pronouns:**

Directions: Write A if the boldfaced word serves as an adjective; write P if the boldfaced word serves as a pronoun.

1. __P__ **Several** will be for sale just before the holidays.
2. __A__ Please bring **several** dollars with you to the event.
3. __P__ **That** is a very unusual parrot.
4. __A__ I didn't know **that** fact about Queen Elizabeth.
5. __P__ **Few** chose to hike Pinnacle Peak.
6. __A__ **Few** beavers live in that creek.
7. __P__ **What** is your middle name?
8. __A__ To **which** public library do you go?
9. __P__ Would you like **these**?
10. __A__ Are **these** cuff links silver?

I. **Pronouns:** **Answers are in boldfaced print.**

Directions: Circle the correct pronoun.

1. (**Who**, Whom) is the judge?
2. They want to color the map (**themselves**, theirselves).
3. Mr. Helman and (us, **we**) have agreed to a settlement.
4. Did the bridal company and (**they**, them) meet to discuss marriage details?
5. With (who, **whom**) are you working?
6. The scout leader gave Kit, Ryan, and (she, **her**) a badge.
7. One of the girls left (their, **her**) luggage at the airport.
8. The owner of the new cafe is (**she**, her) holding the menus.
9. Please give (we, **us**) details about your happy childhood memories.
10. Everyone of the boys needs (**his**, their) jacket.
11. The magazine company sent (they, **them**) a reminder to renew their subscription.
12. The students chose (who, **whom**) as their leader?

Name________________________________ **PRONOUN REVIEW**

Date________________________________

H. Demonstrative, Interrogative, and Indefinite Pronouns:

Directions: Write A if the boldfaced word serves as an adjective; write P if the boldfaced word serves as a pronoun.

1. _____ **Several** will be for sale just before the holidays.
2. _____ Please bring **several** dollars with you to the event.
3. _____ **That** is a very unusual parrot.
4. _____ I didn't know **that** fact about Queen Elizabeth.
5. _____ **Few** chose to hike Pinnacle Peak.
6. _____ **Few** beavers live in that creek.
7. _____ **What** is your middle name?
8. _____ To **which** public library do you go?
9. _____ Would you like **these**?
10. _____ Are **these** cuff links silver?

I. Pronouns:

Directions: Circle the correct pronoun.

1. (Who, Whom) is the judge?
2. They want to color the map (themselves, theirselves).
3. Mr. Helman and (us, we) have agreed to a settlement.
4. Did the bridal company and (they, them) meet to discuss marriage details?
5. With (who, whom) are you working?
6. The scout leader gave Kit, Ryan, and (she, her) a badge.
7. One of the girls left (their, her) luggage at the airport.
8. The owner of the new cafe is (she, her) holding the menus.
9. Please give (we, us) details about your happy childhood memories.
10. Everyone of the boys needs (his, their) jacket.
11. The magazine company sent (they, them) a reminder to renew their subscription.
12. The students chose (who, whom) as their leader?

Name_______________________________ **PRONOUN TEST**

Date_______________________________

A. Directions: Circle the correct pronoun.
Answers are in boldfaced print.

1. (**Who**, Whom) wants to ride a roller coaster?
2. The managers are (them, **they**) standing by the door.
3. A chef gave (**us**, we) a lesson in chopping food.
4. (Me, **I**) intend to explore a cave soon.
5. Her friend writes to (**her**, she) nearly every week.
6. May (**we**, us) boys play now?
7. This discussion will remain between you and (I, **me**).
8. To (who, **whom**) did you give a hamburger?
9. Our dentist gives (we, **us**) patients a toothbrush.
10. The librarian told (he, **him**) to work more quietly.

B. Directions: Write **P** in the blank if the boldfaced word serves as a pronoun.
Write **A** in the blank if the boldfaced word serves as an adjective.

1. ___P___ **Which** do you want?
2. ___P___ Are **those** yours?
3. ___A___ **What** time is it?
4. ___A___ **That** golf cart is broken.
5. ___P___ **Each** must carry his own gear.

C. Directions: Circle the correct word.
Answers are in boldfaced print.

1. (**Their**, They're) dog is loose again.
2. I believe (**you're**, your) right!
3. (**It's**, Its) going to be very cloudy today.
4. A turtle turned (it's, **its**) head slowly from side to side.
5. Please ask if (**their**, they're) dad is coming to get them.

Name________________________________ **PRONOUN TEST**

Date________________________________

A. Directions: Circle the correct pronoun.

1. (Who, Whom) wants to ride a roller coaster?
2. The managers are (them, they) standing by the door.
3. A chef gave (us, we) a lesson in chopping food.
4. (Me, I) intend to explore a cave soon.
5. Her friend writes to (her, she) nearly every week.
6. May (we, us) boys play now?
7. This discussion will remain between you and (I, me).
8. To (who, whom) did you give a hamburger?
9. Our dentist gives (we, us) patients a toothbrush.
10. The librarian told (he, him) to work more quietly.

B. Directions: Write P in the blank if the boldfaced word serves as a pronoun; write A in the blank if the boldfaced word serves as an adjective.

1. _____ **Which** do you want?
2. _____ Are **those** yours?
3. _____ **What** time is it?
4. _____ **That** golf cart is broken.
5. _____ **Each** must carry his own gear.

C. Directions: Circle the correct word.

1. (Their, They're) dog is loose again.
2. I believe (you're, your) right!
3. (It's, Its) going to be very cloudy today.
4. A turtle turned (it's, its) head slowly from side to side.
5. Please ask if (their, they're) dad is coming to get them.

D. Directions: Circle the correct pronoun.

Answers are in boldfaced print.

1. Madge gave Shanna and (he, **him**) several popsicles.
2. Judy and (**I**, me) noticed a flaw in the sweater.
3. Both want (his, **their**) dinners late.
4. The explorers and (**we**, us) want to visit Carlsbad Caverns.
5. Harry and (**they**, them) might be going to Acapulco.
6. The last people chosen were Karen and (**we**, us).

E. Directions: Write the antecedent of the boldfaced word.

1. insect — A small insect spread **its** wings.
2. Marcus — Marcus's farm set is **his** favorite toy.
3. men — The men looked at **their** boss's schedule to determine if they had to work on Tuesday.
4. One — One of the boys left **his** books.
5. Joanna/mother — Joanna and her mother love **their** exercise machines.

F. Directions: Tell how the boldfaced pronoun functions in the sentence.

A. subject B. direct object C. indirect object
D. object of the preposition E. predicate nominative

1. E — The first person to arrive at the restaurant was **he**.
2. A — **They** fly kites on windy days.
3. C — A bakery made **us** a beautiful orange cake.
4. C — A lady in charge handed **me** several T-shirts.
5. A — Has **she** cleaned her carpets?
6. A — Did **you** understand the directions?
7. B — A referee threw **him** out of the game.

D. Directions: Circle the correct pronoun.

1. Madge gave Shanna and (he, him) several popsicles.

2. Judy and (I, me) noticed a flaw in the sweater.

3. Both want (his, their) dinners late.

4. The explorers and (we, us) want to visit Carlsbad Caverns.

5. Harry and (they, them) might be going to Acapulco.

6. The last people chosen were Karen and (we, us).

E. Directions: Write the antecedent of the boldfaced word.

1. ______________________________ A small insect spread **its** wings.

2. ______________________________ Marcus's farm set is **his** favorite toy.

3. ______________________________ The men looked at **their** boss's schedule to determine if they had to work on Tuesday.

4. ______________________________ One of the boys left **his** books.

5. ______________________________ Joanna and her mother love **their** exercise machines.

F. Directions: Tell how the boldfaced pronoun functions in the sentence.

A. subject B. direct object C. indirect object
D. object of the preposition E. predicate nominative

1. _____ The first person to arrive at the restaurant was **he**.
2. _____ **They** fly kites on windy days.
3. _____ A bakery made **us** a beautiful orange cake.
4. _____ A lady in charge handed **me** several T-shirts.
5. _____ Has **she** cleaned her carpets?
6. _____ Did **you** understand the directions?
7. _____ A referee threw **him** out of the game.

Name____________________________________
WORKBOOK PAGE 257
Date____________________________________

CUMULATIVE REVIEW
Pronoun Unit

A. Directions: Write the sentence type.

1. imperative — Please wash off the table.
2. interrogative — How many days are in February?
3. declarative — A rock collection is on the top shelf of his desk.
4. exclamatory — You're right!

B. Directions: Write fifty prepositions.

1. about
2. above
3. across
4. after
5. against
6. along
7. amid
8. among
9. around
10. at
11. atop
12. before
13. behind
14. below
15. beneath
16. beside
17. between
18. beyond
19. but (meaning except)
20. by
21. concerning
22. down
23. during
24. except
25. for
26. from
27. in
28. inside
29. into
30. like
31. near
32. of
33. off
34. on
35. onto
36. out
37. outside
38. over
39. past
40. regarding
41. since
42. through
43. throughout
44. to
45. toward
46. under
47. underneath
48. until
49. up
50. upon
51. with
52. within
53. without

Name________________________________

Date________________________________

CUMULATIVE REVIEW
Pronoun Unit

A. Directions: Write the sentence type.

1. ____________________ Please wash off the table.

2. ____________________ How many days are in February?

3. ____________________ A rock collection is on the top shelf of his desk.

4. ____________________ You're right!

B. Directions: Write fifty prepositions.

1. __________	14. __________	27. __________	40. __________
2. __________	15. __________	28. __________	41. __________
3. __________	16. __________	29. __________	42. __________
4. __________	17. __________	30. __________	43. __________
5. __________	18. __________	31. __________	44. __________
6. __________	19. __________	32. __________	45. __________
7. __________	20. __________	33. __________	46. __________
8. __________	21. __________	34. __________	47. __________
9. __________	22. __________	35. __________	48. __________
10. __________	23. __________	36. __________	49. __________
11. __________	24. __________	37. __________	50. __________
12. __________	25. __________	38. __________	
13. __________	26. __________	39. __________	

C. Directions: Write S if the group of words is a sentence. Write F if the group of words is a fragment. Write R-O if the group of words is a run-on.

WORKBOOK PAGE 258

1. S His head aches terribly.
2. R-O Farnsworth likes to play two-square, his sister enjoys tag.
3. F Jerry during the winter storm.
4. F After the students learned about the Aztecs of Mexico.

D. Directions: Write the twenty-three helping verbs.

has, have, had, do, does, did, may, must, might, should, would, could, shall, will, can, is, am, are, was, were, be, being, been

E. Directions: Write the contraction.

1. will not - won't	4. who is - who's	7. he is - he's
2. cannot - can't	5. they are - they're	8. it is - it's
3. you will - you'll	6. I am - I'm	9. has not - hasn't

F. Directions: Write the plural of each noun.

1. leaf - leaves	3. repair - repairs	5. fly - flies
2. deer - deer	4. tomato - tomatoes	6. proof - proofs

G. Directions: Circle any abstract noun: vapor card egg **joy** **love** **peace**

Answers are in boldfaced print.

H. Directions: Circle any common noun: JOE **HAND** **RABBIT** CO ISLE **ISLAND**

I. Directions: Circle any linking verb: **to feel** to skip to bring **to remain** **to be**

J. Directions: Write the seven adverbs that tell *to what extent*. **not, so, very, too, quite, rather, somewhat**

K. Directions: Circle any proper adjective: a blue pen a **Swiss** knife a hat brim

C. Directions: Write S if the group of words is a sentence, write F if the group of words is a fragment, and write R-O if the group of words is a run-on.

1. ______ His head aches terribly.

2. ______ Farnsworth likes to play two-square, his sister enjoys tag.

3. ______ Jerry during the winter storm.

4. ______ After the students learned about the Aztecs of Mexico.

D. Directions: Write the twenty-three helping verbs.

____

____

E. Directions: Write the contraction.

1. will not - ____________ 4. who is - ____________ 7. he is - ____________

2. cannot - ____________ 5. they are - ____________ 8. it is - ____________

3. you will - ____________ 6. I am - ____________ 9. has not - ____________

F. Directions: Write the plural of each noun.

1. leaf - ____________ 3. repair - ____________ 5. fly - ____________

2. deer - ____________ 4. tomato - ____________ 6. proof - ____________

G. Directions: Circle any abstract noun: vapor card egg joy love peace

H. Directions: Circle any common noun: JOE HAND RABBIT CO ISLE ISLAND

I. Directions: Circle any linking verb: to feel to skip to bring to remain to be

J. Directions: Write the seven adverbs that tell *to what extent*. ____________

____

K. Directions: Circle any proper adjective: a blue pen a Swiss knife a hat brim

L. Directions: Circle any adverbs.
WORKBOOK PAGE 259
Answers are in boldfaced print.

1. I **can't** stay **long anyway**.
2. **Yesterday**, the barn was **suddenly** struck by a **very** large bolt of lightning.
3. We shall **probably** arrive **quite late**.
4. You may **not** go **home yet**.

M. Write the correct possessive form.

1. a pond belonging to Phyllis - Phyllis's pond
2. a bone that their dog has - their dog's bone
3. many experiences shared by the two boys - two boys' experiences
4. the ceiling in a kitchen - kitchen's ceiling
5. a meadow belonging to more than one goose - geese's meadow

N. Directions: Circle any adjectives.

Answers are in boldfaced print.

1. **African** daisies had been planted in **several flower** beds.
2. **Candy's baseball** hat with **the wide** brim is very **dirty**.
3. **That unusual** tree in **our front** yard has **tiny pink** blossoms.

O. Directions: Fill in the blank.

1. **Wow! We're winning!** What part of speech is Wow!? interjection
2. **Kay Lynn should have arrived by now.** The main verb is arrived.

L. Directions: Circle any adverbs.

Suggestion: Cross out any prepositional phrase(s). However, check to see if any adverb telling **to what extent** is in any prepositional phrase. If it is, circle it. Then, underline the subject once and verb/verb phrase twice. Next, go through the sentence looking specifically for any adverbs that tell **how**. Reread the sentence, searching for any adverbs that tell **when**. Next, look for any adverbs that tell **where**. Finally, look for any adverbs that tell **to what extent** and are not located in a prepositional phrase. This process may sound long, but once you do it step-by-step, it will become faster and will definitely help you to determine adverbs.

1. I can't stay long anyway.
2. Yesterday, the barn was suddenly struck by a very large bolt of lightning.
3. We shall probably arrive quite late.
4. You may not go home yet.

M. Directions: Write the correct possessive form.

1. a pond belonging to Phyllis________________________________
2. a bone that their dog has - ________________________________
3. many experiences shared by the two boys - ______________________
4. the ceiling in a kitchen - ________________________________
5. a meadow belonging to more than one goose - ____________________

N. Directions: Circle any adjectives.

1. African daisies had been planted in several flower beds.
2. Candy's baseball hat with the wide brim is very dirty.
3. That unusual tree in our front yard has tiny pink blossoms.

O. Directions: Fill in the blank.

1. **Wow! We're winning!** What part of speech is <u>Wow!</u>? ________________
2. **Kay Lynn should have arrived by now.** The main verb is ________________.

P. Directions: Cross out any prepositional phrases. Underline the subject once and the verb/verb phrase twice. In the space provided, write the tense: *present, past, future, present perfect, past perfect, future perfect, present progressive, past progressive,* or *future progressive.*

WORKBOOK PAGE 260

1. present progressive — Rebecca is planning a surprise party.
2. present perfect — Have you seen the low clouds ~~on that mountain~~?
3. future — Will you finish this ~~within five minutes~~?
4. present perfect — He has flown ~~in a helicopter~~ three times.
5. present — That judge listens carefully ~~to all testimony~~.

Q. Directions: Underline the subject once and the verb/verb phrase twice. Write P if the group of words is a phrase; write C if the group of words is a clause.

1. P — Beside the stream.
2. C — When you finish with that chore.
3. C — His motorcycle needs a new light.
4. P — Standing at the edge of the road.

R. Directions: Circle the correct adjective form.

Answers are in boldfaced print.

1. His big toe is (**smaller**, smallest) than his second one.
2. Jennifer thinks that England is the (more colorful, **most colorful**) country of all Europe.
3. Mrs. Elder is the (friendlier, **friendliest**) Sunday school teacher.

S. Directions: Cross out any prepositional phrases. Underline the subject once and the verb/verb phrase twice. Write D.O. above a word that serves as a direct object; write I.O. above a word that serves as an indirect object.

1. The clown ~~with the red cheeks~~ handed a balloon (**D.O.**) ~~to the smiling child~~.
2. Mr. Hansen laughed and handed me (**I.O**) a large bag (**D.O.**) ~~of groceries~~.

P. Directions: Cross out any prepositional phrases. Underline the subject once and the verb/verb phrase twice. In the space provided, write the tense: *present, past, future, present perfect, past perfect, future perfect, present progressive, past progressive,* or *future progressive.*

1. ______________________ Rebecca is planning a surprise party.

2. ______________________ Have you seen the low clouds on that mountain?

3. ______________________ Will you finish this within five minutes?

4. ______________________ He has flown in a helicopter three times.

5. ______________________ That judge listens carefully to all testimony.

Q. Directions: Underline the subject once and the verb/verb phrase twice. Write P if the group of words is a phrase; write C if the group of words is a clause.

1. ______ Beside the stream.

2. ______ When you finish with that chore.

3. ______ His motorcycle needs a new light.

4. ______ Standing at the edge of the road.

R. Directions: Circle the correct adjective form.

1. His big toe is (smaller, smallest) than his second one.

2. Jennifer thinks that England is the (more colorful, most colorful) country of all Europe.

3. Mrs. Elder is the (friendlier, friendliest) Sunday school teacher.

S. Directions: Cross out any prepositional phrases. Underline the subject once and the verb/verb phrase twice. Write D.O. above a word that serves as a direct object; write I.O. above a word that serves as an indirect object.

1. The clown with the red cheeks handed a balloon to the smiling child.

2. Mr. Hansen laughed and handed me a large bag of groceries.

T. Directions: Write N if the boldfaced word serves as a noun. Write A if the boldfaced word serves as an adjective. Write V if the boldfaced word serves as a verb.

WORKBOOK PAGE 261

1. N This **fall** they will go to the New England states.
2. A The shoppers were all looking for a new **fall** wardrobe.
3. V Did you **fall** over the toys scattered on the floor?
4. N Mrs. Kent suffered a bad **fall** recently.

U. Directions: Write the past paticiple form.

1. to give - (had) given
2. to write - (had) written
3. to sing - (had) sung
4. to take - (had) taken
5. to freeze - (had) frozen
6. to go - (had) gone
7. to lie - (had) lain
8. to steal - (had) stolen
9. to see - (had) seen
10. to lay - (had) laid
11. to fly - (had) flown
12. to bring - (had) brought
13. to swear - (had) sworn
14. to come - (had) come
15. to do - (had) done
16. to spring - (had) sprung

V. Directions: Cross out any prepositional phrases. Underline the subject once and the verb/verb phrase twice.

1. ~~After the beginning of the game~~, several spectators came in and sat down ~~near the team~~.
2. (You) Please applaud loudly ~~for this outstanding performer~~.
3. Many ~~of the zoo animals~~ did not come out ~~of their homes during the rain~~.
4. Will you go ~~with Mary and me to the symphony~~ tomorrow?
5. The cheerleader jumped excitedly and touched her toes.

T. Directions: Write N if the boldfaced word serves as a noun. Write A if the boldfaced word serves as an adjective. Write V if the boldfaced word serves as a verb.

1. ______ This **fall** they will go to the New England states.

2. ______ The shoppers were all looking for a new **fall** wardrobe.

3. ______ Did you **fall** over the toys scattered on the floor?

4. ______ Mrs. Kent suffered a bad **fall** recently.

U. Directions: Write the past participle form.

1. to give - ______________________
2. to write - ______________________
3. to sing - ______________________
4. to take - ______________________
5. to freeze - ______________________
6. to go - ______________________
7. to lie - ______________________
8. to steal - ______________________
9. to see - ______________________
10. to lay - ______________________
11. to fly - ______________________
12. to bring - ______________________
13. to swear - ______________________
14. to come - ______________________
15. to do - ______________________
16. to spring - ______________________

V. Directions: Cross out any prepositional phrases. Underline the subject once and the verb/verb phrase twice.

1. After the beginning of the game, several spectators came in and sat down near the team.

2. Please applaud loudly for this outstanding performer.

3. Many of the zoo animals did not come out of their homes during the rain.

4. Will you go with Mary and me to the symphony tomorrow?

5. The cheerleader jumped excitedly and touched her toes.

W. Directions: Cross out any prepositional phrases. Underline the subject once and the verb/verb phrase twice. On the line provided, write A if the verb is action; write L if the verb is linking.

WORKBOOK PAGE 262

is

1. L That spaniel seems alert.
2. A ~~During the morning hours~~, we split wood ~~for the fire~~.

is

3. L This hot cereal tastes too bland ~~without brown sugar~~.
4. A The mother felt the head ~~of her sick son~~.

X. Directions: Cross out any prepositional phrases. Underline the subject once and the verb/verb phrase twice. Label any predicate nominative - PN Write the proof on the line.

PN

1. A famous composer ~~from Austria~~ was Mozart.

   Proof: Mozart was a famous composer.

PN

2. His new item ~~for his art studio~~ is a large table ~~with a tilted top~~.

   Proof: A large table is his new item.

Y. Directions: Cross out any prepositional phrases. Underline the subject once and the verb/verb phrase twice.

1. Hornets (swarm, swarms) ~~in that area~~.
2. Magazines (is, are) ~~on the table~~ ~~in the family room~~.
3. Someone must have (did, done) my job.
4. Has Earl ever (ridden, rode) five miles ~~on a motor scooter~~?
5. The girls (lay, laid) ~~on their bunks~~ ~~for an afternoon nap~~.
6. One ~~of the ducks~~ (waddle, waddles) ~~around the lake~~.
7. Several conference attendees (want, wants) (to tour) the city.

W. Directions: Cross out any prepositional phrases. Underline the subject once and the verb/verb phrase twice. On the line provided, write A if the verb is action; write L if the verb is linking.

Suggestion: Write *is, am, are, was,* or *were* above each verb to help you decide.

1. _____ That spaniel seems alert.

2. _____ During the morning hours, we split wood for the fire.

3. _____ This hot cereal tastes too bland without brown sugar.

4. _____ The mother felt the head of her sick son.

X. Directions: Cross out any prepositional phrases. Underline the subject once and the verb/verb phrase twice. Label any predicate nominative-PN Write the proof on the line.

1. A famous composer from Austria was Mozart.

   Proof: ____

2. His new item for his art studio is a large table with a tilted top.

   Proof: ____

Y. Directions: Cross out prepositional phrases. Underline the subject once and the verb/verb phrase twice.

1. Hornets (swarm, swarms) in that area.

2. Magazines (is, are) on the table in the family room.

3. Someone must have (did, done) my job.

4. Has Earl ever (ridden, rode) five miles on a motor scooter?

5. The girls (lay, laid) on their bunks for an afternoon nap.

6. One of the ducks (waddle, waddles) around the lake.

7. Several conference attendees (want, wants) to tour the city.

Z. Directions: Select the correct adverb form.
WORKBOOK PAGE 263 **Answers are in boldfaced print.**

1. Of the two cars, this one goes (**faster**, fastest).
2. She can swim underwater (**more easily**, most easily) than on the surface.
3. At the batting cages, Jonathan hit the fourth ball (harder, **hardest**).
4. Jane runs (weller, **better**) after a good night's sleep.
5. Of the triplets, Faith talks (more loudly, **most loudly**).

AA. Directions: Fill in the blank.

1. The three determining (limiting) articles are **a**, **an**, and **the**.
2. The four demonstratives that may help you to determine nouns are **this**, **that**, **those**, and **these**.
3. The possessive pronouns (used as adjectives) that help locate nouns are **my**, **his**, **her**, **its**, **your**, **our**, and **their**.
4. Write an example of a number used as a determining adjective.
   Answers will vary:
   Representative answers: **three** swans, **fifty** meteorites, **seven** dollars
5. Write an example of a possessive noun used to determine another noun.
   Answers will vary:
   Representative answers: **Micah's** dog, **girls'** outing, **Miss Davidson's** daughter
6. Write an indefinite with a noun.
   Answers will vary:
   Representative answers: **no** time, **many** suits, **few** electricians

BB. Directions: Write A if the boldfaced word serves as an adjective. Write P if the boldfaced word serves as a pronoun (stands alone). Write the adjective and the noun on the line after any sentence marked A.

1. A **Few** fireworks were set off during the Fourth of July. few fireworks
2. P **Few** were sitting in the back row. ______
3. P I want **that** for my collection. ______
4. A Who gave you **that** hat? that hat

CC. Directions: Box any nouns.
Nouns are in boldfaced print. (Although directions do not indicate it, determining (limiting) adjectives have been italicized.)

1. **Martha** ate *three* blueberry **pancakes**, *some* **bacon**, and *an* **egg** for *her* **breakfast**.
2. Has **Henry's** older **brother** given you *those* **shoes** with *the* black **stripes**?
3. *Several* team **members** played **basketball** in *that* **arena** during *a* rainy **afternoon**.

Z. Directions: Select the correct adverb form.

1. Of the two cars, this one goes (faster, fastest).
2. She can swim underwater (more easily, most easily) than on the surface.
3. At the batting cages, Jonathan hit the fourth ball (harder, hardest).
4. Jane runs (weller, better) after a good night's sleep.
5. Of the triplets, Faith talks (more loudly, most loudly).

AA. Directions: Fill in the blank.

1. The three determining (limiting) articles are _____, ______, and _______.

2. The four demonstratives that may help you to determine nouns are ___________, ___________, ___________, and ______________.

3. The possessive pronouns (used as adjectives) that help locate nouns are ______, _______, ______, ________, ________, _________, and _________.

4. Write an example of a number used as a determining adjective. _______________

5. Write an example of a possessive noun used to determine another noun. ______ ____

6. Write an indefinite with a noun. ______________________________________

BB. Directions: Write A if the boldfaced word serves as an adjective. Write P if the boldfaced word serves as a pronoun (stands alone). Write the adjective and the noun on the line after any sentence marked A.

1. _____ **Few** fireworks were set off during the Fourth of July. _______________
2. _____ **Few** were sitting in the back row. ___________________________
3. _____ I want **that** for my collection. ___________________________
4. _____ Who gave you **that** hat? ______________________________

CC. Directions: Box any nouns.

1. Martha ate three blueberry pancakes, some bacon, and an egg for her breakfast.

2. Has Henry's older brother given you those shoes with the black stripes?

3. Several team members played basketball in that arena during a rainy afternoon.

Name ______________________________ **CUMULATIVE TEST**

Pronoun Unit

Date________________________________

A. Directions: Write PN in the space if the boldfaced word serves as a predicate nominative. Write PA if the boldfaced word serves as a predicate adjective. Write NO if the boldfaced word does not serve as a predicate nominative or predicate adjective.

1. PA Your hands look very **chapped**.
2. PN Miss Liston is my friend's **aunt**.
3. NO Fran looks for **money** with her metal detector.
4. NO This **old** coin was used in ancient Rome.
5. PN My best friend is **she** in the blue dress.

B. Directions: Circle the correct adverb form.
Answers are in boldfaced print.

1. My sister doesn't ever drive (slow, **slowly**).
2. That first grader writes her name (good, **well**).
3. The children playing in the water yelled (loud, **loudly**) to the passing boat driver.
4. His voice rose (sharp, **sharply**) as he became angrier.

C. Directions: Circle any adverbs.
Answers are in boldfaced print.

1. We **sometimes** go **there** for lunch.
2. **How** did you hurt your wrist **so badly**?
3. A race horse galloped **swiftly by**.
4. The lady has **frantically** searched **everywhere** for the missing money.
5. He dashed **in**, looked **down** at his shoes, and began to chuckle **softly**.

D. Directions: Label any conjunction - Conj.; label any interjection - Intj.

Intj. **Conj.**
1. Yippee! Mark and Mandy are entering the race!

Conj. **Conj.**
2. Either Holly or her sister attends college in North Carolina.

Intj. **Conj.**
3. Hurray! My parents are going to the reunion, but I may go fishing!

Name______________________________

Date______________________________

CUMULATIVE TEST
Pronoun Unit

A. Directions: Write P.N. in the space if the boldfaced word serves as a predicate nominative. Write P.A. if the boldfaced word serves as a predicate adjective. Write NO if the boldfaced word does not serve as a predicate nominative or predicate adjective.

1. _____ Your hands look very **chapped**.
2. _____ Miss Liston is my friend's **aunt**.
3. _____ Fran looks for **money** with her metal detector.
4. _____ This **old** coin was used in ancient Rome.
5. _____ My best friend is **she** in the blue dress.

B. Directions: Circle the correct adverb form.

1. My sister doesn't ever drive (slow, slowly).
2. That first grader writes her name (good, well).
3. The children playing in the water yelled (loud, loudly) to the passing boat driver.
4. His voice rose (sharp, sharply) as he became angrier.

C. Directions: Circle any adverbs.

1. We sometimes go there for lunch.
2. How did you hurt your wrist so badly?
3. A race horse galloped swiftly by.
4. The lady has frantically searched everywhere for the missing money.
5. He dashed in, looked down at his shoes, and began to chuckle softly.

D. Directions: Label any conjunction-Conj.; label any interjection-Intj.

1. Yippee! Mark and Mandy are entering the race!

2. Either Holly or her sister attends college in North Carolina.

3. Hurray! My parents are going to the reunion, but I may go fishing!

E. Directions: Write the sentence type.

1. ___imperative___ Stand up.

2. ___exclamatory___ Look at him stand on his head!

3. ___declarative___ He is standing on his head.

4. ___interrogative___ Can you stand on your head?

F. Directions: Write the tense: *present, past, future, present perfect, past perfect, future perfect, present progressive, past progresive, future progressive.*

1. ___present___ She likes tarantulas.

2. ___future progressive___ I shall be flying to Denver next month.

3. ___present perfect___ The child has fallen off a swing.

4. ___future perfect___ By spring, Ted will have taken all his exams.

5. ___past___ Mayor Loo greeted the ambassador from Peru.

6. ___past progressive___ A newspaper was lying by the road.

G. Directions: Write the contraction.

1. I am - ___I'm___ 3. will not - ___won't___ 5. there is - ___there's___

2. you are - ___you're___ 4. we are - ___we're___ 6. they have - ___they've___

H. Directions: Write A if the noun is abstract; write C if the noun is concrete.

1. ___A___ kindness 2. ___C___ salad 3. ___A___ caution 4. ___C___ harp 5. ___A___ joy

I. Directions: Write C if the noun is common; write P if the noun is proper.

1. ___C___ PLANT 2. ___C___ GRASS 3. ___C___ TOWER 4. ___P___ EIFFEL TOWER

5. ___P___ OREGON 6. ___P___ AMERICA 7. ___C___ ANGEL 8. ___P___ GABRIEL

E. Directions: Write the sentence type.

1. ______________________ Stand up.

2. ______________________ Look at him stand on his head!

3. ______________________ He is standing on his head.

4. ______________________ Can you stand on your head?

F. Directions: Write the tense: *present, past, future, present perfect, past perfect, future perfect, present progressive, past progressive, future progressive.*

1. ______________________ She likes tarantulas.

2. ______________________ I shall be flying to Denver next month.

3. ______________________ The child has fallen off a swing.

4. ______________________ By spring, Ted will have taken all his exams.

5. ______________________ Mayor Loo greeted the ambassador from Peru.

6. ______________________ A newspaper was lying by the road.

G. Directions: Write the contraction.

1. I am - __________ 3. will not - __________ 5. there is - __________

2. you are - __________ 4. we are - __________ 6. they have - __________

H. Directions: Write A if the noun is abstract; write C if the noun is concrete.

1. ___ kindness 2. ___ salad 3. ___ caution 4. ___ harp 5. ___ joy

I. Directions: Write C if the noun is common; write P if the noun is proper.

1. ___ PLANT 2. ___ GRASS 3. ___ TOWER 4. ___ EIFFEL TOWER

5. ___ OREGON 6. ___ AMERICA 7. ___ ANGEL 8. ___ GABRIEL

J. Directions: Write D.O. if the boldfaced word serves as a direct object.
Write I.O. if the boldfaced word serves as an indirect object.
Write APP. if the boldfaced word serves as an appositive.

1. I.O. Dad handed **Tammy** an apple for her lunch.

2. APP. Their friend, **Tammy**, is a great seminar speaker.

3. D.O. A small child hit **Tammy** on the back with a toy.

K. Directions: Cross out any prepositional phrases. Underline the subject once and the verb/verb phrase twice.

1. Several ~~of the crew members~~ took a break and sat ~~in the shade~~.

2. A lion ~~with his ears at attention~~ is lying ~~between two trees~~ ~~near a stream~~.

3. (You) Take this sword ~~to the auditorium~~ ~~for Miss Dormal and Mr. Master~~.

4. Headlights should have been turned on ~~before the tunnel entrance~~.

5. Haven't you ever walked ~~through the woods~~ ~~on a cold, crisp winter day~~?

L. Directions: Circle the correct answer.
Answers are in boldfaced print.

1. A (childrens', **children's**) play area has been added.

2. Has Uncle Marty done that (**himself**, hisself)?

3. Several (boy's, **boys'**) jackets are on sale.

4. One (**lamb's**, lambs') mouth seems to be sore.

5. (You're, **Your**) idea is being considered.

6. Many (**skiers'**, skier's) poles have been slightly bent.

7. (Mrs. Hass, **Mrs. Hass's**) husband is an orthodontist.

8. The peacock was spreading (it's, **its**) beautiful tail.

9. Sooner or later, the (**women's**, womens') club must reach a decision.

J. Directions: Write <u>D.O</u>. if the boldfaced word serves as a direct object.
Write <u>I.O</u>. if the boldfaced word serves as an indirect object.
Write <u>APP</u>. if the boldfaced word serves as an appositive.

1. _____ Dad handed **Tammy** an apple for her lunch.

2. _____ Their friend, **Tammy**, is a great seminar speaker.

3. _____ A small child hit **Tammy** on the back with a toy.

K. Directions: Cross out any prepositional phrases. Underline the subject once and the verb/verb phrase twice.

1. Several of the crew members took a break and sat in the shade.

2. A lion with his ears at attention is lying between two trees near a stream.

3. Take this sword to the auditorium for Miss Dormal and Mr. Master.

4. Headlights should have been turned on before the tunnel entrance.

5. Haven't you ever walked through the woods on a cold, crisp winter day?

L. Directions: Circle the correct answer.

1. A (childrens', children's) play area has been added.

2. Has Uncle Marty done that (himself, hisself)?

3. Several (boy's, boys') jackets are on sale.

4. One (lamb's, lambs') mouth seems to be sore.

5. (You're, Your) idea is being considered.

6. Many (skiers', skier's) poles have been slightly bent.

7. (Mrs. Hass, Mrs. Hass's) husband is an orthodontist.

8. The peacock was spreading (it's, its) beautiful tail.

9. Sooner or later, the (women's, womens') club must reach a decision.

M. Directions: Write the plural.

1. lotus - **lotuses**
2. nursery - **nurseries**
3. clay - **clays**
4. leaf - **leaves**
5. pitch - **pitches**
6. son-in-law - **sons-in-law**
7. laughter - **laughter**
8. circle - **circles**

N. Directions: Circle each correct answer.
Answers are in boldfaced print.

1. The parade had not (came, **come**) down the main street.
2. This opening is (narrower, **narrowest**) of the three.
3. Nancy's grandmother (**serves**, serve) as our church's greeter.
4. (**You're**, Your) the person I most respect.
5. The police officer has (rode, **ridden**) a horse on his beat for several years.
6. The lady with those crying children (**is**, are) very upset.
7. The man scrubbed the floor (**more vigorously**, most vigorously) the second time.
8. A zebra and a giraffe often (**stand**, stands) near a tree in the African meadow.
9. Two-year-olds frequently want to do things (theirselves, **themselves**).
10. Have you (brang, **brought**) a suitcase with you?
11. (**Lie**, Lay) here beside the fire and get warm.
12. He (**sits**, sets) under a tree in the park nearly every evening.
13. The pilot must have (went, **gone**) to the airport already.
14. This matter is between your sister and (I, **me**).
15. Her father must have (laid, **lain**) in his recliner all afternoon.
16. Give (we, **us**) adults a chance to help you.
17. The winner should have been (me, **I**).
18. Many ribbons have been given to (**her**, she) for her athletic talent.
19. Everyone must take (their, **his**) clothes into the laundry room.
20. Several people in the overturned boat had (swam, **swum**) to the river's bank.
21. When the phone rang, he answered, "This is (**he**, him)."
22. The light fixture had been (broke, **broken**) while still in the box.
23. (**We**, Us) will be meeting with a senator from Kansas.
24. You are much taller than (**I**, me).

M. Directions: Write the plural.

1. lotus - ______________________
2. nursery - ______________________
3. clay - ______________________
4. leaf - ______________________
5. pitch - ______________________
6. son-in-law - ______________________
7. laughter - ______________________
8. circle - ______________________

N. Directions: Circle each correct answer.

1. The parade had not (came, come) down the main street.
2. This opening is (narrower, narrowest) of the three.
3. Nancy's grandmother (serves, serve) as our church's greeter.
4. (You're, Your) the person I most respect.
5. The police officer has (rode, ridden) a horse on his beat for several years.
6. The lady with those crying children (is, are) very upset.
7. The man scrubbed the floor (more vigorously, most vigorously) the second time.
8. A zebra and a giraffe often (stand, stands) near a tree in the African meadow.
9. Two year olds frequently want to do things (theirselves, themselves).
10. Have you (brang, brought) a suitcase with you?
11. (Lie, Lay) here beside the fire and get warm.
12. He (sits, sets) under a tree in the park nearly every evening.
13. The pilot must have (went, gone) to the airport already.
14. This matter is between your sister and (I, me).
15. Her father must have (laid, lain) in his recliner all afternoon.
16. Give (we, us) adults a chance to help you.
17. The winner should have been (me, I).
18. Many ribbons have been given to (her, she) for her athletic talent.
19. Everyone must take (their, his) clothes into the laundry room.
20. Several people in the overturned boat had (swam, swum) to the river's bank.
21. When the phone rang, he answered, "This is (he, him)."
22. The light fixture had been (broke, broken) while still in the box.
23. (We, Us) will be meeting with a senator from Kansas.
24. You are much taller than (I, me).

O. Directions: Box any nouns. **Answers are in boldfaced print.**

1. The **desert** is a **habitat** for some **snakes** and various **cacti**.
2. I need a **package** of **napkins**, some paper **plates**, and a few **straws** for our **picnic**.
3. **Lee's aunt** is an aspiring **violinist**; she hopes to play with the **Phoenix Symphony**.
4. These **boxes** containing two **lamps** were sent to the **girls' apartment** by **mistake**.

P. Directions: Circle any adjectives. **Answers are in boldfaced print.**

1. **Several beautiful** models wore **soft, flowing** dresses made of **imported** silk.
2. **Five Dalmatian** puppies scampered friskily among **many** shrubs in **their back** lawn.
3. **The Irish** countryside is **fertile**, very **green**, and **scenic** in **the** summer.
4. **That** man writes **funny short** stories, **Gothic** novels, and **humorous** poetry.

Q. Directions: Read each group of words. Write F for fragment, S for sentence, and R-O for run-on.

1. F Having been chosen as the best.
2. S Jenny and John have been married a year.
3. R-O Pizza was delivered for dinner, unfortunately, it was cold.
4. R-O During the summer, Brian goes to his grandmother and grandfather's house in Nebraska and loves swimming in a creek by their home and going to the local fairs plus he drives the tractor on their farm.

R. Directions: Circle the correct answer. **Answers are in boldfaced print.**

1. They feel (**happy**, happily) about their choice.
2. You painted that wall (quick, **quickly**).
3. Garth does his job (good, **well**).
4. Kimberly's mother looks (**tired**, tiredly) today.
5. He answered the question (weird, **weirdly**).
6. Of the four sandwiches, the beef one was (more delicious, **most delicious**).

O. Directions: Box any nouns.

1. The desert is a habitat for some snakes and various cacti.
2. I need a package of napkins, some paper plates, and a few straws for our picnic.
3. Lee's aunt is an aspiring violinist; she hopes to play with the Phoenix Symphony.
4. These boxes containing two lamps were sent to the girls' apartment by mistake.

P. Directions: Circle any adjectives.

1. Several beautiful models wore soft, flowing dresses made of imported silk.
2. Five Dalmatian puppies scampered friskily among many shrubs on their back lawn.
3. The Irish countryside is fertile, very green, and scenic in the summer.
4. That man writes funny short stories, Gothic novels, and humorous poetry.

Q. Directions: Read each group of words. Write F for fragment, S for sentence, and R-O for run-on.

1. _____ Having been chosen as the best.
2. _____ Jenny and John have been married a year.
3. _____ Pizza was delivered for dinner, unfortunately, it was cold.
4. _____ During the summer, Brian goes to his grandmother and grandfather's house in Nebraska and loves swimming in a creek by their home and going to the local fairs plus he drives the tractor on their farm.

R. Directions: Circle the correct answer.

1. They feel (happy, happily) about their choice.
2. You painted that wall (quick, quickly).
3. Garth does his job (good, well).
4. Kimberly's mother looks (tired, tiredly) today.
5. He answered the question (weird, weirdly).
6. Of the four sandwiches, the beef one was (more delicious, most delicious).

PUNCTUATION

PERIOD: Rule 1: **Use a period at the end of a declarative sentence (statement).**

I like snow cones.

Rule 2: **Place a period at the end of an imperative sentence (command).**

Pass the salt.

Rule 3: **Use a period after initial(s).**

David James Sloan = David J. Sloan or D. J. Sloan
Lisa Marie Fry = L. M. F.

If a sentence ends with an abbreviation and a period, do not add another period.

Rule 4: **Use a period after the letter(s) and number(s) of an outline.**

I. Civil War
    A. Union
        1. Generals
        2. Strategy
    B. Confederacy
        1. Generals
            a. Robert E. Lee
            b. Thomas "Stonewall" Jackson
        2. Strategy
II. Reconstruction

Rule 5: **Place a period after an abbreviation.**

A. **Days of the week**:

Monday - Mon.
Tuesday - Tues.
Wednesday - Wed.
Thursday - Thurs.
Friday - Fri.
Saturday - Sat.
Sunday - Sun.

B. **Months of the year**:

January - Jan.
February - Feb.
March - Mar.
April
May
June
July
August - Aug.
September - Sept.
October - Oct.
November - Nov.
December - Dec.

PERIOD: Rule 5: **Place a period after an abbreviation.***

C. **Times**:

A. M. - (Latin, ante meridiem) before noon

P. M. - (Latin, post meridiem) after noon

D. **Directions**:

N. - North	S.W. or SW. - Southwest
S. - South	S.E. or SE. - Southeast
E. - East	N.E. or NE. - Northeast
W. - West	N.W. or NW. - Northwest

E. **Titles**:

Dr. - Doctor	Pres. - President
Mr. - Mister	Sen. - Senator
Mrs. - Mistress	Rep. - Representative
Lieut. - Lieutenant	Prof. - Professor
Capt. - Captain	Gen. - General

F. **Places** (General):

St. - Street	Dr. - Drive
Rd. - Road	Riv. - River
Ave. - Avenue	Mts. - Mountains
Blvd. - Boulevard	Str. - Strait

G. **Places** (Specific):

N.Y. - New York*	U.S. - United States
Med. Sea - Mediterranean Sea	St. Paul - Saint Paul

***Do not, however, punctuate postal codes (NY).**

H. **Associations and Organizations**:

A. M. A. - American Medical Association
Y. M. C. A. - Young Men's Christian Association
NOW - National Organization of Women*

*If the name of the organization is an acronym, no period is used. (An acronym spells out a word.)

I. Others:

Co. - Company	Bldg. - Building
Am. Rev. - American Revolution	yd. - yard*

***Metric measurements do not use a period (cm).**

***Note: Check a dictionary to determine proper abbreviation and use of a period.** This can be tricky. For example, SA is Seaman Apprentice; S. A. is South America, South Africa, South Australia, or Salvation Army.

Name________________________________

WORKBOOK PAGE 266

Date________________________________

PUNCTUATION

Periods

Directions: Insert needed periods.

1. It's raining today.
2. Please give me your paper.
3. Miss R. E. Talley has arrived.
4. I. Birds

   A. Types

   B. Care

   II. Alligators

   A. Types

   B. Dangers

5. The address is 354 W. Andrew Lane.
6. Is your tour scheduled for Sept. or Nov.?
7. The Bering Str. is located west of Alaska.
8. Do you want to leave Sun. or Mon. for L. A. , Calif.?
9. Was the Stone Age B. C. or A. D.?
10. At 6 o'clock P. M., Capt. John Yust arrived on the <u>U. S. S. Independence</u>.
11. Dr. Angelic Stomb spoke at an A. M. A. meeting in N. Y. last May.
12. The Rocky Mts. are west of the Miss. Riv.
13. During the War of 1812, neither Brit. nor Am. won.
14. On Fri., Oct. 23, Prof. Flang will meet with you.
15. The A. I. Ritter Co. has moved to 2435 N. Orange Dr., Phx., Arizona.

Name________________________________

Date________________________________

PUNCTUATION
Periods

Directions: Insert needed periods.

1. It's raining today

2. Please give me your paper

3. Miss R E Talley has arrived

4. I Birds

   A Types

   B Care

   II Alligators

   A Types

   B Dangers

5. The address is 354 W Andrew Lane

6. Is your tour scheduled for Sept or Nov ?

7. The Bering Str is located west of Alaska

8. Do you want to leave Sun or Mon for L A , Calif ?

9. Was the Stone Age B C or A D ?

10. At 6 o'clock P M , Capt John Yust arrived on the U S S Independence

11. Dr Angelic Stomb spoke at an A M A meeting in N Y last May

12. The Rocky Mts are west of the Miss Riv

13. During the War of 1812, neither Brit nor Am won

14. On Fri , Oct 23, Prof Flang will meet with you

15. The A I Ritter Co has moved to 2435 N Orange Dr , Phx, Arizona

Name________________________________ **PUNCTUATION**
WORKBOOK PAGE 267 Periods
Date________________________________

Directions: Insert needed periods.

1. Our friend will take us down the Hudson Riv. and around N. Y. Harbor on his new boat.
2. On Thurs., Mar. 5, the members of the Y. M. C. A. are invited to a picnic at 9 A. M.
3. We live at 6777 S. Madison Ave., St. Louis, Mo., during the summer.
4. I. Furniture

    A. Antique

        1. Periods

        2. Types

    B. Modern

        1. Periods

        2. Types

5. The Alps Mts. are mountains in Eur. that run from France through Switz.
6. Lieut. Martha Woods wants to move to Brattleboro, Vt., in a few years.
7. Go west on McGrew Blvd. until you come to the International Bldg. on the corner of McGrew and N. 51st Ave. in St. Paul.
8. Dr. and Mrs. T. L. Lewis will visit Den. and Czech. in the spring.
9. He was approx. fifty-six years old on Fri., Apr. 11, 1990.

Name____________________________________

Date____________________________________

PUNCTUATION
Periods

Directions: Insert needed periods.

1. Our friend will take us down the Hudson Riv and around N Y Harbor on his new boat

2. On Thurs , Mar 5, the members of the Y M C A are invited to a picnic at 9 A M

3. We live at 6777 S Madison Ave , St Louis, Mo , during the summer

4. I Furniture

    A Antique

        1 Periods

        2 Types

    B Modern

        1 Periods

        2 Types

5. The Alps Mts are mountains in Eur that run from France through Switz

6. Lieut Martha Woods wants to move to Brattleboro, Vt , in a few years

7. Go west on McGrew Blvd until you come to the International Bldg on the corner of McGrew and N 51st Ave in St Paul

8. Dr and Mrs T L Lewis will visit Den and Czech in the spring

9. He was approx fifty-six years old on Fri , Apr 11, 1990

PAGE 575 = WORKBOOK PAGE 268

APOSTROPHE: Rule 1: **Use an apostrophe in a contraction to show where letter(s) have been omitted.**

can't = cannot
she'll = she will
I've = I have

Rule 2: **Use an apostrophe when the first two digits are omitted from the year.**

'84 = 1984
'99 = 1999

Rule 3: **Use an apostrophe when taking letters or words out of context.** (They will also be underlined.)

You need to cross your t's.
There are too many well's in this paragraph.

Rule 4: **Use an apostrophe to show possession.**

A. **If the word is singular (one), add apostrophe + s ('s).**

barber's chair
blender's buttons
Chris's boots

B. **If the word is plural and ends in s, add the apostrophe after the s (s').**

dogs' kennel
pilots' association
ladies' club

C. **If the word is plural and does NOT end in s, add apostrophe + s ('s).**

women's magazine
oxen's master
children's playground

Note: If two people own something jointly, place the apostrophe after the last person's name.

Joan and Dave's new car

If two people each own items, place the apostrophe after both names.

Bob's and Hannah's new cars

Name________________________________ **PUNCTUATION**
WORKBOOK PAGE 269 Apostrophes
Date________________________________

Directions: Insert needed apostrophes.

1. Didn't you want this magazine?
2. Our swimmers' club meets every Thursday.
3. Those ten cows' watering trough doesn't have enough compartments.
4. They'll see you in San Diego.
5. The two boys' bedroom was a mess.
6. Your 3's look like 8's.
7. Billy's hair is very unmanageable.
8. Couldn't he open the jar?
9. I like Tom and Alice's stories.
10. Some of your and's should be replaced with but's.
11. The street isn't paved yet.
12. One boy's answers were written in ink.
13. You have forgotten to cross your t's.
14. Mr. Greenley shouldn't have spoken so crossly to Susan's brother.
15. Their teachers' lounge was enlarged last summer.

Name________________________________

Date________________________________

PUNCTUATION
Apostrophes

Directions: Insert needed apostrophes.

1. Didnt you want this magazine?
2. Our swimmers club meets every Thursday.
3. Those ten cows watering trough doesnt have enough compartments.
4. Theyll see you in San Diego.
5. The two boys bedroom was a mess.
6. Your <u>3s</u> look like <u>8s</u>.
7. Billys hair is very unmanageable.
8. Couldnt he open the jar?
9. I like Tom and Alices stories.
10. Some of your <u>ands</u> should be replaced with <u>buts</u>.
11. The street isnt paved yet.
12. One boys answers were written in ink.
13. You have forgotten to cross your <u>ts</u>.
14. Mr. Greenley shouldnt have spoken so crossly to Susans brother.
15. Their teachers lounge was enlarged last summer.

Name________________________________ **PUNCTUATION**

WORKBOOK PAGE 270 Apostrophes

Date________________________________

Directions: Insert needed apostrophes.

1. Won't you graduate in '96?
2. Glenda's dog can't walk well.
3. Our ladies' meeting wasn't scheduled until Monday.
4. You have too many <u>but's</u> in the last paragraph.
5. Our mice's tails have strange kinks in them.
6. Don't you think there are many good points in Larry's essays?
7. Hasn't the school's debating team returned?
8. Those <u>5's</u> aren't in the correct column, Joe.
9. James's car isn't a new one, but it's in nice shape.
10. We'd be happier if we found Mother's keys.
11. You'll want to insert synonyms for all the <u>small's</u> in this story.
12. The children's playgrounds haven't been cleaned in that area.
13. The lawyers' association held its annual meeting last week.
14. I haven't seen too many <u>my's</u> in anyone's writing.
15. An article about our city's freeway system appeared in today's newspaper.

Name________________________________

Date________________________________

PUNCTUATION
Apostrophes

Directions: Insert needed apostrophes.

1. Wont you graduate in 96?
2. Glendas dog cant walk well.
3. Our ladies meeting wasnt scheduled until Monday.
4. You have too many <u>buts</u> in the last paragraph.
5. Our mices tails have strange kinks in them.
6. Dont you think there are many good points in Larrys essays?
7. Hasnt the schools debating team returned?
8. Those <u>5s</u> arent in the correct column, Joe.
9. Jamess car isnt a new one, but its in nice shape.
10. Wed be happier if we found Mothers keys.
11. Youll want to insert synonyms for all the <u>smalls</u> in this story.
12. The childrens playgrounds havent been cleaned in that area.
13. The lawyers association held its annual meeting last week.
14. I havent seen too many <u>mys</u> in anyones writing.
15. An article about our citys freeway system appeared in todays newspaper.

PAGE 581 = WORKBOOK PAGE 271
PAGE 582 = WORKBOOK PAGE 272
PAGE 583 = WORKBOOK PAGE 273

COMMA: Rule 1: **Use a comma to set off a noun of direct address (a person spoken to).**

Louise, come here, please.
Have you gone, Michael?
I want to go, Roy, with your group.

Rule 2: **Use a comma to set off introductory words.**

No, I haven't seen it.
Well, I've changed my mind.
Yes, the chimes are new.

Rule 3: **Use a comma to set off interrupters in a sentence.**

The answer, I think, is fifty-four.
This calendar is, in fact, an old one.
However, not all is lost.
These swings, by the way, need to be repaired.

Rule 4: **Use a comma after the greeting of a friendly letter.**

Dear Karla,
My dearest friend,

Rule 5: **Use a comma after the closing of any letter.**

Sincerely yours,
Love,

Rule 6: **Use a comma to set off words or phrases in a series.**

Furniture, linens, toys, and dishes were sold there.
We ran a mile, swam a half mile, and biked a mile.
You may go to the zoo, to the park, or to the carnival.

Rule 7: **Use a comma to clarify (make clear) a sentence.**

In the night time was extremely important.
In the night, time was extremely important.

Rule 8: **Use a comma between two or more descriptive adjectives.**

Bright, sparkling stars twinkled in the dark night.

Do not place a comma between the last adjective and the noun or pronoun.

Note: If one adjective is a color or a limiting adjective, no comma is placed between the two adjectives.

Example: A white fluffy puppy ran by.

<u>COMMA</u>: <u>Rule 9</u>: **Use a comma to set off an appositive from the rest of the sentence.**

Ms. Reno, <u>the bank president</u>, spoke about loans.
The best student is Gregor, <u>the boy in the last row</u>.
We invited Tracy, <u>our best friend</u>, to dinner.

<u>Rule 10</u>: **Use a comma between a city and state or country.**

Miami, Florida London, England

Use a comma to separate the parts of an address.

Bill lives at 567 West Lowe Drive, Tulsa, Oklahoma.

If the city and state or country appear in a sentence, also place a comma after the state or country.

Have you been to Richmond, Virginia, in the fall?
Dallas, Texas, is a growing city.
I moved from 23 Dray Lane, Yuma, Arizona, last fall.

<u>Rule 11</u>: **Use a comma after a month and year or day and year in a date.**

February, 1980 Jan. 1, 1900

Use a comma after the day of the week if the day appears with the date.

Monday, August 3 Friday, Nov. 7, 1999

If the month and year, or day and year, appear in a sentence, also place a comma after the year.

On June 22, 1898, her grandparents were married.

<u>Rule 12</u>: **Use a comma at the end of most direct quotations.**

"I would like a hamburger," Kimi said.

If the person who is making the statement is given first, place a comma after the person's name + the verb that follows it.
Kimi said, "I would like a hamburger."

In a split quotation, place a comma after the first part of the quotation and also after the person + the verb (verb + person).
"I agree," replied Arlo, "that this rocket is ready."

COMMA: Rule 13: **Use a comma to set off a title following a name.**

Gloria Kole, D.D.S., is opening a new office.
Linn Holter, R.N., works at Friedland Hospital.

Rule 14: **Use a comma to invert a name.**

Dickinson, Emily is a famous poet.
His name appeared alphabetically as Sween, Guy.

Rule 15: **Use a comma after a dependent clause at the beginning of a sentence.***

After we ate lunch, we went to a movie.
(Dependent Clause) (Independent Clause)

If I could be there, I would be delighted.
(Dependent Clause) (Independent Clause)

If the dependent clause is at the end of a sentence, no comma is needed.
We went to a movie after we ate lunch.
I would be delighted if I could be there.

Rule 16: **Use a comma before the conjunction that joins two independent clauses (compound sentence).**

Our outing was fun, but we were glad to return.
(Independent clause) (independent clause)

Dad cooked dinner, and I set the table.
(Independent clause) (Independent clause)

Rule 17: **Use a comma after two introductory prepositional phrases or after a long prepositional phrase when a subject follows it.**
In the middle of the night, Frank boarded a plane for Japan.
During the long intermission, everyone chatted.

Rule 18: **Use a comma after an introductory participial phrase.**

Jumping on the bed, the toddler giggled with delight.
Torn into shreds, the red handkerchief hung limply from the bush.

Rule 19: **Use a comma to set off adjectives in apposition.**

Bright and shiny, the gem sparkled in the light.
The gem, bright and shiny, sparkled in the light.

*A review of clauses is suggested.

Name________________________________ **PUNCTUATION**
WORKBOOK PAGE 274 Commas
Date________________________________

Directions: Insert needed commas.

1. In Rome, Italy, there are many beautiful fountains.
2. His entire outlook, it seemed, had changed.
3. Miss Ish, my kitten, has gone to sleep. **or** Miss Ish, my kitten has gone to sleep.
4. Will you help me, Kristin?
5. Yes, we will take Route 91 to the caverns.
6. Dear Matilda,

   I am still your friend.

   Love,

   Holly
7. Blue shimmering lights reflected on the lovely, calm lake.
8. During the night, owls sat in the barn.
9. Our address is 27 Haven Avenue, Boston, Massachusetts.
10. If you become a famous star, remember the folks back home.
11. They were both born on March 3, 1971.
12. Carl plans on going to Yellowstone, and I am going to Yosemite.
13. She said, "Mother, may I have some money?"
14. "I don't have any," replied Mother.
15. "With that in mind," she remarked, "I'll just stay home."
16. Sands, Mary appeared on the application.
17. David Smith, Ph.D., has written a new book.
18. The turkeys, ducks, and chickens have not been fed.
19. Houston, Texas, is one of the fastest growing cities in America.
20. I took a shower, brushed my teeth, and crawled into bed to read.

Name__________________________________

Date___________________________________

PUNCTUATION

Commas

Directions: Insert needed commas.

1. In Rome Italy there are many beautiful fountains.
2. His entire outlook it seemed had changed.
3. Miss Ish my kitten has gone to sleep.
4. Will you help me Kristin?
5. Yes we will take Route 91 to the caverns.
6. Dear Matilda

   I am still your friend.

   Love

   Holly
7. Blue shimmering lights reflected on the lovely calm lake.
8. During the night owls sat in the barn.
9. Our address is 27 Haven Avenue Boston Massachusetts.
10. If you become a famous star remember the folks back home.
11. They were both born on March 3 1971.
12. Carl plans on going to Yellowstone and I am going to Yosemite.
13. She said "Mother may I have some money?"
14. "I don't have any " replied Mother.
15. "With that in mind " she remarked "I'll just stay home."
16. Sands Mary appeared on the application.
17. David Smith Ph.D. has written a new book.
18. The turkeys ducks and chickens have not been fed.
19. Houston Texas is one of the fastest growing cities in America.
20. I took a shower brushed my teeth and crawled into bed to read.

Name________________________________
WORKBOOK PAGE 275
Date________________________________

PUNCTUATION
Commas

Directions: Insert needed commas.

1. When the medication was too strong, she broke out in hives.

2. Dear Mrs. Gunther,

   I will see you on Friday, June 10, 1999.

   Truly yours,
   Fran Mills

3. The attendant screamed, "Get back!"

4. Large, neon letters flashed on the new sign.

5. On January 1, 1980, I was in Chicago, Illinois, on business.

6. Rhonda, will you paint that wall, put new tile in the bathroom, and wallpaper the entry?

7. The knee, bruised and bleeding, needed immediate attention.

8. Well, those oil derricks, in fact, have been operating since last summer.

9. Priscilla cooked pancakes, and everyone ate them.

10. Rose Trost, my grandmother, was married in Tulsa, Oklahoma, by a local minister.

11. The catcher, the third base person, and the pitcher are up to bat.

12. This player piano, for example, is damaged and old, but it's very valuable.

13. The following items are needed for the party: napkins, candles, and paper plates.

14. They had to work late, but they received a bonus for it.

15. "Put these clothes," the housekeeper said, "in your closet."

16. If you can't go, give me a call, Sarah.

17. Broken off at the base, the fountain no longer circulates water.

Name________________________________ **PUNCTUATION**
Commas

Date_________________________________

Directions: Insert needed commas.

1. When the medication was too strong she broke out in hives.

2. Dear Mrs. Gunther

   I will see you on Friday June 10 1999.

   Truly yours
   Fran Mills

3. The attendant screamed "Get back!"

4. Large neon letters flashed on the new sign.

5. On January 1 1980 I was in Chicago Illinois on business.

6. Rhonda will you paint that wall put new tile in the bathroom and wallpaper the entry?

7. The knee bruised and bleeding needed immediate attention.

8. Well those oil derricks in fact have been operating since last summer.

9. Priscilla cooked pancakes and everyone ate them.

10. Rose Trost my grandmother was married in Tulsa Oklahoma by a local minister.

11. The catcher the third base person and the pitcher are up to bat.

12. This player piano for example is damaged and old but it's very valuable.

13. The following items are needed for the party: napkins candles and paper plates.

14. They had to work late but they received a bonus for it.

15. "Put these clothes " the housekeeper said "in your closet."

16. If you can't go give me a call Sarah.

17. Broken off at the base the fountain no longer circulates water.

Name________________________________ **PUNCTUATION**
WORKBOOK PAGE 276 Commas
Date________________________________

Directions: Insert needed commas.

1. Trisha, have you met Meryln Jones, my dance instructor?

2. We are still going, but we won't leave until tomorrow.

3. A stained, cotton shirt is soaking in a prewash solution.

4. The fashion artist has been at her new address of 2109 North 10th Street, Denver, Colorado, since August 23, 1982.

5. The fourth, fifth, and sixth graders will see a film today.

6. These canisters, for example, are sturdier than those.

7. No, my niece from Buffalo, New York, did not attend Harvard College.

8. I wasn't there on July 4, 1984, in the afternoon.

9. "The circus is coming to town," said the child.

10. When you finish with that letter, do you want to play chess?

11. James Russelman, D.D.S., has an office in Sacramento, California.

12. "Our major goal," the president of the company said, "is to expand."

13. On September 30, 1990, they went to Hawaii, Singapore, and New Zealand.

14. The expensive pants, however, fell apart after the first washing.

15. Her name appeared on the list as Martin, Cynthia Ann.

16. His cheeks, red and glowing, appeared very swollen.

17. Standing in a grocery line, the lady thumbed through several magazines.

18. After the long drought during the summer, rain fell steadily for four days.

Name________________________________

Date________________________________

PUNCTUATION

Commas

Directions: Insert needed commas.

1. Trisha have you met Meryln Jones my dance instructor?
2. We are still going but we won't leave until tomorrow.
3. A stained cotton shirt is soaking in a prewash solution.
4. The fashion artist has been at her new address of 2109 North 10th Street Denver Colorado since August 23 1982.
5. The fourth fifth and sixth graders will see a film today.
6. These canisters for example are sturdier than those.
7. No my niece from Buffalo New York did not attend Harvard College.
8. I wasn't there on July 4 1984 in the afternoon.
9. "The circus is coming to town " said the child.
10. When you finish with that letter do you want to play chess?
11. James Russelman D.D.S. has an office in Sacramento California.
12. "Our major goal" the president of the company said "is to expand."
13. On September 30 1990 they went to Hawaii Singapore and New Zealand.
14. The expensive pants however fell apart after the first washing.
15. Her name appeared on the list as Martin Cynthia Ann.
16. His cheeks red and glowing appeared very swollen.
17. Standing in a grocery line the lady thumbed through several magazines.
18. After the long drought during the summer rain fell steadily for four days.

PAGE 591 = WORKBOOK PAGE 277
PAGE 594 = WORKBOOK PAGE 279
PAGE 595 = WORKBOOK PAGE 280

<u>SEMICOLON</u>: <u>Rule 1</u>: **Use a semicolon (;) to join two independent clauses that are closely related.**

The rain stopped; the sun came out.
(independent clause) (independent clause)

His voice was too soft; we couldn't hear him.
(independent clause) (independent clause)

Do not place <u>and</u>, <u>but</u>, or <u>or</u> after a semicolon.

Incorrect: This scarf is pretty; and I might buy it for my sister.
Correct: This scarf is pretty; I might buy it for my sister.

If a word such as <u>therefore</u> or <u>however</u> appears after the semicolon, place a comma after it.

You may go out to play; however, you must wear a jacket.

<u>COLON</u>: <u>Rule 1</u>: **Use a colon after the greeting of a business letter.**

Gentlemen:
Dear Mrs. Atmadi:

<u>Rule 2</u>: **Use a colon in writing the time.**

9:00 A.M.
11:23 P.M.

<u>Rule 3</u>: **Use a colon to set off lists.**

Groceries:
milk
bread
cookies

The following people must attend: Val, Sue, and Ty.

<u>Rule 4</u>: **Use a colon after divisions of topics in a writing.**

COMMAS: Rule 1:
Rule 2:

Name________________________________ **PUNCTUATION**
WORKBOOK PAGE 278 Colons and Semicolons
Date________________________________

Directions: Insert needed colons and semicolons.

1. Farah emptied the trash; Ander set the table.

2. It's now 5:30 P.M.

3. We need the following items: sugar, milk, and eggs.

4. Kannon will drive us to the airport; therefore, we will need to be ready by noon.

5. Dear Sir:

    Please send me three copies of your magazine, <u>Signs of the Times</u>.

    Sincerely yours,

    Coby Stout

6. Rule A: Do not pick any flowers.

    Rule B: Stay off the grass.

7. At 9:00 A.M. we ordered the following: 2 chairs, a table, and three lamps.

8. Fire Safety:
    Rule A:
    Rule B:

9. I want to go; please wait for me.

10. Gentlemen and Ladies of the Board:

    I wish to address the problem of several ineffective computers. May I meet with you on Tuesday, July 4th, at 11:30 A.M.?

    Best wishes,

    Alicia J. Bevins

11. The game has gone into overtime; however, I think our team will win.

12. Things to do:
    -Clean room
    -Take out trash

Name________________________________

Date________________________________

PUNCTUATION
Colons and Semicolons

Directions: Insert needed colons and semicolons.

1. Farah emptied the trash Ander set the table.

2. It's now 530 P.M.

3. We need the following items sugar, milk, and eggs.

4. Kannon will drive us to the airport therefore we will need to be ready by noon.

5. Dear Sir

   Please send me three copies of your magazine, <u>Signs of the Times</u>.

   Sincerely yours,

   Coby Stout

6. Rule A Do not pick any flowers.

   Rule B Stay off the grass.

7. At 900 A.M. we ordered the following 2 chairs, a table, and three lamps.

8. Fire Safety
   Rule A
   Rule B

9. I want to go please wait for me.

10. Gentlemen and Ladies of the Board

    I wish to address the problem of several ineffective computers. May I meet with you on Tuesday, July 4th, at 1130 A.M.?

    Best wishes,

    Alicia J. Bevins

11. The game has gone into overtime however, I think our team will win.

12. Things to do
    -Clean room
    -Take out trash

QUESTION MARK: Rule: **Use a question mark at the end of an interrogative sentence.**

Does her niece live in Kansas.
Have you ever ridden a bull?

EXCLAMATION POINT: Rule 1: **Use an exclamation point after an exclamatory sentence (one showing strong feeling).**

Look out!
We won!

Rule 2: **Use an exclamation point after a word or phrase that shows strong feeling (interjection).**

Yeah! You did it!
Good grief! Someone ate my lunch!

HYPHEN: Rule 1: **Place a hyphen between fractions and certain numbers.**

two-fifths
three-fourths
twenty-one
seventy-seven

Rule 2: **Use a hyphen when dividing a word of two or more syllables at the end of a line. (You must have at least two letters on the first line and three on the following line.)**

________________________________ unhappy ________________________________
____________________________ wonderful __________________________________

Rule 3: **Use a hyphen to combine some prefixes with abase word.**

ex-president self-rising

Check a **dictionary** to determine if a word is hyphenated.

HYPHEN: Rule 4: **Use a hyphen to combine some closely related words.**

two-handed
to-and-fro

Check a dictionary to determine if a word should be hyphenated.

UNDERLINING:

Rule 1: **Underline the names of ships, planes, and trains.**

Do you like the Spirit of St. Louis?
The Silverton Express arrives at nine o'clock.
The U.S.S. Constitution is in Boston Harbor.*

*This may also be written **U.S.S.** Constitution.

Rule 2: **Underline letter(s), word(s), or numeral(s) used out of context.**

You forgot to dot your i!
This sentence has too many and's.
A 7 should appear in the first column.

Rule 3: **Underline the title of books, magazines, movies, newspapers, plays, television shows, record albums, CD's, tapes, long stories, and works of art.**

Have you read the book, Tex?
I like the magazine entitled Coat of Arms.
The old movie, Lassie Come Home, is interesting.
Is The Morning News delivered daily?
The play, Annie Get Your Gun, was amusing.
Many children enjoyed Oscar on Sesame Street, the television show.
Your tape, In His Time, has finished playing.

Rule 4: **In printed materials, any item that should be underlined can be in italics.**

The child's father read My Mother Doesn't Like to Cook at bedtime.

or

The child's father read *My Mother Doesn't Like to Cook* at bedtime.

Name________________________________
WORKBOOK PAGE 281
Date________________________________

PUNCTUATION
Question Marks
Exclamation Marks
Hyphens
Underlinings

Directions: Insert needed punctuation (question marks, exclamation marks, hyphens, and underlinings).

1. Wow! I won the first prize in archery!

2. Did you barbecue the chicken?

3. Three-fourths of the messages were unimportant.

4. We were given a three-pronged fork for the job.

5. Have you ever sailed on the ship, Princess?

6. The ex-chief of police had sailed on the Titanic.

7. Rats! I forgot to include my address on the envelope!

8. When I was twenty-one, I went aboard the Queen Mary.

9. The ex-marine worked for thirty years as a professional bor
der patrol.

10. Have you seen the movie, Gone with the Wind, or read the book, Susannah?

11. He lives in a tri-level that includes seventy-four units.

12. The newspaper, The Penny Stock Journal, interests many people, especially business people.

13. Have you seen the movie, Fiddler on the Roof, or the television series, Alice?

14. The Axter family hasn't seen the play, Oklahoma, for several years.

15. Did you know that Clark Jones was a self-educated man who, in fact, developed a new style of shoe?

Name________________________________

Date________________________________

PUNCTUATION
Question Marks
Exclamation Marks
Hyphens
Underlinings

Directions: Insert needed punctuation (question marks, exclamation marks, hyphens, and underlinings).

1. Wow I won the first prize in archery
2. Did you barbecue the chicken
3. Three fourths of the messages were unimportant.
4. We were given a three pronged fork for the job.
5. Have you ever sailed on the ship, Princess
6. The ex chief of police had sailed on the Titanic.
7. Rats I forgot to include my address on the envelope
8. When I was twenty one, I went aboard the Queen Mary.
9. The ex marine worked for thirty years as a professional bor
   der patrol.
10. Have you seen the movie, Gone with the Wind, or read the book, Susannah
11. He lives in a tri level that includes seventy four units.
12. The newspaper, The Penny Stock Journal, interests many people, especially busi
    ness people.
13. Have you seen the movie, Fiddler on the Roof, or the television series, Alice
14. The Axter family hasn't seen the play, Oklahoma, for several years.
15. Did you know that Clark Jones was a self educated man who, in fact, de
    veloped a new style of shoe.

PAGE 599 = WORKBOOK PAGE 282

QUOTATION MARKS:

Rule 1: **Use some quotation marks (“ ”) to indicate someone’s exact word or words.**

“Are the baseball hats here?” asked Hannah.
Tom said, “Let’s go for pizza.”

A. **In a split quotation, use quotation marks around each part spoken.**

“I see,” said Blake, “that you drive.”
“Jean knows,” said the man, “your idea.”

B. **In a quotation that is not split, do not place the ending quotation mark until speaker is finished. This may involve many sentences.**

“Don’t talk. Look at me.” said Kelly.

C. **In dialogue, each time a person speaks, a new paragraph is begun.**

“I like the mountains of Vermont,” Milly remarked.
Thelma replied, “Let’s go there next winter.”
“I can’t,” said Milly, “because I’m going to England then.”

Note: **If the entire sentence is a quotation, place the end punctuation inside the final quotation mark.**

The instructor asked, “Did you try**?**”

If the entire sentence is not a quotation, place a period or comma inside the quotation mark. All other punctuation is placed outside the quotation mark.

I read the article, “Pain.”

Rule 2: **Use quotation marks to enclose the titles of chapters, articles, poems, essays, short stories, nursery rhymes, and songs.**

I like Kipling’s poem entitled “If.”
Many read “Dear Abby” in the daily paper.

Note: **Any “Item” that is contained within a larger one is usually placed in quotation marks. Chapters are in a book. Articles are in newspapers and magazines.**

Name________________________________ **PUNCTUATION**
WORKBOOK PAGE 283 Quotation Marks
Date________________________________

Directions: Insert needed quotation marks.

1. Barry said, "Hello. How are you?"
2. Our butler replied to the remark, "How dreadful for you."
3. "Who is studying for the exam?" asked Barbara.
4. Donna exclaimed, "I love snow!"
5. Has the baby sitter read "Little Red Riding Hood" to the children?
6. "Is this," asked Jean, "the comb that you want?"
7. "Yankee Doodle" was a popular song during the American Revolution.
8. Wilma exclaimed, "I can't believe that we are finally here!"
9. I love the poem, "Death of a Hired Man."
10. I rapidly read the assigned chapter, "Reconstruction," in my American history class, and then enjoyed the magazine article entitled "What Is Your IQ?" in a psychology periodical.
11. "Don't light the candle," he ordered, "or you will regret it."
12. "These records," Macy replied, "are current ones."
13. Have you ever read the funny story, "Thirteen"?
14. "Stay here," Kent replied, "and I'll go to get help."
15. Peg said that her cat was taken to a veterinarian.

Name________________________________

Date________________________________

PUNCTUATION
Quotation Marks

Directions: Insert needed quotation marks.

1. Barry said, Hello. How are you?
2. Our butler replied to the remark, How dreadful for you.
3. Who is studying for the exam? asked Barbara.
4. Donna exclaimed, I love snow!
5. Has the baby sitter read Little Red Riding Hood to the children?
6. Is this, asked Jean, the comb that you want?
7. Yankee Doodle was a popular song during the American Revolution.
8. Wilma exclaimed, I can't believe that we are finally here!
9. I love the poem, Death of a Hired Man.
10. I rapidly read the assigned chapter, Reconstruction, in my American history class, and then enjoyed the magazine article entitled What Is Your IQ? in a psychology periodical.
11. Don't light the candle, he ordered, or you will regret it.
12. These records, Macy replied, are current ones.
13. Have you ever read the funny story, Thirteen?
14. Stay here, Kent replied, and I'll go to get help.
15. Peg said that her cat was taken to a veterinarian.

Name________________________________

WORKBOOK PAGE 284

Date________________________________

PUNCTUATION

Quotation Marks

Directions: Insert needed quotation marks.

1. Sam asked, " Which way is it to the tropical gardens?"
2. Dad enjoys the newspaper article entitled "Food."
3. "Were you," asked the detective, " at the Hand's house on the night of the incident?"
4. Most people have read the nursery rhyme, " Jack and Jill."
5. Father shouted, "Come back! You forgot your luggage!"
6. The story, "Cat and the Underworld," is interesting.
7. "Who," the unhappy customer asked, " is in charge here?"
8. Did you enjoy the chapter entitled "Living Things"?
9. "Your picture is crooked," said Valerie.
10. "Down in the Valley" is an unusual melody.
11. The lost hikers screamed, "We're over here!"
12. One of Ralph Waldo Emerson's poems is entitled "We Thank Thee."
13. "Some of these," remarked Theda, "have already been eaten."
14. We clipped the magazine article, "Secrets of a Coupon Saver."
15. Tiffany asked, "Did you read the article about crime in today's newspaper?"

Name________________________________

Date________________________________

PUNCTUATION
Quotation Marks

Directions: Insert needed quotation marks.

1. Sam asked, Which way is it to the tropical gardens?
2. Dad enjoys the newspaper article entitled Food.
3. Were you, asked the detective, at the Hand's house on the night of the incident?
4. Most people have read the nursery rhyme, Jack and Jill.
5. Father shouted, Come back! You forgot your luggage!
6. The story, Cat and the Underworld, is interesting.
7. Who, the unhappy customer asked, is in charge here?
8. Did you enjoy the chapter entitled Living Things?
9. Your picture is crooked, said Valerie.
10. Down in the Valley is an unusual melody.
11. The lost hikers screamed, We're over here!
12. One of Ralph Waldo Emerson's poems is entitled We Thank Thee.
13. Some of these, remarked Theda, have already been eaten.
14. We clipped the magazine article, Secrets of a Coupon Saver.
15. Tiffany asked, Did you read the article about crime in today's newspaper?

Name________________________________

WORKBOOK PAGE 285

Date________________________________

PUNCTUATION

Underlining or Quotation Marks?

Directions: Use quotation marks or underlining as needed.

1. the short story, "Cat and the Underworld"
2. the poem, "Why Nobody Pets the Lion at the Zoo"
3. the movie, <u>Raiders of the Lost Ark</u>
4. the play, <u>Annie</u>
5. the chapter, "Living Things"
6. the book, <u>Summer of the Monkeys</u>
7. the television show, <u>Price Is Right</u>
8. the essay, "Land of Opportunity"
9. the ship, <u>Queen Mary</u>
10. the newspaper, <u>Southern Post</u>
11. the airplane, <u>Regal Star</u>
12. the magazine, <u>Horses and Cowboys</u>
13. the magazine article, "Sweet Revenge"
14. the newspaper article, "Dealing with Life"
15. the train, <u>Orient Express</u>
16. the nursery rhyme, "Humpty Dumpty"
17. the song, "How Great Thou Art"
18. the album, <u>Pictures at Eleven</u>
19. the painting, <u>Mona Lisa</u>
20. the book, <u>Autobiography of My Mother</u>

Name________________________________

Date________________________________

PUNCTUATION
Underlining or Quotation Marks?

Directions: Use quotation marks or underlining as needed.

1. the short story, Cat and the Underworld
2. the poem, Why Nobody Pets the Lion at the Zoo
3. the movie, Raiders of the Lost Ark
4. the play, Annie
5. the chapter, Living Things
6. the book, Summer of the Monkeys
7. the television show, Price Is Right
8. the essay, Land of Opportunity
9. the ship, Queen Mary
10. the newspaper, Southern Post
11. the airplane, Regal Star
12. the magazine, Horses and Cowboys
13. the magazine article, Sweet Revenge
14. the newspaper article, Dealing with Life
15. the train, Orient Express
16. the nursery rhyme, Humpty Dumpty
17. the song, How Great Thou Art
18. the album, Pictures at Eleven
19. the painting, Mona Lisa
20. the book, Autobiography of My Mother

Name________________________________

WORKBOOK PAGE 286

Date________________________________

PUNCTUATION

Underlining or Quotation Marks?

Directions: Use quotation marks or underlining as needed.

1. the magazine, Southwest Mining
2. the television show, Electric Company
3. the poem, "Dust"
4. the movie, Apple Dumpling Game
5. the newspaper, Gettysburg Times
6. the ship, U. S. S. Arizona
7. the newspaper article, "Women in the News"
8. the essay, "The Significance of Education"
9. the book, Cat Ate My Gym Suit
10. the song, "Jingle Bells"
11. the book, Rumble Fish
12. the airplane, Spruce Goose
13. the nursery rhyme, "Hickory Dickory Dock"
14. the magazine article, "Let's Go Roller Skating"
15. the play, Cat on a Hot Tin Roof
16. the chapter, "Your Body"
17. the painting, Sunday Best
18. the book, Crafty Bazaar Gifts
19. the poem, "I Knew You Once"
20. the short story, "Thirteen"

Name________________________________

Date________________________________

PUNCTUATION
Underlining or Quotation Marks?

Directions: Use quotation marks or underlining as needed.

1. the magazine, Southwest Mining
2. the television show, Electric Company
3. the poem, Dust
4. the movie, Apple Dumpling Game
5. the newspaper, Gettysburg Times
6. the ship, U. S. S. Arizona
7. the newspaper article, Women in the News
8. the essay, The Significance of Education
9. the book, Cat Ate My Gym Suit
10. the song, Jingle Bells
11. the book, Rumble Fish
12. the airplalne, Spruce Goose
13. the nursery rhyme, Hickory Dickory Dock
14. the magazine article, Let's Go Roller Skating
15. the play, Cat on a Hot Tin Roof
16. the chapter, Your Body
17. the painting, Sunday Best
18. the book, Crafty Bazaar Gifts
19. the poem, I Knew You Once
20. the short story, Thirteen

Name________________________________ **PUNCTUATION**

WORKBOOK PAGE 287

Date________________________________

Directions: Insert needed punctuation.

1. Do you enjoy reading magazines like Redbook or books like Blubber?

2. The U. S. S. Arizona sank Dec. 7, 1941, at eight o'clock in the morning; that was Japan's attack on Pearl Harbor, Hawaii.

3.

5638 E. Crenter Blvd.
Arlington, Virginia
Mar. 4, 20--

My dearest Aunt Joy,

Have you seen the play entitled Music Man? Wouldn't it be great to see that play, visit the Spruce Goose,* and fly to London, England, for a few weeks?

Love,
Netty

4. When you write minister in that sentence, capitalize the m.

5. I haven't any money, but I want to go to Martin Shoe Store's sale.

6. Grip Enterprises
4554 Libby St.
Amarillo, Texas

Dear Sir:

I'll be visiting your office on Monday, Sept. 9, and I hope you can spare a few minutes.

Sincerely yours,
R. H. Durango

7. Waiting for a bus, the young man read for a few minutes, stared at passing cars, and drifted off to sleep.

*name of an airplane

Name________________________________ **PUNCTUATION**

Date________________________________

Directions: Insert needed punctuation.

1. Do you enjoy reading magazines like Redbook or books like Blubber

2. The U S S Arizona sank Dec 7 1941 at eight oclock in the morning that was Japans attack on Pearl Harbor Hawaii

3.

5638 E Crenter Blvd
Arlington Virginia
Mar 4 20--

My dearest Aunt Joy

Have you seen the play entitled Music Man Wouldn't it be great to see that play visit the Spruce Goose* and fly to London England for a few weeks

Love
Netty

4. When you write minister in that sentence capitalize the m

5. I havent any money but I want to go to Martin Shoe Stores sale

6. Grip Enterprises
4554 Libby St
Amarillo Texas

Dear Sir

Ill be visiting your office on Monday Sept 9 and I hope you can spare a few minutes

Sincerely yours

R H Durango

7. Waiting for a bus the young man read for a few minutes stared at passing cars and drifted off to sleep

*name of an airplane

Name__________________________________ **PUNCTUATION**

WORKBOOK PAGE 288

Date__________________________________

Directions: Insert needed punctuation.

1. A large red truck just passed us, Sarah.
2. Dot your <u>i</u> in this word, and your paper will be perfect.
3. Serena likes to dance; most of us would rather sit and watch.
4. We passed a meadow, a brook, and a run-down mill.
5. Gretta Tarkin, her sister-in-law, can't visit Memphis, Tennessee, in June.
6. Although the children's library is five blocks away, we'll go there.
7. Niki asked, "Where is the Grand Canyon?"
8. "Have you seen," asked the sales lady, "our new line of carpeting?"
9. I've always wanted to read the book entitled <u>Megatrends</u> and to see Shakespeare's play, <u>Romeo and Juliet</u>.
10. Dear Alona,

    You're the best friend in the world; we get along well.

    Your friend,
    Jemima
11. Her eyes, red and swollen, looked somewhat blodshot.
12. The article entitled "Speaker for the House" in the magazine, <u>Good Ideas</u>, was intereresting.
13. The giraffes, lions, tigers, and gorillas were the most interesting.
14. I read a novel, and Eli sang the song entitled "Bicycle Built for Two."
15. "May I," asked Mr. Luna, the real estate agent, "help you sell your home?"

Name______________________________ **PUNCTUATION**

Date______________________________

Directions: Insert needed punctuation.

1. A large red truck just passed us Sarah

2. Dot your i in this word and your paper will be perfect

3. Serena likes to dance most of us would rather sit and watch

4. We passed a meadow a brook and a run down mill

5. Greta Tarkin her sister in law cant visit Memphis Tennessee in June

6. Although the children's library is five blocks away well go there

7. Niki asked Where is the Grand Canyon

8. Have you seen asked the sales lady our new line of carpeting

9. Ive always wanted to read the book entitled Megatrends and to see Shakespeares play Romeo and Juliet

10. Dear Alona

    Youre the best friend in the world we get along well

    Your friend
    Jemima

11. Her eyes red and swollen looked somewhat bloodshot

12. The article entitled Speaker for the House in the magazine Good Ideas was interesting

13. The giraffes lions tigers and gorillas were the most interesting

14. I read a novel and Eli sang the song entitled Bicycle Built for Two

15. May I asked Mr Luna the real estate agent help you sell your home

Name________________________________ **PUNCTUATION**
WORKBOOK PAGE 289
Date________________________________

Directions: Insert needed punctuation.

1. Because the door was locked, we couldn't enter Paul's home.

2. Marie said, "Grandma, you're so nice to me."

3. It was a bright, striped scarf that was given to A. J. Snead, the retiring librarian.

4. Our girls' locker room isn't on this floor.

5. We're going tomorrow, and you will come next week.

6. Your t's need to be crossed; otherwise, everything in the essay is correct, Heidi.

7. "Our plumber, Tracy Smith, works long, hard hours," said Jeanette.

8. Derrick isn't my brother; my brother's name is Ralph.

9. No, Janet, the post office address is not 46 Barrow Lane, Cheyenne, Wyoming.

10. There were three selected for the team: Janice, Sam, and Andy.

11. "It seems," said the man quietly, "that you have made a mistake."

12. Her up-to-date ideas earned her a job with Targon Co., St. Louis, Mo.

13. One-fourth of the animals hadn't been given the vaccine prepared by Dr. Sturks, our local veterinarian.

14. The completion date will be August 24, 2057, at 5:00 P. M.

15. You're, without a doubt, one of our group's best swimmers, Ruth.

Name________________________________ **PUNCTUATION**

Date________________________________

Directions: Insert needed punctuation.

1. Because the door was locked we couldnt enter Pauls home
2. Marie said Grandma youre so nice to me
3. It was a bright striped scarf that was given to A J Snead the retiring librarian
4. Our girls locker room isnt on this floor
5. Were going tomorrow and you will come next week
6. Your ts need to be crossed otherwise everything in the essay is correct Heidi
7. Our plumber Tracy Smith works long hard hours said Jeanette
8. Derrick isnt my brother my brothers name is Ralph
9. No Janet the post office address is not 46 Barrow Lane Cheyenne Wyoming
10. There were three selected for the team Janice Sam and Andy
11. It seems said the man quietly that you have made a mistake
12. Her up to date ideas earned her a job with Targon Co St Louis Mo
13. One fourth of the animals hadnt been given the vaccine prepared by Dr Sturks our local veterinarian
14. The completion date will be August 24 2057 at 5 00 P M
15. Youre without a doubt one of our groups best swimmers Ruth

Name________________________________ **PUNCTUATION**

WORKBOOK PAGE 290

Date________________________________

Directions: Insert needed punctuation.

1. The R. E. Polk Co. opened a new office at 17842 N. Andrews Ave., Greensburg, Pa.

2. One-third of Daryl's class had visited Seattle, Washington, at some time.

3. On Tuesday, Feb. 7, 1904, my father was born in Prescott, Arizona.

4. Mary, have you seen this child's purple sweater?

5. Wow! Our team, in fact, scored thirty-nine points!

6. Yes, we are going aboard the <u>Queen Mary</u>* on Friday, Oct.6th.

7. Mr. and Mrs. Hahn, please send me the following: three pencils, six rulers, and a box of crayons.

8. Joan asked, "Who's that?"

9.

322 Deflin St.
Birmingham, Alabama
Mar. 4, 1957

Dear Dorothy,

I'm enclosing twenty-one pictures of my family's vacation.

Love,
Sandy

10. "This day," said Gloria, "is the greatest."

11. No, there aren't too many <u>also's</u> in your first paragraph.

12. Gentlemen:

The first board meeting was held June 2, 1993, at 2:00 P. M. in Chicago, Illinois.

Respectfully submitted,

Wayne P. Coles

*name of a ship

Name________________________________ **PUNCTUATION**

Date________________________________

Directions: Insert needed punctuation.

1. The R E Polk Co opened a new office at 17842 N Andrews Ave Greensburg Pa

2. One third of Daryls class had visited Seattle Washington at some time

3. On Tuesday Feb 7 1904 my father was born in Prescott Arizona

4. Mary have you seen this childs purple sweater

5. Wow Our team in fact scored thirty nine points

6. Yes we are going aboard the Queen Mary* on Friday Oct 6th

7. Mr and Mrs Hahn please send me the following three pencils six rulers and a box of crayons

8. Joan asked Whos that

9. 322 Deflin St
Birmingham Alabama
Mar 4 1957

Dear Dorothy

Im enclosing twenty one pictures of my familys vacation

Love
Sandy

10. This day said Gloria is the greatest

11. No there arent too many alsos in your first paragraph

12. Gentlemen

The first board meeting was held June 2 1993 at 2 00 P M in Chicago Illinois

Respectfully submitted

Wayne P Coles

*name of a ship

Name________________________________ **PUNCTUATION TEST**

Date________________________________

Directions: Insert needed punctuation.

1. Gail's dad lives at 17251 N. Palomino Avenue, Sedalia, CO 80135.
2. Edna, hasn't your family visited Trafalgar Square, Green Park, and Barclay Square in London?
3. "Her father-in-law is that tall, talkative man in the gray jacket," said Mrs. Somerset.
4. Bernard Waber wrote a children's book entitled <u>Ira Sleeps Over</u>.
5. Yuck! The two dogs' dishes are covered with bits of food, and ants are crawling all over the bowls!
6. Jason, their best friend, was born in St. Louis, Missouri, on May 20, 1982, at 2:00 P.M.
7.

   5503 East Blair Lane
   Peoria, Arizona 85345
   March 18, 20--

   Dear Artie,

   The following three will be traveling to summer camp in your van: Joshua, Peter, and Jenny.

   Sincerely,
   Patty

8. When Sally went to a ranch for summer vacation, she read and loved the poem entitled "Stopping by Woods on a Snowy Evening" by Robert Frost.
9. Jackson Co.
   89 W. Marilyn Lane
   Metamora, Illinois 61548

   Dear Miss Hanna:

   Three-fourths of the article entitled "Ultrasound Toothbrushes" was supposed to be continued on page forty-five. However, that part of the article was missing.

   Very truly yours,
   Martin S. Treubell

Name________________________________ **PUNCTUATION TEST**

Date________________________________

Directions: Insert needed punctuation.

1. Gails dad lives at 17251 N Palomino Avenue Sedalia CO 80135

2. Edna hasnt your family visited Trafalgar Square Green Park and Barclay Square in London

3. Her father in law is that tall talkative man in the gray jacket said Mrs Somerset

4. Bernard Waber wrote a childrens book entitled Ira Sleeps Over

5. Yuck The two dogs dishes are covered with bits of food and ants are crawling all over the bowls

6. Jason their best friend was born in St Louis Missouri on May 20 1982 at 2 00 P M

7.

5503 East Blair Lane
Peoria Arizona 85345
March 18 20--

Dear Artie

The following three will be traveling to summer camp in your van Joshua Peter and Jenny

Sincerely
Patty

8. When Sally went to a ranch for summer vacation she read and loved the poem entitled Stopping by Woods on a Snowy Evening by Robert Frost

9. Jackson Co
89 W Marilyn Lane
Metamora Illinois 61548

Dear Miss Hanna

Three fourths of the article entitled Ultrasound Toothbrushes was supposed to be continued on page forty five However that part of the article was missing

Very truly yours
Martin S Treubell

CAPITALIZATION

A review of proper and common nouns is suggested before rules of capitalization are taught. Students need to understand the difference between common and proper nouns so that they can "think through" utilization of particular rules. In addition, a review of proper adjectives is highly advisable.

As stated at the beginning of this book, capitalization needs to be reviewed throughout the year. The following texts are available for daily review of capitalization, punctuation, and grammar concepts:

<u>Daily Grams: Guided Review Aiding Mastery Skills for 3rd & 4th Grades</u>

<u>Daily Grams: Guided Review Aiding Mastery Skills for 4th & 5th Grades</u>

<u>Daily Grams: Guided Review Aiding Mastery Skills for 5th & 6th Grades</u>

<u>Daily Grams: Guided Review Aiding Mastery Skills</u> (6th and above)

If you do not choose to use a daily review, it is suggested that a capitalization unit be taught several times during the school year.

Student writing is also necessary to insure application of rules and to insure mastery learning. Writing should be an integral part of any language curriculum.

PAGE 619 = WORKBOOK PAGE 291

CAPITALIZATION

Rule 1: **Capitalize the first letter of the first word in a sentence.**

Example: **P**earls are very elegant.

Rule 2: **Capitalize the pronoun I.**

Example: Had the captain forgotten that **I** left early?

Rule 3: **Capitalize the first letter of the first word in most lines of poetry.**

Example: **W**hose woods these are I think I know

If the words of a line of poetry will not fit on one line, indent the next line and continue writing. However, do not capitalize the first word of the continuing line.

Example: Whose woods these are I
think I know

Rule 4: **Capitalize the first word, the last word, and all important words in any title.**

Do not capitalize a, an, the, and, but, or, nor, or prepositions of four or less letters unless located as the first or last word of a title. CAPITALIZE ALL OTHER WORDS IN A TITLE.

A. **Always capitalize verbs.**
Example: **E**ight **Is** **E**nough

B. **Capitalize prepositions of five or more letters.**
Example: "**D**on't **S**it **Under** the **A**pple **T**ree"

Rule 5: **Capitalize Roman numerals and the letters for the first major topics in an outline. Capitalize the first letter of the first word in in an outline.**

I. **E**nergy
    A. **T**ypes
        1. **P**hysical
        2. **N**uclear
    B. **V**arious uses
II. **M**atter

Name________________________________ **CAPITALIZATION**

WORKBOOK PAGE 292

Date________________________________

Directions: Supply needed capitalization.
Answers are in boldfaced print.

1. **Has** anyone seen the movie, **Mustang Country**?

2. **Did I** give you "**Jack** and the **Beanstalk**" to read?

3. **I. Fight** for independence

    A. Battles

    B. Important people

    II. Battle of 1812

    A. Events

    B. Historical significance

4. **The** movie, **Snoopy Comes Home**, was playing at the local theater.

5. **He** and **I** don't know where to find **The Witch Tree Symbol** on the shelves.

6. **The** poem began, "**Today**, a red-breasted robin sat upon my **Aleppo** pine..."

7. **That** book entitled **The Adventures of Odyseus and the Tale of Troy** is interesting.

8. "**The Donkey**" is the name of a poem that begins, "**When** fishes flew and forests walked..."

9. **Have** you seen my copy of **Cowboy Songs and Other Frontier Ballads**?

10. **This** story entitled "**Every Dog Should Own** a **Man**" is one **I** want to read.

11. "**A Bird Came** down the **Walk**" is a poem by **Emily Dickinson**.

12. **We** read the action-packed book, **First Through the Grand Canyon**.

Name________________________________ **CAPITALIZATION**

Date________________________________

Directions: Supply needed capitalization.

1. has anyone seen the movie, <u>mustang country</u>?

2. did i give you "jack and the beanstalk" to read?

3. i. fight for independence

   a. battles

   b. important people

   ii. battle of 1812

   a. events

   b. historical significance

4. the movie, <u>snoopy comes home</u>, was playing at a local theater.

5. he and i don't know where to find <u>the witch tree symbol</u> on the shelves.

6. the poem began, "today, a red-breasted robin sat upon my aleppo pine..."

7. that book entitled <u>the adventure of odysseys and the tale of troy</u> is interesting.

8. "the donkey" is the name of a poem that begins, "when fishes flew and forests walked..."

9. have you seen my copy of <u>cowboy songs and other frontier ballads</u>?

10. this story entitled "every dog should own a man" is one I want to read.

11. "a bird came down the walk" is a poem by emily dickinson.

12. we read the action-packed book, <u>first through the grand canyon</u>.

PAGE 623 = WORKBOOK PAGE 293

CAPITALIZATION

Rule 6: **Capitalize the first letter of the first word in a direct quotation.**

Examples: Lyle asked, "**W**here's my comb?"

"**I**n the drawer," replied his father.

In a split quotation, do not capitalize the first letter of the word in the second part unless a new sentence is begun.

Examples: "Did you," asked Joe, "**o**pen this door?"

"I'm finished," yelled Chris, "**L**et's go!"

Rule 7: **Capitalize Mother, Dad, and other titles when they serve as a replacement for the person's name.**

Example: We haven't told **M**other about our plan.

You can insert the person's name for Mother; the **M** is capitalized: We haven't told **M**other (**D**ebra) about our plan.

Example: How are you feeling, **S**on?

You can insert the person's name for Son so the **S** is capitalized: How are you feeling, **D**an?

Capitalize the title if it appears with a name.

Examples: **G**randpa Smith
Aunt Cecilia
Captain Lowe
Judge Worth
Senator Billings
Cousin Lee

Rule 8: **Capitalize the names of organizations.**

Examples: **B**oy **S**couts of **A**merica

American **R**ed **C**ross

Kiwanis **C**lub

Name________________________________ **CAPITALIZATION**
WORKBOOK PAGE 294
Date________________________________

Directions: Supply needed capitalization.
Answers are in boldfaced print.

1. **My Aunt Gail** belongs to **Bingham School Parent Teacher Organization**.

2. **The** child remarked, "**It's** hot in here."

3. **The Women's World Association** meets in **Mayor Larkin's** office.

4. "**Where** have you been?" the upset mother asked.

5. **I** asked **Dad** for his car keys.

6. **Has Councilman Barett** contacted you, **Mother**?

7. "**This** pottery," replied the leader, "was made by **Alice's** nephew."

8. "**Do** you want to join the **Welcome Wagon Club**?" asked **Ms. Partin**.

9. **When** did **Grandmother** see **Representative Kelly**?

10. **My** sister has joined the **National Honor Society**.

11. **The** guest speaker at our **4-H Club** meeting was **Corporal Jenkins**.

12. **Roberta** jumped and yelled, "**Let's** go!"

13. "**Will** you come here, **Son**?" asked **Dad**.

14. "**May I** stay?" commented **Harriet**, "There's plenty of room for me."

15. "**Your** daughter should join the **Maryland Young Executives Club**," said **Martin**.

Name________________________________ **CAPITALIZATION**

Date________________________________

Directions: Supply needed capitalization.

1. my aunt gail belongs to bingham school parent teacher organization.
2. the child remarked, "it's hot in here."
3. the women's world association meets in mayor larkin's office.
4. "where have you been?" the upset mother asked.
5. i asked dad for his car keys.
6. has councilman barett contacted you, mother?
7. "this pottery," replied the leader, "was made by alice's nephew."
8. "do you want to join the welcome wagon club?" asked ms. partin.
9. when did grandmother see representative kelly?
10. my sister has joined the national honor society.
11. the guest speaker at our 4-h club meeting was corporal jenkins.
12. roberta jumped and yelled, "let's go!"
13. "will you come here, son?" asked dad.
14. "may i stay?" commented harriet, "there's plenty of room for me."
15. "your daughter should join the maryland young executives club," said martin.

PAGE 627 = WORKBOOK PAGE 295

CAPITALIZATION

Rule 9: **Capitalize business names.**

Examples:

Fanton **E**nterprises	**A**mazon **A**irlines
Brown **C**ompany	**J**olen's **R**estaurant
Pratt **L**imited	**F**ast **B**ody **S**hop, **I**nc.
Crenton **I**nn	**B**eamer **G**rocery **S**tore

Rule 10: **Capitalize government bodies and departments.**

Examples:

Senate	**C**ongress
House of **R**epresentatives	**C**abinet
Department of **I**nterior	**T**reasury **D**epartment

Rule 11: **Capitalize institution names.**

Examples:

Goldton **H**ospital	**P**ioneer **S**chool
University of **F**lorida	**A**dams **C**ounty **J**ail

Rule 12: **Capitalize names of particular geographic places.**

Examples:

Potomac **R**iver	**C**anada
Andes **M**ountains	**S**unset **P**oint
Lake **S**uperior	**C**ape **C**od
Bering **S**trait	**T**ampa **B**ay
North **S**ea	**G**ulf of **M**exico
Miller **C**reek	**C**arlsbad **C**averns
Atlantic **O**cean	**M**eteor **C**rater
Catalina **I**sland	**M**ammoth **C**ave
Great **P**lains	**N**ew **E**ngland

Rule 13: **Capitalize historical events, periods of time, and historical documents.**

Examples:

Ice **A**ge	**A**merican **R**evolution
Battle of **W**aterloo	**M**iddle **A**ges
Magna **C**arta	**D**eclaration of **I**ndependence

Name________________________________ **CAPITALIZATION**
WORKBOOK PAGE 296
Date________________________________

Directions: Supply needed capitalization.
Answers are in boldfaced print.

1. **From** the corner of **Market Street** and **Central Avenue**, curve around **Bristol Lake** until you come to **Cripton's General Store**.

2. **Last** summer they visited **Yellowstone National Park**, **Fantasy World**, **Markham Ranch**, and **San Francisco Bay**.

3. **The** turning point battle of the **Civil War** was at **Gettysburg**, **Pennsylvania.**

4. **The Asian** hunters crossed the **Bering Strait** and traveled through **North America**.

5. **The Cress Travel Agency** made the family's **Hawaiian Islands** reservations.

6. **When Marco** and his family visited **Washington, D. C.**, they saw the buildings of the **Department** of **Education**, the famous **Potomac River**, and **Georgetown University**.

7. **Our** class studied about the **House** of **Burgesses** and **Jamestown's** early beginnings.

8. **Take Darkston's Limousine Service** to **Los Angeles International Airport** to catch your **Aspen Airline** flight to **Denver, Colorado**.

9. **Our** vacation schedule includes the following: **Niagara Falls**, the **Pocono Mountains**, **Mt. Rushmore**, and **Yosemite National Park**.

10. **In** the morning, we ran errands to **Hartzel's Dry Cleaning Service** and **Himball Department Store**.

Name________________________________ **CAPITALIZATION**

Date________________________________

Directions: Supply needed capitalization.

1. from the corner of market street and central avenue, curve around bristol lake until you come to cripton's general store.
2. last summer they visited yellowstone national park, fantasy world, markham ranch, and san francisco bay.
3. the turning point battle of the civil war was at gettysburg, pennsylvania.
4. the asian hunters crossed the bering strait and traveled through north america.
5. the cress travel agency made the family's hawaiian islands reservations.
6. when marco and his family visited washington, d. c., they saw the buildings of the department of education, the famous potomac river, and georgetown university.
7. our class studied about the house of burgesses and jamestown's early beginnings.
8. take darkston's limousine service to los angeles international airport to catch your aspen airline flight to denver, colorado.
9. our vacation schedule includes the following: niagara falls, the pocono mountains, mt. rushmore, and yosemite national park.
10. in the morning, we ran errands to hartzel's dry cleaning service and himball department store.

PAGE 631 = WORKBOOK PAGE 297

CAPITALIZATION

Rule 14: **Capitalize names of days, months, holidays, and special days.**

Examples: **S**aturday — **C**olumbus **D**ay
Fourth of **J**uly — **H**anukkah
December — **S**t. **V**alentine's **D**ay
Pearl **H**arbor **D**ay — **G**eorge **W**ashington's **B**irthday
February — **T**uesday

Rule 15: **Capitalize a proper adjective but not the noun it modifies unless the noun is part of a title.**

Examples: a **C**olumbus **D**ay parade
our **T**uesday meeting
Hanukkah celebration
Alaskan coast
Swiss village
Labor **D**ay weekend
a **S**cottsdale rodeo

Specific titles are capitalized following the rule: Capitalize the first word, the last word, and all important words in any title. Do not capitalize a, an, the, and, but, or, nor, or prepositions of four or less letters unless those words are the first or last word.

Examples: **C**alifornia **G**old **R**ush **D**ays
Washington **C**herry **B**lossom **F**estival
Pasadena **T**ournament of **R**oses **P**arade
Winter **O**lympics
Kansas **S**tate **F**air

Note: Include the in a title only if the actually would appear on a sign announcing the event.

Examples: Are you going to the **O**range **B**owl **P**arade?
They went to the **I**ndianapolis 500.

Rule 16: **Capitalize brand names but not the product(s).**

Examples: **M**aylord muffins — **G**eneva milk
Healthy **H**aven vegetables — **G**alasea fishing rod

Name________________________________ **CAPITALIZATION**
WORKBOOK PAGE 298
Date_________________________________

Directions: Supply needed capitalization.
Answers are in boldfaced print.

1. **Last Monday** the band marched in a **Memorial Day** parade.

2. **Our** family celebrated **Grandparents' Day** at an **Italian** restaurant.

3. **At** our **Thursday** meeting we will plan a **St. Patrick's Day** party.

4. **Most** baseball fans know if the **World Series** begins on a **S**unday.

5. **Did Alva** participate in the 1983 marathon sponsored by **Luca Company** in **Hawaii**?

6. **The** purchases included **Padco** shortening, **Babyboom** diapers, **Lasic** grated cheese, and **Cottage Inn** ham.

7. **During Friday's** storm, signs of the **Texas State Fair** fell down.

8. **After Thanksgiving** vacation, the convention will meet in a **Palm Springs** hotel.

9. **In July** we will attend the **Biglerville Chamber** of **Commerce Annual Music Festival**.

10. **Do** you know that **Veteran's Day** is the same as **Armistice Day**?

11. **Kissa** and **I** bought **Sunbrew's** coffee, **Fasco** shredded wheat, and **Beemont's** soup.

12. **This Christmas** vacation we will spend two days at a **C**olorado ski resort near **Denver**.

Name________________________________ **CAPITALIZATION**

Date________________________________

Directions: Supply needed capitalization.

1. last monday the band marched in a memorial day parade.
2. our family celebrated grandparents' day at an italian restaurant.
3. at our thursday meeting we will plan a st. patrick's day party.
4. most baseball fans know if the world series begins on a sunday.
5. did alva participate in the 1983 marathon sponsored by luca company in hawaii?
6. the purchases included padco shortening, babyboom diapers, lasic grated, cheese, and cottage inn ham.
7. during friday's storm, signs of the texas state fair fell down.
8. after thanksgiving vacation, the convention will meet in a palm springs hotel.
9. in july we will attend the biglerville chamber of commerce annual music festival.
10. do you know that veteran's day is the same as armistice day?
11. kissa and i bought sunbrew's coffee, fasco shredded wheat, and beemont's soup.
12. this christmas vacation we will spend two days at a colorado ski resort near denver.

PAGE 635 = WORKBOOK PAGE 299
PAGE 638 = WORKBOOK PAGE 301
PAGE 639 = WORKBOOK PAGE 302
PAGE 642 = WORKBOOK PAGE 304
PAGE 643 = WORKBOOK PAGE 305

CAPITALIZATION

Rule 17: **Capitalize religions, religious denominations, religious documents, names of churches, and names for a supreme being.**

Examples:

Hindu religion	**P**rotestant
God	**I**slam religion
Dead **S**ea **S**crolls	**T**orah
Methodist	**L**ady of the **V**alley **C**atholic **C**hurch
Heavenly **F**ather	**A**llah
Ten **C**ommandments	**L**utheran

Notes:

A. a **B**aptist church: Capitalize only **B**aptist because a specific name of a church is not given. Baptist is a denomination and should be capitalized.

Madison **B**aptist **C**hurch: Capitalize the name of a church.

B. Greek or Roman gods and goddesses: Do not capitalize the terms, *gods* and *goddesses*.

Athena and **Z**eus: Capitalize the names of gods and goddesses.

Rule 18: **Capitalize languages.**

Examples:

English	**G**erman	**L**atin
Spanish	**F**rench	**A**rabic

Rule 19: **Capitalize races and ethnic groups.**

Examples:

Caucasian	**P**olynesian	**H**ispanic
Indian	**N**egro	**C**ajun

Rule 20: **Capitalize North, South, East, West, Northeast, Northwest, Southeast**, and **Southwest when they refer to a region of the country or the world.**

Examples: Does your Uncle Ray live in the **E**ast?

The **S**outhwest includes the state of Arizona.

Name________________________________ **CAPITALIZATION**

WORKBOOK PAGE 300

Date________________________________

Directions: Supply needed capitalization.
Answers are in boldfaced print.

1. **My** mother speaks **English**, **Italian**, and **Russian**.

2. **This** basket, made by **Indians**, is of outstanding quality.

3. **The Riverdale Methodist Church** hosted a **Polynesian** luau.

4. **Members** of a **Christian** organization met with a **Jewish** rabbi.

5. **A** class on **Hispanic** culture will be conducted in both **Spanish** and **English**.

6. **Were** the **Dead Sea Scrolls** found in a **Syrian** cave?

7. **The Franklin** family lived in **South Carolina** and in some other state in the **South**.

8. **Has Inga**, your aunt, learned to speak **Swedish** yet?

9. **The Roman Catholic** faith is dominant in **Latin America**.

10. **That Lutheran** church located west of my home held a **Bible** school in **June**.

11. **The Hopi Indians** of the **Southwest** make beautiful jewelry.

12. **Do** you know anything about the **Shinto** religion of **Japan**?

13. **Church** services at **Santiago Baptist Church** are conducted in **Spanish**.

14. **Some** exchange students studied modern art and **Chinese** at a college in the **New England** states.

15. **My United States** ten dollar bill states: ***In God We Trust.***
(Also accept only the word, God, capitalized in the motto.)

Name________________________________ **CAPITALIZATION**

Date________________________________

Directions: Supply needed capitalization.

1. my mother speaks english, italian, and russian.

2. this basket, made by indians, is of outstanding quality.

3. the riverdale methodist church hosted a polynesian luau.

4. members of a christian organization met with a jewish rabbi.

5. a class on hispanic culture will be conducted in both spanish and english.

6. were the dead sea scrolls found in a syrian cave?

7. the franklin family lived in south carolina and in some other state in the south.

8. has inga, your aunt, learned to speak swedish yet?

9. the roman catholic faith is dominant in latin america.

10. that lutheran church located west of my home held a <u>bible</u> school in june.

11. the hopi indians of the southwest make beautiful jewelry.

12. do you know anything about the shinto religion of japan?

13. church services at santiago baptist church are conducted in spanish.

14. some exchange students studied modern art and chinese at a college in the new england states.

15. my united states ten dollar bill states: *in god we trust.*

CAPITALIZATION

Rule 21: **Capitalize specific names of structures.**

Examples: Empire State Building
Golden Gate Bridge
Eiffel Tower
Washington Monument
Yankee Stadium
Astrodome
Grand Central Station

Rule 22: **Capitalize names, initials, and titles appearing with names.**

Examples: Abe
Debra R. Stone
Professor Elik
Admiral James Stevens
Fido

Rule 23: **Capitalize political parties and their members.**

Examples: Republican Party
Democrats
Communist Party
Tories

Rule 24: **Capitalize the first letter only in most hyphenated words that begin a sentence.**

Examples: Twenty-two ducks use that pond.

Fathers-in-law meet in this room today.

Capitalize both parts of a hyphenated word in titles.

Examples: Did you know that Vice-President Mondale ran for President?

Cindy has memorized the "Twenty-Third Psalm."

Rule 25: **Capitalize President when it refers to the leader of the United States.**

Examples: Have you seen that famous portrait of **P**resident George Washington?

The **P**resident has called a press conference.

Rule 26: **Capitalize a specific, well-known area or event.**

Examples: Did President Bush work late in the **O**val **O**ffice?

Her ice skating at the **W**inter **O**lympics was fantastic.

Rule 27: **Capitalize the first word of the greeting and closing of a letter.**

Examples: **D**ear **J**ane,

My dear and favorite niece,

Karla,

Love,

Sincerely yours,

My very best wishes,

Name________________________________ **CAPITALIZATION**

WORKBOOK PAGE 303

Date________________________________

Directions: Supply needed capitalization.
Answers are in boldfaced print.

1. **Does Dr. Shinley** have an office at **Lincoln Medical Hospital**?

2. **The Democratic Party** held a convention in **San Francisco, California**.

3. **We** met **Captain Todd R. Yost** at the police building on **Macaroni Avenue**.

4. **Has Aunt Gloria** or **Dad** ever visited **Sears Tower** in **Chicago**?

5. **Your** pictures of **Lincoln Memorial** are very clear, **Beverly**.

6. **Many** of us would like to visit **Notre Dame Cathedral** in **Paris, France**.

7. **In** the country of **Pakistan**, there is a special province called **North-West Frontier Province**.

8. **Should** this road lead to the **Leaning Tower** of **Pisa**?

9. **A** search is being conducted for **Sergeant Major Glugg**.

10. **My** friend, **T. R. Franklin**, is a stockbroker for that company.

11. **Both** the **Lincoln Tunnel** and the **George Washington Bridge** lead into **N. Y. C.**

12. **If** you, **Clarence**, favored staying with **England** during the **American Revolution**, you probably would have belonged to the **Tory Party**.

13. **The Fiesta Bowl** is held annually at **Sun Devil Stadium**.

14. **Did** you realize that the **Smithsonian Institution** has many buildings?

15. **I** would have liked to have been a colonist in **Plymouth** when **John Carver** was the governor.

Name______________________________ **CAPITALIZATION**

Date______________________________

Directions: Supply needed capitalization.

1. does dr. shinley have an office at lincoln medical hospital?
2. the democratic party held a convention in san francisco, california.
3. we met captain ted r. yost at the police building on macaroni avenue.
4. has aunt gloria or dad ever visited sears tower in chicago?
5. your pictures of lincoln memorial are very clear, beverly.
6. many of us would like to visit notre dame cathedral in paris, france.
7. in the country of pakistan, there is a special province called north-west frontier province.
8. should this road lead to the leaning tower of pisa?
9. a search is being conducted for sergeant major glugg.
10. my friend, t. r. franklin, is a stockbroker for that company.
11. both the lincoln tunnel and the george washington bridge lead into n. y. c.
12. if you, clarence, favored staying with england during the american revolution, you probably would have belonged to the tory party.
13. the fiesta bowl is held annually at sun devil stadium.
14. did you realize that the smithsonian institution has many buildings?
15. i would have liked to have been a colonist in plymouth when john carver was the governor.

DO NOT CAPITALIZE

Rule 1: **Do not capitalize north, south, east, west, northeast, northwest, southeast and southwest when they are used as directions.**

Examples: Go north on 57th Street.

Do you live east or west of the Mississippi River?

However, capitalize the direction when it appears with a geographic place.

Examples: The barber lives at 863 **W**est Hooly Drive.

Do you live on **S**outh Friar Street?

Rule 2: **Do not capitalize school subjects unless they state a language, or they are numbered.**

Examples: I enjoy **E**nglish.

Is **A**lgebra I meeting here?

My favorite subjects are spelling, history, and math.

If a proper adjective appears with the subject, capitalize only the proper adjective.

Examples: **A**merican history.

Greek literature

Rule 3: **Do not capitalize seasons of the year.**

Examples:	spring	winter
	summer	fall/autumn

Rule 4: **Do not capitalize foods, games, trees, musical instruments, animals, diseases, and plants. If a proper adjective appears with the item, capitalize only the proper adjective.**

FOODS:	pizza	ice cream	**S**wedish meatballs
	creamed corn	tuna	**I**talian sauce

Spanish rice Swiss cheese lettuce

GAMES: chess, bridge, football, Chinese checkers, tag, Mexican hat dance, two square, English soccer, polo

However, capitalize the names of trademarked games.

Example: Monopoly

TREES: oak, ash, elm, Mexican fan palm, apple, silk oak

MUSICAL INSTRUMENTS: piano, drums, harp, French horn, violin, guitar

DISEASES: mumps, Hodgkin's disease, chicken pox, measles, cerebral palsy, flu, cancer, German measles, Asiatic flu

PLANTS: tulips, asparagus fern, philodendron, oleander, Bermuda grass, ice plant, cactus, American rose, gardenia

ANIMALS: kitten, poodle, armadillo, palomino, giraffe, German shepherd, Siamese cat, snake, Arabian horse, Asiatic beetle, Clydesdale horse, monkey

Name________________________________ **CAPITALIZATION**

WORKBOOK PAGE 306

Date________________________________

Directions: Supply needed capitalization.
Answers are in boldfaced print.

1. **The** accountant lived in the northern part of **South Dakota**.

2. **A German** shepherd dog patrols **Gorbam Industries** on **Delta Avenue**.

3. **She** purchased her saxophone on **Friday** at **Mernet Music Store**.

4. **Last** fall **Melinda** took a course in **Spanish** literature.

5. **The Rotary Club** met at **Gringo's Mexican Food Restaurant** and feasted on cheese crisps.

6. **In** our front yard, the gardener planted **Italian** cypress, daffodils, chrysanthemums, and **Japanese** anemone.

7. **The** doctor's questionnaire requested to know if **I** had ever had the following: measles, diphtheria, scarlet fever, polio, or **Hong Kong** flu.

8. **Marvin** studies **English**, economics, **American** literature, **Computer Science** I, and psychology at a **Western** university.

9. **When I** had pneumonia last winter, my **British** friend played backgammon with me.

10. **His** favorite foods are **Greek** pie, bologna, onion rings, **Boston** creme pie, and **Danish** pastries.

Name________________________________ **CAPITALIZATION**

Date________________________________

Directions: Supply needed capitalization.

1. the accountant lived in the northern part of south dakota.
2. a german shepherd dog patrols gorbam industries on delta avenue.
3. she purchased her saxophone on friday at mernet music store.
4. last fall melinda took a course in spanish literature.
5. the rotary club met at gringo's mexican food restaurant and feasted on cheese crisps.
6. in our front yard, the gardener planted italian cypress, daffodils, chrysanthemums, and japanese anemone.
7. the doctor's questionnaire requested to know if i had ever had the following: measles, diphtheria, scarlet fever, polio, or hong kong flu.
8. marvin studies english, economics, american literature, computer science I, and psychology at a western university.
9. when i had pneumonia last winter, my british friend played backgammon with me.
10. his favorite foods are greek pie, bologna, onion rings, boston creme pie, and danish pastries.

Name________________________________ **CAPITALIZATION**

WORKBOOK PAGE 307

Date________________________________

Directions: Supply needed capitalization.
Answers are in boldfaced print.

1. **Have** you read **Island of the Blue Dolphins**, **Aunt Barbara**?

2. **In** history, **I** learned that the **U.S. Constitution** replaced the **Articles of Confederation**.

3. **On Easter** we attended the **Lion's Club Fifth Annual Pancake Breakfast** held in the social hall of **Memorial Presbyterian Church**.

4. **Did Mr. Applebee** serve **Sara Lee** cupcakes or **Mississippi** fudge pie for dessert?

5. **The** city of **Port Chester** is in southeastern **New York** on **Long Island Sound**.

6. **The** language of **Poland** is one of the **Indo-European** languages called **Slavic**.

7. **The Pets-Are-Fun Shop** on **Milter Lane** has a **Siberian** husky, various snakes, and two **French** poodles.

8.

45785 **W. Arms Drive**
Reno, Nevada
August 10, 20--

Dear Cousin Steven,

We are enjoying the **West**. **Yesterday**, we visited an **Arabian** horse farm, and on **Saturday** we leave for **Organ Pipe National Monument**.

Your friend,

Clyde

Name________________________________ **CAPITALIZATION**

Date________________________________

Directions: Supply needed capitalization.

1. have you read island of the blue dolphins, aunt barbara?

2. in history, i learned that the u.s. constitution replaced the articles of confederation.

3. on easter we attended the lion's club fifth annual pancake breakfast held in the social hall of memorial presbyterian church.

4. did mr. applebee serve sara lee cupcakes or mississippi fudge pie for dessert?

5. the city of port chester is in southeastern new york on long island sound.

6. the language of poland is one of the indo-european languages called slavic.

7. the pets-are-fun shop on milter lane has a siberian husky, various snakes, and two french poodles.

8.

45785 w. arms drive
reno, nevada
august 10, 20--

dear cousin steven,

we are enjoying the west. yesterday, we visited an arabian horse farm, and on saturday we leave for organ pipe national monument.

your friend,

clyde

Name________________________________ **CAPITALIZATION**
WORKBOOK PAGE 308
Date________________________________

Directions: Supply needed capitalization.
Answers are in boldfaced print.

1. **The Battle** of **New Orleans** at the end of the **War** of 1812 made **General Andrew Jackson** famous.

2. **The Laketon Wildlife Club** meets at **Sunset Park Restaurant** on **Wednesdays**.

3. **The** children watched **Sesame Street** and then read **Winnie the Pooh and the Blustery Day**.

4. **That Brownie** troop visited the **Baltimore Museum** of **Art** last summer during the third week in **July**.

5. **Lillian** asked, "**Have** you planted an **American** rose in this planter?"

6. **The** country of **France** is bordered by **Spain**, the **Mediterranean Sea**, the **English Channel**, **Belgium**, **Switzerland**, **Italy**, **Luxembourg**, and the **Atlantic Ocean**.

7. **My** father entered **General Eisenhower Hospital** on **Eighth Street** during **Christmas** vacation.

8. **In** the **Mexican** history class, we studied **Aztec Indians** and **Chief Montezuma**.

9. **Our** tour of the **White House*** and our trip to the **Jefferson Memorial** were interesting.

10. **The U.S. Figure Skating Association** held competitions last summer.

* particular building where the President resides

Name________________________________ **CAPITALIZATION**

Date________________________________

Directions: Supply needed capitalization.

1. the battle of new orleans at the end of the war of 1812 made general andrew jackson famous.

2. the laketon wildlife club meets at sunset park restaurant on wednesdays.

3. the children watched <u>sesame street</u> and then read <u>winnie the pooh and the blustery day</u>.

4. that brownie troop visited the baltimore museum of art last summer during the third week in july.

5. lillian asked, "have you planted an american rose in this planter?"

6. the country of france is bordered by spain, the mediterranean sea, the english channel, belgium, switzerland, italy, luxembourg, and the atlantic ocean.

7. my father entered general eisenhower hospital on eighth street during christmas vacation.

8. in the mexican history class, we studied aztec indians and chief montezuma.

9. our tour of the white house* and our trip to the jefferson memorial were interesting.

10. the u.s. figure skating association held competitions last summer.

* particular building where the President resides

Name________________________________ **CAPITALIZATION**
WORKBOOK PAGE 309
Date________________________________

Directions: Supply needed capitalization.
Answers are in boldfaced print.

1. **Most** of **Greenland** lies north of the **Arctic Circle** and is bordered by the **Arctic Ocean**.

2. "**Dad**, will you," asked **Yvonne**, "take me to the **San Diego Zoo**?"

3. **I. Literature**

   A. Prose

   B. Poetry

4. **Is Desert Sky Junior High School** near **Union Hills Road**?

5. The article entitled "**Three Days** to the **Desk** of **Your Dreams**" appeared in the **August** issue of <u>**Successful Leadership**</u> magazine.

6.

15 **North Monte Cristo Drive**
San Clemente, **California**
October 21, 20--

Department of **Revenue**
P.O. Box 333
Augusta, **Maine**

To whom it may concern:

Enclosed is the information requested.

Truly yours,

W. T. Sung

Name________________________________ **CAPITALIZATION**

Date________________________________

Directions: Supply needed capitalization.

1. most of greenland lies north of the arctic circle and is bordered by the arctic ocean.

2. “dad, will you,” asked yvonne, “take me to the san diego zoo?”

3. I. literature

    a. prose

    b. poetry

4. is desert sky junior high school near union hills road?

5. the article entitled “three days to the desk of your dreams” appeared in the august issue of <u>successful leadership</u> magazine.

6.

15 north monte cristo drive
san clemente, california
october 21, 20--

department of revenue
p.o. box 333
augusta, maine

to whom it may concern:

enclosed is the information requested.

truly yours,

w. t. sung

Name________________________________ **CAPITALIZATION**
WORKBOOK PAGE 310
Date________________________________

Directions: Supply needed capitalization.
Answers are in boldfaced print.

1. **Last** summer we went to a **Wyoming** ranch, a yacht race, and a **Delaware** beach.

2. **Has Great Aunt Daisy** been to the **Great Wall** in **China**?

3. **The Crusades** were fought between the **Christians** and the **Muslims**.

4. **Send** your copyright form to **Register** of **Copyrights**, **Library** of **Congress**, **Washington**, **D.C**.

5. **Before** leaving the ship, **<u>Mayflower</u>**, the **Pilgrims** drew up their plan of government called the "**Mayflower Compact.**"

6. **Does Carnell Department Store** carry tubas, **Gloria Vanderbilt** perfume, or **African** daisies?

7. A dinner honoring **Lieutenant Colonel Keplinger** will be held at **Snakehorn Restaurant** next **Saturday** evening.

8. **John Ciardi's** poem entitled "**Why Nobody Pets** the **Lion** at the **Zoo**" begins, "**The** morning that the world began..."

9. **A** leukemia patient was transferred to **Good Heart General Hospital** for further blood tests.

10. **The Holland Tulip Festival** is held yearly in **Michigan**.

Name________________________________ **CAPITALIZATION**

Date________________________________

Directions: Supply needed capitalization.

1. last summer we went to a wyoming ranch, a yacht race, and a delaware beach.

2. has great aunt daisy been to the great wall in china?

3. the crusades were fought between the christians and the muslims.

4. send your copyright form to register of copyrights, library of congress, washington, d. c.

5. before leaving the ship, <u>mayflower</u>, the pilgrims drew up their plan of government called the "mayflower compact."

6. does carnell department store carry tubas, gloria vanderbilt perfume, or african daisies?

7. a dinner honoring lieutenant colonel keplinger will be held at snakehorn restaurant next saturday evening.

8. john ciardi's poem entitled "why nobody pets the lion at the zoo" begins, "the morning that the world began..."

9. a leukemia patient was transferred to good heart general hospital for further blood tests.

10. the holland tulip festival is held yearly in michigan.

Name________________________________ **CAPITALIZATION TEST**

Date________________________________

Answers are in boldfaced print.

Directions: Write the capital letter above any word that needs to be capitalized.

1. **When Captain Lovell** and **I** visited the **South**, we saw the **Savannah River** and the site of the **Battle** of **Shiloh**, a famous **Civil War** area.
2. **They** learned **Spanish**, computer science, and **Algebra** 1 at a junior high school.
3. **I. Geographical** locations
   A. Rivers
   B. Mountains
   1. **Located** in **Europe**
   2. **Located** in **North America**
4. **Their** grandfather was given a book entitled <u>**The Prayer** of **Jabez**</u> as a **Father's Day** gift.
5. **Juan** and his **Polynesian** friends attended a play entitled <u>**He Was** with **Me** in the **Den**</u> at **Star Theater** last **Saturday**.
6. **A** child with bronchitis was treated at **Sunset Memorial Hospital** on **Drye Lane**.
7. **Did Mayor Torris** drive across the **Golden Gate Bridge** when visiting northern **California** last winter?
8. **After** buying several gifts at **Swan Gift Shop**, the **American** tourist boarded a **Concourse Airline** flight for **New York City**.
9. "**During Thanksgiving** vacation, **Mother** and **Aunt Kama** helped the **Moon Valley Helpers Club** teach **Spanish** at **Largent College**," said **Kalifa.**
10.

1882 **South Breck Drive**
Atlanta, Georgia 30327
January 4, 20—

Dear Dirk and **Cochise,**

To travel to **Grand Canyon National Park** from your home, take the **Black Canyon Freeway** to **Flagstaff**, **Arizona**, and turn west.

Your friend,
Thang

Name________________________________ **CAPITALIZATION TEST**

Date________________________________

Directions: Write the capital letter above any word that needs to be capitalized.

1. when captain lovell and i visited the south, we saw the savannah river and the site of the battle of shiloh, a famous civil war area.
2. they learned spanish, computer science, and algebra 1 at a junior high school.
3. i. geographical locations
    a. rivers
    b. mountains
        1. located in europe
        2. located in north america
4. their grandfather was given a book entitled <u>the prayer of jabez</u> as a father's day gift.
5. juan and his polynesian friends attended a play entitled <u>he was with me in the den</u> at star theater last saturday.
6. a child with bronchitis was treated at sunset memorial hospital on drye lane.
7. did mayor torris drive across the golden gate bridge when visiting northern california last winter?
8. after buying several gifts at swan gift shop, the american tourist boarded a concourse airline flight for new york city.
9. "during thanksgiving vacation, mother and aunt kama helped the moon valley helpers club teach spanish at largent college," said kalifa.
10.

1882 south breck drive
atlanta, georgia 30327
january 4, 20—

dear dirk and cochise,

to travel to grand canyon national park from your home, take the black canyon freeway to flagstaff, arizona, and turn west.

your friend,
thang

FRIENDLY LETTER

First, teach the **purpose** of friendly letters.

It is suggested that you teach the formal heading. Students should be told that in their personal letters, the first two lines of a heading, and sometimes even the date, are omitted. When you teach your first friendly letter, take ample time to model placement of each line and content of each line.

It is suggested that students be given many opportunities to write friendly letters. After their introduction, it is wise to have students write friendly letters once a week (for at least a month). After that, assign this task periodically as a reinforcement.

Although friendly letters seem easy, some students find them difficult without a sample form. Your goal is **mastery** of friendly letters, including both format and parts. Students need to be able to place all items where they belong and use appropriate capitalization and punctuation. They should also be able to label friendly letter parts.

PAGE 659 = WORKBOOK PAGE 311
PAGE 660 = WORKBOOK PAGE 312
PAGE 661 = WORKBOOK PAGE 313
PAGE 662 = WORKBOOK PAGE 314
PAGE 663 = WORKBOOK PAGE 315

FRIENDLY LETTER

Parts:

The parts of a friendly letter are the heading, the salutation or greeting, the body, the closing, and the signature.

Your Post Office Box
or
Number and Street Name

heading City, State Zip Code

Complete Date

greeting Dear (Person),

The written message in any letter is called the **body**.

closing *Appropriate closing,

signature Your Name

*The closing/signature should be lined up with the heading.

Note: It has become acceptable to abbreviate the state even in formal letter writing. In using the postal codes, both letters are capitalized and no period is used.

FRIENDLY LETTER

Sample:

1087 North Main Avenue

Honolulu, Hawaii

October 23, 2089

My dear friend,

Hi! How are you? It's been a long time since I've written so there's so much to ask you. Did you take your planned trip to St. Louis and Washington, D. C.? Did you visit the White House, the Lincoln Memorial, or the Washington Monument? I'm anxious to hear all about your trip.

Our family didn't do much this past summer. Dad started his own business, and we didn't have much extra cash for anything *big*. We did manage to go up to the mountains for some picnics and to the beach often. That's one nice thing about living here.

Speaking of *here*, when do you think your family can visit us? Write and let me know. I miss the good times we had in our old neighborhood.

Love,

Chris

BUSINESS LETTER

Parts:

The parts of a business letter are the heading, the inside address, the salutation or greeting, the body, the closing, and the signature.

Your Post Office Box
or
Number and Street Name

heading City, State Zip Code

Complete Date

Name of Business

Street Address of Business **inside address**

City, State Zip Code

Person(s) or Business Name: **greeting or salutation**

____

body ______________________________

____

____

closing Appropriate closing,

Written Signature

signature Typed Signature

There are many acceptable business letter formats; this is only one.

BUSINESS LETTER

Sample:

11124 South Drake Drive

Anaheim, California 92827

May 20, 2067

Bristo Enterprises

P. O. Box 35

Phoenix, Arizona 85032

Ladies and Gentlemen:

Last March I ordered several items from your catalog: a red wagon (#LD 2437), a deck of cards (#SP 1030), and a revolving flashlight (#FL 5550). I also enclosed a personal check for the total of the three items: check number 321, City Bank, amount - $46.23. I have not received my goods. Please ship them immediately.

Sincerely yours,

Laura P. Belts

Laura P. Belts

ENVELOPE

The envelope for a friendly letter and a business letter are the same. The block style is shown here; block style means that each line is exactly below the preceding line.

YOUR NAME **********

NUMBER AND STREET ADDRESS **return address** STAMP

CITY, STATE ZIP CODE **********

PERSON TO WHOM YOU ARE SENDING LETTER*

NUMBER AND STREET NAME

CITY, STATE ZIP CODE

---

*or company

Ted Kline **********

2265 Morningstar Lane STAMP

Gettysburg, Pennsylvania 17325 **********

Miss Susan Smith

712 Tabby Lane

Phoenix, Arizona 85308

FRAGMENTS and RUN-ONS

A sentence fragment does not express a complete thought.

Example: Recently, I met Mrs. Valdez**.** Shopping at Park Mall.

Shopping at Park Mall cannot stand alone as a complete thought.

Corrected: Recently, I encountered Mrs. Valdez shopping at Park Mall.
Recently, I encountered Mrs. James, who was shopping at Park Mall.

A run-on sentence expresses too many thoughts. Do not use a comma to separate two or more complete thoughts.

Example: Training for a marathon is time consuming**,** many hours are spent in building endurance.

Corrected: Training for a marathon is time consuming**, and** many hours are spent in building endurance.

Training for a marathon is time consuming**, for** many hours are spent in building endurance.

Training for a marathon is time consuming **because** many hours are spent in building endurance.

Training for a marathon is time consuming**;** many hours are spent in building endurance.

Note: Be aware that the comma is often used to join sentences in journalistic writing such as magazines and newspapers. Professional writers use this for effect. However, in schools, colleges and, usually, businesses, this usage is considered wrong.

CLAUSES

Coordinate Clauses:
Coordinate ideas are of equal rank or importance. **Coordinate clauses** each contain a subject and a verb. These clauses may be classified as **addition**, **contrast**, **choice**, and **result**.

Addition:

Connective words used to join coordinate clauses: **and**, **besides**, **also**, **then**, **furthermore**, **likewise**, **moreover**, and **both...and**

Example: She thinks vintage jewelry is beautiful**, and** she invests in it.

Contrast:

Connective words used to show conflict or contrast: **but**, **however**, **still**, **yet**, and **nevertheless**

Example: He has decided to go**, but** he's not allowed to take his dog.

Choice:

Connective words used to state another possibility: **or**, **nor**, **otherwise**, **either...or**, and **neither...nor**

Example: Either Dr. Roe must resign, or she must take long-term disability.

Result:

Connective words used to express the result of the first clause: **therefore**, **thus**, **consequently**, **accordingly**, and **hence**

Example: We have misplaced our car keys**; therefore,** we will be late.

Use a comma before **and**, **but**, **or**, **nor**, and **yet** when two coordinate clauses are joined.

Example: Each team member received a blue ribbon**, and** the team received a trophy.

When joining two coordinate clauses with a semicolon **and** using one of the following words—**however, therefore, furthermore, nevertheless, moreover, besides, thus, hence, likewise,** or **accordingly**, use a comma after that word. Remember that coordinate clauses are of equal importance.

Example: The jury had deliberated for five days**; thus,** each member believed the verdict was just.

Name________________________________ **Clauses**

Date_________________________________

A clause must contain a subject and a verb.
Coordinate clauses are of equal rank or importance.

Common Coordinating Conjunctions:

and, besides, also, then, furthermore, likewise, moreover, both...and, but, however, still, yet, nevertheless, or, nor, otherwise, either...or, neither...nor, therefore, thus, consequently, accordingly, hence

Use a comma before **and**, **but**, **or**, **nor**, and **yet** when two coordinate clauses are joined.

Example: They like to scuba dive**, and** they will dive this week.

When joining two coordinate clauses with a **semicolon and using one of the following words—however, therefore, furthermore, nevertheless, moreover, besides, thus, hence, likewise,** or **accordingly**, use a comma after that word.

Example: His grandmother is ill; **therefore,** he will visit her.

Directions: Write a coordinate clause to finish the sentence. Then, underline the subject and verb of your clause.

ANSWERS WILL VARY/REPRESENTATIVE ANSWERS:
The subject of the coordinate clause is boldfaced; the verb or verb phrase is italicized.

1. The party will be held next Saturday, and my **friends** *will be* there.

2. She bought a new computer, but **it** *does*n't *work*.

3. You may finish your work now, or **you** *may do* it after supper.

4. Our team won; however, **I** *did*n't *play* very well.

5. I like your idea, yet **I** *need* more time to think about it.

6. The job was completed on time; nevertheless, the **boss** *would*n't *pay* the workers.

7. I don't want to go; besides, **I** *do*n't *want* to buy a new suit for the event.

Name________________________________ **Clauses**

Date________________________________

A clause must contain a subject and a verb.
Coordinate clauses are of equal rank or importance.

Common Coordinating Conjunctions:

> **and, besides, also, then, furthermore, likewise, moreover, both...and, but, however, still, yet, nevertheless, or, nor, otherwise, either...or, neither...nor, therefore, thus, consequently, accordingly, hence**

Use a comma before **and**, **but**, **or**, **nor**, and **yet** when two coordinate clauses are joined.

Example: They like to scuba dive**, and** they will dive this week.

When joining two coordinate clauses with a **semicolon and using one of the following words—however, therefore, furthermore, nevertheless, moreover, besides, thus, hence, likewise,** or **accordingly**, use a comma after that word.

Example: His grandmother is ill**; therefore,** he will visit her.

Directions: Write a coordinate clause to finish the sentence. Then, underline the subject and verb of your clause.

1. The party will be held next Saturday**, and** ________________________________
____
2. She bought a new computer**, but** ________________________________
____
3. You may finish your work now**, or**________________________________
____
4. Our team won**; however,** ________________________________
____
5. I like your idea**, yet** ________________________________
____
6. The job was completed on time**; nevertheless,** ________________________
____
7. I don't want to go; **besides,**________________________________
____

Name________________________________ **Clauses**

Date________________________________

A clause must contain a subject and a verb. **Coordinate clauses** express two complete, related thoughts. Both are of equal importance.

Common Coordinating Conjunctions:

and, besides, also, then, furthermore, likewise, moreover, both...and, but, however, still, yet, nevertheless, or, nor, otherwise, either...or, neither...nor, therefore, thus, consequently, accordingly, hence

Use a comma before **and**, **but**, **or**, **nor**, and **yet** when two coordinate clauses are joined.

Example: Kiki likes to decorate cakes**, and** she plans to start her own business soon.

When joining two coordinate clauses with **a semicolon and using one of the following words—however, therefore, furthermore, nevertheless, moreover, besides, thus, hence, likewise**, or **accordingly**, use a comma after that word.

Example: Kiki wants to open her own cake-decorating business; **however**, she first wants to take a class about starting a business.

Directions: Write a coordinate clause to finish the sentence. Then, underline the subject and verb of your clause.

ANSWERS WILL VARY/REPRESENTATIVE ANSWERS:

The subject of the coordinate clause is boldfaced; the verb or verb phrase is italicized.

1. You may place your paper plate in the trash, or **you** *may place* it on the counter.

2. The artist drew a colorful picture of the Grand Canyon, but **nobody** *has purchased* it.

3. That store is going out of business; therefore, a huge **sale** *is occurring*.

4. I do not like the way that child is behaving, nor *do* **I** *like* her parents' attitude.

5. Josh wants to move out on his own; thus, **he** *has been looking* for an apartment.

6. Micah read a story about identity theft, and **he** *is* now *researching* that topic for an essay.

7. Their mother is a stay-at-home mom; likewise, **many** of her friends **remain** at home with their children.

Name______________________________

Date______________________________

A clause must contain a subject and a verb. **Coordinate clauses** express two complete, related thoughts. Both are of equal importance.

Common Coordinating Conjunctions:

and, **besides**, **also**, **then**, **furthermore**, **likewise**, **moreover**, **both...and**, **but**, **however**, **still**, **yet**, **nevertheless**, **or**, **nor**, **otherwise**, **either...or**, **neither...nor**, **therefore**, **thus**, **consequently**, **accordingly**, **hence**

Use a comma before **and**, **but**, **or**, **nor**, and **yet** when two coordinate clauses are joined.

Example: Kiki likes to decorate cakes**, and** she plans to start her own business soon.

When joining two coordinate clauses with **a semicolon and using one of the following words—however, therefore, furthermore, nevertheless, moreover, besides, thus, hence, likewise**, or **accordingly**, use a comma after that word.

Example: Kiki wants to open her own cake-decorating business; **however,** she first wants to take a class about starting a business.

Directions: Write a coordinate clause to finish the sentence. Then, underline the subject and verb of your clause.

1. You may place your paper plate in the trash**, or** ______________________________

____

2. The artist drew a colorful picture of the Grand Canyon**, but** ____________________

____

3. That store is going out of business**; therefore,** ____________________________

____

4. I do not like the way that child is behaving**, nor** ____________________________

____

5. Josh wants to move out on his own**; thus,** ________________________________

____

6. Micah read a story about identity theft**, and** ______________________________

____

7. Their mother is a stay-at-home mom**; likewise,** ____________________________

____

Clauses

Ideas represented in a clause have both a subject and a verb. However, the idea represented in a clause that expresses a complete thought is of first rank. It is referred to as an **independent** or **main clause**; it can stand alone as a sentence. A dependent clause ranks **under** an independent clause.

A **subordinate clause** contains a subject and verb, but it cannot stand alone as a complete thought. This is a **dependent clause**. It ranks under (*sub*) an independent clause; therefore, it is called a subordinate clause.

A **subordinate conjunction** may begin a subordinate (dependent) clause. There is always a relationship between the independent clause and the subordinate clause. This may take the form of **cause or reason**, **purpose or result**, **condition**, or **time**.

<u>**Cause or Reason**</u>:

Words often used as subordinate conjunctions to express the cause or reason of the independent clause tell *why*. A few of these words are **as**, **because**, and **whereas**.

Example: We can go skiing ***because*** *enough snow has fallen.*

Purpose or Result:

Words often used as subordinate conjunctions for purpose or result from the idea expressed in the independent clause are **in order that**, **that**, and **so that**.

Example: Mario attended law school ***so that*** *he could become a lawyer.*

Condition:

The dependent clause expresses the condition under which the idea in the main clause is true. Words often used as subordinate conjunctions to express condition are **though**, **although**, **even though**, **if**, **unless**, **while**, and **provided that**.

Example: You may go out to play in the drizzle ***if*** *you wear boots.*

Time:

The dependent clause expresses the time under which the idea in the independent clause is true. Words often used as subordinate conjunctions to express time are **before**, **after, when**, **while**, and **whenever**.

Example: The child has his snack ***after*** *he takes a nap.*

Name________________________________ **Clauses**

Date________________________________

A clause must contain a subject and a verb.
An **independent clause** can stand alone as a sentence.
A **subordinate clause** cannot stand alone as a sentence.

Common Subordinate Conjunctions:

after, although, as, as if, as long as, as though, because, before, if, in order that, provided that, since, so that, than, though, unless, until, when, whenever, where, wherever, whereas, whether, while

Directions: Finish each subordinate clause. Then, underline the subject and verb of your clause.

ANSWERS WILL VARY/REPRESENTATIVE ANSWERS:
The subject of the subordinate clause is boldfaced; the verb or verb phrase is italicized.

1. He will go if **he** *can borrow* some money.

2. Sara is sad because her **puppy** *is* sick.

3. Tate is tall whereas his **sister** *is* short for her age.

4. The bank was robbed while my **brother** *was cashing* his check.

5. The bride looked as if **she** *were going* to faint.

6. Dad handed me five dollars in order that **I** *could buy* a hot dog at the baseball game.

7. You may leave when **you** *have done* all of your chores and **have taken** out the trash in your bedroom.

8. Please look where **you** *are going*.

9. We haven't seen him since **he** *came* to our basketball game last winter.

Name________________________________

Date________________________________

Clauses

A clause must contain a subject and a verb.
An **independent clause** can stand alone as a sentence.
A **subordinate clause** cannot stand alone as a sentence.

Common Subordinate Conjunctions:

after, although, as, as if, as long as, as though, because, before, if, in order that, provided that, since, so that, than, though, unless, until, when, whenever, where, wherever, whereas, whether, while

Directions: Finish each subordinate clause. Then, underline the subject and verb of your clause.

1. He will go **if** ________________________________
____
2. Sara is sad **because** ________________________________
____
3. Tate is tall **whereas** ________________________________
____
4. The bank was robbed **while** ________________________________
____
5. The bride looked **as if** ________________________________
____
6. Dad handed me five dollars **in order that** ________________________________
____
7. You may leave **when** ________________________________
____
8. Please look **where** ________________________________
____
9. We haven't seen him **since** ________________________________
____

DEPENDENT CLAUSES

A dependent clause serves as a part of speech and has a relationship with some word or words in the independent clause. **Dependent clauses can functions as adverbs, adjectives, or nouns.**

<u>Adverbial Clauses</u>:

Adverbial clauses (also called adverb clauses) modify a verb, an adjective, or another adverb. They tell **how**, **when**, **where**, **to what extent**, **how much**, **why**, and **under what conditions**.

Examples of adverbial clauses:

He runs ***like*** *someone is chasing him.*
He runs ***when*** *he has an extra half hour.*
He runs ***where*** *the woods are separated by a cow path.*
He runs ***because*** *he is training for a marathon.*
He runs more than he did ***when*** *he was in his teens.*
He runs ***if*** *he doesn't arrive home too late.*

<u>Adjective Clauses</u>:

An adjective clause may serve to explain or elaborate on some idea expressed in the independent clause. An adjective clause usually begins with a relative pronoun: **who**, **whoever**, **whom**, **whomever**, **whose**, **what**, **whatever**, **which**, or **that**. Other words such as **why** can begin an adjective clause.

Example: The dancer wore a gown with feathers, ***which*** *made her look somewhat like a peacock.*

Adjective clauses may help to **emphasize** an idea expressed in an independent clause.

Example A: Thomas Jefferson, ***who*** *wrote the Declaration of Independence*, was America's third leader.

In this sentence, the main idea emphasizes that Jefferson was America's third leader. The fact that he wrote the Declaration of Independence is not as important.

Example B: Thomas Jefferson, ***who*** *was America's third leader*, wrote the Declaration of Independence.

In this sentence, the main idea emphasizes that Jefferson wrote the Declaration of Independence. That he was America's third leader is of less importance; therefore, it is in a subordinate role.

Adjective clauses are dependent clauses; they cannot stand alone as a complete thought. They form a subordinate idea to an independent clause. Joining a subordinate clause and one independent clause forms a complex sentence.

Noun Clauses:

A noun clause is a dependent clause that serves where a noun would typically function.

Subject:	**Truth** is evident. **That he is telling the truth** is evident.
Direct Object:	She likes **spinach**. She likes **that her coach helps her to improve.**
Indirect Object:	Mondo sent **me** a card. (You can insert *to* before *me*.) Mondo will give **whomever asks** a ride home.
Predicate Nominative:	The winner is **that girl.** The winner is **whoever crosses the line first.**

Nonessential Clauses (or Nonrestrictive Clauses):

A **nonessential clause**, a subordinate clause, is one that is not important to the meaning of a sentence.

Example: My neighbor, ***who** is a plumber*, loves to garden.

Note that *who is a plumber* is not important to the meaning of the sentence. Therefore, the clause is set off by commas.

Note: If the word **which** is used to introduce a clause, a comma is used.

Essential Clauses (or Restrictive Clauses):

An **essential clause**, a subordinate clause, is one that is important to the meaning of a sentence.

Example: My brother is the scout ***who** was chosen to lead the pledge*.

Here, the subordinate clause is important to the meaning of the sentence. Therefore, it is not set off by commas.

Note: Use **that** rather than **which** to introduce an essential clause modifying a thing. (Some grammarians argue this point.)

Note: Whether the clause is essential or nonessential is frequently debatable.

Elliptical Clauses:

Elliptical means something omitted. An elliptical clause has some part missing.

Example: You are friendlier *than I*.
(You are friendlier *than I* ***am***.)

Name______________________________

Date______________________________

Clauses

A clause must contain a subject and a verb. An independent clause can stand alone as a sentence. A dependent clause (subordinate clause) cannot stand alone as a sentence. If the independent clause occurs first, a comma is not needed after it.

Example: I like to play the guitar when I am restless.
independent clause — dependent clause

If the dependent clause occurs first, place a comma after it.

Example: When I am restless**,** I like to play the guitar.
dependent clause — independent clause

Directions: Finish each sentence. Be sure to use correct punctuation.

ANSWERS MAY VARY/REPRESENTATIVE ANSWERS:

1. When we attended a dog show, one little dog jumped into the audience.
2. Before she was five years old, she lived with her grandparents in Kansas.
3. Unless you take your time, you may make careless errors.
4. Because he is an only child, he is accustomed to being with adults.
5. Although we enjoy watching soccer games, we don't want to become coaches.
6. After the play ended, the actors came back on stage and took a bow.
7. Whenever Jack sees a sports car, he pretends that he is driving it.
8. Whereas Jana's brother wants to be a jockey, she wants to be a horse trainer.
9. Even though his stock dropped in value, he refused to sell it.

Name________________________________ **Clauses**

Date________________________________

A clause must contain a subject and a verb. An independent clause can stand alone as a sentence. A dependent clause (subordinate clause) cannot stand alone as a sentence.

If the independent clause occurs first, a comma is not needed after it.

Example: I like to play the guitar when I am restless.
(independent clause: "I like to play the guitar"; dependent clause: "when I am restless")

If the dependent clause occurs first, place a comma after it.

Example: When I am restless, I like to play the guitar.
(dependent clause: "When I am restless"; independent clause: "I like to play the guitar")

Directions: Finish each sentence. Be sure to use correct punctuation.

1. When we attended a dog show____

2. Before she was five years old____

3. Unless you take your time____

4. Because he is an only child____

5. Although we enjoy watching soccer games____

6. After the play ended____

7. Whenever Jack sees a sports car____

8. Whereas Jana's brother wants to be a jockey____

9. Even though his stock dropped in value____

Name________________________________ **Clauses**

Date________________________________

You may want to review noun clauses and essential clauses before completing this page.

Note: After completing these exercises, you may have students circle the dependent clause. These have been italicized.

A. Directions: Complete each sentence. **ANSWERS WILL VARY/REPRESENTATIVE ANSWERS:**

1. *That you are angry* is obvious.

2. The toddler *who threw a toy at another child* also bit the teacher.

3. I want you to take *whichever drink you want.*

4. The winner is *whoever throws the ball the highest.*

5. *What you did* was heroic!

6. I understand *that your ancestors were from Ireland.*

7. That knife *that was a gift from the Lu family* needs to be sharpened.

8. The girl *whose essay won first place* read it to the school-board members.

9. You may ask *whomever you wish* to go camping this weekend.

B. Directions: Place commas where needed.

1. The contestant who lays down his cards first wins. (essential clause—no comma needed)
2. Wichita, where my aunt and uncle currently live, was her birthplace.
3. While Dad was cooking dinner, he helped me with spelling.
4. Whoever finishes eating first may start rinsing dishes. (clause serving as subject—no comma needed)

Name________________________________

Date________________________________

Clauses

A. Directions: Complete each sentence.

1. That you are angry____

____

2. The toddler who threw a toy at another child____________________

____

3. I want you to take whichever_________________________________

____

4. The winner is whoever_______________________________________

____

5. What you did____

____

6. I understand that____

____

7. That knife *that was a gift from the Lu family*____________________

____

8. The girl whose essay won first place__________________________

____

9. You may ask whomever you wish_____________________________

____

B. Directions: Place commas where needed.

1. The contestant who lays down his cards first wins.
2. Wichita where my aunt and uncle currently live was her birthplace.
3. While Dad was cooking dinner he helped me with spelling.
4. Whoever finishes eating first may start rinsing dishes.

Assessment Answers

A. Clauses: *(1 pt. each) (4 pts.)*

1. **DC** After you buy your ticket.
2. **No** After dinner at a fast-food restaurant. **(This is two prepositional phrases.)**
3. **IC** After we finish, let's make popsicles.
4. **IC** The team flew to Los Angeles after the game.

B. Sentences, Fragments, and Run-Ons: *(2 pts. each) (10 pts.)*

1. **R-O** Lana doesn't like kiwis, she prefers pineapples.
2. **S** Stop.
3. **F** When their parents went to a neighborhood party.
4. **S** Within two hours of hearing about the flood, rescuers responded.
5. **R-O** Kira drove to the airport, parked, went to ticketing, but she had left her purse in her truck and had to return to it and so she missed her flight.

C. Sentence Types: *(1 pt. each) (4 pts.)*

1. **interrogative** Is Tamarindo in Costa Rica**?**
2. **exclamatory** Yikes! We're lost**!**
3. **imperative** Please remain quiet**.**
4. **declarative** They live on Shell Avenue**.**

D. Business Letters: *(1 pt. each)(2 pts.)*

September 21, 20—

Easy Grammar Systems
Post Office Box 100
Scottsdale, AZ 85255 **inside address**

Dear Mr. Phipps**:**

E. Capitalization: *(1/3 pt. each)(25pts.)*

1. **H**ave **G**overnor **T**. **L**oon and those from the **H**ouse of **R**epresentatives met today?
2. **I**n the summer, they like to eat fish tacos at a **M**exican restaurant on **S**hell **B**each.
3. **T**he oldest **A**frican-**A**merican church was started in the **E**ast in 1813 by **P**eter **S**pencer.
4. **H**e studied **F**rench history, reading, and **B**iology 101 at **C**ambria **C**ollege in **J**uly.
5. **T**he **D**emacane **C**orporation moved just south of **P**innacle **P**eak last **T**uesday.
6. **D**uring **T**hanksgiving weekend, both **D**ad and **I** read **S**trangers from **M**y **N**ative **L**and.
7. **T**ake **V**entura **F**reeway north to see **H**earst **C**astle and to attend the **T**empleton **G**rape **F**estival.

8. **H**is brother, a banker, speaks **J**apanese and flies to **A**sia on **T**hailand **A**irlines.
9. **A D**elaware company that worked with **NASA** is located on **M**oonwalker **R**oad.
10. **D**id **J**ames **C**ook claim the **H**awaiian **I**slands for the **B**ritish **E**mpire?
11. **S**ome pioneers left **N**ew **E**ngland to settle near the **S**alt **R**iver in the **A**rizona **T**erritory.
12. **D**oes the **U**niversity of **V**irginia **F**oundation run the **B**oar's **H**ead **I**nn?

F. Punctuation: ***(1/2 pt. each) (25 pts.)***

1. His address is 10 South Street, Austin, TX 78705.
2. Joy's aunt, a teacher, bought a newly-remodeled home.
3. On May 24, 2006, they were married in a small, country chapel.
4. Emma asked, "Tate, do you need a old branding iron?"
5. Yes, I want to see the movie entitled Struck Twice by Lightning.
6. "During the last week of September, we went to Alaska," said Kim.
7. "Yeah!" Emily exclaimed, "My race is next!"
8. Although Allen is a nurse, he's interested in doctors' rights.
9. "Fight Against Bacteria" is an article in the magazine entitled Health World.
10. The town built the following: a children's hospital, a large park, and a zoo.
11. The team will leave at noon, and the band will follow within two hours.
12. By the way, are you going with us to Missoula, Montana, next fall?
13. The fair is next week; however, I can't attend.

G. Subjects and Verbs: ***(1 pt. for subject/1 pt. for verb or verb phrase)(10 pts.)***

1. I have purchased a new watercolor ~~by a Western artist~~. ***Do not count prepositional phrases!***
2. Did anyone find a cat ~~with long gray fur~~?
3. ~~Before the basketball game~~, several players were given extra practice.
4. I am definitely sad ~~about your lost hamster~~.
5. Your brother shouldn't have gone ~~to the library~~ ~~by himself~~.

H. Contractions: ***(1 pt. each)(6 pts.)***

1. does not - **doesn't**
2. they are - **they're**
3. I have - **I've**
4. how is - **how's**
5. have not - **haven't**
6. you will - **you'll**

I. Subject-Verb Agreement: ***(1 pt. for subject/1 pt. for verb/verb phrase)(10 pts.)***

1. Carmello and Bo (was, **were**) ~~in Ohio~~ recently. ***Do not count prepositional phrases!***
2. Someone ~~in the last few rows~~ (have, **has**) a cell phone turned on.
3. The girls ~~with the cute, little beagle puppy~~ (**like**, likes) to walk him.
4. Neither the ladies nor the man ~~with them~~ (want, **wants**) dessert.
5. One ~~of the watermelons~~ (**is**, are) ready to cut.

J. Irregular Verbs: *(2 pts. each)(46 pts.)*

1. Have you (spoke, **spoken**) to your friends about it?
2. He should not have (did, **done**) that.
3. Carlo has not ever (**ridden**, rode) a horse.
4. I may have (ate, **eaten**) too much.
5. Their alarm clock has (rang, **rung**) three times.
6. They have (drove, **driven**) to the coast.
7. Have you (**drunk**, drank) green tea?
8. A sign must have (fell, **fallen**) during the storm.
9. The couple has (**chosen**, chose) a house with an old barn.
10. (**Lie**, Lay) on the floor by the fire.
11. We should have (took, **taken**) our dogs to the lake with us.
12. The city of Vancouver was (began, **begun**) in 1792 by the British.
13. They may have (went, **gone**) to a baseball game.
14. I should have (brung, brang, **brought**) my camera.
15. Have Mr. and Mrs. Cole (flew, **flown**) to Dover?
16. The sleepy child had (laid, **lain**) on the floor.
17. The church's stained-glass window was (**broken**, broke).
18. That shovel must have (**frozen**, froze) in the snow.
19. Many doctors must have (came, **come**) to the conference late.
20. (**Sit**, Set) beside me!
21. I (saw, **seen**) him at the mall.
22. Many horses have (ran, **run**) in that famous race.
23. A reporter had (wrote, **written**) about the lost diamond mine.

K. Tenses: *(1 pt. each)* ***Do not count subject and verb; they serve to label the tense.*** *(5 pts.)*

1. **present progressive** — I am leaving soon.
2. **past** — I left early.
3. **past perfect** — They had left for New York City at noon.
4. **future** — Chase will leave on vacation next week.
5. **present** — Abigail always leaves food on her plate.

L. Common and Proper Nouns: *(1 pt. each)(2 pts.)*

1. ____ jar 2. ✓ respect 3. ✓ promise 4. ____ air

M. Singular and Plural Nouns: *(2 pts. each)(20 pts.)*

1. loss - **losses**
2. wrench - **wrenches**
3. leaf - **leaves**
4. robbery- **robberies**
5. deer - **deer**
6. display - **displays**
7. excitement - **excitement**
8. potato - **potatoes**
9. badge- **badges**
10. chief - **chiefs**

N. Possessive Nouns: *(2 pts. each)(12 pts.)*

1. a cart used by more than one workman - **workmen's cart**
2. a market set up by more than one farmer- **farmers' market**
3. a home belonging to Tom and Lori- **Tom and Lori's house**
4. computers owned by a company - **company's computers**
5. a playroom used by more than one child - **children's playroom**

O. Identifying Nouns: *(1 pt. each)(4 pts.)*

1. Many strong **winds** blow through this **village** and its **meadows** and into a deep **cave.**

P. Usage and Knowledge: *(1 pt. each)(5 pts.)*

1. Circle the correct answer: Josh did the sanding (**himself**, hisself).
2. Write an interjection: **Ouch!** *Answers Will Vary/Representative Answer*
3. Write a gerund: **Swimming** *Answers Will Vary/Representative Answer*
4. Write the antecedent of the possessive pronoun:
   Someone shouted his name over a loudspeaker. **Someone**
5. Circle a reflexive pronoun: We did it **ourselves**, and nobody helped!

Q. Identifying Adjectives: *(1 pt. each)(5 pts.)*

1. **One glossy** photograph had **French** swans on **a** very **lovely** lake.

R. Degrees of Adjectives: *(2 pts. each)(8 pts.)*

1. The road by my cousin's house is the (curvier, **curviest**) one in the county.
2. She is the (**more talkative**, most talkative) twin.
3. This shell feels (**rougher**, roughest) than that one.
4. Of the entire family, Tara seems (more timid, **most timid**, timider, timidest).

S. Adverbs: *(2 pts. each)(12 pts.)*

1. You did (good, **well**).
2. I don't feel (good, **well**).
3. Ron hardly ever has (no, **any**) extra change.
4. You are speaking too (loud, **loudly**).
5. She doesn't know (**anybody**, nobody) in her new school.
6. Their truck runs (good, **well**).

T. Identifying Adverbs: *(1 pt. each)(4 pts.)*

1. Tammy and her sister **always** play **so nicely together**.

U. Degrees of Adverbs: ***(2 pts. each)(10 pts.)***

1. Of the two girls, Ellen jumps (**farther**, farthest).
2. Mia wins (**more often**, most often, oftener, oftenest) than her friend.
3. The injured player walked (**more lightly**, most lightly) on his right foot.
4. The dog barked (more ferociously, **most ferociously**) at the third car.
5. Bo played (**worse**, worser, worst, worsest) during the second game.

V. Pronouns: ***(2 pts. each) (34 pts.)***

1. Pam and (**she**, her) donated blood.
2. (Who, **Whom**) did you call?
3. The flowers were for Sara and (I, **me**).
4. (Them, **Those**) cookies are too hard.
5. One of the girls left (**her**, their) books by the bench.
6. The coach and (**we**, us) practiced dribbling.
7. (Me and my friend, **My friend and I**, My friend and me) will help.
8. Annie and (**they**, them) walked to the ice cream shop.
9. The first one to present an award was (**he**, him).
10. Lance will call (we, **us**) boys after dinner.
11. Our cousins are (**they**, them) with the sheep dog.
12. The leader handed (she, **her**) a large manila envelope.
13. (**Who**, Whom) has a colored pencil?
14. Both of the street sweepers ate (his, **their**) snacks.
15. The winners are Nat and (me, **I**).
16. The debate was between Karen and (he, **him**).
17. Please give (they, **them**) my message.

W. Nouns and Pronouns Used as Subjects, Direct Objects, Indirect Objects, Objects of the Preposition, and Predicate Nominatives:
(2 pts. each)(12 pts.)

1. **D.O.** Quit bothering **me**!
2. **S** Their **grandparents** live in Florida.
3. **D.O.** Jenny always earns **money** for her school clothes.
4. **P.N.** Tad became a **bricklayer**.
5. **O.P.** Stay away from the **alley**.
6. **I.O.** Give the **waiter** a tip.

NOTE ABOUT SCORING THE ASSESSMENT:

You may want to ascribe a **percentage grade** to your test. **Don't let 275 points confuse you.** You may have a computer program to convert this. If you don't and want to use a percentage grade, you may do the following.

You can divide the number of points scored by 275. (Subtract the number wrong from 275 to obtain the number correct).

Example:

The number incorrect is 75:

$$275 - 75 = 200$$

Take this score of 200 points and divide by 275:

$$\frac{200}{275} = 73\%$$

(This was technically 72.727272 and was rounded to 73%.)

INDEX

CORRELATION OF

EASY GRAMMAR PLUS WORKBOOK
with
EASY GRAMMAR PLUS teacher edition

workbook page 1 - teacher ed. p. 4
workbook page 2 - teacher ed. p. 7
workbook page 3 - teacher ed. p. 9
workbook page 4 - teacher ed. p. 11
workbook page 5 - teacher ed. p. 12
workbook page 6 - teacher ed. p. 13
workbook page 7 - teacher ed. p. 15
workbook page 8 - teacher ed. p. 19
workbook page 9 - teacher ed. p. 21
workbook page 10 - teacher ed. p. 26
workbook page 11 - teacher ed. p. 23
workbook page 12 - teacher ed. p. 25
workbook page 13 - teacher ed. p. 27
workbook page 14 - teacher ed. p. 29
workbook page 15 - teacher ed. p. 31
workbook page 16 - teacher ed. p. 33
workbook page 17 - teacher ed. p. 35
workbook page 18 - teacher ed. p. 37
workbook page 19 - teacher ed. p. 39
workbook page 20 - teacher ed. p. 43
workbook page 21 - teacher ed. p. 45
workbook page 22 - teacher ed. p. 47
workbook page 23 - teacher ed. p. 49
workbook page 24 - teacher ed. p. 51
workbook page 25 - teacher ed. p. 53
workbook page 26 - teacher ed. p. 55
workbook page 27 - teacher ed. p. 57
workbook page 28 - teacher ed. p. 59
workbook page 29 - teacher ed. p. 61
workbook page 30 - teacher ed. p. 63
workbook page 31 - teacher ed. p. 65
workbook page 32 - teacher ed. p. 67
workbook page 33 - teacher ed. p. 69
workbook page 34 - teacher ed. p. 73
workbook page 35 - teacher ed. p. 75
workbook page 36 - teacher ed. p. 77
workbook page 37 - teacher ed. p. 79
workbook page 38 - teacher ed. p. 81
workbook page 39 - teacher ed. p. 82
workbook page 40 - teacher ed. p. 83
workbook page 41 - teacher ed. p. 85
workbook page 42 - teacher ed. p. 87
workbook page 43 - teacher ed. p. 88
workbook page 44 - teacher ed. p. 89
workbook page 45 - teacher ed. p. 91
workbook page 46 - teacher ed. p. 93
workbook page 47 - teacher ed. p. 94
workbook page 48 - teacher ed. p. 95
workbook page 49 - teacher ed. p. 97
workbook page 50 - teacher ed. p. 98
workbook page 51 - teacher ed. p.100
workbook page 52 - teacher ed. p.101
workbook page 53 - teacher ed. p.103
workbook page 54 - teacher ed. p.105
workbook page 55 - teacher ed. p.107
workbook page 56 - teacher ed. p.109
workbook page 57 - teacher ed. p.113
workbook page 58 - teacher ed. p.115
workbook page 59 - teacher ed. p.117
workbook page 60 - teacher ed. p.118
workbook page 61 - teacher ed. p.119
workbook page 62 - teacher ed. p.121
workbook page 63 - teacher ed. p.123
workbook page 64 - teacher ed. p.124
workbook page 65 - teacher ed. p.125
workbook page 66 - teacher ed. p.126
workbook page 67 - teacher ed. p.127
workbook page 68 - teacher ed. p.129
workbook page 69 - teacher ed. p.131
workbook page 70 - teacher ed. p.133
workbook page 71 - teacher ed. p.135
workbook page 72 - teacher ed. p.137
workbook page 73 - teacher ed. p.139
workbook page 74 - teacher ed. p.141
workbook page 75 - teacher ed. p.143
workbook page 76 - teacher ed. p.145
workbook page 77 - teacher ed. p.147
workbook page 78 - teacher ed. p.149

workbook page 79 - teacher ed. p. 151
workbook page 80 - teacher ed. p. 153
workbook page 81 - teacher ed. p. 155
workbook page 82 - teacher ed. p. 157
workbook page 83 - teacher ed. p. 158
workbook page 84 - teacher ed. p. 159
workbook page 85 - teacher ed. p. 161
workbook page 86 - teacher ed. p. 163
workbook page 87 - teacher ed. p. 165
workbook page 88 - teacher ed. p. 167
workbook page 89 - teacher ed. p. 169
workbook page 90 - teacher ed. p. 171
workbook page 91 - teacher ed. p. 173
workbook page 92 - teacher ed. p. 175
workbook page 93 - teacher ed. p. 177
workbook page 94 - teacher ed. p. 179
workbook page 95 - teacher ed. p. 181
workbook page 96 - teacher ed. p. 183
workbook page 97 - teacher ed. p. 185
workbook page 98 - teacher ed. p. 187
workbook page 99 - teacher ed. p. 189
workbook page 100 - teacher ed. p. 191
workbook page 101 - teacher ed. p. 193
workbook page 102 - teacher ed. p. 195
workbook page 103 - teacher ed. p. 197
workbook page 104 - teacher ed. p. 199
workbook page 105 - teacher ed. p. 201
workbook page 106 - teacher ed. p. 203
workbook page 107 - teacher ed. p. 205
workbook page 108 - teacher ed. p. 207
workbook page 109 - teacher ed. p. 209
workbook page 110 - teacher ed. p. 211
workbook page 111 - teacher ed. p. 223
workbook page 112 - teacher ed. p. 227
workbook page 113 - teacher ed. p. 229
workbook page 114 - teacher ed. p. 231
workbook page 115 - teacher ed. p. 233
workbook page 116 - teacher ed. p. 235
workbook page 117 - teacher ed. p. 236
workbook page 118 - teacher ed. p. 237
workbook page 119 - teacher ed. p. 239
workbook page 120 - teacher ed. p. 241
workbook page 121 - teacher ed. p. 243
workbook page 122 - teacher ed. p. 245
workbook page 123 - teacher ed. p. 247
workbook page 124 - teacher ed. p. 249
workbook page 125 - teacher ed. p. 251
workbook page 126 - teacher ed. p. 252
workbook page 127 - teacher ed. p. 253
workbook page 128 - teacher ed. p. 255
workbook page 129 - teacher ed. p. 257
workbook page 130 - teacher ed. p. 259
workbook page 131 - teacher ed. p. 261
workbook page 132 - teacher ed. p. 263
workbook page 133 - teacher ed. p. 265
workbook page 134 - teacher ed. p. 267
workbook page 135 - teacher ed. p. 269
workbook page 136 - teacher ed. p. 271
workbook page 137 - teacher ed. p. 273
workbook page 138 - teacher ed. p. 275
workbook page 139 - teacher ed. p. 277
workbook page 140 - teacher ed. p. 279
workbook page 141 - teacher ed. p. 281
workbook page 142 - teacher ed. p. 283
workbook page 143 - teacher ed. p. 285
workbook page 144 - teacher ed. p. 291
workbook page 145 - teacher ed. p. 293
workbook page 146 - teacher ed. p. 295
workbook page 147 - teacher ed. p. 301
workbook page 148 - teacher ed. p. 303
workbook page 149 - teacher ed. p. 305
workbook page 150 - teacher ed. p. 307
workbook page 151 - teacher ed. p. 309
workbook page 152 - teacher ed. p. 311
workbook page 153 - teacher ed. p. 313
workbook page 154 - teacher ed. p. 315
workbook page 155 - teacher ed. p. 317
workbook page 156 - teacher ed. p. 319
workbook page 157 - teacher ed. p. 321
workbook page 158 - teacher ed. p. 323
workbook page 159 - teacher ed. p. 325
workbook page 160 - teacher ed. p. 327
workbook page 161 - teacher ed. p. 329
workbook page 162 - teacher ed. p. 331
workbook page 163 - teacher ed. p. 333
workbook page 164 - teacher ed. p. 335
workbook page 165 - teacher ed. p. 336
workbook page 166 - teacher ed. p. 337
workbook page 167 - teacher ed. p. 339
workbook page 168 - teacher ed. p. 341
workbook page 169 - teacher ed. p. 343
workbook page 170 - teacher ed. p. 345

workbook page 171 - teacher ed. p. 347
workbook page 172 - teacher ed. p. 349
workbook page 173 - teacher ed. p. 355
workbook page 174 - teacher ed. p. 357
workbook page 175 - teacher ed. p. 359
workbook page 176 - teacher ed. p. 361
workbook page 177 - teacher ed. p. 363
workbook page 178 - teacher ed. p. 373
workbook page 179 - teacher ed. p. 375
workbook page 180 - teacher ed. p. 377
workbook page 181 - teacher ed. p. 379
workbook page 182 - teacher ed. p. 380
workbook page 183 - teacher ed. p. 383
workbook page 184 - teacher ed. p. 385
workbook page 185 - teacher ed. p. 387
workbook page 186 - teacher ed. p. 389
workbook page 187 - teacher ed. p. 391
workbook page 188 - teacher ed. p. 393
workbook page 189 - teacher ed. p. 395
workbook page 190 - teacher ed. p. 399
workbook page 191 - teacher ed. p. 401
workbook page 192 - teacher ed. p. 403
workbook page 193 - teacher ed. p. 405
workbook page 194 - teacher ed. p. 407
workbook page 195 - teacher ed. p. 409
workbook page 196 - teacher ed. p. 411
workbook page 197 - teacher ed. p. 413
workbook page 198 - teacher ed. p. 415
workbook page 199 - teacher ed. p. 417
workbook page 200 - teacher ed. p. 419
workbook page 201 - teacher ed. p. 421
workbook page 202 - teacher ed. p. 423
workbook page 203 - teacher ed. p. 425
workbook page 204 - teacher ed. p. 427
workbook page 205 - teacher ed. p. 429
workbook page 206 - teacher ed. p. 431
workbook page 207 - teacher ed. p. 433
workbook page 208 - teacher ed. p. 435
workbook page 209 - teacher ed. p. 437
workbook page 210 - teacher ed. p. 439
workbook page 211 - teacher ed. p. 441
workbook page 212 - teacher ed. p. 443
workbook page 213 - teacher ed. p. 445
workbook page 214 - teacher ed. p. 447
workbook page 215 - teacher ed. p. 453
workbook page 216 - teacher ed. p. 455
workbook page 217 - teacher ed. p. 457
workbook page 218 - teacher ed. p. 459
workbook page 219 - teacher ed. p. 461
workbook page 220 - teacher ed. p. 463
workbook page 221 - teacher ed. p. 474
workbook page 222 - teacher ed. p. 475
workbook page 223 - teacher ed. p. 477
workbook page 224 - teacher ed. p. 479
workbook page 225 - teacher ed. p. 481
workbook page 226 - teacher ed. p. 483
workbook page 227 - teacher ed. p. 485
workbook page 228 - teacher ed. p. 487
workbook page 229 - teacher ed. p. 489
workbook page 230 - teacher ed. p. 491
workbook page 231 - teacher ed. p. 493
workbook page 232 - teacher ed. p. 495
workbook page 233 - teacher ed. p. 496
workbook page 234 - teacher ed. p. 497
workbook page 235 - teacher ed. p. 499
workbook page 236 - teacher ed. p. 501
workbook page 237 - teacher ed. p. 503
workbook page 238 - teacher ed. p. 505
workbook page 239 - teacher ed. p. 507
workbook page 240 - teacher ed. p. 509
workbook page 241 - teacher ed. p. 511
workbook page 242 - teacher ed. p. 513
workbook page 243 - teacher ed. p. 515
workbook page 244 - teacher ed. p. 517
workbook page 245 - teacher ed. p. 519
workbook page 246 - teacher ed. p. 521
workbook page 247 - teacher ed. p. 523
workbook page 248 - teacher ed. p. 524
workbook page 249 - teacher ed. p. 525
workbook page 250 - teacher ed. p. 527
workbook page 251 - teacher ed. p. 529
workbook page 252 - teacher ed. p. 531
workbook page 253 - teacher ed. p. 533
workbook page 254 - teacher ed. p. 535
workbook page 255 - teacher ed. p. 537
workbook page 256 - teacher ed. p. 539
workbook page 257 - teacher ed. p. 545
workbook page 258 - teacher ed. p. 547
workbook page 259 - teacher ed. p. 549
workbook page 260 - teacher ed. p. 551
workbook page 261 - teacher ed. p. 553
workbook page 262 - teacher ed. p. 555

workbook page 263 - teacher ed. p. 557
workbook page 264 - teacher ed. p. 568
workbook page 265 - teacher ed. p. 569
workbook page 266 - teacher ed. p. 571
workbook page 267 - teacher ed. p. 573
workbook page 268 - teacher ed. p. 575
workbook page 269 - teacher ed. p. 577
workbook page 270 - teacher ed. p. 579
workbook page 271 - teacher ed. p. 581
workbook page 272 - teacher ed. p. 582
workbook page 273 - teacher ed. p. 583
workbook page 274 - teacher ed. p. 585
workbook page 275 - teacher ed. p. 587
workbook page 276 - teacher ed. p. 589
workbook page 277 - teacher ed. p. 591
workbook page 278 - teacher ed. p. 593
workbook page 279 - teacher ed. p. 594
workbook page 280 - teacher ed. p. 595
workbook page 281 - teacher ed. p. 597
workbook page 282 - teacher ed. p. 599
workbook page 283 - teacher ed. p. 601
workbook page 284 - teacher ed. p. 603
workbook page 285 - teacher ed. p. 605
workbook page 286 - teacher ed. p. 607
workbook page 287 - teacher ed. p. 609
workbook page 288 - teacher ed. p. 611
workbook page 289 - teacher ed. p. 613
workbook page 290 - teacher ed. p. 615
workbook page 291 - teacher ed. p. 619
workbook page 292 - teacher ed. p. 621
workbook page 293 - teacher ed. p. 623
workbook page 294 - teacher ed. p. 625
workbook page 295 - teacher ed. p. 627
workbook page 296 - teacher ed. p. 629
workbook page 297 - teacher ed. p. 631
workbook page 298 - teacher ed. p. 633
workbook page 299 - teacher ed. p. 635
workbook page 300 - teacher ed. p. 637
workbook page 301 - teacher ed. p. 638
workbook page 302 - teacher ed. p. 639
workbook page 303 - teacher ed. p. 641
workbook page 304 - teacher ed. p. 642
workbook page 305 - teacher ed. p. 643
workbook page 306 - teacher ed. p. 645
workbook page 307 - teacher ed. p. 647
workbook page 308 - teacher ed. p. 649
workbook page 309 - teacher ed. p. 651
workbook page 310 - teacher ed. p. 653
workbook page 311 - teacher ed. p. 659
workbook page 312 - teacher ed. p. 660
workbook page 313 - teacher ed. p. 661
workbook page 314 - teacher ed. p. 662
workbook page 315 - teacher ed. p. 663
workbook page 316 - teacher ed. p. 664
workbook page 317 - teacher ed. p. 665
workbook page 318 - teacher ed. p. 667
workbook page 319 - teacher ed. p. 669
workbook page 320 - teacher ed. p. 670
workbook page 321 - teacher ed. p. 671
workbook page 322 - teacher ed. p. 673
workbook page 323 - teacher ed. p. 674
workbook page 324 - teacher ed. p. 675
workbook page 325 - teacher ed. p. 677
workbook page 326 - teacher ed. p. 679